Olympias

Modern conventional wisdom knows Olympias as a pitiless and savage woman, a practitioner of barbaric Dionysiac rites compelled by jealousy and ruthless ambition to the murder of her rivals in order to secure her son's succession to the throne of Macedon. In this way she is credited for Alexander the Great's unprecedented achievements—yet the scale of her son's epic story has obscured her own.

Such critical accounts of Olympias' actions have made unforgiving and often unfounded judgments of her motivations. This myth, however, originates from later ancient writers, to which her strength and tenacity represented an abhorrent contradiction to contemporary gender roles. Later historians have all too often perpetuated this ancient sexual stereotyping by failing to question these sources.

In this, the first modern biography of Olympias, Elizabeth Carney penetrates myth, fiction and sexual politics to reveal a fascinating and wholly misunderstood figure. Through a close and critical assessment of the sources, Olympias is humanized as she is placed in the context of her own brutal political world.

Olympias examines:

- the role of Greek religion in Olympias' life
- literary and artistic traditions about Olympias found throughout the later ancient periods
- varying representations of Olympias found in the major ancient sources.

This book will be the definitive guide to the life of the first woman to play a major role in Greek political history as well as a compelling read for students, scholars and anyone with an interest in Greek, Classical or women's history.

Elizabeth Carney is Professor of Ancient History at Clemson University in South Carolina. She is the author of *Women and Monarchy in Ancient Macedonia* (2000).

Women of the Ancient World
Series editors: Ronnie Ancona and Sarah Pomeroy

The books in this series offer compact and accessible introductions to the lives and historical times of women from the ancient world. Each book, written by a distinguished scholar in the field, introduces and explores the life of one woman or group of women from antiquity, from a biographical perspective.

The texts will be authoritative introductions by experts in the field. Each book will be of interest to students and scholars of antiquity as well as those with little or no prior knowledge of ancient history or literature, combining rigorous scholarship with reader-friendly prose. Each volume will contain a guide to further reading, a brief glossary, and timelines, maps, and images, as necessary.

Women of the Ancient World will provide an opportunity for specialists to present concise, authoritative accounts, uncovering and exploring important figures in need of historical study and advancing current scholarship on women of the past. Although there is a growing body of excellent scholarship on the lives and roles of women in the ancient world, much work remains. This series will be the first of its kind.

Olympias, Mother of Alexander the Great
Elizabeth Carney

Julia Domna, Syrian Empress
Barbara Levick

Julia Augusti, The Emperor's Daughter
Elaine Fantham

Olympias

Mother of Alexander the Great

Elizabeth Carney

Routledge
Taylor & Francis Group

NEW YORK AND LONDON

First published 2006
by Routledge
270 Madison Ave, New York, NY 10016

Simultaneously published in the UK
by Routledge
2 Park Square, Milton Park, Abingdon, Oxon OX14 4RN

Routledge is an imprint of the Taylor & Francis Group, an informa business

© 2006 Elizabeth Carney

Typeset in Sabon by
Keystroke, Jacaranda Lodge, Wolverhampton
Printed and bound in Great Britain by
Antony Rowe Ltd, Chippenham, Wiltshire

Library of Congress Cataloging in Publication Data
A catalog record for this book has been requested

British Library Cataloguing in Publication Data
A catalogue record for this book is available from the British Library

ISBN10: 0–415–33316–4 (hbk)
ISBN10: 0–415–33317–2 (pbk)
ISBN10: 0–203–41278–8 (ebk)

ISBN13: 978–0–415–33316–0 (hbk)
ISBN13: 978–0–415–33317–7 (pbk)
ISBN13: 978–0–203–41278–7 (ebk)

In Memoriam
James Francis Carney

Contents

Preface

I have written about Olympias, on and off, since the summer of 1979. That means that I have been living with Olympias longer than I have lived with my husband and that my interest in her is older than my daughter, by several years. Nonetheless, only in my first article on her did I attempt to construct a unified and self-contained analysis of her entire career. I am grateful to Ronnie Ancona and Sarah Pomeroy, the editors of this series, and to Richard Stoneman of Routledge, for the opportunity to write a monograph on this remarkable woman and for the encouragement to return, after so many years, to a comprehensive consideration of her life. There is no lengthy, modern, scholarly study of her career.

No one accomplishes scholarly work without the assistance of many others. Stan Burstein was kind enough to read over and comment on the entire manuscript. Like everyone else who works on royal women in the late Classical and Hellenistic period, I owe a debt to my distinguished predecessor, Grace Harriet Macurdy. I was lucky enough to help to direct Kate Mortensen's dissertation on Olympias. Conversations and letters with Kate, as well as her own scholarship, have often given me new ideas. Bob Milns, Bill Greenwalt, Peter Green and Waldemar Heckel have patiently read much of what I have written about Olympias, sometimes helping by disagreeing. Daniel Ogden and Jeanne Reames-Zimmerman have opened up new ways of looking at sexuality and competition at the Macedonian court. Gene Borza and Ernie Fredricksmeyer have always offered broad insight on matters Macedonian. John Oates and Philip Stadter, who gave me my initial understanding of the reign of Alexander, have continued to offer every assistance. Pierre Briant, Sylvie Le Bohec, Olga Palagia, Dolores Mirón-Pérez, Bruno Tripodi, Argyro Tataki, and Miltos Hatzopoulos have all offered help by email and kindly sent me material otherwise difficult to obtain. My colleagues in the history department have listened to and commented on my stories of ancient Macedonian melodrama. Without the efficient work of our inter-library loan librarians, this book would never have been possible.

My family has always encouraged my research. My husband William Aarnes has often functioned as an editor of my more wordy pieces and my daughter, Emma Aarnes, so empathized with her mother's work that, as a third grader, she produced an entertaining and accurate report on Olympias. But I would like to offer particular thanks to my father, to whose memory this book is dedicated. His love of Latin led to my first interest in the ancient world.

Significant events

331   Alexander visits Siwah and begins to assert his divine sonship
       Battle of Gaugamela
       Revolt of Agis
       (Fall or winter 330) Death of Alexander of Molossia
       Olympias leaves Macedonia for Molossia

330   Antipater's defeat of Agis
       Death of Darius
       Elimination of Philotas and Parmenio

328   Death of Cleitus

327   Alexander's marriage to Roxane
       Hermolaus conspiracy

326   Alexander's troops refuse to march further

325   (Or winter 324) Cleopatra leaves Molossia for Macedonia

324   Alexander marries daughter of Darius amid mass marriages
          of Macedonians and Greeks to Asian women
       Alexander appoints Craterus to succeed Antipater

323   Cassander arrives in Babylon
       (June 10) Alexander dies
       Settlement in Babylon
       Birth of Alexander IV
       Outbreak of Lamian War
       Cleopatra (and Olympias) negotiate marriage alliance with
          Leonnatus

322   Leonnatus dies raising siege of Lamia
       (?) Aeacides becomes king (or co-king) of Molossia
       Cleopatra leaves for Sardis

320   Perdiccas killed
       Antipater regent

319   Antipater returns to Macedonia with the kings
       (Late summer) Antipater dies; Polyperchon regent

317   Cassander invades Macedonia and allies with Adea Eurydice
       (Fall) Olympias and Polyperchon return to Macedonia
       Deaths of Adea Eurydice and Philip Arrhidaeus
       Surrender and death of Eumenes (late fall or winter 316)

316   (Spring) surrender and death of Olympias; Cassander takes
          over

310–309 Murders of Alexander IV and Heracles

c. 308   Murder of Cleopatra, daughter of Olympias

c. 295   Murder of Thessalonice, half sister of Alexander the Great

The Aeacid dynasty in the era of Olympias

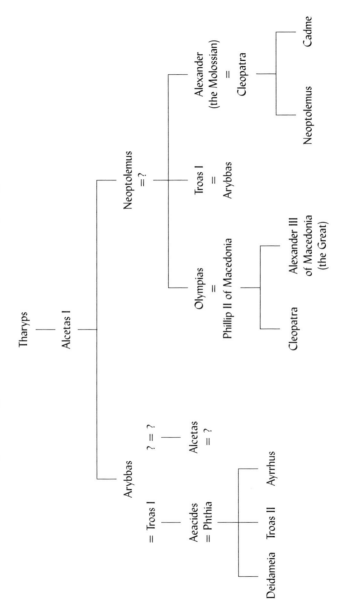

The Argead dynasty in the era of Olympias

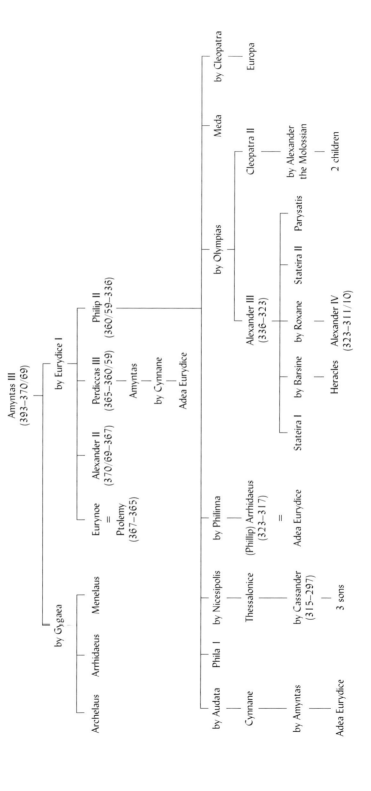

Abbreviations

AAA	*Athens Annals of Archaeology*
AC	*L'Antiquité classique*
AE	*Archaiologika Ephemeris*
AEMTH	*To archaiologiko ergo ste Makedonia kai Thrake*
AHB	*Ancient History Bulletin*
AHR	*American Historical Review*
AJA	*American Journal of Archaeology*
AJAH	*American Journal of Ancient History*
AJP	*American Journal of Philology*
AM	*Archaia Makedonia/Ancient Macedonia*, Proceedings of the International Symposia on Ancient Macedonia.
AncW	*Ancient World*
AncSoc	*Ancient Society*
AnnPisa	*Annali della Scuola Normale Superiore di Pisa*
AR	*Archaeological Reports*
ArchN	*Archaeological News*
BCH	*Bulletin de correspondance hellénique*
BSA	*Annual of the British School at Athens*
BSRAA	*Bulletin de la Société Royal d'Archéologie d'Alexandrie*
CA	*Classical Antiquity*
CAH	*Cambridge Ancient History*
Choix	F. Dürrbach, *Choix d'inscriptions de Délos*, Paris, 1921
CJ	*Classical Journal*
CP	*Classical Philology*
CQ	*Classical Quarterly*
CW	*Classical World*
EchCl	*Echos du monde classique/Classical Views*
Ergon	*Ergon tes archaiologikes Etaireias*
EtPap	*Études de papyrologie*
FGrH	F. Jacoby, *Die Fragmente der griechischen Historiker*, Leiden, 1993
FHG	C. Müller, *Fragmenta Historicorum Graecorum*, Paris, 1849–51

FlorIlib	*Florentia Iliberritana*
G&R	*Greece and Rome*
GHI	M. N. Tod, *A Selection of Greek Historical Inscriptions*, Vols. 1 and 2, Oxford, 1946 and 1948
GRBS	*Greek, Roman and Byzantine Studies*
HSCP	*Harvard Studies in Classical Philology*
HThR	*Harvard Theological Review*
ID	F. Dürrbach, *Inscriptions de Délos*, Paris, 1929
IG	*Incriptiones Graecae*
JHS	*Journal of Hellenic Studies*
LCM	*Liverpool Classical Monthly*
LSJ	H. G. Liddell, R. Scott, and H. Stuart Jones, *Greek–English Lexicon*, 9th edn, Oxford, 1940
MDAI(A)	*Mitteilungen des Deutschen Archäologischen Instituts Abteilung Athens*
NC	*Numismatic Chronicle*
OGIS	W. Dittenberger, *Orientis Graecae Inscriptiones Selectae*, Leipzig, 1903–5
PCPhS	*Proceedings of the Cambridge Philological Society*
P&P	*Past and Present*
PF	*Philosophical Forum*
PP	*La Parola del Passato*
RE	A. Pauly, G. Wissowa, and W. Kroll, *Realencyclopädie des classischen Altertumswissenschaft*, Stuttgart, 1893–
REA	*Revue des études anciennes*
REG	*Revue des études grecques*
RendIstLomb	*Rendiconti. Istituto lombardo, Accademia di scienze e lettere*
RFIC	*Rivista di filologia e d'istruzione classica*
RhM	*Rheinisches Museum*
RIDA	*Revue internationale des droits de l'antiquité*
RN	*Revue numismatique*
RSA	*Rivista storica dell'antichita*
SEG	*Supplementum Epigraphicum Graecum*
SIG	W. Dittenberger, *Sylloge Inscriptionum Graecarum*, 3rd edn, Leipzig, 1915–24
TAM	K. Ninou, *Treasures of Ancient Macedonia*, Athens, 1980
TAPA	*Transactions and Proceedings of the American Philological Association*
WS	*Wiener Studien*
ZfN	*Zeitschrift für Numismatik*
ZPE	*Zeitschrift für Papyrologie und Epigraphik*

Abbreviations of ancient authors and works are those used by the *Oxford Classical Dictionary*.

Introduction

Olympias (c. 373–316 BCE), daughter of a Molossian king, wife of Philip II of Macedon, and mother of Alexander the Great, lived a remarkable life. Though comparatively obscure during her husband's reign (359–336 BCE), her son's reign (336–323 BCE) transformed her into a powerful political force in the entire Greek peninsula. After her son's unexpected death, Olympias tried to guarantee that her grandson Alexander IV, the child king, would live long enough to rule in his own right. She was able to sway the Macedonian home army away from loyalty to a rival branch of the Argead (royal Macedonian) dynasty and over to support for herself and her grandson. In the end, however, the military failure of the forces supporting her led to her capture and execution and, ultimately, that of her grandson as well. Ruthless and tenacious, she was the first woman to play a major role in Greek political history.

The sources for the life of this extraordinary woman are problematic at best. Ancient writers were not kind to politically active and powerful women. Of course, the ancient world, particularly the ancient Greek world, had views and expectations about women that are very different from our own. Nonetheless, not infrequently, modern writers do little better than their ancient predecessors. Stereotypes that appear in Greek and Roman authors remain potent, particularly when embedded in compelling, if highly colored, narrative. Some of the least plausible tales are told simply because they are fun, guilty pleasures we continue to indulge. A peculiar feature of sexual stereotyping about political women is the insidious "niceness" factor. Whereas modern and ancient writers tend to treat even the most brutal actions of male rulers in matter-of-fact terms, often failing to comment at all on the morality of their actions, similar actions by women virtually never pass without moralizing There is an unstated presumption that women should/ought to be/are nicer, kinder than men. That this is an implicit standard makes it more dangerous; made explicit, it sounds as silly as it is. One reason that male atrocities comparatively rarely generate comment is the assumption that men commit such crimes out of policy, for rational reasons, out of Realpolitik. Paradoxically, often in the same writer who expects women to be more kindly than men appears the presumption that personal passion lies behind female brutality. Somehow, women are both more and less "nice" than men. As a consequence of the expectation of personal motivation (typically again sexually stereotypical in nature), the possible policy of the woman is not even addressed. Men take vengeance for a reason; women are simply vengeful.

Moreover, in her own day Olympias was a controversial figure, a person who produced extreme reactions in those who knew and dealt with her. Even if many more contemporary accounts of her actions and motivations had survived the centuries, difficulty in arriving at a clear and full understanding of her career would persist.

Sexual prejudice and controversy are not the only factors that make understanding Olympias' career difficult. Most contemporary authors, typically southern Greeks, were unfamiliar with and hostile to the society and culture of the northern Greek kingdoms of Molossia and Macedonia, inclined to view them as barbaric, irrational and mysterious. Monarchy itself, let alone more exotic phenomena like the polygamy of Macedonian kings or royal women who were politically active, was seen as primitive and mistaken.

In the years after Olympias' death and that of her son, accounts of their lives and actions became tools in power struggles of the Macedonian generals (commonly termed the Successors of Alexander) that followed Alexander's death and led to the fragmentation of his empire. The virtues, vices, and relationships with others of both mother and son were minimized, exaggerated, or distorted to serve short-term propaganda goals. Writers of later antiquity had little ability or inclination to sort out partisan observation from more objective statements. As the number of centuries separating the author from the world of the fourth century grew, the degree of misunderstanding could only increase, even for the writer who genuinely tried to understand a world very different from his own. Yet, with comparatively few exceptions (largely Athenian orators, often hostile to Macedonia), other than fragmentary quotations and paraphrases, it is the work of Greek and Roman writers many centuries removed from the world of Alexander and Olympias that survives, not the once abundant material from contemporary writers.

These layers of hostility and misunderstanding compound a more essential problem. Nothing survives that one can, with absolute confidence, conclude that Olympias said or wrote herself. Although she may well have produced some remarks attributed to her by our extant sources, one cannot simply assume that she did, and sorting out the genuine from the fabrication or, worse yet, from the elaboration, is no easy task.

I refer the reader to the Appendix for a more detailed discussion, author by author, of the treatment of Olympias in our major surviving sources, but I offer the following guidelines for my own decisions involving the weighing of contradictory, fragmentary, or obviously hostile evidence. Documentary evidence deserves the most credence. In terms of Greek history, this usually means inscriptions, formal statements or governmental decrees inscribed in stone. Archaeological evidence, where relevant, should have nearly similar weight. Statements by contemporary writers like the Athenian orator and politician Demosthenes (famously an enemy of Philip, Alexander, and Olympias) can be trusted when they refer to public actions by Olympias, much less so when they ascribe motivation to her. Much the same applies to material about her found in later historical narratives, biographies, and essays. Many such works include letters or parts of letters from the correspondence of Olympias. The general scholarly view has been to treat each letter on its merits, acknowledging that real letters did once exist but that fictional collections were also created. Some letters clearly serve a political or propaganda agenda, but those that do not (or portions that do not) deserve more credence (see further Chapter 3). The most dubious evidence of all is the body of anecdotal material about Olympias. One could simply reject all of it out of hand, but anecdotal material often contains credible information, even when the main thrust of the story is not. For instance, Plutarch's assertion (*Alex.* 2.1) that Philip fell in love with Olympias at first sight, that theirs was a love match, is almost certainly a romantic fiction, but the setting he provides for their first encounter, that they were fellow initiates in the cult of the Great Gods of Samothrace, is likely accurate, for reasons I will discuss later (see Chapter 1).

Only Olympias knew why she chose to act as she did, but I have begun with the presumption that she had reasons for what she did and then considered what those reasons might have been, just as historians generally do when speculating about the motivation and policy of male historical figures. More emotional and irrational factors may also have affected Olympias' choices, as they do those of most people (and certainly those of her male contemporaries), but I see no reason to presume, *a priori*, that they alone, or largely, motivated her.

When one looks at Olympias' entire career, several themes recur, some of them interrelated. Many royal women married foreign rulers and never saw their homelands or families again, but Olympias returned to her homeland, resided there for many years, and derived political and military support from it. Even more important than her Molossian identity, though, was her identity as an Aeacid and the dynastic ties and pride her famous lineage offered her. I will suggest that her heroic lineage may have shaped her public conduct at critical moments in her life (and perhaps that of other royal women), that epic and tragic images of royal women functioned as models and a script of sorts for how this woman, who believed herself to be the linear descendant of Achilles, Andromache, and Hecuba, shaped her public presentation. Epic and tragedy often deal with the rise and fall of dynasties, family curses, heroic deaths, and cycles of vengeance worked out over generations. Many of these elements are central in Olympias' life. More particularly, what may have begun as a personal dispute between Olympias and Antipater, the man her son had left in some sort of administrative charge over Greek and Macedonian affairs, was transformed into a multi-generational vendetta between the Aeacid and Antipatrid clans. Finally, throughout her life, the position of women in the Hellenic world limited Olympias' accomplishments, requiring her, like other royal women, to do indirectly what royal men could do directly. In an era where command of troops was critical, no royal woman managed to maintain control over a large body of troops for any significant length of time. The result was the ultimate limitation: male generals or kings murdered not only Olympias but all of Alexander's sisters and wives.

Olympias seemed larger than life to her contemporaries and has, over the centuries, continued to seem so. The goal of this biography is to place Olympias in her historical and cultural context and to determine, as much as possible, why she acted as she did. I want to make her life-sized.

1 Olympias the Molossian

Olympias was born the daughter of Neoptolemus, king of Molossia, a region of Epirus. Although almost no material directly dealing with Olympias' childhood and life before her betrothal and marriage survives, information about her family and her country is available, enough to indicate how her background continued to influence her throughout her eventful life. Her identity as a Molossian and as a member of the Aeacid (descendants of Aeacus) dynasty endured; her son embraced that same identity to a remarkable degree, considering the patriarchal and patrilineal nature of Macedonian society and the Hellenic world in general.

Ironically, we know more about the mythic than the historic past of her family. In a sense, it is more important anyway. The development of a heroic genealogy by the Molossian royal house played an early role in the Hellenization of Epirus.[1] Tradition had long associated Neoptolemus (alternatively called Pyrrhus), son of Achilles, with rule of Epirus (Pind. Nem. 4.51–53, 7.38–39). Perhaps as early as the days of Pindar (late sixth, early fifth century BCE),[2] but certainly by the time Euripides composed his *Andromache* (in the 420s), the rulers of Molossia asserted that they were the descendants of Neoptolemus through a son of his by Andromache, widow of Hector (*Andr.* 1246–49).[3] Euripides may have chosen to popularize this genealogy for reasons of current Athenian political advantage.[4] By Olympias' day a subsequent addition to the genealogy made Priam, through his son Helenus, an ancestor of the Aeacids as well; in this version the kings also descended from a son of Andromache by Helenus.[5] As the fourth century progressed, the name choices of the dynasty indicated growing emphasis on this heroic genealogy. In the reign of Olympias' father Neoptolemus they became, in effect, the rule.[6] The peculiarly Trojan quality of the names of Neoptolemus' children[7] has led some[8] to conclude that their mother must have been Chaonian since the ruling house of that Epirote tribe claimed descent from Andromache and Helenus (Just. 17.3.6).

This Aeacid genealogy gained wide acceptance in the Greek world; clearly it colored the careers of Olympias' son Alexander and of her great-nephew, Pyrrhus. The memory of the greatest Homeric hero shaped the image both men presented to the ancient world: being a descendant of Achilles helped explain themselves to themselves and to the world.[9] While the generally Homeric nature of Macedonian society and monarchy, as well as the influence of Aristotle, also contributed to Alexander's emulation and imitation of Achilles, Olympias was unquestionably the original source of his fascination with Achilles.[10] We know (Plut. *Alex.* 5.5) that Leonidas, a kinsman of hers who was chosen as Alexander's earliest tutor, called himself "Phoenix" (Achilles' foster father and tutor), Alexander "Achilles," and even referred to Philip as "Peleus" (the father of Achilles). Apparently he reinforced the Aeacid point of view,[11] in effect transforming Philip himself into an Aeacid. A fragment of Theopompus, however, confirms what this story implies. Theopompus (*FGrH* 115 F 355) notes that Olympias proclaimed Achilles (as well as Helenus, son of Priam) as her ancestor.

Indeed, although the influence of Achilles (as well as other heroic ancestors) on the character and image of Alexander has been much discussed,[12] with good reason, little attention has been paid to the effect of heroic ancestry on the character, image, and actions of Olympias and other royal women. It should be no surprise that an Aeacid woman would stress the claim of descent from Achilles for herself and her children, particularly in the competitive Macedonian court. Olympias' ancestry distinguished her from Philip's other wives. Her Aeacid lineage meant more to her than simply a way to get ahead of her rivals at court. Written references to Aeacid genealogy mention heroic males, a natural consequence of the Greek tendency to reckon patrilineally, but, as the "Trojan" name (Polyxena) suggests, female members of the line may have been models as well, at least for the women of the clan. Moments in the life of Olympias, her daughter, and her rivals, as described in extant narratives, resemble scenes from Greek tragedy. Even allowing for considerable fictionalization and embroidery by our sources, it is likely that the "tragic queen" aspect of Olympias' life actually was shaped by the cycle of Trojan stories, as developed in the Homeric poems and in Athenian tragedy, particularly that of Euripides.[13] Even otherwise hostile sources treat her death as heroic. Hecuba, Andromache, and Polyxena—her supposed ancestresses— may have been her models.[14] If her mother or maternal grandmother were indeed the source of the Trojan part of the Aeacid genealogy, then Olympias herself may have identified to a greater degree with her maternal ancestry.

As my discussion of mythic/Homeric models suggests, it is important to consider what the expectations for royal female behavior were in Molossia, in order to understand the background for Olympias' actions. More specifically, we need to place the position of royal women in Molossia in the broader context of the position of women generally in the Greek world. That is no longer an easy task.

A scholarly generation ago, generalizations came more easily. We talked about a black-and-white divide between the world of men and that of women, about parallel polarities: women/private/*oikos* versus men/public/ *polis*. We stressed inequality and difference. To my mind, these generalizations remain extremely valid, but can easily be applied too broadly.[15] Prescription should not be mistaken for description.[16] Because of the comparative abundance of evidence and the importance of Athenian democracy, scholarship on women focused nearly exclusively on Athens, its middle and upper citizen classes (the minority), and on the fifth century BCE. As a consequence, the most extreme situation of women in the Greek world was often taken as the norm. Olympias was no Athenian.

In terms of the role of women in Molossia and Macedonia, the most obvious point to make is that these were non-urban, more or less tribal monarchies, and that many of the familiar dichotomies just mentioned were products of the *polis* world, more particularly of democratic Athens. The situation of elite women as shown in Homer and as evidenced in the Archaic period much more closely resembled the situation of Molossian and Macedonian female elites[17] than it did what Athenian males claimed to be the truth about their wives and daughters. In Thucydides' (1.136–137.3) version of a tale about the flight of Themistocles[18] (the famous Athenian general exiled for treason) and his appearance as a suppliant at the court of the Molossian king Admetus, the king's wife Phthia plays a pivotal role by giving advice to Themistocles about how to win her husband's support. Whatever the historicity of this story, let alone this variant, it confirms a southern Greek understanding of the role of Molossian women, royal ones anyway, as Homeric. Phthia's advice recalls that of Nausicaa (*Od.* 6. 304–315). Like Penelope or Helen or Arete, she converses with males not related to her, does not seem to be secluded, and takes an active role in events.

Women in Greek elites often dominated the religious establishment in their regions and might journey considerable distances to panhellenic shrines.[19] Andromacha, wife of Arybbas (almost certainly an Aeacid and probably the uncle of Olympias; see below), traveled to the shrine of Aesclepius at Epidaurus (*IG* IV² 1.122 iama 31). Olympias and other royal women made dedications at major shrines and dominated their religious world (*SIG* I³ 252N 5ff; Hyp. *Eux.* 19). I shall discuss Olympias' religiosity at length later in this book (see Chapter 5), but suffice to say here that she tried to play a dominant role in some aspects of Macedonian religion.

Olympias would not have expected to cope with the degree of masculine control that women in southern Greece experienced. An assortment of documents from Epirus suggest that women there were less legally and culturally circumscribed than in Athens, other Greek cities, and perhaps even Macedonia.[20] In Molossia, women could independently own and alienate property and act as guardians for their minor children. Apparently women, at least once they were adults, had no legal guardians.[21] They could receive grants of citizenship and pass that citizenship on to their children.[22]

The legal situation of ordinary Molossian women may have a parallel in the situation of royal Molossian women. While no woman is known for a certainty to have acted as regent in Macedonia (see Chapter 3), at least two and perhaps three women (Olympias' daughter Cleopatra, possibly Olympias herself, and Olympias II) did so in Molossia. In southern Greece, formal entertaining not related to family events was sexually segregated; respectable women did not attend *symposia* (drinking parties). In Macedonia, literary evidence offers no reason to think that Olympias or other women of her status attended *symposia*,[23] but Plutarch (*Pyrrh.* 5.5) tells a tale about the younger generation of Olympias' family that has a brother and sister dining, drinking and plotting together. Olympias and her daughter Cleopatra, wife of Alexander I of Molossia, corresponded with various important political figures of their day.[24] Particularly because of the frequent need for confidentiality in this correspondance,[25] it is likely that they were literate.[26] Literate or not, female Aeacids would have known Homer and very likely Pindar and Euripides.[27] The evidence is slender, but it seems reasonable to conclude that Olympias grew up in a world which had less narrow expectations for women than did the Athenians or even the Macedonians.

Let us now turn to what Olympias' homeland was like in other respects. Around the time of Olympias' birth, Molossia was an inland kingdom in northwestern Greece, part of the region known as Epirus. Southern Greece had long been organized in terms of urban centers called *poleis*, but northern Greece in the fourth century BCE, with the exception of some coastal regions, was not urbanized. In many areas, the older governmental form, monarchy, not the *polis*, dominated populations that were still tribally organized. In this period, many southern Greeks considered the general population of Epirus and Macedonia barbarians, although some ruling dynasties (including the Aeacids) had managed, via heroic genealogies, to acquire a degree of recognition for their own Hellenic identities.[28]

Molossia—and, indeed, most of Epirus, with the exception of coastal regions—was a very different physical world from that of southern Greece.[29] Molossia was initially an inland, mountainous kingdom, largely cut off from the coast, not easily reached from southern Greece, although comparatively accessible by means of several mountain passes (during the summer) from the western parts of Macedonia.[30] The climate was continental, not Mediterranean. Rainfall and snow were abundant; swift-flowing streams remained lively and difficult to ford even during the summer, when streams in southern Greece dried up. In Olympias' day, forests dominated by oaks probably covered most of her homeland. Granted the mountainous terrain and harsh winters, cereal agriculture was not successful but herding was. Today Epirus is one of the poorest parts of Greece. In antiquity the situation was probably relatively similar.[31] Despite this, individual members of the Aeacid clan, judging by the actions of various members in the fourth century, commanded sufficient wealth[32] to enable them to engage in activities similar to those of others in Greek elites.[33] Molossia was a green and pleasant place to grow up, but it was remote from the rest of the Greek world, a primitive backwater and not always a safe place, especially for members of the royal family. The seat of the royal family, let alone the location of its palace, is uncertain, though it seems reasonable to conclude that by Olympias' day, the Aeacids must have spent considerable time at Dodona.[34]

Ancient sources pay scant attention to Molossian history. Apart from inscriptions, most of our knowledge of Molossian events comes from a few critical passages in ancient authors[35] and passing mention in narratives more interested in southern Greek and Macedonian affairs. Sources often contradict each other about the identities and relationships between various members of the royal clan.[36] As a consequence, any Aeacid family tree is based on conjecture and should be treated with caution. For similar reasons, the chronology of Molossian events is often unclear. With such scrappy sources, one can only sketch in a picture of the political world in which Olympias grew up, only surmise what her experience and expectations were as she arrived in Macedonia, the latest bride of its much married king.

Consequently, we know only a little of Molossian events and Olympias' family's history. As we have already noted, Phthia, wife of the Molossian king Admetus, supposedly persuaded her husband to save Themistocles, helped him escape his enemies, and allowed him to flee to Macedonia and from there to the Persian Empire.[37] During the Peloponnesian War, Molossian armies, commanded by the regent Sabulinthus, fought on the Spartan side early in the war (Thuc. 2.80. 6). The young king, Tharyps,[38] for whom the regent acted, was sent to Athens for education (Just. 17.3.11) and was apparently given Athenian citizenship (Tod *GHI* 2.173, l. 4–5). Upon his return to Molossia, Tharyps sponsored some degree of Hellenization in his kingdom (Just. 17.3.12–13; Plut. *Pyrrh.* 1.3).[39] His son, Alcetas, was at some point exiled. Dionysius of Syracuse (*c.* 385) attempted to restore Alcetas with Illyrian aid; the Illyrians inflicted a massive defeat on the Molossians but were ultimately driven out with Spartan aid (Diod. 15.13.1–3). In 377, Alcetas was a signatory of the second Athenian confederacy and his son, Neoptolemus, also signed for the alliance (Tod *GHI* 2.123, l.109, 110). Alcetas' son Neoptolemus at first reigned alone,[40] but, in the end, shared rule with his brother Arybbas.[41] Neoptolemus had three children: Alexander (in terms of Molossian history he is Alexander I), Olympias, and her sister Troas (Just. 7.6.10–11, 8.6.5; Plut. *Alex.* 2.1; Diod. 16.72.1). The name or ethnicity of the mother/mothers of Neoptolemus' children is unknown, though scholars often assume that the mother of Olympias and her siblings was a Chaonian princess (see above). At some point prior to the marriage of Olympias (Just. 7.6.11; Plut. *Alex.* 2; 1–2), Neoptolemus died[42] and Arybbas ruled alone, marrying Troas, by whom he had a son, Aeacides, and acting as guardian for his brother's other two children. Arybbas had an older son as well, another Alcetas (Paus. 1.11.5). Shortly before Olympias' marriage to Philip, Arybbas had, by guerrilla tactics, repelled an incursion by Illyrian tribes (Frontin. 2.5.19). Such is our sketchy knowledge of the historical past of Olympias' dynasty.

The Aeacids were kings, but governmental structure and custom limited the power of fourth-century Molossian monarchs.[43] The kings functioned primarily as war leaders, although they conducted religious ceremonies as well. Molossians chose annual chief magistrates and representatives for each

Molossian tribe. Over time other offices developed.[44] After sacrificing to Zeus Areius, kings exchanged annual oaths with their people, the kings promising to rule according to *nomos* (custom or law) and the people to maintain the monarchy by *nomos* (Plut. *Pyrrh*. 5.2). This annual practice gives the impression that this was a kind of constitutional monarchy, although actual events suggest a less tidy reality.[45] The nature of the terrain, governmental structure, and political events imply that royal control of the tribes was limited. During the first half of the fourth century, Molossia was an expansionist state. For instance, around the time of Olympias' birth, Molossia finally acquired control of some coastal territory.[46] Much later in her life, Molossia became part of a more complex structure, the Epirote League or Alliance, but the Aeacids, though they became the war leaders of the alliance, were not Epirote kings (see Chapter 3).

Olympias became the wife of Philip, a man famous for his many wives. It would be helpful in terms of understanding her career to know whether she had grown up in a household where the kings had multiple wives. However, if Molossian kings practiced polygyny before the day of Pyrrhus (Plut. *Pyrrh*. 9.1, 10.5), Olympias great-nephew, we do not know it.[47] Some aspects of Aeacid history hint that kings prior to Pyrrhus may have practiced polygyny. Brothers, or branches of descent from royal brothers, frequently contended for the throne.[48] Struggles between men with the same father but different mothers were often a consequence of the polygamy of royal males.[49] Warring Aeacid brothers could have been only half-siblings.[50] Nonetheless, even if there could be certainty that these were indeed half-brothers in conflict, it would prove only that kings married more than once, not that they married more than one woman at the same time. Olympias grew up in a contentious and comparatively unstable court, but it may not have been one where the kings had many wives simultaneously.

Would Olympias have expected to marry a ruler from so comparatively far away, from a kingdom on the other side of the Pindus Mountains? It is difficult to say much about Aeacid marriage policy since, prior to the reign of Olympias' uncle Arybbas, we know the name of only one Molossian royal wife and the ethnicity of none. Most likely it was comparatively localized and brides were taken from and offered to other Epirote tribes and neighboring peoples like the Thessalians and the various peoples of Upper Macedonia (western, mountainous Macedonia). It may even be that close-kin marriages within the dynasty, like that of Arybbas and his niece, Olympias' sister Troas, were common.

As the career of Olympias' father demonstrates, her family did not maintain a set pattern for succession to the throne and they were even less consistent in terms of keeping a ruler on the throne, once he had assumed power. True, those who write about ancient Molossia tend to assume that the Aeacids practiced primogeniture.[51] Judging by events, however, there is no evidence for regular succession by older sons. Pausanias (1.11.5), for instance, reports that Arybbas' son Aeacides, who became king after his father, was not Arybbas' eldest son and that Aeacides' eldest son, Alcetas, became king only after the death of his younger brother. When the Epirotes became dissatisfied with Alcetas, they killed him and his children and brought in Pyrrhus, the son of his younger brother. Granted, however, the inevitable limits of ancient life expectancy, the oldest surviving son clearly had a working if not a theoretical edge. Whatever the initial basis for selection, considerable second-guessing seems to have occurred. The Molossians frequently expelled their kings, sometimes recalled them, and occasionally compelled them to shared rule with another member of the dynasty. The judgment of the previous king (Paus. 1.11.5), military victory or defeat (Plut. *Pyrrh*. 5.7), popular opinion (Paus. 1.11.5), and military assistance by foreign powers (Plut. *Pyrrh*. 5.1), all played a part on one occasion or another. Until after the death of Olympias, however, though Aeacid kings were hardly in a strong or stable position and dynastic infighting happened more often than not, its severity had limits: there is no certain instance of the murder of one Aeacid by another until Pyrrhus murdered Neoptolemus (Plut. *Pyrrh*. 5.6–7). Prior to Pyrrhus, Aeacids victorious in dynastic contention made do by forcing their rivals to share rule or by expelling them.[52]

Indeed, before we turn to the circumstances and significance of Olympias' marriage, it is helpful to consider both the similarities[53] and differences between the Molossian world in which she grew up and the Macedonian court she joined when she married. Both were northern monarchies, less urban, more tribal, more dependent on pastoral transhumance than cereal agriculture.[54] The dynasties claimed descent from major Greek heroes but the people they ruled were not yet widely considered Greek. Both kingdoms dealt constantly with incursions from Illyrian tribes; their efforts made them buffer states,[55] saving those further south from similar experiences, but limiting their own ability to develop. The intervention of major Greek powers also contributed to this situation. The kingdoms remained warlike societies with unstable monarchies.

On the other hand, major differences existed. Macedonia was a country richer in population and mineral resources and had much better access to the sea and its markets. Its coastline bordered a major grain route; Molossia's did not. Molossian monarchy originated away from the sea, in the mountains and only gradually reached the coast. Macedonian monarchy actually began on the coastal plain and gradually asserted control over mountainous regions. Centralization and Hellenization moved more rapidly in Macedonia. Though both dynasties changed allegiances with major southern Greek powers from time to time, out of weakness, the Aeacids had something of a tradition of alliance with the Athenians and the Argeads did not. Internal dynastic conflict in Macedonia had a much more violent and bloody history than in Molossia. Despite this, ordinary Macedonians manifested a much greater degree of dynastic loyalty to the Argeads than Molossians and Epirotes did to the Aeacids. It comes as no surprise that the Epirotes ultimately abolished the monarchy while the Macedonians, after the end of the

Argead dynasty, comparatively quickly embraced a new royal dynasty and stayed loyal to it until the Romans took their independence from them. In Macedonia, monarchy and nationalism were one, but in Molossia and Epirus they were not. Macedonian kings had virtually no structural checks on their power whereas the power of Molossian kings was distinctly more limited. The degree of difference between the two monarchies grew greater as the fourth century progressed.[56] One can only wonder whether Olympias found the wider role apparently available to royal women in Molossian monarchy more appealing than the greater absolutism of Macedonian monarchy. The later period of her life (see Chapter 4) might suggest that, in effect, she tried to combine these two traditions to her own advantage, and that this attempt was, ultimately, unsuccessful.

It would be interesting to know how old Olympias was when she first encountered the intrigues and complexities of Philip's court, but her age at the time of her marriage and the dates of her betrothal and wedding to Philip are unknown. The only comparative certainty is that Alexander was born in the summer of 356. That granted, the wedding must have taken place by late summer, early fall of 357, although it could have happened earlier.

Plutarch's account (*Alex.* 2.1) of the betrothal of Philip and Olympias implies that some time passed between betrothal and marriage: Plutarch says Philip was still a *meirakion* (youth, a person around twenty) and Olympias an orphan child. Philip would have turned twenty around 362, so one could imagine that years passed between betrothal and wedding, but a number of factors suggest that was not the case. Philip did not rule in his own right until 359 and a betrothal to a foreign princess while his brother still ruled would seem unlikely. Although he certainly did marry several times at the beginning of his reign and so could have taken yet another bride very quickly, the political situation with the Illyrians, the probable context for the marriage (see below) makes it likely that both marriage and betrothal happened in 357. Athenian girls tended to marry between the ages of fourteen and eighteen, but female members of the Argead dynasty tended to marry later, and Aeacid habits may have been similar.[57] If one takes Plutarch's statement seriously but assumes his diction is either vague or exaggerated, then it seems reasonable to conclude that Olympias was no more than eighteen at the time of her marriage in 357 and certainly could have been a bit younger. So she was probably born between 375 and 371.

The circumstances of Olympias' first encounter with Philip were probably distinctly less romantic than Plutarch would have it. As we have noted, he asserts that the two young people met as initiates of the cult at Samothrace, that Philip fell in love with her and arranged the betrothal. The love-story part of Plutarch's account is quite unlikely to be true.[58] Members of Greek elites, let alone kings, married for political reasons, to mates whose wealth and family connections would be beneficial. Philip was particularly famous for using his marriages to seal or establish alliances (see Chapter 2). Even ordinary Greeks did not marry for romantic love; the prime purpose of marriage was the procreation of children, and virtually all marriages were arranged.[59]

Moreover, the location of this first encounter implies considerable forethought on the part of all parties. Samothrace was an extremely isolated island and its cult comparatively unknown at the time, especially to mountain people of northwestern Greece. Elite women like the Molossian Andromacha (see above) certainly did travel to major shrines for religious purposes. That a king's daughter would be escorted by her guardian would be unsurprising. But it is implausible to believe that Olympias and Arybbas simply happened on Philip at the initiation to a cult with which no Molossian was likely familiar.[60] They were not there by accident.

Since the marriage alliance benefited both rulers,[61] either king might have initiated negotiations for the union. Philip's tendency to marry in connection to political alliances hints that he could have been the initiator. Virtually everyone agrees that this marriage alliance was intended to create a unified Molossian/Macedonian front against the Illyrian menace. Philip came to the throne when his brother fell in a massacre the Illyrians had inflicted on the Macedonians and Arybbas had barely driven the Illyrians out of his kingdom.[62] Despite his brother's disastrous end and other early troubles, Philip had succeeded in winning a major victory against Illyrian forces. His success was the primary context for the alliance.[63] Arybbas probably hoped that Philip's aid would enable him to expand his own kingdom (Just. 7.6.12). Philip may well have seen the possibility for other benefits to be derived from the alliance,[64] most notably the potential to exploit and ultimately dominate the neighboring kingdom. Philip's was the mind of a conqueror: he had a knack for finding and exploiting open-ended situations. That being so, it is hard to mark the point when potential becomes plan.[65]

Although the marriage alliance brought advantages to both kings, it is likely that, whichever initiated the alliance, it was Philip who dominated it. At the time, the two kings must have looked quite similar to southern Greeks, and Arybbas may even have had greater prestige among Greeks. But the fact that the engagement happened at Samothrace almost certainly signifies that arrangements were made to please Philip, not Arybbas. The trip from inland Molossia to Samothrace, whether by land or sea, was neither easy nor short. Until around the time of the reign of Philip, Samothrace had been a poor and remote sanctuary with only local significance. Philip was responsible for the first stone building at the site[66] and it continued to be patronized by the Argead and later dynasties. The alliance was arranged on his ground, not neutral ground and certainly not Arybbas'.[67] Secrecy was probably not a factor in the choice of meeting place.[68] Betrothals were formal and public affairs and the presence of two kings at Samothrace was, if anything, more likely to attract attention than their presence at one of the better-known panhellenic shrines. The betrothal may have occurred in the very public context of an annual festival held there in mid-June.[69] The cult permitted initiation at times other than the festival, but a connection between the betrothal and the festival is particularly appealing because, at least in Hellenistic times and quite possibly earlier, the festival included a re-enactment of the wedding of Cadmus and Harmonia.[70]

Plutarch's language makes it clear that the betrothal was an agreement between two men. Olympias probably did not consent; it is unlikely that her views on the subject were solicited. Had she been a widow, not a young girl, it might have been different. Widowed women in Molossia had consider-able legal independence and in Macedonia several widowed royal women acted as their own marriage brokers or tried to arrange marriages for their daughters.[71]

Did Arybbas negotiate, in any sense, with Olympias' interests in mind? Military alliance apart, it seems plausible to assume that Arybbas would have been concerned about anything that would affect Aeacid honor and improve Molossian interests or his personal ones. Aeacid clan pride certainly could be a potent force. When, many years later, Philip did act in a way that Olympias' son Alexander considered dishonored her, he and his mother exiled themselves to Molossia (Alexander went on to the Illyrians), trouble did brew between the two dynasties, and only a second Molossian–Macedonian royal marriage soothed this affront to Aeacid pride (see Chapter 2). It seems much less likely that Arybbas would have cared about Olympias' personal welfare (after all, he had presumably forced her father to share the throne with him, a situation unlikely to produce warm feelings between uncle and niece, and his marriage to her sister may or may not have improved relations). It has been hypothesized[72] that Arybbas asked for and received certain guarantees: that Olympias be given greater status at court than existing wives, that a son born to her be treated as heir, and that she be given an unprecedentedly prestigious wedding in Macedonia. While all of these possible guarantees accord, in varying degrees, with what I have suggested were Arybbas' interests, the first and second suggest a certainty about future complications and about Philip's willingness to honor the terms that seems implausible.[73] The third, because it directly connects to family pride and involved an event in the immediate future, is more believable. However, as we shall see, it is not certain that Olympias got a big public wedding and even less certain that, if she did, it was unprecedented.

What role, then, did Olympias play in this alliance? First and foremost, she had to produce babies, preferably male and preferably more than one. A childless wife risked divorce and certainly lost status. The production of children, central to any ancient marriage, was particularly vital in royal marriages. Not only property but also succession to the throne and thus political stability were at issue. The central importance for women is demon-strated by the actions of Andromacha, probably Olympias' aunt. She made a trip to the distant shrine of Asclepius in Epidaurus in order to become pregnant, and perhaps a second, in gratitude for the birth of a son.[74] Marriage alliances arranged by two males were, among other things, agreements to have common descendants. Philip, Arybbas and Olympias all benefited from the production of children from the alliance: Philip could get more heirs and marriageable daughters; Arybbas could get greater prestige and perhaps closer relations if a child of the marriage became king; and Olympias got immediate precedence over any childless royal wives, yet more if she produced male children, and the greatest prestige of all if she produced the heir to the throne.[75] In other contexts in the Greek world, the production of children rather than the wedding itself confirmed a marriage and made it seem permanent (e.g., Lys. 1.6). This would be especially true in a political marriage alliance.

Many historians treat all royal brides involved in such alliances as mere tokens, soon forgotten by both the families of their births and their marriage, particularly if they produced no children. Judging by the evidence, that probably was the situation of some royal women, but by no means all.[76] One must, first of all, reflect on the implications of Greek marriage practice. In terms of general Greek marriage patterns, one family in a sense loaned a woman to another family; she never became part of her husband's family and (as in the case of Olympias' return to her family, mentioned above) even quarrels, let alone divorce or death, might send her back to the family of her birth. Any children of the marriage belonged to her husband's family, not hers, and would not follow her if she left the marital household. Her birth family might arrange a marriage to yet another family.[77] Women, therefore, were likely to retain a significant degree of identity with their birth families and were likely to maintain, as much as possible, close relations with them. In practice, in royal dynasties, this meant that women functioned as intermediaries between two royal families. Olympias' connection to Molossia and the Aeacid dynasty remained strong throughout her life. Royal fathers, brothers and uncles often expected that the new wives would act as ambassadors in a foreign court for the interests of the family of their birth, even in opposition to those of their husbands (e.g., Just. 16.2.4). Husbands sometimes had the reverse expectation (e.g., Plut. *Demetr.* 2.3). Negotiating these contradictory expectations was a given for royal women. Such expectations could, of course, create conflicts in loyalty, but the alliances themselves could also help to resolve them.

For royal women confronted with a situation in which they were not the only wife, continued ties to birth families were even more likely. Family status could increase their personal status compared to other wives and birth family members could function as their advocates and supporters against the interests of other wives. Olympias' career offers examples of both: she stressed her heroic genealogy and passed on that focus to her son. As we shall see, several members of the Aeacid clan played important roles in the court of Philip (see Chapter 2). She would not be the lone Molossian at court.

Throughout this chapter I have referred to the daughter of Neoptolemus as "Olympias," yet that is unlikely to have been the name she was known by during her girlhood in Molossia. Plutarch (*Mor.* 401) noted that nicknames often obscure real names and asserted that Alexander's mother, Polyxena, was later called Myrtale, Olympias, and Stratonice.[78] Justin

(2.7.13) insists that Myrtale was the name she was known by as a child. Since other royal women either changed their names or took on additional epithets, it seems likely that this Molossian king's daughter had different names or epithets at different periods and that the changes came at significant moments in her life.[79] Name changing and the choice of politically significant names marked the comparatively public status of royal women. These significant names may sometimes have functioned as quasi-titles in an era before actual titles were employed.[80]

Various scholars have developed explanations for the four names of Olympias. (We shall return to the issue of her name changes in Chapter 5, in the context of their relationship to her religiosity.) This is what seems likely to me. At first she was known as Polyxena, a Trojan name like those of her sister and brother, appropriate choices if their mother was a member of the Chaonian dynasty that claimed descent from the royal house of Troy, yet a name with connections to Neoptolemus as well.[81] At some point before her marriage she acquired the name Myrtale, almost certainly in connection to some religious experience, whether a rite of passage,[82] Samothracian ritual,[83] or some other, as yet unknown, mystery cult. Olympias, the name the sources always employ about her, must date from the early days of her marriage to Philip, most likely to a wedding somehow connected to the festival of Olympian Zeus, although possibly to Philip's Olympian victory in the following year (see Chapter 5). Stratonice ('victory' in military matters) is probably the last name, more like an epithet, employed in the brief period in 317 between her victory against Adea Eurydice and Philip Arrhidaeus and her own defeat by Cassander.[84]

Sarah Pomeroy raises an interesting question about Olympias' name changes. How would she herself have felt about them? Pomeroy wonders whether Olympias would have experienced a "loss of identity" or, alternatively, would have seen the changed name as "an affirmation of his [Philip's] bond with her."[85] The assumption seems to be that all these changes in name/epithet were imposed upon her by her father (and perhaps her mother, granted the Chaonian connection), uncle, and husband. Whereas "Polyxena" and "Olympias" were likely chosen by others, Olympias could possibly have chosen her other two names herself. She could have selected "Myrtale" herself, as part of a coming-of-age ceremony or as part of her betrothal, in the same way that those about to receive communion for the first time can choose for themselves an additional name. "Stratonice," probably selected long after the death of Philip, is, of all these names, the one most likely to have been her own decision.

Ancient sources tell us nothing directly about the personality, character, world view or even the appearance[86] of the daughter of Neoptolemus as her wedding entourage set off over the Pindus Mountains in the direction of her new kingdom. However, based on what is known about her life and background, we can speculate about her views and circumstance as she began her public career.

Though only in her mid- to late teens, this young woman had already experienced a great deal. While still a young child, she had seen her father lose sole control of his kingdom. A possibly tense period of uncertain duration followed in which he and his brother shared rule. Then her father Neoptolemus died, leaving his children in what may well have seemed the sinister guardianship of their uncle. Probably soon after that, her uncle married her sister. Shortly before Olympias' betrothal, the Illyrians invaded her country. Frontinus (2.5.19) reports that Arybbas sent the non-combatants as refugees into Aetolia, while he and whatever army he could gather withdrew to the mountains in order to utilize guerrilla tactics against the much larger invading force. Presumably Olympias and her sister would have endured the danger of the invasion and the uncertainty of evacuation. More recently yet, Olympias had made the long journey to Samothrace. Even before her entry into Macedonia, Olympias had dealt with political intrigue, physical danger, and the loss of her most powerful protector, and had traveled to two different foreign territories. Her life began, much as it would end, in uncertainty and danger.

Despite her early entry into the world of power politics and violence, as my comparison and contrast of the two kingdoms should have implied, the society Olympias would encounter in Macedonia, though likely much less alien to her than that of Thebes or Athens, would have been different from her previous experience. Philip's court was certainly richer and more cosmopolitan than that of Arybbas, or at least it became so soon after her arrival. Military activity and success mattered more in the Macedonian court. The climate and terrain around Pella and Aegae, the Macedonian capitals, was much milder than that of Olympias' homeland. Philip had more power over the Macedonians than her uncle did over the Molossians. As we shall see, Philip already had several wives and children (and may have had concubines in residence, as well). Despite the fact that Olympias had grown up in a court that was itself not without intrigue, the level of complexity that she would encounter in the court of Philip would be far greater than that of Arybbas (although Olympias would surely have been warned to expect the presence of the other wives).

It is particularly difficult to assess Olympias' probable attitude toward her coming marriage. Literature written by Greek women stresses the pain and loss of identity the break between the world (family and friends) of a young unmarried girl and a bride occasioned. Olympias' distance from the land of her birth could have exacerbated this feeling.[87] However, since her father was dead, her mother may have been, and we do not know how well she got on with her uncle and how comfortable she was at his court, we cannot tell whether she would have been glad to leave.[88]

What we do know is that she brought her pride in her lineage with her. Hers was a more prestigious marriage than that of any previous Aeacid woman and, if her wedding were indeed held at a major Macedonian festival, her nuptials were more elaborate and public than those of previous Molossian royal women. Olympias' Aeacid descent would continue to be a support and source of identity to herself and both her children.

In her subsequent career, Olympias consistently pursued her son's and then her grandson's political interests, tending to regard any check on their power, the prominence of any other figure, as a threat to them. Herself the product of a relatively weak monarchic system, she regularly attempted to create a situation which enabled both her male kin and herself to act more absolutely. This response was probably instinctive, certainly not at first a conscious plan or policy, though it would become one. Olympias was, like Philip, a person with a knack for seeing the possibilities for exploitation in a situation. Even early on in her Macedonian career, she demonstrated that. If Olympias the young girl was anything like Olympias the mature woman, then she would have been aware of many of the dangers and complications awaiting her, but she would not have been fearful and she would not have been timid.

2 Olympias, wife of Philip II

Olympias, the young princess from a remote mountain kingdom, became the wife of Philip II (r. 359–336) of Macedon, probably in the fall of 357. Olympias would need to find her own way through the intrigues, shifting alliances, and power plays of a court that was at once cosmopolitan and yet profoundly provincial. The complexities of a polygamous marriage to a king who was rapidly becoming the most powerful man in the Greek world made this task even more difficult. Nonetheless, Olympias became the most important woman in the Macedonian court since, about midway through his reign, Philip began to treat her son Alexander as his heir. However, shortly after Philip's great victory of Chaeroneia in 338 established his domination of the entire Greek peninsula and as he planned a Graeco-Macedonian invasion of the Persian Empire, a series of events relevant to Alexander's relationship with Philip threatened to jeopardize the succession of her son and thus Olympias' position. Despite the fact that Philip arranged a public reconciliation with his son (and almost certainly with Olympias as well), his murder triggered charges that mother and son were involved in his assassination. Notwithstanding continuing suspicions about their role in Philip's death, Alexander succeeded his father, and Olympias became the most influential woman in the Greek world and would remain so until her death. While Philip's initial preference for her son may have had little to do with Olympias or her actions (Philip's only other son had mental limitations), Alexander's successful negotiation of the threats to his position as heir may have owed much to his mother's efforts on his behalf. Certainly it is during this troubled period that the sources first report her taking an active role in events, as her son's advocate.

Olympias arrived in Philip's court at a turning point in the reign of her husband and in the history of Macedonia and the entire Greek peninsula. Two years before, Philip had come to the throne in a moment of great crisis. The Illyrians had invaded Macedonia and massacred a Macedonian army. Among the dead was its commander, Philip's older brother Perdiccas III. Three different pretenders to the throne (two supported by foreign powers) threatened Philip's rule and the kingdom itself.[1] Although this was one of the worst moments in Macedonian history, Macedonia had never been stable:

Argead rulers lacked real control over the mountainous areas of the kingdom. Invasions, particularly by Illyrian tribes, happened with some regularity. Bitter rivalries within the royal Argead clan frequently led to royal exile and assassinations. The years since the death of Philip's father Amyntas III had proved particularly rocky; the kingdom seemed to lurch from one crisis to another.[2]

At the time of Philip's accession, no one would have been surprised if his kingdom had been partitioned, but instead, within only two years, Philip dealt with all the pretenders and staved off the threatened invasions. He did this by a combination of military success (having begun a reform of the Macedonian army) and diplomatic skill. Olympias' arrival roughly coincided with a basic change in Philip's efforts: he moved from the defensive to the offensive. Philip had already begun to centralize his kingdom and consolidate his borders, and now he moved to expand the realm he had inherited. His combination of military and political acumen brought him increasing wealth and renown and would ultimately enable him to defeat all comers in Greece. Thus Olympias appeared in Macedonia at the very time it was ceasing to be a backward and remote kingdom, much like the one in which she had grown up, and was becoming a more urban, wealthier, and much more Hellenized realm ruled by a king who had already accumulated more control than had any Argead ruler before him.

Macedonian monarchy had no structural limits, unlike Molossian monarchy, but it had previously had many circumstantial ones. Rival claimants to the throne, invasions, and assassinations had prevented the development of much centralized power, as had the comparative lack of urbanization. Macedonia had a large population and rich timber and mineral resources but the only Macedonian king who had begun to take advantage of this potential, Archelaus, was assassinated, and Macedonia once more sank into instability. The result of this chaotic history was a personal monarchy of a nearly Homeric sort, one with little ceremony. The king was chief administrative, religious, and military leader. He was always escorted, as were Homeric leaders, by *Hetairoi* (Companions), who accompanied him at court and in battle. They were part of a warrior elite who fought on horseback; until the reign of Philip they were virtually the only Macedonian military force. The king's Companions hunted, drank, and sometimes had sexual relations with the king. The intimate relationship between king and elite began early. By Philip's day and quite possibly sooner, the custom had developed of sending the sons of great families to court (though often termed "Pages" the members of this group are more accurately called "Royal Youths") where they served the king as personal attendants and bodyguards.[3] Although the distinction between the ruler and the rest of the elite was not great, the rule of the Argead clan was the only fixed element in a country where virtually every other political aspect of life was unstable.[4] Even the royal residence was changeable: Archelaus had created a new capital at Pella, close to the coast but Aegae, the old capital on the slopes above the coastal plain, was still where the Argeads were buried and where they spent considerable time.[5]

Although some earlier Argead kings had probably practiced polygamy, Philip did so on an unprecedented scale.[6] In the end, he married seven women. Most of these marriages were clearly part of his initial move to stabilize the kingdom and secure its borders. Much of what we know about Philip's marriages and the children they produced comes from a famous passage[7] in Athenaeus' *Deipnosophistai* (13.557b–e) that contains a fragment of Satyrus' life of Philip II.[8] The passage makes a generalization about the connection between Philip's marriages and his wars (this initial statement is that of Athenaeus, not Satyrus), the quotation (or paraphrase) from Satyrus then begins with the list (in apparent chronological order) of his wives and the children he had by each, and concludes with material about events toward the end of Philip's reign. Since this fragment is crucial to understanding the circumstance in which Olympias found herself, I offer a translation of the entire passage:

Philip of the Macedonians did not lead women into war, as did Darius (the one deposed by Alexander), who, throughout the whole campaign, led around three hundred concubines, as Dicaearchus records in the third book of his *History of Greece*. But Philip always married in connection to a war. Anyway, in the twenty-two years in which he reigned, as Satyrus says in his *Life* of him, Philip, having married Audata an Illyrian woman, had by her a daughter Cynnane and he also married Phila the sister of Derdas and Machatas. Wishing to govern the Thessalian nation as well, he begot children by two Thessalian women, of whom one was a Pheraean, Nicesipolis, who bore to him Thessalonice, the other the Larissan Philinna by whom he fathered Arrhidaeus. And, in addition, he also gained the kingdom of the Molossians, having married Olympias, by whom he had Alexander and Cleopatra. And when he conquered Thrace, Cothelas the king of the Thracians came over to him, bringing his daughter Meda and many gifts. Having married her also, he brought her in beside Olympias. In addition to all of these, having conceived a passion for her, he married Cleopatra, the sister of Hippostratus as well as the niece of Attalus. And, having brought her in beside Olympias, he troubled every aspect of his life, for right away, during the actual wedding festivities, Attalus said, "Now, at any rate, genuine not bastard kings will be born." And Alexander, having heard this, threw the cup which he held in his hands at Attalus and thereupon he threw his cup at Alexander. And after these things, Olympias went into exile among the Molossians and Alexander among the Illyrians and Cleopatra bore a daughter to Philip called Europa.

Scholars continue to debate many aspects of this passage. The phrase I have translated "in connection to a war" is vague and could refer to a marriage

made at the end of a war, but also to one before or during a war. It is therefore not really possible to date Philip's marriages by his wars[9] and the rest
of the passage, in fact, fails to connect Philip's marriages to wars, although
it often connects them to political aims.[10] Satyrus intended the list that follows
to be in chronological order, but he may not have known the exact order
of some of the earlier marriages, which could be why his language is vaguer
in those sections.[11]

Despite all this uncertainty, several things relevant to Olympias' situation
seem either certain or very likely. Olympias' name appears fifth on the list;
it is probable that she was Philip's fifth bride; if she was not, then she was
his fourth and the fifth marriage came soon thereafter.[12] What this means
is that Philip married at least four women and more likely five within a two-
year period. Even if his fifth marriage was not to Olympias but Nicesipolis,
as is sometimes suggested, a long gap would still exist between that marriage
and his last two. Since his early marriages produced five children fairly
quickly but did not continue to do so, one must also note a long gap in the
production of children. After the birth of Thessalonice, none of his wives
bore any children until Philip's last wife, Cleopatra, produced a baby girl on
the eve of his murder. Philip's marriage alliances came in three stages: the
initial period in which he quickly married five women, primarily to stabilize
Macedonia and its borders; a long intermediate period (probably from
357 until 342 or even 339[13]) in which he made no new marriage alliances;
and a third period (339–336), shortly before his planned invasion of Asia,
in which he involved himself in a number of marriages (his own and those
of other family members), primarily to stabilize the dynasty before his
departure to the east.[14]

Olympias' co-wives were, like herself, products of political alliances, some
with external powers, some with internal. All contributed to the unprecedented internal and external stability that characterized the reign of Philip.
Audata, an Illyrian possibly related to the king Bardylis, likely married Philip
as part of a settlement after his defeat of Bardylis. Philip's two Thessalian
marriages speak to the importance of Thessaly (a region bordering Philip's
own with excellent cavalry and a culture comparatively similar to that of
Macedonia) to the growth of Philip's military machine. Phila, apparently
a member of the Upper Macedonian house of Elimeia, was clearly married
as part of Philip's successful efforts to incorporate the mountainous regions
of Macedonia into royal control in a thoroughgoing way. The marriage
of Meda, the daughter of a Getic king, connects to stabilizing the Thracian
border after Philip's conquests in that region.[15] Though some scholars
continue to believe that Philip's last marriage to Cleopatra, niece of Attalus,
was a love match,[16] this too was a political marriage intended to conciliate
a powerful faction and stabilize Macedonia prior to Philip's departure for
Asia (see below for further discussion).

When a man is polygamous, particularly when he is a ruler, the relative
status of his wives inevitably becomes an issue. Some polygamous ancient

monarchs, like Egyptian pharaohs, chose an official chief wife or queen whose unique status was indicated by a title, but even the king, in Philip's day, did not use a title, and certainly none of his wives did.[17] Earlier scholars used to sort through the women on Satyrus' list, categorizing some as wives and others as mere concubines or worse, but most would now agree that this approach was a mistake, borne out of our own monogamous prejudices, those of southern Greeks, and the innuendos that arose from the rivalries of Philip's wives and their factions. The list Athenaeus preserves, as we have seen, explicitly refers to marriages.[18]

While nothing indicates any institutionalized ranking of Philip's wives, functional ranking of wives tends to develop in polygamous circumstances and certainly this seems to have happened at Philip's court. Several factors contributed to the status of wives.[19] First and foremost was the production of a male child treated as heir to the throne, but the production of any male children, the earlier the better, was clearly vital. As in Molossia there was a tendency toward primogeniture, but no really regular pattern of succession.[20] Being the mother of a daughter or daughters was less prestigious but still vital: it suggested fruitfulness and thus the possibility of future male children and provided the king with daughters who would be useful in marriage alliances. A childless wife was in a weak position, but was not necessarily without any status at all at court because childbearing, though the preeminent source of status for royal wives, was not the only one. The prestige of a woman's family certainly mattered since this was the reason that the marriage happened in the first place, and family prestige continued to be significant throughout the duration of the marriage. Prestige could also connect to another factor affecting a royal wife's place in the court pecking order: her ability to intrigue. A woman's ability to function as a succession advocate for her son, to scheme, to work against rivals and build alliances, was critical, but a wife with powerful and eminent family members at court would inevitably have an advantage in this area. Although some scholars believe that the ethnicity of a king's wife could influence her status, my view is that it did not in an absolute way (in the sense of an ethnic prejudice), but it could situationally as it related to a woman's family and its continuing influence. Audata, for instance, would have been affected by the current importance of her Illyrian family, but not by the mere fact that she was Illyrian.[21] (We will return to this issue in the context of the troubles Olympias and Alexander experienced late in Philip's reign, troubles some link to Olympias' ethnicity.)

Although I believe that one personal quality, a woman's ability to scheme, contributed to the achievement of status at court, Philip's sexual interest in (let alone affection for) a wife probably did not play a significant role in her status. There is no evidence that Philip actually liked any of his wives, though he may have. Ancient sources (Plut. *Alex.* 2.1, 9.4; Satyr. *ap.* Athen. 557d) speak of his erotic interest in Olympias and later Cleopatra but, quite apart from the uncertainty of their testimonies, it is unlikely that this erotic interest had any lasting effect on the status of individual wives. Believing that it did derives from the false presumption that ancient marriage, let alone royal marriage, existed for the reasons and on the terms that modern ones do. The purpose of any wife, certainly a royal one, was to produce children.[22] Philip had many lovers, a number of them male. An erotic relationship with the king, as we shall see, definitely led lovers (especially male lovers) to expect reward and prestige, but lovers were not wives. Short term, catching the king's eye could have given temporary advantage to one wife over another, if both were otherwise in the same circumstance.[23] But the only possible way the king's erotic interest might make a lasting difference in the status of a wife would be when two women had produced male children of similar age and equal ability.[24] This did not happen in the reign of Philip II.

Though Philip's wives competed for status, particularly because no fixed status marked out a chief wife or heir,[25] one should not exaggerate or stereotype the degree of this competition. Generally speaking, competition for rank in polygamous marriages tends to decrease and coalitions tend to develop as the number of wives increases.[26] If wives' interests are not antagonistic, then alliances are apt to appear. The mother of royal sons might, for instance, ally with the mother of a royal daughter. Family ties and friendships could play a role. For instance, the Aeacids had traditional ties to Upper Macedonia, so Olympias might easily have established ties to the childless Phila. A childless wife with powerful connections might play the role of peacemaker.[27] Both men and women in the Macedonian court were extraordinarily competitive, but women, like men, did not necessarily compete with everyone. We should expect alliances as well as enmities.

Olympias became the dominant woman at court though she probably did not become so immediately.[28] Philip's formidable mother Eurydice may well have survived into the early years of Philip's reign; if so, she would have been a force to reckon with. Generally royal women had greater influence during their sons' reigns than their husbands', primarily because the mother–son relationship often meant that the mother was an advocate in her son's accession. Eurydice had proved a formidable succession advocate for her sons and she apparently played a prominent role in cult in Macedonia, probably primarily during the reigns of her sons.[29]

Apart from Philip's mother, only one other woman at court could, during most of Philip's reign, have rivaled Olympias' prestige in any lasting way. Philip's only other son, Arrhidaeus, roughly the same age as Alexander,[30] was the son of a Thessalian woman, Philinna. As Arrhidaeus grew older, his mental limitations became apparent: he was probably mildly retarded.[31] According to Plutarch (*Alex.* 77.5), however, these limitations were either not apparent earlier or did not originally exist. In the light of my discussion of determinants of the status of royal wives, it should be obvious that Philinna would, for some years, have been Olympias' greatest rival.

Several features of the tradition about her, her son, and Olympias confirm this deduction and imply the existence of a rivalry of some length until, presumably, the clear manifestation of Arrhidaeus' handicap inevitably gave the victory to Alexander and Olympias.[32] Some sources assert that Philinna was not respectable: Justin (13.2.11) and Ptolemy, son of Agesarchus (*ap.* Athen. 13.578a) claimed that she was either a prostitute or something close to it, and Plutarch (*Alex.* 77.5) maintains that she was lower class and without repute. None of these claims is likely to be true,[33] but they are the sorts of slander that appear in struggles for the succession between royal sons with different mothers.[34] Plutarch also reports (*Alex.* 77.5) that Olympias caused Arrhidaeus' disability by means of *pharmaka* (drugs or spells). Again, the charge is unlikely to be true, but suggests the existence of hostile propaganda and thus rivalry. Moreover, charges of witchcraft accompany rivalries in polygamous situations in many cultures, and Daniel Ogden has recently suggested that our tradition preserves the remnants of counter-charges of witchcraft by Philip's rival wives.[35] Although the evidence for Philinna is tenuous at best, two passages in Plutarch (*Alex.* 2.5, 77.5) explicitly connect Olympias to the use of *pharmaka*.[36]

Olympias had certainly established her dominant position by 340, when Philip left the sixteen-year-old Alexander as regent while he was on campaign (Plut. *Alex.* 9.1); by then the king was clearly treating Olympias' son as his heir. Alexander's, and thus Olympias', dominance was, however, likely established several years before that. Aristotle tutored Alexander for about three years, starting about 343 (Plut. *Alex.* 7.2–3; Diog. Laert. 5.10; Strabo 13.608). The choice of a distinguished royal tutor and the establishment of a separate "school" for him at Mieza seem to indicate the distinctive treatment given an heir. A letter of Isocrates (*Ep.* 5), *c.* 343, implies that Alexander was, by this year, widely regarded as Philip's heir. But if Arrhidaeus' mental limits had become obvious by the time he was ten, as seems likely,[37] then Alexander's position may have been clear as early as 346.[38]

Shortly after his great victory at Chaeroneia, Philip conceived of a monument, the Philippeum. Among other things, this embodied Olympias' and Alexander's victory in the struggle for succession. Constructed within the sacred precinct at Olympia, in a building that looked like a temple, the Philippeum contained gold and ivory (a material previously reserved for images of divinities) statues of Philip, his father Amyntas and his mother Eurydice, Alexander and Olympias (Paus. 5.17.4, 20.9–10). The general significance of this ambiguous structure has been much debated, though it clearly hinted at the divinity of not only Philip but his immediate family. In any event, since the Philippeum includes only one wife for each king (Amyntas had two) and only one son for each, it selects an official royal family and singles out Olympias and her son from the other wives and from Arrhidaeus.[39]

Ironically, within months of conceiving of this dynastic monument, Philip's last marriage jeopardized the status that the Philippeum seemed to commemorate. Even in her most secure years, however, as Philip's wife, Olympias would always have had to be vigilant to slights and mood changes on his part. In the absence of fixed titles and defined positions for chief wife and heir, succession and status were fluid by definition and mother and son would have had to keep a weather eye on the king. The chronic uncertainty of the situation of even the most dominant royal wife inevitably colored her relationships with her husband and her children. In effect, a degree of paranoia was a practical necessity for survival at Philip's court, but this same instinct to look for plots and hostility could not only preserve a royal mother and her son but could lead them to self-destructive behavior.

We know almost nothing about Olympias' relationship with her husband, and what little we do know relates to the troubled last two years of Philip's reign. There is no good evidence for an estrangement between them prior to that period. Granted that Philip continued to make indications that Alexander was his heir, there probably was no estrangement. That Olympias had only two children by Philip, probably born within a year or two of each other, is not evidence of estrangement after Cleopatra's birth, *c.* 355. The fertility of women in polygamous marriages tends to decline for a variety of factors,[40] but the more important point is that Olympias is the only wife of Philip generally acknowledged to have had more than one child by the king (see below for the possibility, rejected by most scholars, that his last wife, Cleopatra, had two children). Unless one concludes that he became "estranged" from all his wives shortly after a child was born to each, one must conclude that Olympias' failure to produce more children is not proof of estrangement. Indeed, as late as 341, Philip had an agent doing shopping for her in Athens, suggesting that no estrangement existed at that time.[41]

True, Plutarch (*Alex.* 2.4) does tell a tale (one that endured for many centuries) in which the sight of a snake sleeping with Olympias so disturbs Philip that he rarely has sexual relations with her again, fearing either spells or that the snake was a god. Some scholars consider this serious evidence about their relationship, although it clearly derives from the period of Alexander's belief that he was the son of Zeus Ammon and deserves no more credence than the assertion earlier in the same passage (*Alex.* 2.2) that the night before her marriage Olympias dreamed that her womb was struck by lightning. Even if we reject Plutarch's implausible claim that Philip's impulse to marry Olympias was erotic (*Alex.* 2.1) rather than political, it could be true that the relationship early on had an erotic charge—here were two able and absolutely ruthless young people with strong characters and passions. If so, then Olympias might, in the early years of her marriage, have experienced sexual jealousy when Philip's attention turned to other women and men, but after nearly twenty years of that sort of thing (including a possible sexual relationship between her husband and her brother; see below), it was unlikely to be a factor in Olympias' reaction to the threat posed by his last marriage.

As elsewhere in Greece, elite males had sexual relationships with both men and women. This seems to be true of both the kings and members of the elite. There are a number of indications, however, that masculine sexuality was differently constructed in Macedonia than in southern Greece and that the distinctively Macedonian take on sexual norms for elite males often played a critical role in the life of the court and in political events.[42] At least four Macedonian kings, including Philip,[43] are known to have had sexual relationships with other males and, in the case of each king, at least some of these relationships occurred or at least persisted into the adulthood of the king. Sexual relationships between males were often important in the context of assassination plots against the kings; in some they seem at least partially causative. It is unlikely that Olympias (or any other wife) would have felt herself to be in competition with Philip's male lovers and not implausible that she could have allied herself with one of his male lovers or former lovers. As Philip's assassination demonstrates, sexual tensions were an intrinsic part of court intrigue, and Olympias had years to learn to cope with them.

In any event, whatever their relationship had been earlier, dealings between Philip and Olympias were clearly filled with suspicion in the last year or two of his reign (see below for further discussion). Nonetheless, the fact that Philip effected a public reconciliation with Alexander and Olympias and arranged the marriage between Olympias' daughter and brother in the context of a grand panhellenic religious festival suggests that, in a formal and public way, on the day of Philip's death, Olympias was once more his dominant wife, if not his most trusted one.

Conventional wisdom says that Olympias was close to her son;[44] indeed, it often implies that the relationship was unhealthily close, that it explains Alexander's supposed lack of interest in women, that the world conqueror was a "mama's boy."[45] The truth is more complex and not easily fitted to popular psychological stereotypes. Alexander demonstrably had some interest in women, more in men (like many elite Greek males, including his own father), but limited interest in sex in general and more in power.[46] It is very likely that Alexander was closer to his mother than to his father, but the reasons for this circumstance were largely practical and functional. In the competitive polygamous situation described above, a king's son inevitably drew closer to his mother than to his father because the former was his succession advocate since her status derived from his success whereas his father probably had other sons and might prefer them. Plutarch (Mor. 178e) actually relates an anecdote in which Alexander complains to Philip because he is producing children by multiple women, and Philip replies by claiming that a contest for the succession would be good thing, demonstrating that he was worthy to inherit. Though the anecdote is probably not literally true, it recognizes a reality of royal father–son relations. A king's son had reason to distrust his father or at least to worry that he might not be able to count on his father's favor, whereas his mother's support was guaranteed out of her own self-interest.[47]

A fact of life in monarchy exacerbated this distrust: a son who reached or neared adult years was, in effect, waiting for his father to die, and royal fathers would always feel the breath of the heir just behind them.[48] Philip's constant departures on campaign inevitably increased this distance between father and son.[49] When serious trouble between Alexander and Philip developed in 338 or 337, it became apparent that Alexander could and did trust his mother and did not and could not trust his father to the same degree. Once Alexander became king, his relationship with his mother grew more complex (see Chapter 3), but its essence did not change: in a court riddled with suspicion, hostility and danger, these two could trust each other and watch each other's back. This fact may explain why, though he certainly honored his Argead ancestor Heracles and emulated his deeds, it was his mother's heroic ancestor who was Alexander's more compelling model. In a patrilineal world, his identification of himself as an Aeacid (and the tendency of our sources so to identify him) is striking. Arrian (1.11.8), for instance, has Alexander say that he was descended from the *genos* (clan, family) of Neoptolemus.[50]

What little the sources preserve about Olympias' relationship with her only daughter, Cleopatra, relates to the period after the death of Philip. Indeed, information about relationships between mothers and daughters in general, granted the male voice of most Greek written sources and Athenian reluctance to mention respectable women is public, is not easy to come by. Nonetheless, mother–daughter relationships may well have been closer than our largely male sources allow us to demonstrate. What little literature written by women we do possess focuses on the difficulty of leaving home; for young women, home meant, more than anything, their mother. The "returnable" quality of Greek women means that many, widowed or divorced young, might have returned to their mother's household. The centrality of the Demeter/Persephone myth and its role in women's festivals like the Thesmophoria that would have reunited mothers and married daughters is suggestive.[51] There is some evidence that Olympias and her daughter were close, at least at times. Later in life they demonstrably acted in concert. That her daughter became the wife of a Molossian king (Olympias' brother) probably intensified the relationship as another marriage might not have. Cleopatra's status was also tied to that of her brother, so to some degree these three formed a sub-unit, a succession unit, within the royal family. Once Alexander was king, he paid more attention to Cleopatra than to his half-sisters. Unlike Alexander, Cleopatra would most likely have stayed at her mother's side until her marriage.[52]

Olympias' most complex family relationship was probably that with her brother, Alexander of Molossia. Unfortunately, it is the one about which we have the least evidence, particularly because of the chronological uncertainties of the sources. He was probably younger than Olympias, though possibly not much younger.[53] At some point after Olympias' marriage, he arrived at Philip's court (where he may have been one of the Royal Youths) and Justin (Just. 8.6.3–6) insists that he also became Philip's lover. His arrival at court could demonstrate Olympias' influence over her husband and concern for her brother's safety[54] as he neared adulthood or it could simply signify that Philip continued to be interested in close ties to Molossia. Philip may already have been planning to replace Arybbas with Alexander of Molossia (as Justin 8.6.4–5 implies). Such a plan would doubtless have pleased Olympias, but her pleasure may have had nothing to do with Philip's actions. If Philip chose to put Alexander on the throne, he must have had considerable confidence in his control over him. In this context, the story that the young Molossian prince became his lover makes sense,[55] though this does not guarantee that it happened.

In our world, coping with the fact that one's husband and brother had a sexual relationship would be bizarre and painful.[56] In the Greek world, where sexual relationships between males, especially elite males, were widely accepted, it may not have been so unusual. Sexual relationships between males were probably not unknown at the Aeacid court and thus not unfamiliar to Olympias even before her arrival in Macedonia.[57] She could possibly have understood her brother's sexual relationship with Philip as confirmation of the prestige and influence of her family. On the other hand, it could have made her jealous or left her with a sense that her family had been humiliated.[58] I believe that Olympias' view and that of her brother would have depended on whether, having established the relationship, Philip then showed his esteem for Alexander by giving him honors. In Macedonian history, as in the case of Philip's assassin and the assassins of Archelaus (Arist. *Pol.* 1311b), failure to provide honors, support, and gifts to the beloved compromised the honor of the young man and might lead to violence. Since Philip did, in effect, give young Alexander Molossia, he would seem to have conducted what in context was an honorable relationship.

In any event, Alexander's arrival in Macedonia almost certainly signifies that relations between Philip and Arybbas had begun to deteriorate. After some military hostilities, Philip finally drove Arybbas into exile and put young Alexander of Molossia on the throne (Just. 8.6.7–8; Diod. 16.72.1[59]). This fact would complicate the situation that developed at the end of Philip's reign, when trouble with Philip drove Olympias' son and Olympias herself to her brother's court. On the other hand, initially it could only have increased Olympias' prestige at court.

In all likelihood, at least three other Aeacids (other than Olympias' brother) played roles in the Macedonian court. Doubtless they were there because of the importance of Philip's Molossian alliance, but their presence probably meant that Olympias, in addition to the female attendants who doubtless accompanied her, had other allies at court.[60] Though Alexander's wet nurse was a member of the Macedonian elite,[61] his earliest chief tutor was an Aeacid named Leonidas (Plut. *Alex.* 5.4).[62] Much more important was a royal bodyguard named Arybbas (Arr. 3.5.5); no source says that he was a kinsman of Olympias, but it is quite likely he was.[63] If so, his presence would surely have been helpful to Olympias since his was a position of great prestige. In addition, it is likely that the Neoptolemus whom Arrian calls an

Aeacid (Arr. 2.27.6) was already present in Philip's court, perhaps as a Royal Youth who accompanied Olympias' brother when he came to court.[64] Other court figures may have had kinship ties to Olympias. The Aeacids and Argeads both had close connections to elite Thessalians, and the Aeacids may well have intermarried with some of the princely houses of Upper Macedonia.[65] In sum, Olympias would not have had as many kinsmen and supporters at court as royal wives from within Macedonia itself, but neither was she entirely isolated and without any kind of support network of close kin.

It is more difficult to determine what, if any, influence she had in the larger court. Later in life she and her daughter trusted Eumenes, probably Philip's secretary. The beginning of this close political tie may well have been forged during the reign of Philip. Late in his reign, Philip sent several of his son's closest associates into exile. During her son's reign, the sources portray Olympias as jealous and suspicious of Alexander's associates, but in this early period she may have associated herself with the men who endured exile for her son's sake. (As we shall see, features of the "Pixodarus incident" might confirm this deduction.) From early in Alexander's reign until his own death, Antipater, general and diplomat for Philip and later regent for Alexander, was her arch enemy. This enmity lasted into another generation and evolved into a feud between the Antipatrid and Aeacid clans. Nonetheless, since Antipater aided Alexander in his youth and probably did much to ensure his succession at the time of Philip's murder, the troubles between Olympias and Antipater likely did not begin in her husband's reign but rather in her son's. The sources indicate some tension between Alexander and the family of Philip's best general, Parmenio. A marriage alliance to Attalus, guardian of Philip's last bride Cleopatra, the man who threatened to deprive Alexander of the throne, would also suggest that Olympias would not have been close to him and his, but no direct evidence then or later confirms it. Within the world of women, Olympias developed some renown because of her public leadership role in some cults (see Chapter 5) and she may also have worked out accommodations of sorts with some of Philip's other wives. In general, however, no evidence intimates that Olympias played a prominent or important role in her husband's court, at least not until the last two years of his reign.[66]

It would be satisfying to provide some physical context for the life of Olympias and her co-wives or, more generally, for the court of Philip. Unfortunately, virtually none exists. No literary source describes the living circumstances of royal women or clarifies their physical accessibility to the court as a whole, particularly to male courtiers. Archaeology does not solve the problem, even if the palace at Vergina (ancient Aegae) dates to the reign of Philip, as has recently been suggested.[67] The complexity of the remains of the palace at Pella prevents any clear conclusions.[68] Granted that recent scholarship has argued that the "women's quarters" of ordinary southern Greek women had no physical existence,[69] it seems unwise to assume that

royal Macedonian women, whose actions were demonstrably less circumscribed than women in *poleis* to the south, dwelled in something like the
Oriental harem of nineteenth-century Europeans' imaginings. More likely
they had households and suites of their own, possibly even separate buildings.[70] Both sons and daughters, until at least the age of six, would probably
have been part of their mothers' households, although sons would begin to
be introduced into the wider court and integrated into their father's company
sooner and to a much greater degree than their sisters. However, Olympias
and her daughter knew and corresponded with numerous elite Macedonian
males, a circumstance that implies that, like Homeric royal women, they
appeared in public at court, as well as at the kind of public occasions at which
all women appeared.[71] Perhaps royal women of earlier generations actually
performed domestic tasks, but the size and complexity of fourth-century
Macedonian palaces suggest that they were run by an extensive staff, probably partly slave, and that royal women could, at most, have had only
a supervisory role. Olympias and her daughter seem to have owned slaves
and employed various staff members of their own. In one letter preserved in
Athenaeus (14.359f), Olympias urges her son to buy a slave in her possession
who has special skills in ritual cooking. Childcare, as we have seen, was also
delegated to some degree. Royal women may, like Penelope, have done fine
work in cloth, but most of the fabric used in the royal household would have
been the work of others. Olympias and her daughter were probably literate
and certainly would have been familiar with Homer and Attic drama (see
Chapter 1).[72]

Let us now turn to the event that destroyed the comparative security and
prestige that Alexander and his mother had enjoyed for a number of years.
It is only with this event that we can do more than comment on her general
situation because we can, to a limited degree, see Olympias taking specific
actions: actions that imply certain priorities. In summer or perhaps early
autumn of 337,[73] Philip married his last wife, a young woman named
Cleopatra[74] whose guardian, her uncle, was named Attalus.[75] Though doubtless all of Philip's marriages caused some renewal of tension and uncertainty
among his other wives and children,[76] until the male drinking party after the
wedding Alexander (and therefore Olympias) had little reason to feel concern
about this latest union. Any son born as a result of it would be far too young
to threaten Alexander's chances at the throne, and only months before Philip
had entrusted to his teenage son a critical position at Chaeroneia, the battle
that brought Philip control of Greece. After the battle, Philip reconfirmed
the importance of Alexander by sending him, along with the experienced
Antipater, to negotiate with the defeated but still vital Athenians. No wonder
that Alexander attended the *symposium* celebrating his father's most recent
marriage.

Three accounts of events at the wedding *symposium* survive. According
to Plutarch (*Alex.* 9.4–5), Attalus told the Macedonians to beg the gods for
a legitimate successor to the monarchy. Alexander, enraged, asked Attalus

if he, Alexander, seemed to be a bastard, and then threw a wine cup at him. Philip rose and turned his sword against his own son, but his drunkenness made him fall. Alexander, after mocking his father for his failure to cross from one couch to another when he hoped to cross from one continent to another, then left Macedonia, leaving Olympias in Epirus and himself going on to his father's enemies, the Illyrians. Satyrus' version of the incident, as preserved in Athenaeus (13.557d–e) is similar but not identical. Attalus boasted that now legitimate, not bastard, princes would be born. Not only did Alexander throw a cup at Attalus, but Attalus then threw one back. Satyrus mentions the departure of Olympias for Molossia and Alexander for the Illyrians, but says nothing of Philip's reaction to either Attalus' words or Alexander's actions, though one could consider the absence of any reaction significant. Justin's account (9.7.3–6) puts responsibility for the beginning of the drunken argument on Alexander's quarrelsomeness because of his fear that a son born of the marriage would eclipse him, but it also stresses Philip's enmity to his son. Justin's Philip first quarrels with his son and then tries to kill him but is prevented not by his own drunkenness but by the pleas of his friends. Again Alexander takes his mother to his uncle and then goes on to Illyrian territories.

Despite the variations in the accounts, collectively they are telling. All three versions agree on two points: Philip failed to defend his son against Attalus and Alexander took himself and his mother into self-imposed exile. Two of the three accounts maintain that Philip not only failed to defend his son but actually took Attalus' part and attacked Alexander. Thus the departure of Alexander and Olympias was occasioned not so much by Attalus as by Philip's failure to support his son and, if Justin and Plutarch are credible, his active support of Attalus. All three accounts make it clear that the quarrel between Alexander and Attalus somehow involved Alexander's ability, relative or absolute, to succeed his father. Whether on his own initiative or in response to Alexander's complaints, Attalus somehow questioned Alexander's legitimacy. One may doubt details of any of the accounts—Alexander's witticism to Philip in Plutarch, for instance—but the appearance of *gnesios* (legitimate) and *nothos* (bastard) in both Plutarch and Satyrus should be taken quite seriously. Witnesses, especially drunken ones, might be mistaken about many things and a source might add embellishments, but people would tend to remember these words when used with respect to the young man everyone had expected to follow his father to the throne.

Thus, the sources demonstrate that it was not the marriage itself, but Attalus' interpretation of its significance—an interpretation Philip either accepted or, at the very least, failed to reject—that suddenly transformed the situation of Alexander and his mother. Despite the fact that Macedonian *symposia* were very drunken and sometimes violent affairs, important decisions were made at them; they were essential to the functioning of the Macedonian court.[77] The vital importance of Attalus' remarks and Alexander's reaction to them should not be underestimated simply because they, and

Philip, were probably quite drunk. Attalus' remarks were almost certainly not casual, and Philip's reaction to them, though doubtless unplanned, since he may well have found them unexpected, was nonetheless revealing.

The incident profoundly affected the last years of Philip's reign. It had a lasting effect on the personalities of Alexander and Olympias. Some, as we shall see, believe that the quarrel also led to Philip's murder. Perhaps the most puzzling aspect of the affair is Philip's role in it. With his departure for Asia imminent, he would hardly have wanted to destabilize the political situation in Macedonia by suggesting that Alexander was not his intended heir. Any son born to Cleopatra would be roughly eighteen years away from any ability to rule on his own. Child monarchs did not last long in Macedonia, as Philip knew from personal experience. His subsequent efforts to effect a public reconciliation, efforts that must have begun soon after the departure of his son and Olympias, confirm the idea that he had intended no change in the succession.[78] Philip may, by this point, have found Alexander irritatingly ready to take over and might, had he lived long enough, have preferred sons of Cleopatra because their much greater youth would postpone the feeling that his heir was breathing down his neck; but in 337, these potential advantages were far away. For years to come, let alone at this critical moment, Philip cannot have contemplated a change in the succession.[79] This would be so even if (see below) Cleopatra herself had Argeads in her genealogy.

The mere fact that Philip chose to marry again, after a long period without taking any new wives, certainly does not imply that he no longer meant Alexander to follow him on the throne. Now in middle age, Philip had only two sons, one of them incompetent and the other possibly meant to accompany him on his Asian campaign. His brother Perdiccas III's son Amyntas[80] could have functioned as a back-up, but Philip clearly needed more sons. His father had produced six sons and three of them had ruled. In this same period Philip arranged marriages for a number of other family members, partly to generate more political stability but certainly also to generate more Argeads.[81]

If Philip's last marriage signified nothing negative in terms of Alexander's succession (and thus Olympias' status), why then did he allow the public questioning of Alexander's ability to inherit and actually side with the person who questioned it against his own son? The answer must surely lie with the political significance of Attalus and his ward Cleopatra (perhaps supplemented by possible tension and rivalry between father and son and the effects of heavy drinking on Philip's ability to reason).[82] The difficulty, however, is that Attalus makes his first appearance in the sources with this incident. He is clearly already an important figure but we know nothing of his past history. As we shall see, Philip not only supported him against his own son, but, not long after, supported him against the interests and claims of his own former lover Pausanias, a failure or betrayal that was the catalyst for Philip's assassination. Moreover, though we know of no previous military commands of Attalus, Philip appointed him to a shared command with Parmenio, the preliminary expeditionary force Philip dispatched to Asia. While it is doubtless the case that a royal marriage brought prestige and influence to the bride's family, all of Philip's other marriages were made because the family of the bride was already important. It is unlikely that his marriage to Cleopatra was any different.[83] Whoever he was, it was deemed so vital to conciliate Attalus that Philip twice had to put placating him above his obligations to others and even above what appeared to be his own self-interest. While there is no direct proof, I have suggested that Cleopatra and probably Attalus too were Argeads.[84] Irrespective of whether this suggestion is correct, Philip apparently thought that his marriage to Cleopatra would be enough to placate them, but it was not. Attalus (and presumably Cleopatra) wanted more. While giving precedence to an infant heir would not have been attractive to Philip, Attalus doubtless saw himself as the obvious guardian and regent for such a baby king. Naturally he wanted his kin, not Olympias' son, to be treated as heir. This brings us to another mystifying and controversial aspect of the incident. I have suggested that the language of legitimacy and illegitimacy present in two of our sources, the *gnesios/nothos* opposition, deserves to be taken seriously. What, then, does this language signify?[85] Is Olympias being accused of adultery, Alexander of not being the son of Philip? Or does the diction in the sources constitute an ethnic slur, the implication that because Alexander's mother was not Macedonian, any son born of the Macedonian Cleopatra would be more legitimate? Neither of these possibilities seems likely to be true in a literal sense, though the second merits more attention than the first.

Though the idea that Attalus was charging Olympias with adultery and Alexander with literal bastardy has gained limited support,[86] this interpretation lacks credibility. Despite source hostility, only one ancient historical source clearly suggests that Olympias was unfaithful.[87] Justin alone (11.11.5) asserts that Philip publicly denied that Alexander was his son, that Olympias was guilty of adultery, and that Philip therefore repudiated Olympias. One wonders if the *Alexander Romance* (a historical novel about Alexander that developed in antiquity and endured in a plethora of forms until the Renaissance) influenced his view (see Chapter 6 and the Appendix). Since Philip continued to treat Alexander as his son, despite their differences, until the day of his death (see below), Justin's first statement is demonstrably untrue. That being the case, the second is unlikely to be and the third, as we shall see, is contradicted by the bulk of the evidence. Moreover, as Ogden has noticed, Attalus' language "bastardised" both Alexander and Arrhidaeus since Attalus' remarks implied that no legitimate sons had yet been born; it seems unlikely that Attalus meant to accuse both Olympias *and* Philinna of adultery.[88] Attalus' remarks may well have played to Macedonian xenophobia.[89] Macedonians likely did prefer royal mothers to be Macedonian too (Alexander's Asian wives certainly got little respect from them[90]), but Philip's own mother was probably not entirely Macedonian[91] and yet three of her sons reigned in Macedonia. It is therefore unlikely that any general rule or expectation required that a king's son have a Macedonian mother.[92]

A much more viable solution involves the realization that Attalus' legitimacy language should not necessarily be taken literally and certainly should be understood in a comparative context. Today, if a person labels someone with a common street epithet, that person means to insult the individual at whom the insult is directed but hardly intends to accuse the victim of incest with his mother, even though the insult is meant to slur the mother as well. Attalus intended to insult, but he may not have intended his insult to be taken literally. More important, as the sources make clear, Attalus' comment is comparative and the comparison lies between the son of Olympias and any son of Cleopatra; in Attalus' view the latter's sons would be more legitimate than the former's. If that is the case, then Attalus' slur is not necessarily ethnic, but it does imply that his family is the one with greater prestige. In short, the remarks were Attalus' opening salvo in a struggle to give priority to his candidate in the competition among Philip's wives. Attalus forced the opening of a question that had seemed settled for nearly a decade.

Let us turn to consideration of the reaction of Olympias and her son. Olympias, of course, was not at the *symposium*; it was Alexander whose actions defined those of Attalus and Philip as unacceptable. He did so by his angry words and gestures and by his decision to leave Macedonia with his mother. Despite this, Plutarch comes close to blaming the incident on Olympias, although he allots some blame to what he considers bad Macedonian court practice. He begins by saying that upheavals in Philip's household caused many accusations and major disagreements, and he blames these upheavals on Philip's marriages and erotic relationships: they caused the entire kingdom to be contaminated by the women's quarters. Olympias, Plutarch explains, made the troubles worse because she was difficult, jealous, and indignant and so provoked her son. The evidence does support a connection between Philip's affairs and marriages and political upset, and might be said to bolster the view that royal polygamy caused more problems than it solved. It does not, however, support Plutarch when he blames not polygamy but the role of women in monarchy generally and more specifically that of Olympias. (See the Appendix for a discussion of Plutarch's hostile picture of Olympias in *Alexander*.) As we have noted, the quarrel began in the world of men, at the *symposium*. Plutarch, nonetheless, may be figuratively if not literally right in suggesting that Alexander's reaction to Attalus' insult came, at least in part, out of the values and world view his mother had inculcated. Just as Achilles could not bear even the most temporary slight to his *timé* (honor, often external in nature, signifying the esteem of others), neither could his supposed descendant, Olympias' son.

Alexander and Olympias did not overreact; their departure from Macedonia was reasonable granted the nature of the incident. They may have feared for their physical safety but, in any event, dared not tolerate the public questioning of Alexander's ability to rule.[93] Their departure forced Philip to make a public reconciliation and public gestures of reaffirmation of Alexander as his heir. Staying put in Macedonia and perhaps accepting a private apology would have made them look dangerously weak and would not have remedied the offense to their honor. Olympias' departure for her family in Molossia seems the obvious alternative for her; her son's ultimate choice of the Illyrians as his hosts is more problematic. He may simply have chosen a place where he had kin through his grandmother Eurydice, but his choice may have been meant to irritate Philip or perhaps worse.[94] They may both have felt personally betrayed (as, arguably, a certain irrationality in their behavior on their return implies), but the political aspect of their estrangement from Philip was probably the dominant concern in their actions.

Olympias was doubtless furious but not, as some assume or assert,[95] because of sexual jealousy of the new and younger wife. She was not repudiated by Philip[96] because to repudiate her in this situation would be to deny that Alexander could inherit and to accept Attalus' claim to the priority of Cleopatra's possible sons. All the evidence suggests that Philip had no such plans, or at least no immediate plans, to do that. Plutarch and Justin say not that Philip sent Olympias away but that Alexander took her (Plut. *Alex*. 10.5; Just. 9.7.5).[97] The insult that would have infuriated her was not sexual but a challenge to her son's ability to inherit and in some sense an insult to her entire clan. Olympias and the Aeacids made much of their distinguished heroic ancestry yet Attalus had somehow slighted it and Philip had tolerated or perhaps even embraced the slight. Justin claims (9.7.7), somewhat convincingly, that once Olympias reached Molossia she tried to persuade her brother to make war on Philip. Her brother Alexander was, indeed, in a difficult situation. Philip's actions compromised Aeacid honor, particularly if Attalus' insult referred not to adultery but, as I have suggested, to Olympias' family.[98] All of this would be true regardless of whether brother and sister were fond of each other. The problem was not their opinions of each other but rather public opinion about the family.

Alexander of Molossia's personal honor would have been a tender issue anyway if he were indeed a former lover of Philip or even if it were merely rumored that he was. As we have seen, ancient sources make it clear that sexual relationships between rulers and ruled were potentially explosive: past lovers expected rewards and influence and easily came to believe that the ruler had exploited them sexually and so dishonored them. The result was sometimes violence and attempted regicide.[99] On the other hand, Alexander of Molossia owed his throne to Philip. Calling him Philip's puppet would be an exaggeration, but Philip's army and military might were much greater, so for Alexander of Molossia to contemplate action against the Macedonian king, however satisfying to Aeacid and masculine honor, was hardly sensible. Justin (9.7.6) says that young Alexander of Macedon was barely persuaded to accept reconciliation by the encouragement of his relatives; one wonders if the most important of those was his uncle, Alexander of Molossia, caught between a rock and a hard place.[100]

If, as I have suggested, Philip had never meant to jeopardize either Alexander's place in the succession or the honor of his ally Alexander of Molossia, then it follows that Philip would soon attempt a reconciliation with his wife and his son. Plutarch (*Alex.* 9.6; *Mor.* 70b, 179c) suggests that his primary motivation for the reconciliation was the desire to end public comment about his household when he wanted a unified effort for the campaign on which he was about to embark. This reconciliation involved Olympias as well as her son and brother, as Plutarch (*Mor.* 179c) specifically asserts.[101] It had to because both men understood the initial insult to involve her. Arrian (3.6.5) says that Alexander was suspicious of Philip because he had married Cleopatra and dishonored Olympias. It was the dishonor, the loss of *timé*, that had to be coped with, that required compensation.

Philip arranged a marriage between Olympias' brother Alexander and his own daughter by Olympias, Cleopatra (Diod. 16.91.4). This marriage was clearly part of the reconciliation with Alexander and Olympias and part of Philip's attempt to stabilize the rocky Molossian alliance by a new marriage that could only bring honor to Olympias, her son, and her brother.[102] Since its object was to convince the Greek world that Philip's household troubles were over and to offer a very public demonstration of the restoration of the Molossian alliance and confirmation of Aeacid honor, he turned this wedding into an international religious festival, complete with pubic performances and processions in which Philip marched between the two Alexanders. It is difficult to imagine a gesture more calculated to salve wounded Aeacid pride. That the wedding proved to be the setting for his murder in no way negates its importance: Philip staged a public demonstration of the importance of the Molossian alliance, his wife, and his son Alexander.

An incident preserved only in Plutarch (*Alex.* 10.1–3), however, suggests that this reconciliation was, at best, only partial and possibly entirely hollow. Plutarch reports that Alexander heard that Pixodarus, the satrap (Persian governor) of Caria (a region on the coast of Asia Minor), was trying to make an alliance with Philip by offering his daughter in marriage to Alexander's half-brother Arrhidaeus. Plutarch claims that Alexander's friends and mother, supplementing their comments with further tales and accusations, persuaded him that the projected marriage meant that Philip intended to leave the kingdom to Arrhidaeus. Alexander then attempted to substitute himself for his half-brother as prospective groom. Philip, however, discovered what had happened, scolded Alexander publicly in very strong terms, imprisoned the agent Alexander had employed, and sent some of Alexander's *Hetairoi* into exile. (Alexander would later reward these men once he was king.) Despite the fact that only Plutarch preserves the episode, it deserves credence. No obvious reason exists for the invention of the incident[103] and Arrian (3.6.5–6) does confirm the exile of Alexander's friends in the context of the troubles relating to Philip's last marriage, although he does not connect it to the Pixodarus episode since he does not mention that at all. Certainly, granted the disarray at the Persian court in the years just before the invasion, a satrap might well have wanted to hedge his bets by an alliance with Macedonia, and Philip would have welcomed the acquisition of friendly territory in western Turkey. It is also true that Pixodarus had a daughter but no sons.[104]

If the story is true, what does it mean and why did it happen? Clearly it signifies that Olympias, the group of Companions around Alexander, and Alexander himself feared that Philip no longer intended that Alexander would succeed to the throne or, at the very least, they thought he was trying to hedge his bets. The incident therefore occurred because they no longer trusted Philip. The Attalus affair had generated distrust between father and son that the public peacemaking had not eliminated. Attalus' continued prominence may have contributed to the reaction of Alexander's camp. Moreover, though Philip arranged a number of royal marriages in this period, he did not find a bride for Alexander, his supposed heir. That omission does seem odd, whether Philip planned to take Alexander with him to Asia or whether he intended to leave him behind. It is, however, perfectly possible that Philip, who probably continued to fault Alexander for their recent troubles, may have planned the Pixodarus arrangement as a kind of rap on the knuckles to an overly independent son, not a serious indication of his viability as heir.

Whereas the reaction of Alexander and Olympias to the Attalus episode seems appropriate and effective in the context of the Macedonian court, their response to Philip's marriage plans for Arrhidaeus can more reasonably be characterized as an overreaction. More to the point, even if their reading of the proposed alliance was correct, their solution could and did only make matters worse. Philip lost a valuable ally, Alexander lost much (though hardly all[105]) of his support base, angered his father, and yet failed to gain even a Carian bride. Even if the marriage had taken place, Philip's anger would surely have been greater than any possible benefit. If Plutarch is right that Olympias and her son's friends advocated this foolish strategy, then, despite the diplomatic victory of Alexander's recall, they remained rattled and perhaps angry and so offered advice that weakened rather than strengthened his position. They called Philip's bluff only to find it was no bluff.[106]

Just a short time can have passed between the collapse of the proposed Carian alliance and departure of Alexander's companions for exile and the murder of Philip.[107] As has been noted, he was murdered in the midst of the wedding festivities for his daughter Cleopatra and his brother-in-law, and now son-in-law, Alexander of Molossia. Though our sources for the assassination are poor,[108] the identity and motivation of the assassin are clear enough. Pausanias, a young Macedonian noble and former lover of Philip, having become involved in a dispute with another of Philip's young lovers, was gang-raped at the command of Attalus and Cleopatra,[109] who were associates of Pausanias' rival. Pausanias had expected justice from his former royal lover but Philip, thanks to the importance of Attalus, failed to punish his new bride's guardian and tried to placate Pausanias in other ways. His honor in jeopardy, Pausanias planned and carried out the assassination of

Philip, choosing to stab or spear him in the midst of a public procession. Although it is not certain, Pausanias was probably killed soon after the regicide. Alexander, with the likely support of Antipater, was recognized as king and he, rather than his father, led the great Graeco-Macedonian expedition to Asia.

Immediately suspicions arose that Pausanias had not acted alone but that he was supported or even employed by Olympias and/or Alexander (Plut. *Alex.* 10.4; Just. 9.8.1–14). Two factors explain why contemporaries suspected that they were implicated in the murder. First, past Macedonian history, especially recent Macedonian history, was full of regicides and attempted regicide of one Argead against another, whereas only the assassination of Archelaus, more than sixty years earlier, may have involved non-Argeads who acted for reasons somewhat similar to those of Pausanias. So the first and natural assumption was that Argeads lay behind Pausanias' crime.[110] That assumption seemed to be confirmed by the recent troubles between Philip and his wife and son, particularly since Olympias and Alexander shared with Pausanias the same enemies, Attalus and Cleopatra. It was easy to deduce that mother and son found in Pausanias a handy means to extract vengeance against their enemies and guarantee Alexander's succession at a time which meant that he, not his father, would command the great Asian expedition.[111]

Our sources permit no certainty about the innocence or guilt of Alexander and his mother. Probably few at the time knew in any absolute way whether they had played a role in Philip's death, but it is impossible to deny that they might have been involved. Both later committed acts of political violence and proved capable of public acts of anger and vengeance. Philip had given them, even if unintentionally, reason to doubt their futures and perhaps reason to fear for their lives. Not only Alexander but Olympias benefited from Philip's elimination. She exercised much more influence, as we shall see, as the mother of a king than she had as the wife of one.

Nonetheless, though Alexander and Olympias may not have much regretted Philip's murder, they were not likely to have been involved in it, for a number of reasons. First, though his death brought advantages to both, their involvement would have put at risk everything each of them wanted. As things had stood, no matter how much they had come to distrust Philip and he they, the king had no viable alternative heir in the immediate future. Philip was a middle-aged man committed to years of dangerous campaigning with a high level of personal danger. Alexander continued to stand an excellent chance of inheriting the throne, quite possibly in the near future. If, however, the Macedonians had discovered that Alexander had killed his father, they would not have accepted him as their king; the same would be true if evidence implicated Olympias.[112] (One could, perhaps, imagine that Alexander and Olympias at some point became aware of Pausanias' plot and, though not directly involving themselves, failed to inform Philip. However, even this possibility seems remote for some of the reasons discussed below.)

Moreover, the circumstances of the murder strongly argue against their participation.[113] Olympias and Alexander had easy access to Philip, both in person and via agents. They had no need to commit a public murder and had considerable reason to avoid it. Alexander and Olympias were not likely to humiliate young Cleopatra and her Aeacid groom on their wedding day, a day meant (among other things) to restore the good repute of Olympias' family with a grand show. The assassination seriously threatened Macedonian domination of Greece and hardly guaranteed that Alexander would replace his father as commander of the joint Graeco-Macedonian expeditionary force. Indeed, it could have led to the collapse of the planned invasion, and it did cause internal instability (see Chapter 3). Alexander had to work very hard to establish his control over Macedonia, the Greeks, and the expeditionary force. No matter what group Greeks blamed for the assassination, the very fact that it happened seemed to show that Macedonia really was the barbaric, chaotic, and unstable kingdom that Philip had tried so hard to convince his southern neighbors that it was not. The regicide made it appear that Macedonia had returned to the bad old days of weakness and instability and thus encouraged the Thebans and others to attempt the overthrow of the existing order so newly established by Philip. Alexander and Olympias, if they intended harm, had every reason to arrange a discreet murder at home or on some convenient battlefield. They had no need to humiliate both royal dynasties and threaten the destruction of things they held dear by this embarrassing episode that seemed to confirm southern Greek stereotypes about the peoples of northern Greece.

Though mother and son undeniably benefited from Philip's death, they were hardly the only ones to do so. Moreover, some of the other beneficiaries of Philip's demise risked virtually nothing if their participation in or support of Pausanias' plot were to be revealed. The Athenians and Persians would not have been embarrassed if they had participated and their participation were exposed. Philip's death did delay the invasion of the Persian Empire for two years. Members of the Persian elite had spent time at Philip's court and could easily have found agents to collaborate with Pausanias.[114] Indeed, if, as the evidence suggests, Pausanias had hoped to survive his regicide, he must have had reason to expect that some power not formally allied with Philip would take him in. That power would most likely have been the Persian king.

Furthermore, elements within Macedonia itself benefited and yet did not share the risk of exposure that Alexander and Olympias did. Separatist elements within Macedonia, most likely members of one of the formerly independent dynasties of Upper Macedonia, may have felt that the cost to Macedonian prestige was much less important than the chance to eliminate the man who had ended their liberty, before he set off to cover himself with yet more glory. Philip's nephew Amyntas, though a less likely conspirator than the others, cannot be ruled out.[115] Uncles and nephews had murdered each other in Macedonia before, but no king had been killed by his own son.

Finally, Pausanias really could have been a lone assassin. The humiliation of his unavenged gang-rape, the failure of his former lover to punish the guilty, and the increasing prominence of those responsible were powerful motives in a culture that endorsed tyrannicide. The mere attempt would have helped to restore his public honor and reputation.

Whatever the truth, Alexander and Olympias tried to direct suspicions away from themselves and toward some of the groups just mentioned (see Chapter 3 for further discussion). Their official line on the murder of Philip seems to have been that Pausanias did not act alone. As we shall see, this approach not only provided other people to blame but enabled them to eliminate a number of inconvenient rivals.

If my reconstruction of events and motivation is correct, the evening after the assassination of Philip would have found Alexander and Olympias surprised, possibly even somewhat grief stricken, but surely also very relieved. They had negotiated the dangers and complexities of Philip's court successfully—Olympias may well have credited herself for her son's accomplishment—and the throne was now Alexander's. In a sense, though, it was theirs, his and Olympias'. That, at least, was almost certainly Olympias' opinion. The last-minute threat to Alexander's succession may have made mother and son closer than they would have been had events proceeded as they had expected. Their close political bond, forged by the unusual circumstances of the last months of Philip's reign, would endure, though it would also grow more complex.

3   Olympias, mother of the king, Alexander the Great

During the reign of her son (336–323), Olympias managed to play a significant role in in the public life of Macedonia, her homeland Molossia, and the Greek peninsula in general. The contrast to her comparative obscurity during her husband's reign is striking. Assessing the degree of her power during this period presents many difficulties, only some the result of the prejudices and omissions of the sources. Whatever her personal mix of feelings at the time of her son's departure for the Asian campaign, Olympias' actions imply that she regarded his absence as an opportunity to exercise greater authority than would have been possible if Alexander had remained in Macedonia.[1] Her influence with her son fluctuated during his reign, depending, to some degree, on the issue at hand. As we shall see, she had greater clout with him in the earliest and latest stages of his reign, less when his campaign was at its glamorous height and Antipater (the man to whom he had entrusted supreme military control of Macedonia and Greece) was most critical to him. If the issue was a potential threat to his throne, Alexander paid considerable attention to his mother's views, but if it was not, he sometimes treated her much as he did other members of the highly competitive and rancorous Macedonian elite, appearing to keep an amused distance between himself and their quarrels, consequently allowing them to fester, and occasionally even encouraging them, all for reasons of his own. Nonetheless, mother and son remained a political unit. So long as Alexander lived, Olympias might not always have got what she wanted, but she was always physically safe, and those who opposed her in even the smallest matter must have needed to keep a weather eye on the king, uncertain as to whether he would take offense.

The beginning of Alexander's reign proved even less stable than the troubled final years of his father's. Plutarch (*Alex.* 11.1) commented that at his accession the young king faced "great jealousies, terrible hatred, and danger everywhere." Alexander had to confront grave external and internal problems. Successions in Macedonia were always moments of uncertainty, likely to produce foreign invasions and alternative Argead candidates, often backed by foreign powers. Such a scenario was especially likely to develop after an assassination. Philip's unprecedented power within Macedonia and over the entire Greek peninsula, the tensions of the last years of his reign, and the rumors about the possible involvement of Alexander and/or Olympias in his death only increased the chance that Alexander's succession as Macedonian king, let alone as *hegemon* (leader) of the Corinthian League (the Greek alliance his father had formed and led), would be opposed.

In less than two years, between Philip's murder and his own departure, Alexander had to handle threats to both positions. Externally, he dealt with a Greek revolt, gained recognition as *hegemon*, campaigned against the Thracians, crushed an Illyrian invasion, and put down the revolt of the Thebans.[2] Internally, he caused the deaths of a number of prominent Macedonians. A rash of such deaths typically occurred in the context of royal succession in Macedonia. Usually it is impossible to determine if those eliminated had conspired against the king, whether the king eliminated them in order to prevent such plotting, or whether fear of the latter precipitated the former. Moreover, the degree to which those killed were said to be (or actually were) part of a common conspiracy remains murky. This is particularly the case in terms of Alexander's reign because the chronology of these deaths is unclear. Alexander seems to have justified their deaths on the grounds that they had been involved in the plot against Philip and/or plotted against Alexander himself. Plutarch (*Mor.* 327c) said that at the beginning of Alexander's reign, all of Macedonia was unstable and looked to Amyntas and the sons of Aeropus. Alexander eliminated his cousin Amyntas (son of Philip's predecessor, and presumably the Amyntas to whom Plutarch referred[3]) and two of the three sons of Aeropus.[4] Perhaps the most inevitable[5] death was that of Attalus, the uncle and guardian of Philip's last bride, the man who had publicly questioned Alexander's ability to succeed. Attalus was in Asia at the time of Alexander's accession, having been sent as one of the commanders of Philip's preliminary force. Alexander arranged the death of Attalus on the grounds that he was, in collaboration with Athenians, planning a revolt.[6]

Alexander's post-accession purges affected the life of Olympias because she took part in them. She probably murdered Attalus' niece Cleopatra and Cleopatra's baby daughter, Europa, by Philip. The evidence for the crime is poor,[7] apparently because it did not take place in public.[8] Only one of the major Alexander narratives clearly mentions it: Justin (9.7.12) asserts that Olympias first killed the daughter in her mother's arms and then forced Cleopatra to hang herself out of a desire for revenge (see below). Later, Justin (12.6.14) lists Alexander's murdered stepmother (as well as unnamed brothers) among those whose deaths he had brought about, thus implying that Alexander was also complicit in the crime. Plutarch (*Alex.* 10.4) cryptically reports that Alexander was vexed with his mother because, while he was absent, she "treated Cleopatra savagely." Plutarch's choice of words could mean that he was not aware of the accusation of murder or might even suggest that Alexander reproached his mother not for the fact but the manner of Cleopatra's death, but more likely it constitutes a euphemistic reference to murder. Like Justin, Plutarch does not implicate Alexander in the murder directly, but implies that he was complicit: he attributes a quotation from *Medea* (289) to Alexander that hints the king brought about the deaths of Philip, Attalus, and Cleopatra. Finally, the second-century CE geographer Pausanias (8.7.5) claims that Olympias killed Cleopatra and her infant son by dragging them over a burning brazier. Thus the only extant sources that refer to the incident disagree about the method of the murders and the sex of the murdered infant (Plutarch omits all mention of the child) and are uncertain or unclear about Alexander's involvement in the crime. Granted the absence of a standard account and the probability that this was a secret crime, one could even suppose that Cleopatra killed herself and her child out of despair.

Certainly none of these sources inspires much confidence in their veracity. Pausanias' version is the least credible. The method of execution (lurid but inconvenient), the supposed sex of the infant,[9] his hostility to the Macedonian royal house, and his generally poor reputation for accuracy all engender doubts.[10] Plutarch's discussion is so vague (one cannot determine which of the two methods of execution inspires his remarks) and ambiguous as to be useless. Justin's narrative is never especially accurate or trustworthy and his reference to the murder follows his particularly over-the-top account of Olympias' behavior immediately after Philip's death. Nonetheless, one piece of external evidence suggests that his version of the death of Cleopatra and her child deserves more respect than the other accounts. Diodorus (19.11. 2–7) recounts that nearly twenty years later, Olympias forced another royal woman, Adea Eurydice (Philip's granddaughter and then wife of Alexander's successor Philip Arrhidaeus), to kill herself by hanging. The Diodorus episode lends credibility to Justin's account.[11] In sum, it is likely that Olympias somehow arranged the death of the baby and forced Cleopatra to hang herself.

In terms of understanding Olympias' life, it would be useful to know why she wanted the mother and child to die and how her actions might or might not fit into the context of her times. Only Justin mentions her motivation— revenge (*ultio*). But revenge for what? Justin (9.7.1, 12) connects it to Philip's supposed repudiation of Olympias in favor of Cleopatra. Apart from the fact that Justin's belief in Olympias' divorce is almost certainly mistaken, his own narrative, by involving Alexander in both the murder of Philip (9.7.1) and the death of Cleopatra (12.6.14), implies that something more than simple sexual jealousy was involved. As we have seen, the entire series of events at the time of Philip's wedding clearly threatened Alexander's position as heir and therefore his mother's status. Attalus and Cleopatra had threatened the position of mother and son and now mother and son punished them for that threat. But, just as Alexander's elimination of Attalus was intended not only to punish past bad actions but prevent present and future acts, so was that of Cleopatra. Eliminating her and her child meant eliminating one line of descent in the royal family, a line that had already demonstrated its hostility to Alexander and Olympias.[12] Cleopatra could have claimed that she was pregnant with a son by Philip. She and her daughter could have become tools or actors in subsequent battles for the throne.

Olympias' murder of the pair was a fairly typical piece of post-succession royal politics, remarkable only because the murderer and the victims were all female. Granted the trouble that another royal woman and her child later caused Olympias and her family, one can hardly claim that perceiving Cleopatra and child as a threat was unreasonable or that the murder lacked any motivation other than anger or desire for revenge.[13] Olympias was unlikely to underestimate what a determined royal woman could do, particularly one who had already demonstrated some will and ability to do harm.

Quite apart from her presumed involvement in Attalus' attempt to cut Alexander out of the succession, Plutarch offers evidence that Cleopatra had indeed done harm. He reports (*Alex.* 10.4) that Pausanias' rape—critical to the murder of Philip—was ordered by Attalus and Cleopatra. Although no other ancient author connects Cleopatra to this ugly incident, Plutarch's report is credible. While it is possible that Plutarch mentions Cleopatra as well as her uncle only because he thinks of them together, as a dynastic succession unit, that is not likely. The reference follows his account of the Pixodarus incident and precedes his account of the death of Philip, so there is no obvious reason to link Cleopatra to her uncle's role unless she were indeed involved. Whitehorne[14] believes that Olympias and her supporters may have invented Cleopatra's involvement in the rape in order to "excuse" Olympias' subsequent murder of Cleopatra and her child. Indeed, the tendency for royal sons by different mothers to attempt to bastardize their rivals[15] could suggest that Alexander and Olympias might have generated negative stories about Cleopatra even before her murder. However, no trace of a hostile tradition about Cleopatra survives. In fact, the sources portray her quite favorably. Moreover, Plutarch's remark is so much in passing, so without rhetorical embroidering or moralizing, that it is difficult to attribute it to hostility. If her inclusion in the incident were fabricated to excuse Olympias' later presumed murder of her, one would expect more to be made of it. Certainly Cleopatra's pregnancy (if she were indeed pregnant at the time) would not have prevented her involvement in what looks like a clan vendetta.[16] (Even the final stages of pregnancy offer no physical limitation on evil thoughts and plots. Plutarch (*Alex.* 77.4), for instance, reports that Roxane, in the last month or two of her pregnancy, colluded with Perdiccas to arrange the murders of Stateira and her sister.)

It would be a mistake to assume that most victims of dynastic violence were themselves innocents; more often than not they had been plotting too, but failed to move as quickly as their enemies. Cleopatra and her child were doubtless victims of Olympias' merciless brutality, but only one of them was likely a genuinely innocent victim. Although the deaths of Cleopatra and Europa are the first known Macedonian examples of dynastic murder of women (or girls), many more followed. In essence, Olympias' assumption that female royals were fair dynastic game seems to have become the common one.[17] In my view, then, Olympias' murder of mother and daughter was an act of calculation; it may have satisfied a thirst for revenge or fed Olympias' anger, but it was not simply an act of passionate violence. She was and remained till her death a calculating person.

We would consider a woman who killed another woman and her infant a brutal murderer. Today, most people still find violence perpetrated by women more shocking than that perpetrated by men. Despite changing patterns of criminality, men continue to commit more violent crimes than women. A female murderer counters societal norms. Similarly, the sex and ages of Olympias' victims would make the crime more disturbing from our point of view. Granted our understanding of children, especially infants, as innocents and our recognition of the rights of even neonates as individuals, most people would consider the murder of the baby even more upsetting and cruel than the murder of the mother.

But how would her own culture have judged Olympias' actions? To some degree, Greeks and Macedonians shared the expectation that women are, or ought to be, less violent than men (generally connected to perceived greater physical weakness of women) and more likely to pity others, but (see the Introduction) they often combined this expectation with the somewhat contradictory one that women were more emotional and irrational than men and prone to bad actions associated with these weaknesses.[18]

Several factors indicate that contemporaries were not particularly surprised or bothered by Olympias' actions. The mere absence of the incident from most accounts is suggestive; it was not an attention grabber. Unlike other acts of violence committed by Alexander or Olympias, the sources do not mention them again, at least in terms of Olympias. Dynastic murders were a dime a dozen before and after these particular deaths,[19] and some of those murdered were children (see below). Philip's mother had been accused, albeit almost certainly unjustly, of dynastic murders.[20] One suspects that many thought that Attalus and Cleopatra could hardly have expected anything else once Philip was dead. They had committed themselves to what proved to be the losing side in a dynastic struggle and past reigns demonstrated what happened to those who made such a poor choice.

In two respects, Olympias and her son may have been perceived as acting comparatively moderately. Apparently, they limited their revenge/justice to those two members of the family; the rest of the clan was probably spared, though Macedonian custom might have justified more widespread retribution.[21] The manner of death Olympias chose for Cleopatra, forced suicide by hanging (assuming that Justin's version is correct), respected the status and gender of the victim: a private and thus modest death appropriate to a woman, particularly a royal woman, as both literary and historical examples demonstrate. Olympias spared Cleopatra public humiliation.[22] It is even possible that convention made it more appropriate for a woman to kill another woman rather than for a man to commit the act.²³ Presumably Olympias treated Cleopatra in this fashion because she wanted to respect the status of a royal wife, certainly not out of any personal affection or respect for Cleopatra. As we shall see, her enemies would not grant Olympias herself such a private and feminine death.

The murder of the baby, surely the most repugnant of Olympias' crimes by our standards, probably mattered less than that of Cleopatra to Olympias' contemporaries. Plutarch's failure to mention it is telling. The murder of a male baby might have attracted more attention, but not, I think, much more. Greeks were hardly indifferent to the death of young children, even female infants, but they were more pragmatic about them, as the practice of child exposure surely indicates.²⁴ Moreover, perhaps because children were understood not as individuals but as extensions of parents and families, they tended to be killed almost automatically when the rest of their kin were.²⁵ A death that would seem not only inhuman but gratuitous to us would make a kind of cruel sense to them. Significantly, Justin's version of the murders of mother and child seems to focus on the horror for Cleopatra of having the baby killed in front of her rather than on the fact of infanticide itself, as though the baby's murder was most poignant because of the mother's pain.

Both mythic and historical examples of child murders in the context of dynastic struggle occur. In one version of the aftermath of the fall of Troy, Olympias' mythic ancestor Neoptolemus killed Hector's infant son (*Little Iliad* 14), whereas in Euripides' *Trojan Women*, the child's death is the consequence of a joint Greek decision, though one urged by Odysseus. At least three young Argeads were murdered by dynastic rivals.²⁶ In the next generation of Olympias' own dynasty, several child murders occurred or were attempted. The Molossians slaughtered Alcetas (Olympias' cousin and perhaps nephew) and his children (Paus. 1.11.5). According to Justin (17.3.18), the people plotted to kill Olympias' great-nephew, Pyrrhus, then aged only two, because of their hatred for his father, but Plutarch (*Pyrrh.* 2.1) recounts that it was supporters of another Aeacid faction (that of Olympias' grandson) who pursued the infant Pyrrhus.

Finally, in a world untainted by Judeo-Christian ethics, the concept and practice of revenge were much less problematic, more likely to be considered the enactment of justice. The proverbial Greek injunction to help friends and harm enemies generated a very different moral imperative, one that Olympias observed.²⁷ Feuds passed from generation to generation in Greek aristocratic society, as we shall see in Macedonia and Molossia.²⁸ Attributions of vengeance as motivation are, however, problematic. Many violent acts, like Olympias' murders, could have been inspired by revenge, but would also have conveyed practical benefits to the perpetrators. I am reluctant, however, to assume that revenge was the prime determinant unless there is some indication that an act was publicly announced as revenge (see Chapter 4).²⁹

By her actions at the very start of Alexander's reign, Olympias showed herself to be ruthless and savage, but no more so than the rest of the Macedonian elite. Coupled with enduring uncertainty about her role in the death of Philip, this perception meant that Olympias' contemporaries had reason to fear betraying her. Nothing suggests that those contemporaries saw her as irrational or erratic; indeed, they may even have assumed that she had simply followed her son's bidding.

One important aspect of Alexander's early reign was a non-event: he did not marry and so did not produce any children before his departure for Asia. Diodorus (17.16.2) claims that Antipater and Parmenio tried to persuade Alexander to remedy this omission and that he refused. Certainly years passed before he married and many more years before he produced any children. If Parmenio and Antipater really did try to get Alexander to marry, doubtless each hoped he would marry a daughter of theirs. Alexander's initial postponement of marriage probably sprang from a reluctance to choose one man's daughter over the other's and, more generally, from his experiences in Philip's reign, experiences that led him to view marriages as sources of trouble, factionalism, and complexity.[30] Mothers in the Greek world generally had no formal or legal role in the marriages of sons, but we know that Olympias had once involved herself in Alexander's marriage prospects (see Chapter 2) and she may well have done so again. His long delay in marrying (in addition to the fact that when he did marry, his brides were Asian) gave his mother and, to some degree, his full sister, greater prominence than they would otherwise have had. It is certainly possible that Olympias, pursuing her self-interest, supported the idea of marital delay.[31]

My focus is on Olympias, but one cannot consider her life without some reference to her son's career from the time of his departure for Asia in the spring of 334 until his premature death in Babylon on June 10, 323. The brilliant trajectory of Alexander's campaign is well known, but a brief summary, with stress on those events most relevant to his mother's life, is necessary in order to provide a context for Olympias' career during the same period.[32]

Between 334 and 331 Alexander fought and won three major victories against Persian armies. In that same period he began to claim to be legitimate ruler of the Persian Empire and, after a visit to the oracle of Ammon at Siwah in Egypt, came to believe that he was the son of Zeus Ammon. The next year was critical. Darius was killed. Alexander dismissed the Greek allies and his army discovered that they were not going home any time soon. Claiming that he had been part of an assassination plot, Alexander executed Philotas, son of Parmenio, and then had Parmenio himself murdered.

The elimination of the most powerful member of the Macedonian elite on the campaign was a sign of Alexander's increasingly absolute rule. Combined with his developing "Persianizing" of the monarchy and court, the result was growing resentment among both the elite and ordinary soldiers, resentment that often flared into violence or the threat of it.[33] The following years of uncertainty (no one knew how far east Alexander planned to go) and difficult guerrilla warfare were the backdrop for two famous incidents: Alexander's slaughter (328) of Cleitus, an important Macedonian officer who had saved Alexander's life in battle, and the conspiracy (327) of Hermolaus (the so-called Pages conspiracy), a plot hatched by Royal Youths, younger than Alexander and his friends, who (among other things) resented Alexander's changes in Macedonian kingship. In this period, Alexander finally married for the first time, his bride a Bactrian woman named Roxane. In 326 he invaded India, fought a hard-won victory against an Indian ruler, but finally had to yield to the demands of his troops to halt his eastern advance. During the period of Alexander's return from India, he continued to experience difficulties with discipline. Once back in the heart of the empire he had conquered, he eliminated a number of the governors he'd left in charge, married two Persian princesses and arranged mass marriages of his officers and men with Asian women, and coped with another serious outbreak of indiscipline among his Macedonian troops. He issued the Exiles' Decree (a decision that generated political turmoil in Greece) and decided to replace Antipater with Craterus. In the last year of his life, he made Babylon his base. At the time of his death, Antipater remained in Macedonia and had yet to yield up his office.

Uncertainty surrounds nearly every aspect of Olympias' public life in the period from Alexander's departure till his death. Her private life is another matter. Mother and son certainly remained in communication. In many respects, they acted as a conventionally devoted and doting mother and son. Alexander sent booty home to Olympias (*FGrH* 151 F 1; Plut. *Alex.* 25.4). She made an offering at the shrine of Hygieia in Athens, probably for her son's health (Hyp. *Eux.* 19), and arranged for splendid offerings at Delphi (*SIG* I 252N 5ff., with n.3[34]), probably funded from the plunder Alexander had given her. Ancient sources plausibly insist that they maintained a regular and considerable correspondence (see below for further discussion) and tend to mention their letters when the contents are political, but much of it may have had to do with mundane family affairs.[35]

Olympias' public role, in Macedonia, Molossia, and Greece, was far less conventional and proves much harder to categorize. To what degree did her son authorize her role and to what degree did she take advantage of Alexander's long absence for her own aggrandizement? Lack of clarity about her physical location, position, power, and authority vis-à-vis both her daughter Cleopatra and Antipater, Alexander's general, further complicates these questions.

Though Antipater exercised supreme military control over Macedonia and Greece during Alexander's absence,[36] Olympias exerted considerable public authority as well. Alexander may not have defined their duties and spheres of influence before his departure; Macedonian offices in general—if they existed at all—seem undefined at this period and Olympias probably held no office as such anyway. Alexander's failure to define the roles of Olympias and Antipater would cause problems, ones Alexander chose not to resolve.[37] Granted the military aspect of Antipater's role, the fact that no woman had ever acted as sole substitute king in Macedonia, and the absence of a clearly defined office of regent, Olympias' actions were not motivated by a frustrated desire to be regent.[38] Her public role had three sources: her personal relationship with her son, a relationship that inevitably led others to see her as, to some degree, Alexander's agent; her membership in the royal dynasty, in whose *axioma* (reputation) and religious sanction she shared; her membership in the Aeacid dynasty of Molossia, whose rule she shared and whose traditional alliances may have worked to her benefit. While these three sources of power always mattered, they came to matter more as the years of Alexander's absence increased.

Many signs indicate Olympias' public power, despite the fact that Plutarch (*Alex.* 39.7) claimed that Alexander did not allow her to interfere in his affairs or military matters. The second part of Plutarch's claim, however, may have been correct. Although Olympias certainly did play a military role after Alexander's death (see Chapter 4), we know of no such activity during her son's reign. Military matters apart, however, Olympias certainly did "interfere" (it is not clear, as we shall see, that Alexander would have understood it as interference) in her son's affairs. She (and her daughter) not only played a role in the internal politics of their two kingdoms, but also participated in international diplomacy. The prominence of women, particularly elite women, in Greek religion[39] has been understood in terms of piety and conventional gender roles, despite the fact that, in the Greek world, international ties were often created, maintained, or, at the very least, interpreted in terms of religious ties.[40] Female involvement in international religious activities should therefore be understood as diplomatic activity as well (see further Chapter 5).

The participation of royal women in the diplomatic process derived from the international presentation of Macedonian monarchy (in the Argead period, as the rule of a clan) and from Greek understanding of relations between foreign powers in terms of kinship and *philia* (friendship), an understanding particularly likely to develop in dealings between monarchs.[41] Today diplomacy is the work of professionals, but in the Greek world, especially in monarchies, it was individualized and highly personal; personal ties, not public ones, often defined those designated, especially by rulers, to conduct international dealings.[42] Indeed, the world of the family, not the state, inspired many of the terms used in international relations.[43] Relationships involving *philia* included women. Since expectations of reciprocity are a fundamental aspect of the notion of *philia*,[44] women involved in such international relationships,[45] by definition, were expected both to convey benefits and to receive them.

Olympias and her daughter performed benefactions of international scope, actions much more public in nature than Olympias' temple dedications.[46] Such benefactions had a diplomatic aspect since they could initiate or confirm a relationship between benefactor and recipient.[47] Her name and Cleopatra's (each without either a patronymic or a reference to Alexander) appear on a list of major recipients of grain from Cyrene (*SEG* IX.2). In fact, Olympias' name appears twice, most likely as a recipient of grain for Macedonia.[48] This grain was probably not a free gift, but bought by those listed at the usual rather than famine price, perhaps to keep prices low despite the shortage.[49] All the other names on the list belong to states, but only the personal names of Olympias and Cleopatra appear. Parallel male usage suggests that the two women were functioning as heads of state. As is often the case with acts of female benefaction (euergetism) or piety,[50] we cannot be certain whether Olympias paid for this grain on her own initiative, with her own funds, or whether she and her daughter were merely Alexander's agents.[51] Even if Alexander had privately ordered and funded his mother's benefaction, the inscription highlights her role and omits any mention of her son.[52] Antipater performed no action so formally authoritative as the role of mother and daughter commemorated in the inscription.[53]

Other indications of Olympias' international role exist. Hyperides, a contemporary orator, pictures Olympias and Alexander (apparently jointly) inflicting harm on the Athenians, and he makes a similar link between the interests of Olympias and the Macedonians (Hyp. *Eux.* 20). On the other hand, Hyperides also reports that Olympias, apparently speaking in her own interest, stated that Molossia belonged to her (Hyp. *Eux.* 25; see below for Olympias' role in Molossia). Diodorus (17.108.7) claims that Antipater and Olympias (whether in concert or in opposition to each other is unclear) demanded that the Athenians extradite Harpalus, Alexander's absconding treasurer.[54] Conceivably, control of the money Harpalus had taken with him motivated either or both.[55] Antipater and Olympias may each have been eager to dissociate themselves from Harpalus[56] and the dual request may also reflect concern (on their part or Alexander's) to reach various Athenian political factions. Alexander's Exiles' Decree (Diod. 18.8.4), with its threat that the Athenians would have to return Samos, would have made Antipater a controversial figure in Athens. At this moment, Olympias may have had wider appeal there. Her popularity in Athens doubtless varied with the period and the sources' politics. Hyperides, for instance, notoriously anti-Macedonian, speaks of Athenian hatred of Olympias, but in a context that tends to depersonalize the sentiment, associating it with resentment of Macedonian influence in general (*Eux.* 20–1). On the other hand, perhaps in part because of the Aeacids' traditional friendship with them (see Chapter 1), the Athenians sometimes saw her too as a friend. Diodorus (18.65.2), speaking of a period after the death of Alexander, comments that they had always respected her[57] and her previous honors and now hoped that she would help them to restore their autonomy.

Many of the international dealings of royal women relate to *philia*. Some sources make this explicit, but in others, a *philia* relationship is implicit, most obviously in the case of women's dealings with their families, since familial relationships constituted the closest sort of *philia*. Here one needs to recall the importance of the expectation of reciprocity in *philia*. The *philia* created by marriage was a continuing bond, one that involved royal women in international relations.[58] Charitable acts or dedications by royal women initiated or confirmed *philia* for themselves and/or male kin. Royal women participated in the bonds of *philia* that tied the powers of the Greek world together as well as in the enmities that tore it apart.

At some point after Alexander's departure for Asia but before his death, Olympias abandoned Macedonia for her homeland of Molossia. The date of her departure is uncertain, but most likely it was no sooner than 331 and probably around the time of the death of her brother Alexander, the Molossian king (fall 331/winter 330), and Antipater's defeat of Agis, king of Sparta (spring 330).[59] Diodorus (18.49.4) asserted that she fled Macedonia because she had quarreled with Antipater.[60] Her departure was probably voluntary (Plut. *Alex.* 68.3 suggests this),[61] but was the consequence both of her inability to establish supremacy over Antipater in Macedonia itself and the potential she saw for greater power in her homeland.[62] This moment was probably the height of Antipater's power and influence with Alexander, who depended on him for reinforcements and for the defeat of Agis. Alexander's innovations in monarchy and growing absolutism (developments that tended to distance him from the aging general) had only begun to appear. At least in Macedonia, in 330 Antipater was in a stronger position than Olympias.

The situation in Molossia was complicated and our evidence about it is poor. Olympias' daughter had, as we have seen, married her uncle, Alexander of Molossia. Around the time that the Macedonian Alexander left on his Asian campaign, the Molossian Alexander departed for a campaign in Italy, during which he died. Cleopatra almost certainly functioned as regent for her husband during his absence. She probably had two children—a son, Neoptolemus, and a daughter, Cadmeia—by Alexander[63] and she most likely acted as regent for young Neoptolemus. Such a role would be in keeping with the legal situation of widowed Epirote women generally;[64] much later in the Aeacid dynasty, another royal woman also became regent for her children.[65] Molossia had become, as we have seen, something like a puppet state of Macedonia, and Cleopatra, like her mother, bought grain, doubtless for Molossia, but likely in accord with her brother's and mother's wishes.[66] Cleopatra remained in Molossia for some time after the arrival of her mother.[67] Mother and daughter probably worked in concert, as they evidently did after the death of Alexander the Great.

Some time during the reign of Alexander the Great,[68] the political framework of Molossia changed: the Epirotes formed an alliance and the Molossian kingdom joined it. The Aeacids never became kings of the alliance and remained kings of Molossia, but they did function as the military leaders of the alliance.[69] Historians disagree as to whether the formation of the alliance was a sign of the strength or the weakness of the Aeacids.[70] Judging by what was observable at the time, the Epirote Alliance may well have seemed a positive development to the Aeacids, offering the potential for wider power. The feud between Olympias and Antipater, however, had surely begun by this date and subsequent Antipatrids generally acted to limit Aeacid power (see Chapter 4), so one cannot rule out the possibility that Antipater fomented the alliance to limit Aeacid power.[71] Whatever the short-term benefit of the alliance, long term, its birth marked the beginning of the gradual decline of the prestige of the Aeacid dynasty, a decline that would end with the abolition of Aeacid monarchy itself.[72]

An odd passage in Plutarch (*Alex.* 68.3) states that a desire for gaining one's own advantage (presumably Plutarch is speaking about prominent Macedonians since he has just referred to Alexander's troubles with his army, satraps, and generals) and wanton violence spread everywhere, and Olympias and Cleopatra, having formed a faction against Antipater,[73] divided the realm, with Olympias taking Epirus and Cleopatra Macedonia. Plutarch has a seemingly indifferent Alexander approve his mother's choice rather than his sister's, on the grounds that Macedonians would not accept rule by a woman.[74] The passage cannot be literally true in all its details since Antipater remained in his position—whatever exactly that was—until Alexander's death,[75] but it probably means that Cleopatra left Molossia while her mother remained there. Certainly it implies that Antipater's power was fading and that both mother and daughter tried to exploit his growing vulnerability.[76] The time-frame for the situation Plutarch describes is not specified, but its context suggests that he refers to the last few years of Alexander's reign, roughly 325/4.[77]

Our sources often refer to the contents of letters of Olympias sent to Alexander and occasionally contain material taken from Alexander's replies or his verbal reactions to his mother's correspondence. These fragments do not inspire much confidence in their authenticity, particularly because the *Alexander Romance* probably began as an epistolary historical novel (see Chapter 6). Indeed, the credibility of the correspondence preserved in Plutarch and other Alexander historians is part of the wider issue of the dependability of all letters quoted or paraphrased in the text of ancient writers.[78] Scholarly tradition about the treatment of Alexander's correspondence has been to evaluate each letter on its individual merits.[79] Nearly all the letters relating to Olympias portray her in a negative fashion, but the negative image generated has comparatively little to do with factional politics, as such, whether in Alexander's reign or later.[80] Instead, the letters often employ Greek gender stereotypes to define Alexander in contrast to his mother, to demonstrate that he was a conventional Hellene, not a "mama's boy". Greek hostility to monarchy often connected to the view that in a monarchy women, especially royal mothers, had too much influence. The correspondence copes with this prejudice by suggesting that Olympias did try to act as people feared women in monarchies did, but that Alexander, though treating his mother respectfully, sternly resisted this un-Hellenic pattern and preferred male advice or his own good sense.[81] Typically,

Olympias offers bad or partisan advice and tries to "interfere" and Alexander rejects her advice and interference. Though it might at first seem that the "bad advice of Olympias theme" in the correspondence resembles the "bad advice theme" in our sources about Parmenio,[82] more of the Olympias material is usable, if one reads with care (see further the Appendix).

Despite the sources' focus on Olympias' enmities with various members of the elite, it is worth reflecting on her friendships, a topic in which the sources display no interest. If one reads carefully, however, the sources do suggest some possibilities, ones we can probably augment with the names of those who worked with Olympias after her son's death. The young men who went into exile for Alexander's sake as a consequence of their role in the Pixodarus affair (Harpalus, Ptolemy, Nearchus, and Erigyius) were likely allies, since Olympias and they supposedly collaborated on that project.[83] One should surely add to that list Arybbas, one of the royal bodyguards and almost certainly an Aeacid, as well as yet another Aeacid, Neoptolemus, a brave warrior, subsequently a commander of the Hypaspists (the elite infantry guard unit) and a satrap.[84] Eumenes (secretary first to Philip and then to Alexander), Polyperchon (an infantry commander), and three more of Alexander's royal bodyguards (Leonnatus, Aristonous, and Perdiccas) may have been friendly to Olympias during Alexander's life, since, after his death, they certainly were.[85] Members of the elite frequently abandoned friendships and even their king when self-interest led them in another direction, so I do not mean to imply that all of these individuals were friends of Olympias (or each other) at the same time,[86] but, taken as a group, my hypothetical list is suggestive. The names tend to be kin of Olympias or the Argeads, members of Upper Macedonian dynasties (thus quite possibly Aeacid kin or allies; see Chapter 2) or, failing that, sons of Greek immigrants. Five were royal bodyguards. Thus all were men with markedly personal ties to Alexander and many had quasi-royal birth. Other evidence (see below) indicates that Olympias fiercely guarded Alexander's royal status and considered anyone who threatened to compromise either his wealth or power as threats to her son. My list is a good fit for that apparent pattern.

Olympias' life, her friendships and hatreds, transpired in a social context remote from our own political world. It is difficult for us to understand the intimate, claustrophobic nature of the Macedonian court. Generally, it is harder for historians to demonstrate ties of friendship at court than the reverse, partly because strife is more interesting and makes a better story. References to specific enmities between individuals point to the simple fact that many of the court figures hated each other (though only some of these antagonisms would have endured).[87] The generally competitive ethos of the court and Alexander's own administrative style (see below) also generated strife. Still, one must recall that many of the major figures of the era of Philip and Alexander and the Successors had known each other all their lives (as had their grandparents) and were bound together by blood and marriage as well as by shared experience. We can reconstruct only a small fragment of these once powerful ties and attempt to determine which were ephemeral, which endured, which were deeply personal, which essentially formal. Moreover, only occasionally can we be certain when and why these bonds failed, when those once allied now felt betrayed and acted accordingly.

The letters demonstrate that Olympias tried to use her correspondence with Alexander to exert her influence at his mobile court, despite the growing physical distance between them. They depict her employing two methods and imply a third: Olympias attacks individuals or groups at court; she offers information and advice; and she takes full advantage of her son's affection for her. None of these methods seems implausible when compared to the better-attested public actions of Olympias. Her actions after Alexander's death against the Antipatrids (see Chapter 4) certainly demonstrate her willingness to make attacks (physical, verbal, symbolic) against those she considered hostile to her interests. Many incidents in her career imply that she kept herself well informed about both domestic and foreign affairs. Her dedications at shrines in southern Greece, her movement from Macedonia to Molossia and back again, her apparent communication with states and individuals, and her ability to respond quickly to events all confirm this. Moreover, it seems natural that Alexander would expect his mother to tell him about what was going on and to look out for his interests. It is harder to demonstrate—and less certain—that she manipulated her son's affection for her own ends, but several factors certainly suggest that she counted on her son's affection and had little fear of losing it. Certainly we should not accept without question the collective implication of the letters, that Olympias was less successful in exercising political influence with her own son than she was on the Greek peninsula.

The sources indicate that Olympias may have had mixed success when she offered advice to her son or tried to warn him. In the aftermath of the execution of Philotas, Alexander tried some of Philotas' associates, including Amyntas, son of Andromenes. Arrian's account attributes the trial of Amyntas and his brothers to their friendship with Philotas; no mention is made of Olympias (Arr. 3.26.1–3). Curtius' narrative of the trial, however, contains the supposed defense speech of Amyntas which claims (7.1.36–40) that Olympias had warned Alexander by letter that Amyntas and his brothers were enemies. According to Curtius, her maternal anxiety motivated her in part, but her primary reason for warning her son derived from the fact that, on Alexander's instructions, Amyntas had removed young men from her household for military service, putting the king's needs before a "woman's favor." Curtius asserted that Olympias' accusations (7.1.11) and Amyntas' friendship with Philotas led to his trial (7.1.26–35). On the advice of the troops and his companions, Alexander pardoned Amyntas and his brother (Curt. 7.2.7–10).

One could assume that Olympias' role in the affair was solely Curtius' invention or that of his source: it occurs in a speech, a notoriously dubious circumstance, and is couched in terms that play on sexual stereotyping.

Nonetheless, the idea that Olympias had a large household and resented the loss of any of its members is credible,[88] and she had several reasons to dislike the friends and family of Philotas.[89] Alexander's pardon of Amyntas and his brothers, however, had little to do with the degree of his mother's influence: practical politics dictated the king's actions; though the brothers never regained their prominent position.[90]

More problematic is Olympias' role in the downfall of Lyncestian Alexander, the son of Aeropus. Lyncestian Alexander, probably a scion of the formerly independent Lyncestian royal house, was, by any definition, an important figure.[91] After the death of Philip, Alexander had his two brothers killed but not only spared the other Alexander, but gave him important duties.[92] Lyncestian Alexander had married a daughter of Antipater (Curt. 7.1.7; Just. 11.7.1, 12.14.1). Although Antipater's influence may have contributed to the king's distinctive treatment of Lyncestian Alexander,[93] Alexander spared the Lyncestian primarily because he had been among the first of his friends to support him (militarily and politically) at the time of Philip's death (Arr. 1.25.2; Just. 11.2.2 ; Curt. 7.1.6).[94] While Arrian (1.25.1–10) claims that Lyncestian Alexander was arrested in winter 334/3 on information provided by Parmenio (based on his interception of an agent with an incriminating letter) about the Lyncestian's treasonable dealings with the Persian king, Diodorus (17.32.1–2) has been understood to date the arrest to the fall of 333.[95] Curtius (only some of his account of the saga of Lyncestian Alexander survives) seems to follow the dating of Diodorus but attributes the arrest to two unnamed informers (Curt. 7.1.6).[96] He says that the mother of the king[97] wrote to her son about many useful things and warned him to be on his guard against Lyncestian Alexander. Diodorus adds that a number of other credible circumstances contributed to his arrest.[98] Whatever the solution to the chronological problems about the arrest of the Lyncestian, the long delay between his apprehension and death confirms his importance. That granted, a number of factors, some related to his activities in Asia with the Persians and some to past and present connections in Macedonia, may have led to his arrest; in this case, both Olympias and Parmenio may have played roles.[99]

Another supposed letter of Olympias, again found in Plutarch (*Alex.* 39.4–5), relates to Alexander's many expensive gifts to ordinary soldiers and particularly to courtiers. Plutarch comments that the extent of the arrogance Alexander's friends and bodyguards derived from sharing in the king's wealth is clear from a letter Olympias wrote to her son. An apparent quotation follows in which Olympias urges Alexander to find another way to reward his friends and high officials. Currently, she says, "you make all of them equal to kings and enable them to have many friends, but leave yourself isolated."[100] Plutarch adds that Olympias often wrote similar things to Alexander and that he kept her writings secret, with the exception of one occasion involving Hephaestion (see below). This letter, like all of them, could be rejected as a fabrication, though it is usually considered genuine.[101]

While the passage certainly refers to the tremendous wealth Alexander's military success had given him and the extent to which the elite shared in it, it is also an observation about politics at the Macedonian court, and an important one. According to Plutarch, Olympias was worried not simply that Alexander give so much away that he himself was no longer as wealthy, but that the gifted wealth empowered others, by making it possible for them to build a network of friends or companions, while, at the same time, leaving him with fewer. The implication is that friends/Companions are connected to distribution of wealth[102] and that one needed to draw a fine line between giving one's Companions enough to please them and yet ensure they continue to recognize the king's superiority—a basic requirement for a Macedonian king[103]—and giving them so much that they became independent of the ruler.[104] In terms of understanding Olympias' views about others at Alexander's court, the passage is interesting. However personally jealous she may have been, the passage demonstrates a concern for the maintenance of her son's power and a suspicion about the self-serving aspirations of many in the elite that seems savvy, sensible, and well warranted by events. One could read it into her reported reactions to Amyntas, Philotas, Lyncestian Alexander, and, as we shall see, Antipater himself. Olympias wanted to make very sure that no one had more power/wealth than her son.

Did Olympias quarrel with Hephaestion, probably Alexander's lover or former lover and the king's closest personal associate on the campaign?[105] Whatever Hephaestion's character, others in Alexander's inner circle certainly envied his intimacy with the king and quarreled with him (Plut. *Alex.* 47.5–7, *Eum.* 2.1–2, 4–5). The Macedonian court was an extremely competitive place and Alexander's often contradictory treatment of his associates exacerbated this. It would hardly be surprising if Olympias too had resented Alexander's relationship with Hephaestion, particularly since he accompanied her son while she stayed behind. Diodorus (17.114.3) says that Olympias became hostile to Hephaestion out of jealousy and wrote letters to him of a harsh and threatening nature. Hephaestion supposedly wrote back, reproaching her. Diodorus includes an apparent quotation from the letter of Hephaestion, a quotation that bizarrely employs the "royal we."[106] This is the only evidence for strife between Hephaestion and Olympias, though Plutarch preserves four different versions of a story about Hephaestion reading Olympias' letters to her son and being enjoined to secrecy about their contents.[107] None of Plutarch's many versions of the story, however, say anything about relations between Hephaestion and Alexander and they vary as to whether they consider Hephaestion's reading of Olympias' letters unusual. Tension between Olympias and the man closest to Alexander would be unsurprising, but the evidence for it is much poorer[108] than for her notorious and much more important dispute with Antipater.

Whatever one thinks of the historicity of Olympias' other squabbles, most of them seem petty, typical of the quarrelsome and envious nature of Macedonian court life. Olympias' disagreement with Antipater, however, is of a different category. Almost all the major ancient sources for the reign of Alexander allude to the antagonism between Olympias and Antipater. It may well be that these references were affected and exaggerated to some unknown degree by the propaganda wars of the Successor era and perhaps by an inclination to date the origins of the more violent conflicts of that period to an earlier time, but there is no good reason to doubt that Olympias and Antipater feuded throughout most of Alexander's reign. We have already seen one reason why contention arose: Alexander had not clearly defined their relative spheres. Perhaps Alexander intended from the beginning that Olympias function as a kind of counterweight to the authority of Antipater. Throughout his life Alexander had a tendency to play favorites off against each other. The lack of definition in the extent of each one's responsibilities made it easy for each to see the other as overstepping what was appropriate.[109] Alexander generated "an environment of distrust" at his court and often placed people who had conflicting political goals in neighboring territories in order that each would check the other.[110] This could explain the origin of the notorious quarrel between Antipater and Olympias.

It would be helpful to know the exact terms of their dispute (waged through parallel correspondence with Alexander). Unfortunately, most of the sources fail to clarify the motivation of the two disputants, though they are more helpful about the impact of the complaints of each. Virtually all discussions of the dispute connect in some degree to the issue of Antipater's demotion and/or Alexander's death. Only Arrian (7.12.6–7) discusses the motivation of the disputants (see further discussion of this passage in the Appendix). He begins by denying that Alexander's order to Antipater to give up his position in Europe and report to him in Babylon was the consequence, as rumor said, of Alexander's yielding to his mother's accusations about Antipater. Arrian believed that Alexander did not really want to remove Antipater from Macedonia or disgrace him but wanted to prevent the argument from reaching a point past his ability to heal it. Arrian says that Olympias displayed *authadeia* (stubbornness or perhaps willfulness), *oxutes* (sharpness), and *polupragmosune* (meddlesomeness or officiousness). He then comments, to the amusement of the modern reader, that these were qualities not the least suitable for the mother of Alexander![111] He adds an anecdote that implies that the king either agreed with this view or at least found his mother troublesome.[112] More helpfully, Arrian then lists Olympias' charges against Antipater: he was *huperogkon* (immoderate, excessive) on account of his rank and the attention (*therapeia*) paid him, and he was forgetting who had appointed him, claiming himself to be first among Macedonians and Greeks. Arrian then, in apparent contradiction to his earlier statement, adds that these accusations were gaining strength with Alexander because they were exactly the sort of thing to worry a ruler. Nonetheless, he notes that Alexander said or did nothing to suggest that his regard for Antipater was not as great as ever.[113] Clearly Olympias did not act as Arrian/Antipater thought a woman should act, and Arrian seems to assume that her only motive was personal contrariness. Nonetheless, his account implies that Antipater and Olympias each thought the other was taking more power and authority than was appropriate. Olympias' concerns about Antipater echo those Plutarch ascribed to her about a number of prominent members of the court, a fear that others might compromise Alexander's monarchy.

Diodorus and Justin connect the quarrel to their belief that Antipater arranged the death of Alexander. Diodorus (17.118.1) simply states that they quarreled, that Antipater initially treated Olympias with disdain because Alexander did not respond favorably to her charges against him, but that later, as their enmity increased, Alexander wished to gratify his mother in all respects on account of piety and Antipater gave many indications of his estrangement. This, combined with the deaths of Parmenio and Philotas, inspired Antipater's conspiracy. Justin (12.14.3) lists Olympias' accusations as one factor in a long list that inspired Antipater to regicide. Plutarch (*Alex.* 39.7) believed that Alexander was more bothered by Antipater's accusations against his mother than he was by hers against Antipater.

The sources do not intimate that Olympias' influence was the sole factor in the deteriorating relationship between Alexander and Antipater (and they disagree about the degree of deterioration that had occurred[114]) but they generally recognize that Olympias' views were an important element in the mix. Alexander's Asianizing of the monarchy, his interest in divine sonship and then divine monarchy, the violent removal of Parmenio, Philotas, Cleitus, and Lyncestian Alexander, all must have contributed to misunderstanding and distrust. As we have seen, Alexander had commanded Antipater to step down from his position (and yield it to Craterus) and to come to Babylon (Arr. 7.12.4; Just. 12.12.9). Nonetheless, at the time of Alexander's death, though months had passed, Antipater had failed to obey. Long term, Olympias' critique of Antipater's operations gained credibility with Alexander. In a sense it was simple: Alexander knew that he could trust his mother to be concerned about his interests because they were also hers, whereas he could not trust Antipater to the same extent because the two men's interests were increasingly different.

Whether the consequence of a conspiracy headed by Antipater, or, more likely, the result of a combination of disease, grief, and excessive consumption of wine,[115] one can only imagine the stunned horror with which Olympias received the news of her son's death, how unimaginable it must have seemed. If she was as able and as tough minded a person as I have suggested, she must have known that his death spelled disaster for her family and that her chances for a calm old age and retirement in Molossia were poor. No wonder she blamed her son's death on Antipater and his sons (see further Chapter 4). The death of Alexander would transform what had begun as a personal struggle between Antipater and Olympias into an increasingly deadly dynastic dispute.

4   Olympias on her own, 323–316

Olympias now had to cope with the loss of the son whose mere existence and subsequent astonishing success had defined nearly every aspect of her adult life. She had to do so in a world of bewildering political complexity, one characterized by much greater internecine violence than the era that had preceded it. Alexander's unanticipated death left the empire he had forged in political chaos. For more than forty years the Macedonian elite fought over the territory he had conquered. His generals (the Successors) waged war against each other; some of the most brilliant fell early in this seemingly endless struggle, while some of the least competent managed to survive into old age. In 281, two of the last of the group of able but ruthless young men who had gone east with Alexander, now elderly but still tough and battle-hardened, faced each other in battle. Within a few years of that event (277/6), the political structure of Alexander's former empire achieved some measure of stability; of the many original competitors, three dynasties created by the Successors would endure.[1]

By the time some rough equilibrium had been reached,[2] Olympias was long dead, along with all the other Argeads (whether by birth or marriage). A new dynasty ruled in Macedonia. Although she ultimately failed to achieve her political goals and her enemies murdered her, Olympias contrived to live nearly seven years into the tumultuous period of the Successors, to play a role in the great events of the day unprecedented for a woman, and to die a death that was at once heroic and, many would say, deserved. Certainly it suited the life she had lived. This final phase of her career was the most adventurous. During Alexander's reign, her power, her ability to exact her will, ultimately derived from that of her son. After his death, Olympias largely acted on her own and determined her own policy. Her ability to do so depended on her son's and husband's repute, but they themselves were no longer there to decide matters. To the end of her life Olympias retained the character she had first demonstrated as a young woman: wily, brutal to her enemies and loyal to her friends, calculating, indomitable in her determination to secure the throne for her heirs.

Before we turn to an examination of Olympias' policy and actions in these last years, we need to have a brief look at the major conflicts and events of the period immediately after Alexander's death in order to make Olympias' choices and motivation intelligible. Naturally, we will focus on issues most relevant to her and on events on the Greek peninsula, since she never left it. Unfortunately, the ancient sources for this era are much poorer than for Alexander's reign.[3] Consequently, the chronology of events is often disputed.[4] Moreover, as we shall see in the case of Olympias, the problem for historians is often not so much when something happened in relation to other events, as it is when others who could be affected by an event came to know of it. As a consequence, it sometimes proves impossible to determine whether a given figure initiated a series of events or rather reacted to something that another person had done.

When Alexander breathed his last, those who survived him had to re-conceive their world and imagine it without him. This was no easy matter, even for those who had hoped for his death, let alone for those whose success and well-being had depended upon his. Successions in Macedonia had always been rocky and violent, but the succession crisis precipitated by Alexander's death proved far more chaotic and destabilizing than any that had preceded it, and not just because of the vast extent of Alexander's impact.

The point of all previous succession struggles had been to determine which Argead came out on top, an issue because there were often so many plausible contenders and no tidy method to select among them. On the other hand, any violence was therefore previously largely limited to the Argeads; non-Argeads were killed only if they got in the way. Otherwise there was no point in killing them, since they could not hope to be king. Now there were no immediately plausible heirs. Arrhidaeus, Alexander's mentally limited half-brother, was in Babylon. His contemporaries treated him as a permanent minor; he could not rule on his own.[5] When Alexander died, his first wife, the Bactrian Roxane, was well along in a pregnancy, but those in Babylon did not yet know the baby's sex. They could not even be sure it would be born alive. Alexander's two other wives had produced no children. (Barsine, the half-Greek daughter of the famous Artabazus, had borne a son by Alexander [Heracles], but Alexander had never married her.[6])

The problem of the absence of a viable heir was compounded by the fact that the Macedonians had failed to develop any sort of institutionalized sub-stitute kingship, an important issue granted that the most the Macedonians could hope for in the current circumstance was that a son of Alexander would rule after many years of some sort of regency. No Macedonian child-king had ever retained the throne for any length of time. Alexander's generals must have known from the start that it was unlikely that any child of Alexander would live long enough to rule on his own. But one wonders if any of them really wanted that to happen, since, with his death, any of them might hope to rule; and, indeed, many of them did. The Successors long postponed (until 306) the formality of assuming a royal title, but they began to act like kings soon after the death of Alexander.[7] One consequence of this political reality was a dramatic increase in political violence; if any of the generals might be king, then it would be worth his rivals' while to kill him and his male and female kin.[8]

Another factor that intensified the succession crisis was the much expanded scope of Macedonian rule. In earlier contested successions, foreign powers had often supported royal rivals, a pattern in keeping with the historically weak nature of Macedonian power. Invasions might happen even without the excuse of a pretender. But now, the issue was not simply control of Macedonia but control of a vast empire. The great distances involved prolonged and complicated the struggle for power.

As Alexander's corpse lay unburied, disorder and discord descended on the Macedonian court and camp in Babylon.[9] Great dissension existed within the elite and even more between the elite and the mass of the army. In general, ordinary Macedonian soldiers favored the selection of Alexander's half-brother Arrhidaeus while the elite (though many within it found the idea of sharing rule attractive) ultimately gave grudging support to Roxane's son, should she have one. The parties did not disagree simply about who should rule but also about what mechanism should be used to make that determination. Civil war threatened and some people were quickly killed. Generals and troops changed sides, in some cases multiple times. Another complicating factor was that two of the most important generals, Antipater and Craterus, men in control of a large number of troops, were not present at Babylon but could not be ignored. The lack of a dependable source for these events exacerbates the problem of trying to understand what must have been a messy, absolutely terrifying, and probably fairly long-drawn-out series of alarms and excursions.

That being the case, I will simply describe the result of this scary historical moment. The Macedonians soon had two kings, not one, and neither was competent. Arrhidaeus (hereafter referred to as Philip Arrhidaeus, since he took his father's name when he assumed the throne) was king but so, as soon as he was born and his sex was known, was Roxane's son, Alexander IV.[10] Perdiccas, the closest of Alexander's associates once Hephaestion was dead, and the man to whom the dying king had given his signet ring, acquired greater authority than the other generals. For the moment he functioned as both regent and guardian of the two kings. Constitutional niceties, as usual with the Macedonians, were not observed, primarily because they did not exist. Those present at Babylon generally confirmed officers and governors in the positions they had at the time of Alexander's death. Then the generals rushed off to muster their troops, find allies and position themselves as best they could. On top of everything else, there were revolts in the empire, most notably in Greece and in the eastern provinces.

Far off in Molossia, Olympias heard the news of her son's death. She was denied the traditional role of Greek women at the funerary ritual since Alexander's remains were never returned to his homeland. As the years passed, first one and then another of the generals gained control of her son's corpse. Alexander was buried, exhumed, and reburied several times over, but always in Egypt. Unable to act out her grief in the ordinary manner with a funerary procession and tomb, Olympias may nonetheless have raised the lament, another characteristically female responsibility. If so, apart from celebrating the great deeds of her son and the extent of her own loss, her lament may well have named and blamed those she believed had killed him. All three topics characterize laments and Olympias came from a place where they were likely still an important part of the culture.

Dirges tend to be most dominant where vendettas are common; the leader of the lament, typically the mother or wife of the dead man, might include the wish that his enemy suffer the same fate, thus generating another cycle of vengeance.[11] In the Archaic period, women, especially elite women, had played a dominant role in public funerary ritual, but in southern Greece, by the fifth century BCE, cities began to limit their participation and privatize it, partly because they wanted to limit the power of aristocratic clans and their ancestor cults and partly to control the desire for vengeance often inspired by laments.[12] The elite, however, still dominated in Macedonia and Molossia in the fourth century. No similar legislation is known for this period in either kingdom. Moreover, the role of elite women in Macedonia (and probably in Molossia as well) resembled that of elite women in southern Greece in the Archaic period,[13] when large public laments occurred and elite women were more valued as items of exchange between aristocratic clans.[14]

Olympias, I have argued, may have found models for her behavior in epic and tragedy. She may have recalled the words of her supposed divine ancestress Thetis about the premature death of her own son Achilles, also buried far from his homeland: "Not again will I receive him come home to the house of Peleus" (*Il.* 18.59–60). She may have thought of the laments and hopes for vengeance of her female Trojan ancestors. A variant of the Armenian *Alexander Romance* has the dying Alexander write to his mother requesting that she "gather together the women chanters and lament Alexander the pitiful short-lived son of yours." The narrator then reports that Olympias did organize "great lamentation for the noble spirit of her son Alexander."[15]

I would suggest that she first voiced her belief that Antipater and his sons had killed Alexander in public lament for her son, though she may also have employed other means to advance her views. We do know that Olympias blamed Antipater and his sons, but the sources do not clarify when and how she communicated this belief. Although Diodorus (19.11.8) and Plutarch (*Alex.* 77.1) refer to her charges of Antipatrid involvement in Alexander's death in the context of events in 317, Olympias probably immediately suspected Antipater and his sons. If so, she could have used her lament for her son's death as the first occasion for the broadcasting of her belief in the culpability of the Antipatrids.

Certainly, despite Plutarch's implausible assertion that no one thought of death by poison until five years later, assassination must have been suspected from the start. Curtius (10.10.14, 18) reports that rumors about Antipater's role began immediately. Hyperides (*ap.* Plut. *Mor.* 849f) seems to have referred to the stories soon after Alexander's death. Deaths of Macedonian kings, especially ones so comparatively young, generated thoughts of regicide. The timing of Alexander's death certainly benefited Antipater and so seemed suggestive. Moreover, Alexander's seeming invincibility made acceptance of a natural death difficult. Granted the past history of regicide in Macedonia, the assassination of Philip II, the many conspiracies against the life of Alexander, the recent crisis in relations between Alexander and Antipater occasioned by the latter's refusal to honor the king's command to give up his position and come to Babylon, and the general tendency in the ancient world to suspect poison in the deaths of the famous, no matter their age and ill health, Plutarch cannot be correct. Olympias' conviction that the Antipatrids had murdered her son was hardly surprising and seems perfectly reasonable. After all, the modern medical science that has made most scholars doubt her conviction was not available to her. She was hardly alone in her conviction (Curt. 10.10.14–17; Arr. 7.27.1–2; Just. 12.14.1–9). How easy and logical to blame those she already hated. I see no reason why Olympias would not have been convinced from the start that Antipater caused her son's death.

Bereaved people, however, often react to loss by trying to understand the death of a loved one in terms that enable them to explain it and (often) enable them to formulate an action in response to this explanation. Accidental or random death often seems less acceptable than death "for a reason." The reason appears to give meaning to the death that would otherwise be lacking. Parents of those who die in car accidents find odd comfort in the notion that their child's death was the result of the unscrupulous actions of automobile manufacturers rather than chance. Those whose sons (and now daughters) die in war often insist that the war must be just and noble, fearing that, if the war is not justifiable, their child's death is somehow rendered meaningless. Alexander's ironically unwarlike death, not the heroic end he and Olympias would doubtless have preferred, probably made the imposition of "meaning" even more important. Olympias needed to believe that her son was murdered and nothing was easier and more plausible than supposing that those she most hated were responsible.

This supposition, however, did more than satisfy an emotional need. It justified her past views—Antipater really had wanted rule for himself—and laid out an agenda for her future action: vengeance/punishment for those responsible. Her enemies had become her son's as well.

Though she would remain in her native kingdom until 317, Olympias started to act, probably as a response to the news of her son's death, fairly soon after she must first have heard of it. Her actions imply that she understood that her situation (and that of her daughter) had changed radically, that Alexander's demise had robbed them of the guarantee of physical safety that had been theirs while he lived. Not only did they have many Macedonian enemies with whom to contend, but a new Greek revolt from Macedonian control (the Lamian War, begun in the fall of 323) added to the imminent dangers.

Now Olympias and Cleopatra needed male support, primarily military support. While each might appear in front of an army (see below), neither woman could have hoped actually to command one. Their financial resources may also have limited their ability to acquire military forces of their own. As we have seen, Alexander had enriched both with plunder, and assorted evidence demonstrates their ability to function as patrons in command of wealth.[16] Their long-term sources of that wealth, particularly after the death of Alexander, are unknown. Both apparently possessed enough riches to allow them to travel great distances, but the circular relationship between monarchy, generalship, plunder, and legitimacy that characterized the period[17] suggests that their wealth may now have been more restricted, and this, in itself, prevented them from maintaining extensive numbers of troops.

Cleopatra may have returned briefly to Molossia at the time of her brother's death, but regardless of whether she and her mother were physically united again, their policy seems to have been. Cleopatra, as we have seen, had previously joined her mother in opposition to Antipater. Thus she may also have shared her mother's belief in Antipatrid guilt in Alexander's death.

Although Cleopatra had been quite young at the time of her husband's death in about 330, neither she nor her brother, in the years since, had displayed any interest in her remarriage. But within a few months of her brother's death, Cleopatra changed her views and entered what proved to be the brisk post-Alexander elite Macedonian marriage market. Many members of the Macedonian elite, in response to the instability created by Alexander's death, pursued security via new and sometimes conflicting marital ties.[18] While we do not know for certain that Cleopatra's first projected marriage alliance received her mother's approval, her second effort definitely did. Most likely, Olympias was involved in both.

Plutarch (*Eum.* 3.5) reveals that Cleopatra had sent Leonnatus letters in Asia inviting him to meet her in Pella and marry her.[19] He was a reasonable choice: kin to the royal family, a *Somatophulax* of Alexander, brave, and hostile to Cleopatra's and Olympias' enemy Antipater.[20] According to Plutarch, Leonnatus, though claiming that he wanted to leave Asia in order to aid Antipater in the Lamian War, really coveted Macedonia. The implication is that marrying Cleopatra would have assisted him in that goal. Since he arrived to raise the siege of Lamia in the spring of 322, Cleopatra's correspondence with him must date to fall 323 or early 322. Though Olympias is not mentioned in connection with this episode, it is usually assumed that she was behind it.[21] This is especially likely since Cleopatra's suggestion was probably offered to counter a similar one Antipater had made to Leonnatus of one of his daughters in marriage (probably in the fall of 323).[22] Unfortunately for Cleopatra, Leonnatus raised the siege, but died doing so. Although his early elimination voided this marital initiative, it typifies the policy Olympias and her daughter demonstrably pursued: military aid from one of the Successors obtained through marriage to Cleopatra (who was still young enough to bear children with Argead blood) and opposition to the goals and interests of the Antipatrids.

Next (summer or fall 322), Olympias dispatched Cleopatra to Sardis in Asia Minor (the location of much of the Macedonian army, the two kings, and the regent Perdiccas) in order to stymie another of Antipater's marital initiatives, the marriage of his daughter Nicaea to Perdiccas (*FGrH* 156 F 9, 21–6). Since Nicaea and Cleopatra arrived in Sardis about the same time (Diod. 18.23.1), their respective parents must have sent them off at about the same time. Perdiccas had asked for Nicaea soon after Alexander's death, when he desperately needed Antipater's support. Now, supposedly, he preferred Cleopatra because of her Argead blood, but could not afford to offend Antipater. He therefore married Nicaea but continued to negotiate with Cleopatra secretly (Diod. 18.23.3, 25.3; Just. 13.6.4–8). The discovery of Perdiccas' dealings with Cleopatra (winter 322/1) led to a war against him by Antipater, Craterus, Ptolemy, and others. Justin (13.6.12–13) claims that Perdiccas consulted with his friends as to whether to pursue the war in Macedonia or in Egypt, against Ptolemy. Some advised him to choose Macedonia, where Olympias would add significant force to their faction and gain the favor of the Macedonians because of the reputations of Alexander and Philip. In the end, he went to Egypt, experienced a series of political and military defeats, and his own officers assassinated him.[23]

This second projected marriage alliance had been more ambitious and certainly more risky. The fall of Perdiccas left Cleopatra in Sardis, in what proved to be a deteriorating position. By staying, she kept close to her possible marriage market, but also remained close to danger. Many of Perdiccas' associates, including his sister, were killed or under sentence of death. Eumenes, who had been Cleopatra's advocate in her marriage negotiations with Perdiccas, and who was now outlawed, appeared in Sardis. According to Justin (14.1.7–8), he hoped to use Cleopatra's influence as Alexander's sister further to secure the loyalty of his officers. Plutarch (*Eum.* 8.4) offers a very different motive for his arrival in Sardis: he wanted to confront Antipater and impress Cleopatra. She, however, fearful to give Antipater any cause for accusations, asked him to leave and he did so. Arrian (*FGrH* 156, F 11.40) more plausibly asserted that, rather than fearing Antipater, Cleopatra feared the blame of the Macedonian people if she encouraged civil war. When Antipater arrived, rather than prizing her restraint, he upbraided her for her *philia* with Perdiccas and Eumenes; she defended herself vehemently in a manner, says Arrian, not customary for women, and made accusations of him in turn (one wonders if she too accused him of complicity in Alexander's death). Arrian thinks the encounter ended peacefully. In a sense it did: Antipater did not kill her.

After this, Cleopatra remained in Sardis, but ultimately lost her independence. She died many years later when, apparently by then under a kind of house arrest by Antigonus, she tried to break out and escape to Ptolemy and yet another marriage alliance.[24] Cleopatra may have continued to correspond with her mother until Olympias' death, but they never saw each other again. However she felt about her daughter's fate, Olympias would now have to turn to others to pursue her personal and dynastic goals. Though Diodorus (20.37.4) says that because of the fame of her family all the Successors sought to marry Cleopatra since an alliance with the royal house would lead to rule of the whole empire, she never married again. Her attempted marriages, however, demonstrate that what had begun as a struggle between two important individual members of Alexander's court, Olympias and Antipater, had now become a broader struggle, a bitter enmity between two dynasties.

Olympias did have access to a source of military support in the years after her son's death other than that potentially offered by various Macedonian generals. Despite or perhaps because of her daughter's departure, Olympias remained in Molossia, and it was from a Molossian and another Aeacid that she found aid. As usual, our information about events in Molossia is poor. I have suggested (see Chapter 3) that during the years of Alexander of the Great's reign, first his sister, then his mother and sister, and finally his mother alone had acted as regent in Molossia and that some time during that period the Epirote Alliance was formed. When Cleopatra forsook Molossia for the last time, she probably left behind a son and daughter, presumably in her mother's care. No ancient source calls Neoptolemus and his sister Cadmeia the children of Cleopatra and her uncle/husband Alexander, but a number of factors make it likely that they were.[25] Cleopatra's son, of course, would still have been far too young to rule on his own, and now he lacked the powerful support of his famous uncle. Once the Aeacids lost their powerful Argead supporter, a child-king with a female regent was too precarious a situation to be allowed to continue.[26] The collateral branch of the royal family returned from exile and Aeacides, son of Olympias' uncle Arybbas and her sister Troas, became king, perhaps co-king with Cleopatra's son Neoptolemus.[27]

When Aeacides began to rule is uncertain, as is the exact circumstance. These issues are complicated by the fact that in the fall of 323, when the Lamian War began, some Molossians joined the alliance against Antipater (Diod. 18.11.1). One could certainly conclude that Olympias, newly bereaved, eager to do harm to the man whom she blamed for her son's death, acting as regent, dispatched Molossian troops to take part in the war against Antipater. Diodorus, however, describes the Molossians involved as "those around Aryptaeus"[28] and adds that Aryptaeus treacherously changed sides and went over to the Macedonians. Some believe that "Aryptaeus" was in fact Olympias' uncle Arybbas and that it was he, not his son, who began to rule after the death of Alexander the Great, this despite Diodorus' earlier assertion (16.72.1) that Arybbas was already dead (*c.* early 340s) after a ten-year rule, and Justin's assertion (7.6.12) that he grew old in exile.[29] Aryptaeus' change in sides is surprising: it could mean, if Olympias were still regent or influential with "Aryptaeus," that the Molossians in question switched sides when Cleopatra began to negotiate with Leonnatus, who was fighting on the opposite side; or it could be (if Aryptaeus was really Arybbas) that the change came when Arybbas was recognized as king. One can imagine a scenario in which Arybbas got to be king again because Antipater had offered his support in return for Arybbas' changing sides.[30] In any event, Arybbas' son Aeacides was soon king. One cannot believe that Aeacides assumed the throne with help from Antipater, granted that the rest of his life he supported Olympias (Paus. 1.11.3), at some cost to himself, and opposed the Antipatrids.[31] It is far more likely that Olympias invited her nephew to return in order to buttress her now less secure position, especially against Antipater,[32] and that Aeacides felt that he was in her debt.[33] I have already noted the power of Aeacid dynastic loyalty.[34]

In any event, by 320, with the murder of Perdiccas and Antipater's assumption of the regency and personal control of the kings, any hope Olympias had to gain greater power and influence through her daughter had faded. Her enemy was now supreme. Antipater's stay in Asia was brief, and when he returned, he brought with him both kings. Perhaps Olympias had hoped from the start that she would be able to become her grandson Alexander IV's guardian and ensure that he lived long enough to rule in more than name, but so long as he remained in Asia, that could be only a dream.[35] Antipater brought the young king much closer to his grandmother, although, naturally, that was hardly his goal.

Then, in the next year, Antipater did Olympias a much greater favor: he died. One can only imagine Olympias' glee at the news that her long-time enemy was dead, but his death conveyed more benefits to her than the simple fact of it. The dying old general had left the kings and supreme command to Polyperchon rather than to his own son Cassander (Diod. 18.48.4). As we have seen, Olympias believed that Cassander, with his brother and father, had caused her son's death. That an Antipatrid was no longer regent would have seemed a good thing in itself to Olympias (though Antipater had made his son second-in-command to Polyperchon), but Polyperchon soon made his choice seem good in a more particular way for Olympias. Shortly after he became regent, he invited Olympias to return to Macedonia, take over responsibility for her grandson, and assume some sort of public role (Diod. 18.49.4). She refused Polyperchon's offer at least once and probably twice (Diod. 18.49.4, 57.2) before finally agreeing.

Let us consider why he made such an offer to her, why she rejected it for a year or two,[36] and why she ultimately accepted it, embarking on a path that would lead to her death. By the time of Antipater's death, after four harrowing years of civil and foreign war full of betrayals and reversals, Macedonians must have felt that they could count on nothing. Indeed, the old general's death would only have intensified that sentiment. Whatever strengths and weaknesses Antipater had as general or administrator, whatever his popularity with the Macedonian people, he had provided the only order in Macedonia for nearly a generation. He represented continuity with the past, with the world before Alexander's conquests. Almost all the other major Macedonian leaders, including Polyperchon, had been gone for fourteen years, seeing and experiencing things that were alien to those Macedonians who had stayed at home. Here was a people whose only political order had been provided by Argead monarchy, but there had been no monarch for all this time and the only male Argeads available were a dimly remembered mentally limited man and a half-Asian four-year-old.

In this situation, Olympias stood for the monarchy, for the Argeads, and she reminded Macedonians of their great dead leaders, that remarkable father and son, of more secure and successful days. As male Argeads became scarce, legitimacy resided in the women of the clan and none could claim greater renown than the mother of the conqueror. She had a great lineage of her own and had long exercised considerable influence throughout the entire peninsula, as Justin's remarks (see above) indicated. Olympias and the remaining Argeads offered greater legitimacy than any of the regents. As a number of incidents in the early post-Alexander era demonstrated, the mass of Macedonian troops (both those in Asia and those in Macedonia) and probably Macedonian civilians as well remained loyal to the royal house to a much greater degree than did members of the elite, many of whom already saw themselves as kings-in-the-making. In addition, granted prejudice against Asian culture and women, Macedonians probably wanted to see Olympias rather than Alexander IV's hapless Bactrian mother in charge of the heir.

Until Antipater made his fateful decision, Polyperchon had been a comparatively minor figure in Macedonian affairs, typically functioning as second-in-command to some better-known member of the elite.[37] Once he took center stage, he proved to lack the nerve and competence in the field that characterized so many in the Macedonian elite. Because of that, he did not inspire loyalty in his troops and certainly he would demonstrate little of that quality himself. Though responsible for a series of military blunders that led to the collapse of the Argead dynasty, his political skills were stronger than his military ones. Antipater, aged and fatally ill, may have overestimated Polyperchon's talents, but they did exist. (Moreover, Antipater may have based his decision at least as much on his doubts about his own son as on his confidence in Polyperchon's strengths.) Polyperchon's offer to Olympias was a sensible one. Diodorus' narrative of events after the death of Antipater (18.49.1–4, 54.1–57.4) usually represents Polyperchon as a reasonable and competent leader attempting to cope with a man (Cassander) who was determined from the outset to undermine and overthrow him. According to Diodorus, Polyperchon's offer to Olympias did not precipitate a rupture with Cassander but rather followed it. In this case, Polyperchon gained no new enemies and, by means of the offer, acquired the support and prestige he had previously lacked.

What exactly Polyperchon was offering to Olympias may never be clear, particularly since neither Justin nor Diodorus ever tells us when or on what terms Olympias finally accepted his invitation. (The narrative of events rather than an explicit statement in a source indicates that she must finally have accepted.) Still, the terms those authors use to describe Polyperchon's offer and Olympias' actions in the period may be meaningful, bearing in mind that I have suggested that Macedonians did not yet think in terms of specific, defined offices (see above). On three different occasions, Diodorus (18.49.4, 57.2, 65.1) associates Olympias with the *epimeleia* of her grandson. All the people the sources say exercised *epimeleia* of the kings had personal control and responsibility for them. This responsibility had been shared in the past and Polyperchon, presumably, was offering to do so again since nothing indicates that Olympias would also have been responsible for Philip Arrhidaeus. While those responsible for the safety of the kings had to protect them and so had to have some military power, when men like Antipater or Perdiccas had *epimeleia* but also commanded a large number of troops, the sources usually employ other terms to indicate these additional responsibilities. Several other terms employed with respect to Olympias and Polyperchon's offer indicate that he was offering more than simple physical responsibility for her small grandson. On the first occasion, Diodorus mentions, in addition, royal *prostasia*. The significance of this term has been much debated. My own view is that it was not a specific office but rather undefined prominence and power. Another passage in Diodorus (18.65.1) says that when Olympias returned to Macedonia, she would have her former *apodoché* (favor) and *timé* (honor). These two terms may paraphrase what *prostasia* meant in this circumstance, in which case it was a general term, not an office.[38]

As we have seen, Olympias did not immediately accept Polyperchon's offer, even though Cassander's resistance to Polyperchon continued to grow. She turned for advice to Eumenes. By this time, Polyperchon had rehabilitated him (he had previously been outlawed for supporting Perdiccas), given him supreme command in Asia, granted him money and entrusted to him the best soldiers in the Asian armies, the Silver Shields, Alexander's invincible veterans (Diod. 18.58.1). Eumenes, the sole non-Macedonian among the Successors, demonstrated atypical loyalty to Olympias and to the royal family in general. We have already noted his friendly dealings with Cleopatra. When Antigonus, after the death of Antipater, tried to make Eumenes an ally and had him swear an oath of loyalty, Eumenes insisted that the oath he swore include the name of Olympias and those of the kings (Plut. *Eum.* 12.2). Later, Plutarch says (*Eum.* 13.1) that Olympias invited him to take charge of her grandson and protect him because she feared plots against him. She also reinforced his authority, writing to the commanders in Asia to tell them that they should continue to obey Eumenes as the senior general (Diod. 18.62.2).

Diodorus (18.58.3–4) summarizes the content of the letter Olympias sent to Eumenes but also includes his reply. In this passage, Polyperchon's offer is not specifically mentioned, but Olympias' letter, in essence, seems to be about it, as well as the wider political situation *c.* 318. Diodorus says that she kept begging Eumenes to give aid to the kings and herself, stating that he was the most trustworthy of their remaining friends, and the most able to alleviate the isolation of the royal house. More specifically, she asked him whether it would be wiser for her to go to Macedonia or to remain in Epirus, and stated that she distrusted those who claimed to be the guardians of the kings but who actually wanted to bring the monarchy over to themselves. Eumenes sensibly advised Olympias to bide her time, waiting until the outcome of the war between Polyperchon and Cassander was clear. The content of the letter is a good fit for the other actions of Olympias in this period (i.e., her search for military support), demonstrating as it does that she was aware of the dangers inherent in the move back to Macedonia. The letter also suggests that her faith in Polyperchon was limited, as it was in all the other Successors. Olympias was an experienced dynastic politician and recognized how poor her grandson's chances were and how comparatively safe she would remain if she remained in Molossia. Eumenes' advice therefore confirmed her own view of the situation.[39]

That being the case, one wants to know why, rejecting his advice and her demonstrable previous caution, Olympias agreed to go back to Macedonia in the fall of 317, putting herself, her grandson, her nephew, and the future of the Argead house on the line, albeit with the help of Polyperchon's forces and her nephew Aeacides' Molossian forces. Olympias, by this point a woman in her late fifties, an old woman by the standards of the ancient world, must have had a compelling reason to reverse her previous policy and put herself and all she held dear in harm's way.

Almost certainly her enemies' actions (or rumor of the imminence of these actions) precipitated her reversal of course. Before we turn to what these actions may have been, let us consider the identity and nature of each of her two chief foes. One of these enemies has already been mentioned, Cassander, eldest son of Antipater. Though of comparable age to Alexander, Cassander had not shared in the great Asian expedition but, late in Alexander's reign, his father had sent him as his representative to the king at the court in Babylon.[40] Apparently Cassander had to negotiate with Alexander about his plans for Antipater's projected replacement in Macedonia. Cassander resembled his father in his pragmatism and competence but proved capable of much greater brutality and violence than had Antipater. He lacked the glamour of service with Alexander in the Asian campaign and the heroic, Alexander-like style in battle that endeared so many of the Successors to their troops and helped them to build monarchies,[41] but he was an able and efficient commander and administrator who had capitalized on his father's military and political connections throughout the peninsula.

Whether or not the struggle between Olympias and Cassander began as a feud between two dynasties, it certainly developed into one. Diodorus reports (18.57.2) that when Polyperchon took over, Olympias remained in Molossia because of her enmity against Cassander. Since she was convinced of Cassander's guilt in her son's death, her quarrel had not ended with

Antipater's death. Cassander probably resented Olympias' accusations about the death of Alexander, but more certainly he wanted his father's role as the most powerful man in the peninsula, and, by this point, it is likely that he also wanted to be king. Cassander had supposedly disliked Alexander (Paus. 9.7.2) and would ultimately kill the king's mother, wife, and both of his sons. Pausanias puts these events in the context of a dynastic dispute, noting that Cassander destroyed the whole *oikos* of Alexander, and proclaimed (9.7.4) that the subsequent collapse of Cassander's own dynasty was a kind of divine punishment. Whether Cassander initially understood his conflict with Olympias as dynastic is more problematic. At first it may have seemed to him a simple struggle for power between two individuals who wanted control of the same area,[42] but years of violence and reprisal transformed the antagonism into something more than that.[43]

Olympias' other major adversary was Adea Eurydice,[44] the wife of the non-competent king, Philip Arrhidaeus. She was an Argead by birth as well as marriage, but her heritage tended to put her at odds with Alexander's branch of the royal clan. Adea Eurydice's mother was Alexander's half-sister Cynnane,[45] Philip's daughter by the Illyrian Audata. Cynnane had married Philip's nephew, Amyntas, the son of Perdiccas III. Both of Adea Eurydice's parents were therefore Argeads. As we have seen (Chapter 3), when Adea Eurydice was probably little more than a baby, Alexander had her father Amyntas killed, either because he actually had plotted against the king or because Alexander found it convenient to claim he had. Cynnane did not marry again. She trained her daughter in the skills of a warrior, something apparently traditional in the Illyrian elite. (Audata must have done the same for Cynnane herself, since Cynnane fought in at least one battle during Philip's reign.[46])

The death of Alexander opened up the possibility that Cynnane could move her branch of the Argeads back into power. Taking with her some military force, she and Adea Eurydice (now a teenager) evaded Antipater's troops in Macedonia and managed to approach the Macedonian army in Asia. Like Olympias (though a little later), she took the initiative in order to arrange a marriage for her daughter in Asia.[47] This time the intended groom was Philip Arrhidaeus. Faced with the threat this marriage might pose to his position as regent, Perdiccas dispatched his brother Alcetas to prevent the women from reaching the main army. Alcetas apparently killed Cynnane in front of the army, but instead of thwarting her plan, the murder brought it to pass. The army, enraged at the slaying of Philip's daughter, revolted and demanded that the marriage take place.

Despite her youth, Adea Eurydice was not cowed by her mother's murder. Once Perdiccas was dead, she tried to woo the army away from its loyalty to the male officers. Even the arrival of Antipater did not end her influence; in fact, she was able to use his failure to provide the soldiers with their back pay to gain yet greater support from the army. Only the support of some of the other Successors saved Antipater and enabled him, finally, to leash the young woman's ambitions. Antipater, now regent, brought her back to Macedonia with her husband and young Alexander IV.

For Adea Eurydice, as for Olympias, the death of Antipater occasioned new possibilities. Clearly she, not her husband, initiated policy. Somehow— we do not know how—she and her husband left Polyperchon and reached Macedonia. Adea Eurydice may have plotted a successful escape from Polyperchon's custody, her husband may have been persuaded to insist, or she may have convinced Polyperchon to let them go. Once free of his control, Adea Eurydice, despite her earlier enmity with Antipater, dismissed Polyperchon and established an alliance of sorts with Cassander. The latter had probably conducted a brief military expedition into Macedonia while Polyperchon was in southern Greece, so she may have established this relationship while that had taken place. The specifics of their dealings are unclear: Cassander was certainly acting as their general but whether Adea Eurydice or Cassander was regent for Philip Arrhidaeus we do not know.

Thus, by 317, a confrontation loomed between Olympias' branch of the royal family and that of Adea Eurydice. The younger woman had apparently long known of Polyperchon's offer to Olympias. It is unclear whether Adea Eurydice, once she was an independent agent, turned to Cassander simply because she knew the offer had been made, as Justin claims (14.5.1–2), or because she had heard that Olympias had finally accepted it and was about to return to Macedonia, as Diodorus (19.11.1) asserts.[48] (Olympias may have accepted Polyperchon's offer by the time of Adea Eurydice's departure for Macedonia.)

In a sense, though it does not matter which of these women made the first move because a confrontation had been inevitable since the bizarre compromise of Babylon—the creation of two kings, neither competent—had been made. The passage of time pushed each of these two remarkable women toward a dynastic showdown, one driven by their "biological clocks." In the case of Olympias, the biological issue was age. She could not reasonably hope that her grandson could rule on his own until he could command an army, probably at the age of eighteen. The difficulty was that by the time he reached that age, Olympias, if she had survived, would be in her late sixties or even seventy. If she could not count on living long enough to ensure Alexander IV's independent rule, then the next-best thing would be to eliminate the most obvious threat to his survival while she had allies and military forces to do so. Polyperchon may not have been the most able Macedonian general, but he seems to have been the only one immediately available to Olympias.

Adea Eurydice faced a different kind of biological deadline. In the five years or so since her marriage, she had produced no children. If Alexander IV reached adulthood, Adea Eurydice's power (and probably her life) would end.[49] Worse yet, since she was herself an Argead, like Alexander's sisters, she was vulnerable to a forced marriage if Philip Arrhidaeus were eliminated; many of the Successors would have liked to have children who carried the blood of Macedonian kings as well as their own.

Some aspects of the crisis that loomed in the fall of 317 resemble previous events in Macedonian history while others had no precedent. Argeads had fought among themselves for the throne time and again, sometimes with armies, sometimes through assassination plots. What was new, of course, was who was in charge of the struggle this time. As Duris (*ap.* Athen. 13.560F) observed, this was the first war between women. Though we do not know why, Adea Eurydice did not wait for Cassander to return to Macedonia with his forces and his greater military experience.[50] She and her husband marched the Macedonian army out to meet the forces with Olympias at the Macedonian–Molossian border. If Duris' testimony is correct, Adea Eurydice dressed as a soldier and may well have commanded the army that accompanied her; certainly her husband could not. Though she had spent much of her life around soldiers and had frequently addressed the troops, unlike her mother she had no practical military experience, and certainly no experience of command.[51]

The nature of Olympias' alliance and her role in the army that accompanied her are no clearer than the position of her rival. As has been said, we know comparatively little about the specifics of Polyperchon's offers and nothing of the terms to which Olympias (presumably) finally agreed. Duris implies that Olympias as well as Adea Eurydice commanded an army, although he attributes a very different, non-military attire to Olympias, but one nonetheless that may have alluded to past Macedonian victories.[52] According to Duris, she went into battle dressed as a Bacchant or worshiper of Dionysus. Diodorus' narrative (19.11.2–4), however, implies that while Adea Eurydice literally exercised command, Olympias did not. He reports that Polyperchon, having made Aeacides (Olympias' nephew) his partner, gathered a force in order to restore Olympias and her grandson to *basileia* (rule or kingdom). Diodorus' subsequent narrative (19.11.4–9), though, indicates that, after the battle, Olympias was in political control. Justin (14.5.1–10) is somewhat less clear: initially he reports that Polyperchon intended to return to Macedonia and had sent for Olympias, thus intimating that Polyperchon was in charge, but in terms of the confrontation itself, he omits any mention of Polyperchon and says that Olympias returned accompanied by Aeacides.[53]

So the aging Olympias, probably following the same mountain passes by which she, as a young bride, had crossed the Pindus Mountains, returned to Macedonia. Despite her years and previous cautious policy, she set off on one last adventure, a final throw of the dynastic dice. It was a glorious moment. When the two armies were arrayed against each other, the Macedonian army caught sight of Olympias. Despite Adea Eurydice's gifts and promises to the most prominent, the army defected to Olympias without a battle. Diodorus (19.11.2) attributes their action to respect for her reputation (*axioma*) and memory of the benefits Alexander had conveyed to them. Justin (14.5.10) is not sure whether to explain this sudden reversal because of the troops' memory of Olympias' husband or the greatness of her son and the consequent shame involved in opposing her.[54] In any event, at this moment Olympias reached the zenith of her power and influence.

However, from this high point, her decline was precipitate. Within a year Cassander had engineered her death and any chance that her grandson might ever rule in any true sense of the word died with her. When one turns to the question of why Olympias so rapidly lost the power and support she enjoyed when she first returned to Macedonia, many historians have answered that she failed because of a series of brutal actions she undertook soon after her return, actions they believe cost her popularity and support. According to this view, her bad actions led to her downfall. I shall argue that events in Macedonia at any point, let alone at this moment, rarely resembled a morality play where the good were rewarded and the unjust punished, that many of the male Successors committed similar or worse atrocities yet suffered no significant consequences (or the condemnation of historians ancient or modern), and that military losses (her own and others') led to her failure, not the brutality of her actions. These actions did cost her some support, but they played no decisive role in her defeat.[55]

Let us begin with exactly what she did. Diodorus says (19.11.4–9) that when she captured the royal pair, she not only imprisoned them but, contrary to law (or custom), walled them up (apparently having them fed through an opening). When the Macedonians expressed pity for the sufferers, she consigned each a gender-appropriate death, ordering that Philip Arrhidaeus be stabbed, in keeping with the expectation that men die by the blade, and giving Adea Eurydice a choice of methods to commit suicide, thus ensuring her the private death suitable for a woman. Adea Eurydice chose hanging, the most appropriate option for her gender, the preferred method of royal women in tragedy. (Diodorus mistakenly sees Adea Eurydice's punishment as the greater.[56]) Diodorus stresses that, in the light of these actions, Olympias deserved the death she would soon get and provides a play-like account of Adea Eurydice's last moments.[57] After Olympias had eliminated the royal pair, Diodorus reports that she killed Cassander's brother Nicanor and overturned the tomb of another brother, Iolaus; all punishment, she said, for Alexander's death. Finally, she selected a hundred of Cassander's friends for slaughter. According to Diodorus, once she had satisfied her rage by these lawless acts, many Macedonians came to hate her savagery and recalled Antipater's supposed deathbed warning against letting a woman be predominant in the kingdom.

Other sources provide fewer details. Justin's (14.5.10–6.1) account of these events is quite brief though similarly hostile. He simply reports that she killed Philip Arrhidaeus and Adea Eurydice and then comments that, acting more like a woman than a king, she transformed support into hatred because she killed the nobility indiscriminately. Plutarch (*Alex.* 77.1) offers a more grisly version of Olympias' treatment of Iolaus: she scattered about his remains. Pausanias (1.11.3–4) remarks mysteriously that Olympias did "unholy" (*anosia*) things to Philip Arrhidaeus (he does not mention Adea

Eurydice) and that she was even more unholy to many others. His diction could signify that he believed she had left Philip Arrhidaeus and others unburied, but more likely refers to the manner of their deaths, or, perhaps, to the sense that she, as a woman, had no right to kill a king. It is unlikely that other authors would have omitted to mention it if Olympias had actually failed to bury the king. If, however, she buried him but did not cremate (the more expensive and prestigious method) him, both Pausanias' choice of words and the omissions of other sources would be explained.[58] Pausanias insists that her actions meant that she deserved what she later got from Cassander.

Were Olympias' actions peculiarly savage, atypical of the time, as both Justin and Diodorus say (and Pausanias perhaps implies)? The winning side in Macedonian succession disputes typically killed the leadership of the losing side. The Argeads had done this for generations and now, in the age of the Successors, each round in their wars tended to precipitate more deaths in similar circumstances. Granted past behavior, Macedonians must surely have expected that Olympias would kill both Philip Arrhidaeus and Adea Eurydice.

If, however, we accept Diodorus' more detailed account, then one aspect of Olympias' treatment of them was unusual. Instead of immediately killing them off—apparently the traditional approach—she walled them up for a while first. A careful reading of Diodorus suggests that this was what made her unpopular, since, when she realized the effect her action was having among the population, she immediately ordered the death of the royal couple. Torture was employed by the Macedonians, as witnessed by the treatment of Philotas. As torture goes, walling someone up seems fairly mild, but if Olympias wanted Philip Arrhidaeus to relinquish the throne, she might have chosen this method to extract an abdication. Compared to some of the Successors, her methods of execution were positively genteel. For instance, Antigonus had Antigenes burned alive (Diod. 19.44.1) and Perdiccas had elephants trample a large group to death (Curt. 10.9.11–18).

Let us consider the other bad deeds of Olympias. Justin, as we have seen, does not mention the murder of Cassander's brother Nicanor or the dishonoring of the tomb of Iolaus. Nonetheless, these actions may well have occurred. A son of Antipater named Nicanor is otherwise unknown.[59] Still, if there were a son of Antipater accessible to Olympias, it seems likely enough that she would have killed him. If so, such an act was fairly typical of the period. Iolaus, the youngest son of Antipater, had been Alexander's cupbearer at the time of his death. Unsurprisingly, those who believed that Antipater had arranged Alexander's death typically believed that Iolaus had administered to the king poison that had been conveyed to Babylon by Cassander at Antipater's behest.[60] Disturbing a grave was serious business, though simply overturning a tomb (Diodorus' version) would have been less upsetting than disturbing the remains of the dead (Plutarch).[61] If, however, Olympias did both, she would not have been the only one. Pausanias (1.9.7–8) cites Hieronymus of Cardia for the information that

Lysimachus, while warring with Pyrrhus, destroyed the graves and scattered the remains of Aeacids. Pausanias, however, probably incorrectly, insists that the story is false.[62] Diodorus (22.12) and Plutarch (*Pyrrh.* 16.6–7) both say that some of Pyrrhus' Gaulic troops plundered the royal graves at Aegae and scattered abroad the bones; though Pyrrhus had no prior knowledge of their action, he failed to punish them and took the matter lightly. Surely these two incidents were parts of a continuing vendetta, applied even to the dead of the two royal houses. Olympias' treatment of Iolaus' grave conforms to the same pattern of blood feud that was common in Macedonia[63] and remains a feature of life in some parts of the Balkans to this day. One could also interpret her actions as a retroactive refusal to bury. In the Hellenic world, refusal to allow burial was often associated with charges of treason (see below), and that could have been the import of her deed.

Were the multiple murders our sources attribute to Olympias unprecedented? The details of this episode are not, of course, clear. Diodorus, Justin, and Plutarch all mention the deaths of a number of unnamed members of the Macedonian elite. Diodorus specifies the round number of a hundred, specifically said to be friends of Cassander. Justin simply asserts that Olympias slaughtered many in the elite (apparently randomly). Plutarch, though similarly vague, connects these multiple deaths to Olympias' charges that Alexander was assassinated. Curtius (6.11.20, 8.6.28) mentions a Macedonian "*lex*" (law) requiring that the kin of those who plotted against the king should be killed as well. In fact, the Macedonians do not seem to have had national written laws at this period, but Curtius could be roughly correct in believing that relatives of assassins were frequently eliminated, along with the assassins themselves. In a world where kin often (though hardly always) functioned as a kind of political party, such a practice would not be surprising.

In any event, it seems likely that Olympias tried to weaken Cassander's faction in his absence, probably claiming that those she executed who were not Cassander's kin had also contributed to the plot against her son. If large-scale purges like this had happened prior to Alexander's death, we have no record of them. After the death of Alexander, however, the murder/execution of groups of people became more common. Soon after Olympias' death, one of Cassander's generals burned five hundred of Polyperchon's followers to death and killed a few more by other means (Diod. 19.63.2). The people Perdiccas eliminated by elephant trampling numbered at least thirty and possibly three hundred (Curt. 10.9.11–18).[64] After the fall of Perdiccas, the assembly condemned to death more than fifty of his followers and they also killed his sister and unspecified numbers of his most trusted friends (Diod. 18.37.2; Arr. *FGrH* 156 F 9.30).[65] Olympias may have been the first to conduct such a purge in Macedonia proper, but otherwise her ferocity mirrored that of her rivals and allies alike.

Should or can we distinguish legalized violent deaths (executions) from those that lack legitimacy (murders)? If such distinctions existed, how should we characterize Olympias' actions? More particularly, even if her authority was legitimate, did she have a right to kill Macedonians without trial, let alone kill a king? Quite apart from the general argument about the nature of the Macedonian "constitution," royal power in the matter of trials is particularly unclear.[66] Alexander tried some but not all of those he had killed. Procedure varied, apparently based on whether or not the ruler would benefit from involving others in responsibility for an execution. The status of the accused mattered. Some tradition involving groups of Macedonians in trials for capital crimes existed, but a king could ignore it. This might cause the ruler political problems but did not precipitate a constitutional crisis. In a proto-legal system like Macedonia's, the purpose of political trials may not have been to discover a legal truth but to settle disputes between powerful figures, and "mustering of support" may have mattered more than establishing the facts of the case.[67] This was even more true after the death of Alexander, when, for practical purposes, there was no king.

As we have seen, categorizing the nature of Olympias' authority is difficult at any time in her life, but particularly so after the death of Antipater. If, as appears likely, she held the *epimeleia* for her grandson, then she probably had the right to hold trials, but chose not to.[68] The legitimacy of virtually all the Successors after Perdiccas seems dubious, as the series of outlawings and rehabilitations should indicate. Olympias had at least as much right as any of the others to eliminate dissidents, but, like the others, she had to cope with the consequences. Killing a king, however nominally he ruled, was unusual; generally they died in battle or were assassinated. Legality was probably not the main issue—it never was in Macedonia—but Olympias' somewhat postponed murder/execution of Philip Arrhidaeus could have seemed different from the usual form of royal violence.

Although Olympias' actions were comparatively typical of those of Alexander's generals, did they, nonetheless, generate more negative reaction simply because a woman had performed them?[69] Despite the fact that Diodorus' narrative indicates that she lost support primarily for military reasons (see below), shock that a woman had done such violent deeds could have contributed to her loss of popularity. This would be particularly likely for southern Greeks who entertained narrower expectations about the role of women than those in the north. Her actions would have fit the paradoxical stereotype of women as both more and less violent than men (see above), and the association of women with acts of vengeance.[70] Granted the importance of women's role in the care of the dead, Olympias' dishonoring of Iolaus' remains and possible dishonoring of Philip Arrhidaeus' corpse might have seemed particularly heinous, but no source claims this. Macedonians, who generally allowed elite women considerably more leeway than did the southern Greeks and who could have seen Olympias' violence as legitimate revenge, may not have been much bothered by any of her actions. Certainly, Antipater's supposed deathbed warning that the Macedonians should never allow a woman to be first in the kingdom (Diod. 19.11.5), in the unlikely event that he actually uttered it,[71] spoke to his personal enmity with Olympias.[72] One can hardly doubt which woman was the subject of his warning. No good information exists to indicate that Olympias' actions, simply because they were the work of a woman, cost her support of Macedonians who were not already partisans of the Antipatrids.

Olympias' post-victory violence did have consequences, but the narrative of Diodorus (see below) demonstrates that the moralizing ancient sources exaggerate their importance. Cassander was already Olympias' enemy, but her actions may have pushed those merely inclined towards Cassander further into his camp and frightened others previously friendly to Antipater, but not necessarily to Cassander, enough to push them into his son's faction. Her attack on Cassander's supporters was necessarily polarizing. While her desecration of Iolaus' remains enraged Cassander,[73] it may not have had wider impact. The manner in which she dealt with Philip Arrhidaeus is the most problematic, as we have seen. Her treatment of him (and his wife) prior to death may have seemed inappropriate for royalty, and certainly, if she did indeed leave royal remains unburied, that would have been upsetting to Macedonians. The loyalty of the mass of Macedonians to the royal family was a powerful force, one that could help or hurt Olympias. While her other actions would, primarily, only have further offended those who were already her enemies, it is possible that her treatment of the king (and possibly his body) alienated some who would not otherwise have disapproved.

One might suppose that Olympias' motivation for this series of brutal acts was obvious: eliminating the opposition before they could eliminate her. More specifically, she almost certainly hoped that her pre-emptive strike against Cassander's faction would ensure a more stable situation for her grandson. Had her brutal acts been followed by military victories, that might well have happened. If Diodorus is correct, Olympias may have made, in relation to these acts, some public announcement about her belief that the Antipatrids had engineered her son's death. In short, she may have proclaimed these acts to be vengeance for Alexander's death. As I have suggested, she may well have believed them guilty. Our evidence about Olympias and many others is simply not good enough to demonstrate whether they acted out of personal thirst for revenge and/or out of pragmatic policy, the need to eliminate the opposition. Those, modern and ancient, who simply assume that Olympias' motivation was only personal and emotional, and further assume that murders committed for policy are somehow more admirable[74] than those committed for personal satisfaction, indulge in sexual stereotyping. In her willingness to employ remorseless political violence, Olympias showed herself to be just like, rather than different from, the male Successors.[75]

Knowing what happened next, let alone understanding it, is not easy. Most historians agree that Olympias' victory and the deaths she inflicted happened in the fall of 317, but there is no consensus on the chronology of subsequent events. Diodorus (19.35.1) reports that Cassander abandoned his campaign in the Peloponnese and marched north as soon as he heard the news of events in Macedonia. While I accept this chronology, many scholars believe that Cassander did not march north until the spring of 316.[76] In terms of the life of Olympias, my chronological view means that she was dead by late spring 316, whereas those who take the other view believe that the campaign that brought about her capture and death developed more slowly.

It is hard to know what Olympias and Polyperchon planned to do next. Even before his invasion of Macedonia, Polyperchon had already lost most of his dominance of the southern Greek peninsula, thanks to Cassander's superior political and military skill.[77] Diodorus' narrative makes it clear that a series of successes of Cassander and failures of Olympias (and her supporters) led to her surrender and death. Olympias had no military experience, in battle or in command, and she had traveled to Macedonia with a group of non-combatants, children and women.[78] It seems unlikely that she and Polyperchon had ever expected her to play a military role. They must surely have anticipated that Cassander would return to Macedonia when he heard what Olympias had accomplished. Indeed, Olympias' actions after her victory seem almost calculated to bring about the return of Cassander. Nonetheless, from this point forward, Polyperchon took only a peripheral role, Olympias appears to have made many command decisions, and both Polyperchon and Olympias acted in ways that indicate they were unprepared for Cassander's rapid advance.[79]

Olympias' position unraveled quickly. Though the Aetolians, allies of Olympias and Polyperchon (Diod. 19.35.2), blocked the famous pass at Thermopylae, Cassander, by means of naval transport, managed to move his forces into Thessaly anyway. Polyperchon waited for Cassander in Perrhaebia, on the Macedonian border, but Cassander sidestepped Polyperchon's army and headed straight for Olympias. Meanwhile, Callas, one of Cassander's generals, besieged Polyperchon and ultimately bribed his troops to desert (Diod. 19.35.3, 36.5–6). Polyperchon was therefore never able to come to Olympias' aid or that of other forces supporting her. (One wonders about the comparative sizes of his forces and those of Cassander.)[80] Olympias herself dispatched troops to prevent the advance of Cassander's army through the passes into Macedonia but they found them already held by Cassander's forces (Diod. 19.35.3).

Realizing that Cassander was near, Olympias ensconced herself in Pydna,[81] accompanied by a large group of non-combatant courtiers but only a small and motley military force.[82] Though she appointed Aristonous, Alexander's former *Somatophulax*, her general and ordered him to fight it out with Cassander, he seems to have done little and ultimately withdrew some distance, to Amphipolis (Diod. 19.36.4–5, 50.3).[83]

Despite the fact that Olympias found herself besieged in a city ill-prepared for such an ordeal, Diodorus observes that she consciously decided to remain. Although she knew the risk, he says she hoped that if she remained, Greeks and Macedonians would provide aid by sea (Diod. 19.35.6). As it turned out, aid did not come from her two closest allies (Eumenes and her nephew

King Aeacides), although Olympias could not have known that this would be the case when she made her decision.[84] Eumenes' brilliant military career in Asia suddenly spiraled downward. He surrendered and was murdered about the same time that Olympias herself died.[85] Faithful Aeacides called up the Molossians to march to Olympias' aid, but once more Cassander's troops had taken early control of critical passes into Macedonia. Diodorus says that most of Aeacides' troops had not wanted this campaign anyway and now revolted where they were camped.[86] While he was still determined to help Olympias, the revolt forced Aeacides to allow most of his force to depart and he was able to do little with his small remaining army. Meanwhile, the dissidents returned to Epirus and inspired a political revolution. They decreed exile for Aeacides and temporarily abandoned Aeacid monarchy for an alliance with Cassander and rule by one of his generals (Diod. 19.36.2–5). According to Pausanias (1.11.4), the Epirotes abandoned Aeacides on account of their hatred of Olympias, but Justin (13.3.16–18) blames it on Aeacides' frequent military opposition to Macedonia and Epirote hatred of him (see further Chapter 6).[87] In any event, Olympias' personal antagonism with Antipater had, certainly by this stage if not years earlier, been transformed into a multi-generational feud between the Aeacids and the Antipatrids.[88]

Diodorus' narrative indicates that the Greek and Macedonian support Olympias had hoped for eroded as the military victories of her enemies increased. Generally, he describes people reluctant to abandon Olympias but fearful of the consequences of supporting the losing side. He says (Diod. 19.36.5) that only after the Epirotes had allied with Cassander did people throughout the country who had favored Olympias despair and turn to Cassander too. As we have noted, Polyperchon's troops had to be bribed to go over to Cassander; they had no inclination in his favor otherwise. When the siege of Pydna proved disastrous and the troops were starving to death, many of the soldiers under Olympias' command begged her to let them go and she did. This presumably means that they did not want simply to desert (Diod. 19.50.1). Cassander treated those who departed well, sending them off to their homes. Diodorus comments that Cassander did this in the hope that when people found out about the weakness (*asthenia*) of Olympias, they would desert her cause. This, he says, happened. Those who had been determined to continue to fight on the side of those besieged now changed sides to Cassander, leaving Aristonous in Amphipolis and Monimus in Pella as the only resistance to Cassander outside Pydna. Monimus, of whom no more is known, surrendered only when he heard that Olympias had yielded to Cassander; Aristonous held out yet longer, surrendering only when commanded to do so by Olympias herself (Diod. 19.50.1–8). Diodorus' account is clear. Though Olympias' earlier brutal acts may have cost her some support, the main reason her cause failed was the military failure of the generals supporting her and the consistently successful performance of the forces of Cassander.[89] The behavior of Macedonians at the time of

Olympias' death (see below) confirms the conclusion that she lost support because of the defeat of her forces, not because people had lost sympathy for her.

Recognizing that her situation was hopeless, after the failure of an escape attempt,[90] Olympias submitted to Cassander on a promise of her personal safety (Diod. 19.50.6; Just. 14.6.5). A similar promise was made to Aristonous, but Cassander later reneged on it and arranged his death (Diod. 19.51.1).[91]

It is hard to believe that Olympias or anyone else doubted that Cassander would bring about her death, despite his guarantee of her safety. The surprise is what a comparatively difficult time he had in accomplishing this task. He arranged a trial or judicial proceeding of some sort in front of what Justin (14.6.6) calls a popular assembly and Diodorus (19.51.1) the assembly of the Macedonians.[92] We do not know where this assembly took place, but quite possibly it was at Pydna; if so, then those in attendance would have been the men who had just fought against Olympias.[93] Both authors report that Cassander urged the relatives of those whom Olympias had murdered to come forward with charges (their nature unspecified) against her (Justin seems to say that he bribed them), and the assembly condemned her to death.

At this point the accounts diverge. They differ about the context of her death, its perpetrators, and its method. Pausanias (9.7.2) simply says that Cassander turned Olympias over to those Macedonians who were irritated with her so that she could be stoned to death.[94] Justin, complaining that the Macedonians had forgotten the wealth, power, and security that her husband and son had brought them, reports that when Olympias saw armed men approaching her, she went out to meet them, dressed in royal attire and supported by two maids. This action surprised her would-be assassins and reminded them of her former majesty and the names of all the kings she called to mind, and they did not kill her. Instead, Cassander had to send other men to stab her. Rather than trying to avoid the sword and its wounds or crying out "like a woman," Justin claims that Olympias faced death in the manner of brave men, in keeping with the glory of her ancient lineage, so that "you could see Alexander even in his dying mother." By going out to meet her killers, Justin's Olympias defined her death and rendered it a kind of forced suicide since she, in effect, chose it and chose to make it a public death. Finally, Justin reports that as she died, she arranged herself to maintain the modesty of her body.[95]

Diodorus proceeds with a more complex and confusing version of events than that of the others, but his is probably closer to what really happened. Even though Olympias had already been condemned through Cassander's contriving, he sent his friends to try to lure her into a second escape attempt, not out of concern for her safety but in order to, in effect, condemn herself to death and so appear to experience a just punishment. Cassander, says Diodorus, was concerned about Olympias' reputation and the changeability of the Macedonians.[96] This time, though, Olympias refused to flee, hoping to defend herself in public.[97] Fearful that the Macedonians might indeed change their minds if they heard Olympias has defended herself and if they recalled what her husband and son had done for them, Cassander dispatched two hundred soldiers with orders to kill her quickly. Although they broke into the royal dwelling, on seeing Olympias the soldiers were overcome by her reputation (*axioma*) and left without killing her. Diodorus says that in the end the relatives of those whom Olympias had slaughtered, hoping to gain favor with Cassander as well as to avenge those who had died, killed her. Diodorus, like Justin, comments that the dying Olympias said nothing unworthy of her birth or "womanish."

The oddities and discrepancies in these accounts of an event that must have been famous in its day are puzzling, but hardly unusual. Diodorus' narrative offers a confused and confusing picture of the political/judicial proceedings. Perhaps he misunderstood his presumed source Hieronymus or so fore-shortened it as to make it unintelligible. Cassander, despite having engineered one guilty verdict, apparently had to face the possibility of another sort of trial, one in which Olympias would be allowed to speak. Rather than risk that, he turned to what appear to be extra-legal means to eliminate Olympias without another public decision. As kings had often done, he tried to involve and thus implicate a larger group in the killing of a famous person, but his attempt failed and he was forced to consign to the relatives of those Olympias had killed the business of her death; and even they required encouragement.

Various solutions to the apparent contradictions of Diodorus' narrative have been proposed. Some have suggested that the first trial was for Olympias' murder of members of the elite (thus the role of the kin of the murdered as accusers and executioners) and the second trial, the one Cassander avoided, would have been for treason, for killing a king.[98] Others have argued that Diodorus should be understood to mean that, at the time Cassander took alternative action, the Macedonians had not yet condemned Olympias, though they intended to, but that Cassander broke off the trial before she could speak in order to prevent a possible favorable verdict if she did so.[99] Still others have concluded that two different deliberative bodies were at work, both of which somehow had a right to participate.[100] Diodorus, however, twice refers to the Macedonians changing their minds (19.51.3, 4), suggesting that the same or some of the same people would have been involved in both the first and second procedures.

Whatever the character, legality, and legitimacy of these proceedings (or lack of same), some conclusions are still possible. Cassander probably wanted a public event in order to involve large numbers of people in the decision to kill Olympias,[101] and he must originally have been confident of her con-viction, but something went wrong with his plan. If I have read Diodorus correctly, minds changed during the trial itself. In any event, both Justin and Diodorus indicate a subsequent reversal of opinion on the part of those delegated to kill her. Apparently, Cassander never tried to involve the whole army (his whole army, after all) in her death, unlike other Macedonian executions.[102] In the end, her death looked more like a vendetta on the part of the kin of Olympias' victims and Cassander himself than a judicial punishment.[103] The similar fate of Olympias' general Aristonous confirms this view. As has been said, like Olympias, Aristonous had surrendered on a promise of physical safety (Diod. 19.50.8); a promise, like that made to Olympias, that was subsequently ignored. Cassander had the kinsmen of Cratevas kill him (19.51.1), a particularly outrageous act of vengeance since, when Aristonous had recently defeated and captured Cratevas, he had allowed him to go free (19.50.7). Cratevas' family members were apparently taking vengeance for Cratevas' defeat, hardly for his mistreatment. The surprising trouble Cassander experienced in the process of eliminating Olympias clearly testifies to the existence of continuing support for her and doubts about Cassander.

I do not mean to suggest that this support was entirely or perhaps even primarily for Olympias personally, though some of it probably was. Olympias, as we have seen, symbolized the royal house and the great deeds of her husband and son.[104] Surely no one, at this stage, could have doubted that the death of Olympias meant the end of the Argeads, and Cassander's actions immediately after her death (Diod. 19.52.1–5; Just. 14.6.13) would certainly have confirmed this view. Cassander imprisoned Roxane and Alexander IV, having deprived the latter of all signs of his royal status and treated him like a private person,[105] and he refused to allow proper burial of Olympias' body (see below). Thus, by his actions, he tried to categorize the "Alexander branch" of the Argeads as illegitimate. At the same time, he attempted to link himself to other branches of the royal house and thus to legitimacy by burying Adea Eurydice and Philip Arrhidaeus with royal splendor[106] and by marrying Thessalonice (a half-sister of Alexander whom he had captured at Pydna, along with the rest of Olympias' entourage). Years would pass before the cautious Cassander (worried about popular reaction to the killing of Olympias and uncertain about the military success of his allies) thought it was safe to murder Alexander IV and his mother,[107] and several more years before he formally took the royal title, but Diodorus is surely right to say he aimed to be king, sooner or later.[108] The Macedonians hesitated to kill Olympias because they hesitated to abolish the royal house.

Justin's account of Olympias' last actions and even Diodorus' more abbreviated and sober version have a literary feel: the notion that a high-born woman died a death worthy of her male kin is a recognizable classical *topos* (theme) and the concern for the propriety of the female body at the time of death is something one finds elsewhere, too.[109] As I have noted, accounts of the death of Adea Eurydice resemble some aspects of those dealing with Olympias' death and have, as well, other literary aspects. The play-like, even epic, feel of the stories about the ends of these two royal women need not, however, render them entirely false. Alexander and many of the Successors acted like Homeric heroes, often in order to gain the support and approval of their troops. In effect, Homer and tragedy gave them a script, one that was genuinely meaningful to them but also something they could manipulate to their own ends.[110] Olympias, her daughter Cleopatra, and Adea Eurydice may have done much the same. Olympias believed herself to be the linear descendant of both Achilles and Priam. The heroic tradition gave her a model for how she ought to die and she may well have followed it. Surely she would have thought that her *axioma* demanded it. The irony is that Olympias did not die the private, appropriately gendered death she had granted her female enemies. Men killed her with swords, perhaps even in public.[111] She died the death of a male hero.[112]

We must conclude with a consideration of the immediate fate of Olympias' corpse. Diodorus (17.118.2)[113] says that Cassander, having murdered her, cast her out unburied, and attributes this treatment to Cassander's bitter opposition to Alexander's policies. In other words, he puts Cassander's refusal of burial in the context of the quarrel between the two families. Surely it must also have been a reaction to Olympias' treatment of Iolaus, a reaction similar to the violation and counter-violation of Molossian and Macedonian royal graves.

While most Greeks had a genuine horror of the idea of treating human remains like domestic refuse, based more on human dignity than concern for the wandering souls of the unburied dead,[114] this is not the only historic Macedonian example of refusal to bury. Several years earlier Antigonus had first maltreated the body of Alcetas, brother of Perdiccas, and then left it unburied (Diod. 18.47.3). Refusal of burial, either historic or mythic, seems to occur when the dead have either been involved in a peculiarly bitter struggle or have acted in a way that the winners consider irreligious or immoral. Moreover, despite generic Greek horror of non-burial, many Greek peoples employed it as a legal punishment, the most extreme one, for sacrilege, treason, or attempted tyranny.[115] Legality, however, particularly since we do not know if the assembly decreed the punishment or whether Cassander simply decided it, is probably not the issue.

Perhaps more compelling, particularly for Macedonian society, are mythic and especially Homeric examples of refusal to bury and bad treatment of corpses. Achilles' maltreatment of the corpse of Hector and refusal to bury it (*Il.* 22.395–404, 23.20–3, 24.14–21) is the most famous instance, but hardly the only one. Patroclus hoped to dishonor the body of Sarpedon (*Il.* 16.559–60), Hector planned to cut off Patroclus' head and give it to the dogs (*Il.* 17.125–7), and, once Achilles had killed Hector, the other Greek heroes gathered round the corpse and stabbed it (*Il.* 22.371–4). While it is true that in the *Iliad*, heroes imagined or threatened non-burial but did not generally follow up on the threat (after all, even Achilles allows the burial of Hector in the end),[116] the idea of it is an important aspect of Homeric battle, not an extreme notion limited to Achilles in his "feral" period following the death of Patroclus. Nor is maltreatment of a corpse.[117] Homeric heroes hoped to deprive their enemies of graves for a variety of compelling reasons: revenge, symbolization of victory, but perhaps most importantly, denial of the memory and fame of the dead.[118]

Legalities, particularly questions of treason, are dubious in any civil war period, especially in Macedonia, where treason and legitimacy were in this period determined by military success alone. Olympias' treatment of Iolaus' grave (particularly if she, in effect, "unburied" him) and Cassander's refusal to allow her burial, as well as the denial of burial to Alcetas, could all be understood as judicially inspired, but these acts really have much more to do with the world of Homer and a society in which clan and family (the living and the dead) mattered a great deal and vengeance went on past death itself. I have argued that legality was never a major issue in Macedonian society generally. After the death of Alexander and certainly after that of Perdiccas, legitimacy is simply not a useful or viable concept for historians to apply. Arguably, none of the Successors had any genuine legitimacy, but one can certainly imagine a legal basis for all three actions. Olympias probably believed that Iolaus had committed treason since she believed that he had killed her son. Cassander doubtless thought that Olympias had committed treason by killing Philip Arrhidaeus and sacrilege by dishonoring Iolaus. For example, after the murder of Perdiccas, the Macedonian army condemned Eumenes, Alcetas, and other Perdiccas supporters to death (presumably their support for Perdiccas was now seen as treason; Diod. 18.37.2), though Perdiccas had been Alexander's chosen representative.

The world of Homer, and more particularly the figure of Achilles, is the more meaningful context. Macedonians might treat the remains of a dead enemy, particularly a former *philos*, honorably, as Eumenes did the body of Craterus (Nep. *Eum.* 4.4) and Antigonus that of Eumenes (Diod. 19.44.2; Plut. *Eum.* 19.1). These were not personal enemies but political ones. It was different when the conflict was personal and bitter. Diodorus (18.47.3) reports that once Antigonus was given Alcetas' body, he maltreated the body for three days and then threw it out unburied. Curtius (4.6.25–9)[119] claimed that Alexander dragged Batis, the commandant of Gaza, around the city by his heels, going one better than Achilles since Batis was alive at the beginning of this process. This story is more likely to be true than not,[120] irrespective of whether, as Curtius claims, Alexander actually announced that he did this in imitation of his ancestor Achilles. Olympias believed herself to be the linear descendant of Achilles, too; Cassander, like Alexander, had much of Homeric epic by heart (Athen. 14.620b); and the Macedonian elite generally "chose to present themselves in Homeric behavioral patterns."[121]

The point of a refusal to permit burial was not simply to dishonor one individual and that individual's memory, but to do harm to an entire family, to the *philoi* of the dead, to the *kleos* (fame) of the family. The dead were still members of the *oikos* and their remains could be exiled or allowed to return along with living members of the clan.[122] Burial of the dead was the peculiar responsibility of the family and refusal to allow them to perform their duty (or exhumation) dishonored them, too.[123] In their treatment of the dead, Olympias acted against the clan of Antipater, not simply his sons, and Cassander against not only Olympias, but the Aeacids and, to some degree, one branch of the Argeads.[124] Because of the powerful nature of familial obligation for burial, one suspects that the family (or sympathizers) buried most people who were supposedly left unburied. Certainly Diodorus (18.47.3) reports that Alcetas did ultimately receive honorable burial by supporters (his family having all been murdered). And, despite Cassander's decision, Aeacids did manage to bury Olympias and raise a tomb over her remains (see Chapter 6). In the Hellenic world, even those on losing sides tended to have kin or friends willing to play less heroic versions of Antigone's role. By his action, Cassander tried to destroy the *kleos* of Olympias and her line. His success in that regard, as we shall see, proved ephemeral at best.

Olympias died, as she had mostly lived, trying to acquire as much power for herself as she could while attempting to safeguard the continued rule of her descendants. She pursued these goals with ruthlessness and violence, as did her friends and enemies. These qualities did not, however, precipitate her murder and the final collapse of the Argead house. Olympias certainly miscalculated on several occasions in her life, most notably when she supported Alexander's intervention in Pixodarus' marriage alliance, something that could easily have cost her son and herself even more than it did. One could argue that putting her trust in Polyperchon was a fatal miscalculation, but such an assessment assumes that better alternatives were available to her and I doubt that they were. Had Olympias spurned involvement with Polyperchon, she might well have died in bed of old age in Molossia, but Cassander would surely have eliminated her grandson, most likely more rapidly than he actually did. Whether or not Olympias initially grasped how poor an ally Polyperchon would be, she had no other available supporters with an army. If she had eliminated Philip Arrhidaeus and Adea Eurydice in a more discreet and/or conventional way, had resisted the temptation to dishonor the grave of Iolaus, and had quelled her impulse to eradicate the most important supporters of Cassander, she might have retained the support of some Macedonians for longer, but her failure and that of the dynasty were ultimately military. Untrained in military matters herself and lacking the support of a male relative who was not only loyal but an able commander of a large, experienced, and effective army, Olympias lost. One doubts that any royal woman in such parlous times could have done better. Her career demonstrates how much a royal woman of ability, nerve, ruthlessness, and ambition could accomplish; and, at the same time, how little any royal woman could do in the face of male monopoly of military power.

5   Olympias and religion

Many aspects of Olympias' life relate to religious experience and ritual. In this, she was typical of Hellenic women. Indeed, religion may have played a central role in Olympias' identity. The impersonal nature of our sources cannot prove that it did, but one must recognize the possibility. Although Greeks, particularly southern Greeks in the classical period, curtailed female public action in virtually every other aspect of life, women, especially elite women, continued to play a prominent role in the public religious life of the community, as well as in the private cult of the family.[1] Macedonian monarchy, still primarily a household monarchy in the Argead period, tended to give royal women an even more prominent role in religious matters because the line between public and private was not as clear as the line between *oikos* and *polis* in the south. As a consequence, religious activity of royal women could have an internal political dynamic. All over the Greek world, religion often furnished the basis for the creation, perpetuation, and interpretation of international relationships.[2] This meant that women like Olympias could be involved, through religious matters (as well as *philia*; see Chapter 3), in diplomacy. In order to put the function of religion and religious issues in the life of Olympias in proper perspective, we must first address the general role of Greek women in religion and the more particular topic of female cult activity in Macedonia.

Within the *oikos* (household), women performed ritual alone and with other family members. The care of the dead (preparation for burial and the rites at the tomb) was a peculiarly female task. Outside the household, women made dedications to deities, alone, with other women, with family members, or with fellow workers. Women of means traveled considerable distances to make such offerings.[3] Female dedications ran the gamut from simple spindle whorls to entire buildings. Women served as priests, in some cases for the most prominent cults in the cities. Typically female deities had female attendants. Some communal festivals involved men, women, and children while others, though public, included only women as direct participants. In addition, women or men might make the personal choice to be initiated into one of the so-called mystery religions. Women's religious experience centered on female deities, on cults and rituals that promised healing or fertility, offered protection in childbirth and for children, and that enabled them to cope with the stressful transitions of their lives.[4]

Greek culture offered strong approval and praise for women's religious actions. Fathers and husbands, for instance, might be compelled by law to pay women's expenses for participation in festivals and for dedications.[5] Proud parents erected statues of their daughters on sacred ground when the young girls had been chosen to perform important roles in annual rituals.[6] Female religiosity, particularly as experienced in the more emotional cults, provided a way for women to express the frustrations of lives otherwise so closely controlled and to feel free, if only momentarily. This freedom, of course, was largely illusory, a temporary reversal of their ordinary powerlessness that, by permitting a brief release, actually reinforced the existing cultural power structure.[7] Nonetheless, women's religious role in the life of the *oikos* and the *polis* bound the two parts of the community together.[8]

We need to know how much Macedonian religious practice in general, let alone in terms of the specific issue of the role of women, differed from that of other Greek communities. Cult practice varied widely at the individual, family, and communal levels across the Hellenic world. Archaeology and inscriptions are only gradually illuminating the nature of Macedonian religious practice. Any conclusions on this subject must be tentative, particularly as they apply to the Argead period, but currently many differences between Macedonian religion and the Hellenic world look like differences in degree, not kind.[9] However, influence from non-Hellenic Balkan cultures, particularly the Thracian, was vital. Archaeology has discovered traces of the cults of the familiar Olympian deities and other deities worshiped in the wider Hellenic world. Macedonians had their own cult to Olympian Zeus based at Dion, on the slopes of Mount Olympus. The cult of the god worshiped there resembled that of many southern cities.[10] What little we know about the role of ordinary Macedonian women (and royal women as well) indicates that they participated in activities similar to those of women in the south.

Nonetheless, Macedonian evidence does suggest particular areas of religious interest. In Macedonia, the various cults of Dionysus were unusually popular, as were the cults of Zeus, the Mother of the gods, the Muses, the Great Gods of nearby Samothrace, and Heracles, the supposed ancestor of the royal family. As we shall see, the royal family, particularly the king, played a role in religious cult, though its extent and importance are difficult to determine. Judging by the large and elaborately outfitted tombs of the elite, Macedonians took the possibility of the afterlife more seriously and perhaps more literally than did some other Greeks. At least one Macedonian burial has preserved parts of an Orphic papyrus meant, among other things, to enable the dead to reach a blessed afterlife.[11] Two tombs from Vergina, both likely to be royal burials and possibly burials of royal women, contain objects or decorations with themes taken from the myth of Persephone, again confirming a hope for rebirth.[12]

Evidence indicates that earlier Argead women had played prominent roles in cult in Macedonia. The contents of burials at Vergina (ancient Aegae), which some archaeologists believe to be those of royal women, may indicate that Argead women of the Archaic period were priestesses.[13] We know some specifics of the religious activities of Olympias' most important predecessor, her mother-in-law Eurydice, mother of Philip II and two other Macedonian kings. Eurydice, like Olympias, was a controversial figure. As has been said, her ethnicity is uncertain, but she was probably partly of Illyrian descent.[14] Although Justin (7.4.7, 5.4–8) paints her as a nearly demonic villainess out to murder her own sons and commit adultery with her daughter's husband, more plausible contemporary evidence depicts her as a loyal royal mother devoted to securing the throne for her sons. Current common opinion now prefers the latter version.[15] Evidence survives about dedications Eurydice made to two different cults.

A passage preserved in Plutarch's essays (*Mor.* 14c) is our source for one of these dedications. This passage praises Eurydice for becoming educated, past the usual age, for the sake of her children's education, comments that an inscription she dedicated in association with the Muses demonstrates her love for those children, and then includes the text of the inscription, which has now been considerably emended. In the emended text, Eurydice says that she makes the dedication[16] to or for the sake of women citizens in association with the Muses.[17] The tone of the inscription is personal and there is no reference to a husband. (It may have been made after her husband's death.) This dedication presents a picture of Eurydice that is a far cry from the villainous murderess of the same children referred to in this dedication as the objects of her devotion.[18] The cult of the Muses was associated with women's concerns in Greece and Macedonia. In sum, the inscription suggests that Eurydice took some leadership role in association with the Muses—why else would the dedication be made to or for the sake of female citizens?—and that she did so on her own, possibly as a counter to the hostile stories her political enemies generated, commemorating herself as a loving rather than a loathsome mother.

Excavations at Vergina have revealed the foundations of an extensive temple complex in the agora, and within the complex the remains of two statue bases with the identical inscription, "*Eurydika Sirra Eukleiai*" (Eurydice, daughter of Sirras, to Eucleia).[19] One surviving statue[20] has been found.[21] Thus, it appears that the statues and probably the temple complex itself were dedications made by Eurydice,[22] probably during the reign of one of her sons, most likely either Perdiccas III or early in the reign of Philip II.[23] Eurydice may well have been a priestess of the cult.[24] "Eucleia" means "good repute" and the Vergina cult apparently involved a personification of that concept. Scholars have disputed the nature of the cult and the context for Eurydice's dedication. The current excavator has associated it with one of Philip's military victories or, more plausibly (and more recently), a political/dynastic victory of Eurydice.[25] Another scholar has argued that the

Macedonian cult was similar to Artemis Eucleia cults elsewhere in Greece: girls made offerings before marriage at temples often found in market places like the one at Vergina.[26] Granted that Eurydice had, as I have explained, troubles with her *kleos* (reputation), I wonder if she intended the shrine to reestablish and celebrate her reputation, particularly since she probably made her foundation in the period of her widowhood, in the course of which all three of her sons became kings.[27] Both dedications appear to date from the years of Eurydice's widowhood, when she acted as a succession advocate for her three sons. Both look like attempts to shape public opinion and respect through piety in order to make herself, her family, and her sons look more attractive and legitimate and to counter rumors suggesting anything sinister.

Before we turn to Olympias' religious experience and actions in Macedonia, it is important to consider her Epirote religious background. While many cults found a home in the region, we know that Olympias had ties to the best known of Epirote sanctuaries, the oracle of Zeus at Dodona. Tradition made it the oldest of the Greek oracles; Achilles made a libation to Dodonian Zeus (*Il.* 16.233). The original cult at Dodona may have honored a goddess, but by the Historic period, Zeus Naos dominated the site, although a female deity, now called "Dione," shared worship with him.[28] Accounts differ as to the mechanics of the oracle,[29] but the sacred oak was always central to the cult, and three priestesses, the Peleiades (Doves), served the oracle. Despite its remote location, the oracle attracted international patrons, though the majority of its clients seem to have been individuals looking for solutions to personal problems rather than Greek states.[30] Nonetheless, the Athenians sometimes patronized the shrine. The first permanent structure appeared in the first half of the fourth century BCE, about the time that Molossians came to control the site. Most likely, therefore, the Hellenizing Aeacid house had become the patrons of Dodona.[31] The association with Achilles would have made its patronage especially attractive to them. In the third quarter of the fourth century, a separate temple to Dione appeared.[32] Olympias' connection to Dodona relates to the cult statue of Dione.

According to Hyperides (*Eux.* 24–6), the Athenians had consulted the Dodona oracle for reasons unknown and the oracle had instructed them to honor or decorate the image of Dione. The Athenians accordingly had an especially beautiful face constructed for the goddess (as well as some other expensive accouterments) and dispatched these with sacred envoys and a sacrifice, all in a manner worthy of the goddess and the Athenians. Olympias then sent off complaining letters to the Athenians, stating that the land of Molossia, in which the temple was located, belonged to her and so it was not proper for them to meddle there. Hyperides argues that, if they objected to Olympias' gift to an Athenian shrine (see below), they would be justifying her accusations and exaggerations, but if they accepted her dedication to their temple, then she could not object to theirs, particularly since they acted at the behest of the oracle. Clearly this incident has a political context. The time-frame seems to be *c.* 330, around the time of the death of Alexander of Molossia and Olympias' return to Molossia,[33] about the time the Dione temple was built (or soon after), and perhaps about the time that the Epirote Alliance was created (see Chapter 4).

Olympias clearly is using patronage and the denial of patronage at a major sanctuary to assert her own power and prestige, but the specifics of the situation are unclear. The timing suggests a connection to regime change, apparently one that affected the oracle: clearly Olympias' policy and that of the original oracle were at odds, quite possibly because the oracle had been promulgated before she dominated Molossia. Perhaps her view differed from that of her daughter or brother (the previous rulers of Molossia), or perhaps the episode offers an early indication of friction between the Aeacids and the new alliance. One wonders if Olympias herself, perhaps in concert with her daughter, had dedicated the new structure.[34] Political interest as well as religious concern probably motivated both sides in this dispute. The Athenians had reasons of their own for cultivating the oracle.[35] Olympias employed her control of the famous shrine to advance her power and prestige (and that of her family[36]) in central Greece.

Passages from Plutarch imply that Olympias brought with her to Macedonia other quasi-religious experiences, magic,[37] and the use of snakes in ritual and perhaps domestically. His testimony should be treated with caution since it derives from his general hostility to Olympias and his more specific objections to some forms of religiosity,[38] but it cannot be ignored, if only because it provides an important part of the basis for much of his sexual stereotyping of Olympias. He (*Alex.* 2.4) reports the story that Philip lost most of his erotic interest in Olympias because he saw a snake sleeping by her side, whether from fear of her magic and *pharmaka* (drugs or spells[39]) or from his conviction that her sleeping partner was really divine. He then proceeds to discuss Olympias' Orphic and Dionysian experience (see below), but his diction (*Alex.* 2.5) reveals that he considers this experience related to her magical ones. Much later in his life of Alexander, Plutarch includes the claim (77.5) that Olympias used *pharmaka* to destroy Philip Arrhidaeus' mental capacity.[40] The first Plutarch passage implies that Olympias arrived in Macedonia with habits exotic to Macedonians related to snakes and knowledge of spells. Aelian (*N.A.* 15.11) reports that Epirotes had a bad reputation as poisoners and casters of spells.[41]

Sorting the historical from that which is not and distinguishing contemporary propaganda from later accretions in these passages are not easy. Plutarch includes these stories about Olympias and magic but does not say that he believes them.[42] Clearly Philip's alleged suspicion that Olympias was having sexual relations with a god in the form of a snake is a product of Alexander's reign since it relates to Alexander's claims of divine sonship (see below).[43] While real Macedonians and Molossians practiced magic, the reference to Olympias' use of magic or spells, particularly in connection to Philip Arrhidaeus' mental problems, likely derives from the succession rivalry between the mothers of Philip II's two sons, Olympias and Philinna, Philip

Arrhidaeus' mother.[44] Accusations of witchcraft are common, cross-culturally, in polygamous situations, and the northern Greek origin of both women probably facilitated such charges and counter-charges.[45]

While one must regard Plutarch's references to Olympias' practice of magic as dubious at best, her fondness for snakes, whether kept in her living space or used in ritual, deserves more belief.[46] Snakes played a prominent role in many cults, often with phallic significance.[47] As we have seen, Plutarch specifically associates Olympias' use of snakes with Orphic and Bacchic rites. The phallic connotation of the snake in Plutarch's tale could fit a Dionysiac context, too.[48] Moreover, Plutarch describes her provision of snakes for baskets and wands used in Macedonian women's Bacchic activity in terms that suggest that the use of snakes in this context was an innovation of Olympias.[49] The popularity of snake imagery on Dodona votives and the use of living snakes in Epirus in a prophetic cult of Apollo (Ael. *N.A.* 11.2) may mean that Molossians used them in Dionysiac worship and that Olympias imported the practice to Macedonia.[50] Olympias could have kept snakes for personal as well as ritual purposes.[51]

Before we turn to Olympias' religiosity after her marriage, two issues already alluded to in a more political context (see Chapter 1), her name change and the significance of her initiation at Samothrace, need to be addressed more specifically in terms of religion. As we have seen (Plut. *Mor.* 401a–b), Olympias probably changed her name from Polyxena to Myrtale prior to her marriage to Philip, at which point it may well have changed again, to the name by which she is generally known, Olympias.[52] Name changes typically relate to changes in identity. A bewildering variety of cults and cult-related experience employed the myrtle plant,[53] the apparent source for Olympias' new name.

It seems reasonable to connect her name-change to a religious ritual somehow connected to an alteration in status or identity prior to her marriage. However, neither of the solutions so far proposed is persuasive. One suggestion links "Myrtale" to Olympias' betrothal and the mysteries at Samothrace. Aphrodite may have had a role in the cult at Samothrace, at least by a later period, but it is not certain.[54] According to this view, Olympias' new name was linked to her Samothracian initiation (see below) and/or her betrothal.[55] But nothing links myrtle with the Great Gods of Samothrace,[56] and myrtle's association with marriage or betrothal is not common.[57] Evidence does exist that associates the Samothrace cult at a later period with the marriage of Cadmus and Harmonia, and thus, perhaps, with marriage in general.[58] Philip and Arybbas, by opting to stage the betrothal at Samothrace, certainly chose to associate the cult and the betrothal, but their reasons may well have been practical and political, not religious.

The alternative hypothesis[59] suggests that Olympias took the name Myrtale as part of a coming-of-age ceremony (common enough elsewhere in Greece), in this case dedicated to Aphrodite. Since myrtle was sacred to Aphrodite and strongly associated with sexuality,[60] and, by the third century, a temple to Aphrodite had been established at Dodona, this suggestion is more convincing than the first. However, no evidence of such a rite in Molossia, connected to Aphrodite, exists. Granted the growing association between myrtle and mystery cults and beliefs about rebirth, Olympias' new name may suggest initiation into an as yet unidentified mystery cult, perhaps in association with her coming of age.[61] In any event, Olympias' name-change implies the acquisition of a new, additional identity, connected to Dodona, Samothrace, or some other cult.[62]

Although one should regard the romantic details about the betrothal of Philip II and Olympias (Plut. *Alex*. 2.1) with great skepticism (see Chapter 1), Plutarch's account of their initiation into the mysteries of the Great Gods of Samothrace and the location of her betrothal deserve greater acceptance.[63] Initiate lists indicate that group initiations—of family members, citizens of the same *polis*, passengers on the same boat—were common,[64] and Plutarch's account indicates that Arybbas, Olympias' uncle and guardian, had accompanied her to Samothrace. Elite women, probably including members of Olympias' own family (see Chapter 1), traveled considerable distances to major shrines. On the other hand, as we have seen, the choice of this particular sanctuary implies that Philip II chose the location since he was its main developer, likely responsible for the first stone building at the site,[65] and it continued to be patronized by the Argead and later dynasties. It is possible that the betrothal occurred in the very public context of an annual festival held at Samothrace in mid-June.[66] The cult permitted initiation at times other than the festival, but a connection between the betrothal and the festival is particularly appealing because, at least in Hellenistic times and quite possibly earlier, the festival included a re-enactment of the wedding of Cadmus and Harmonia.[67] Much later in his life, Philip combined his daughter Cleopatra's marriage with a religious festival (Diod. 16.92.1). As we shall see, he may have associated his wedding to Olympias with another festival, so it is tempting to think he might have chosen to connect this betrothal to a religious festival.

Nothing tells us what young Olympias' feelings were about initiation into what would have been an unfamiliar cult for a Molossian. Apart from the difficulty for Molossians to reach the island sanctuary,[68] one must also note that it focused on providing safety for those who traveled by sea (not much of a Molossian problem[69]), though protection from other sorts of danger, perhaps even after death, was also offered.[70] Unfortunately, initiates of the Great Gods of Samothrace so thoroughly kept the secrets of the rites that discussion of the nature of the cult is highly speculative at best, particularly what, if any, relationship it had to the Cabiri.[71] Though the names of more male initiates survive, women, even by themselves, did join the cult, and two women, one of them a royal Macedonian woman of a later generation, paid for two large structures at the site.[72] Olympias' known interest in Dionysiac experiences might suggest that cults with similar qualities would appeal to her in a personal way, if, indeed the cult at Samothrace had such qualities.

Curtius (8.1.26) actually has Alexander condemn his father for his focus on the cult, on grounds that it delayed his plan to invade Asia. Nonetheless, a building program did continue at Samothrace during Alexander's reign. Nothing indicates who managed or paid for this work, though it may well have been funded by wealth from the Asian conquests. It could have been Olympias, though Philip Arrhidaeus is also a possibility.[73] Certainly an inscription demonstrates that, after the death of Alexander, both Philip Arrhidaeus and Alexander IV, Olympias' grandson, dedicated a building there.[74]

The third of the additional names Plutarch (*Mor.* 401b) says were employed about Alexander's mother was, of course, Olympias. This name, rather than commemorating the victory of her husband's chariot team at Olympia,[75] more likely relates to a Macedonian festival in honor of Olympian Zeus at which Olympias' marriage to Philip was celebrated.[76] Like Myrtale, this name correlated to an important change in Olympias' life and status and to a cult, one much patronized by the Macedonian royal family.[77]

If Olympias' new name implies that she played a conventional female role in terms of her marriage and religious issues, then evidence from the reign of her son would appear to confirm this view. Olympias so frequently did things unprecedented for women that it is easy to miss the fact that she did a number of quite conventional things as well; although, being Olympias, they were done on a grand scale and attracted attention. Olympias may have made an inquiry at an oracle of Apollo in Asia Minor about the success of her son's Asian campaign that received a positive response.[78] A letter from Olympias sent to Alexander urged him to buy from her a cook who was experienced in sacrifice, specifically Alexander's ancestral rites, both Argead and Bacchic, and those that Olympias rendered (Athen. 559f–660a). Since the specialist chef belonged to Olympias, one must conclude that she made certain sacrifices herself and that (at a minimum) she had some supervisory role in dynastic as well as Dionysiac ritual.[79] Like many ordinary Greek women, Olympias played her part in family cult but also in ritual associated with more public cults. (See below on her fondness for Dionysus.)

Her two known dedications resemble those of other women (if on a grand scale) but probably also relate to Olympias' political aims. As we have already noted, she made a dedication of a *phiale* (a shallow libation cup or bowl, most often made of terracotta but sometimes of precious metal) to the cult statue of Hygieia in Athens (Hyp. *Eux.* 19). Hygieia, the daughter of Aesclepius and often associated with him in cult, personified health.[80] Almost certainly Olympias' offering was made on behalf of her much wounded and sometimes unhealthy son.[81] Women frequently patronized the healing deities,[82] looking for protection of their children's health.[83] The *phiale* was a typical female dedication,[84] primarily because women usually held the *phiale* before a man took it, then a woman poured liquid into it before the man poured the libation on the ground.[85] The dedication of a *phiale* seems to stress the submissive, secondary role of women in this form of worship.

Nonetheless, Euxenippus was held accountable in an Athenian court for allowing Olympias to make this dedication. Even if, as Hyperides implies (*Eux.* 19, 27), the charge was specious, primarily intended to do harm to Euxenippus by manipulating current Athenian hostility to Alexander and Olympias, that it could be made at all indicates the political aspect of religious pilgrimage and dedication, as did Olympias' complaints to the Athenians about Dodona. It is also likely that Olympias arranged for a dedication at the great pan-Hellenic shrine at Delphi of golden crowns (*SIG* 252 N, 5–8, with n.3). Since she gave the sanctuary 190 darics (Persian gold coins), she quite possibly paid for this gift from the plunder Alexander had dispatched to her after the siege of Gaza (Plut. *Alex.* 25.4).[86] Hyperides' language implies that Olympias may have traveled to Athens to make her dedication in person,[87] but Olympias' indirect method of arranging for Apollo's crowns could suggest that she did not do so. On the other hand, it could signify simply that she was rushed.[88] While one cannot establish an exact chronology for either these dedications or her arrival in Molossia, all three events must have happened within a comparatively short time period.[89] Apparently, whether in person or indirectly, Olympias moved to establish her presence and prestige in central Greece about the time she removed herself to Molossia. Her dedications appear to have a political connection.

Olympias' employment of religious ritual and belief to shape her own public image (something her husband, son, and many male political figures also did) does not necessarily mean that she (or they) lacked genuine piety: self-interest and sincere belief are hardly incompatible. As we have seen, Olympias' religious activities generally resembled those of other Hellenic women, albeit on a grander scale. Female members of the royal *oikos* were both more and less free than ordinary women. Their involvement in ritual offered the same chance to express, in comparatively unrestrained ways, their feelings and yet exercise a leadership role, as elite women did throughout the Greek world. On the other hand, as we have already observed, political concerns could complicate their religious activities. As we turn to consideration of Olympias' Dionysiac religiosity, perhaps the most individualized of her cult activities, we should expect to find, once more, both sincerity and the pursuit of self- (and family) interest.

Comparatively little evidence, all of it from literary sources, supports the general belief that Dionysus (and associated cults) played a central role in Olympias' religious experience and activity. One we have already mentioned (Athen. 559f–660a): the letter to her son in which Olympias tries to sell a cook experienced in Alexander's ancestral rites, both Argead and Bacchic. This letter does not even connect Olympias directly or personally to these rites, though the fact that she owns a slave with such skills implies an indirect connection.[90]

Another passage in Athenaeus (13.560f) offers more intriguing evidence. The author cites Duris of Samos for the statement that the first war between women was that between Olympias and Adea Eurydice. Duris claimed that

Adea Eurydice went forth to battle dressed as a Macedonian soldier, having been trained in matters of war by her mother Cynnane, and Olympias marched out like a Bacchant, to the beat of a tympanum (a drum used in Dionysiac rites). As our earlier discussion indicated (see Chapter 4), Duris' picture of Adea Eurydice, even if she had never previously participated in combat, fits the public image she and her mother had constructed. The woman buried in the antechamber of tomb II at Vergina had a warrior's burial;[91] that woman, as is increasingly obvious, was probably Adea Eurydice.[92] We cannot know in any absolute way that she went into battle dressed as a soldier (though I think she did) but, minimally, Duris' story conforms to the persona she had created. Indeed, it sums it up.

Much the same can be said about his description of Olympias: she may actually have appeared in front of the army dressed as a Bacchant (since, as I have argued, she certainly did not plan to fight, such garb would not have been inconvenient), but even if she did not literally dress as Duris insists, his description sums up the persona she had created as a Dionysiac worshiper, by implication a leader in such worship. The army, of course, went over to Olympias for a number of reasons, but her Dionysiac image, irrespective of whether Duris was right to have her acting it out on the scene of the battle, probably helped to sway them because of the popularity of the cult, as we shall see.

Plutarch (*Alex.* 2.5) provides the most extensive description of Olympias' Dionysiac activities. The description appears in the midst of the passage already discussed in terms of Olympias' alleged fondness for snakes, and in the context of Alexander's claim to be the son of a god. Let us begin with a purposefully literal translation of the section about Olympias and Dionysus:

> Concerning these matters there is another tale that goes like this. All of the women in this region, since ancient times, were inclined to Orphic rites and to the secret rites[93] of Dionysus and have the name Klodones and Mimallones[94] and performed many rites similar to the Edonian women and the Thracian women around [Mount] Haemus, from whom, it seems, the word *threskeuin* came to be used for intense [or immoderate] and superstitious [or odd in an excessive way] religious services [or sacrifices]. Now Olympias who, more than the other women, strove after[95] these inspirations and carried out these frenzies more barbarically, introduced to the celebrating groups great tame serpents who, often raising their heads from the ivy wreaths and sacred baskets or twining around the wands and garlands of the women, astonished [or terrified] the men.

Despite Plutarch's obvious hostility to Olympias in particular, northern Greeks, and women in general, and his need to emphasize Olympias' non-Hellenic qualities in order to highlight Alexander's Hellenic ones (a need pursued, as we shall see, at the expense of literal truth; see Appendix), the passage provides specific information about Olympias and Dionysiac worship in Macedonia (and elsewhere). Dionysiac and Orphic rites (see below on their association) were particularly popular among women in northern Greece. Olympias acted as participant, patron, and probably organizer (she provides the snakes and seems to introduce them into the ceremony as an innovation, possibly of Molossian origin) of a public Dionysiac festival; only women participated but men were present as observers.[96] Granted that the entire passage implies that Olympias played a leadership role in these activities, she may well have been a priest of Dionysus,[97] but, if so, Plutarch does not state it. Evidence from other sources, however, indicates that female Dionysiac participation more heavily involved women in the elite, especially in leadership roles.[98]

Nonetheless, while Plutarch may have been right to say that such rites were particularly popular with women in northern regions, it is important to understand that they were very popular with men of this region as well[99] and that, elsewhere in Greece, both men and women participated in Dionysiac cults,[100] although they were particularly associated with women.[101] Objects with Dionysiac significance appear in Macedonian elite houses and tombs, and several temples to Dionysus are known.[102] The royal tombs, in particular, contain many items associated with Dionysus.[103] Euripides spent time at the court of the Macedonian king Archelaus and there is a good likelihood that, possibly influenced by practices he saw while there, he wrote the *Bacchae* in Macedonia.[104] As we have seen, Olympias' letter indicates that ancestral Dionysiac rites were celebrated by the royal family. Certainly Philip and Alexander both paid considerable attention to this cult.[105]

Greek ambivalence about Dionysus, as well as the variety and complexity of the worship of this god of transcendence (through wine, theater, ecstatic religion), complicates any attempt to understand what Olympias' Dionysiac connections might have meant to herself or to her contemporaries. Despite the antiquity of Dionysus worship in the Greek peninsula, many Greek sources insist on the exotic, Oriental nature of the deity and cult, in effect transmuting the "otherness" of transcendence into an understanding of the god and cult as Other,[106] even though most Greeks would have participated in some form of Dionysiac experience. This was a god of many aspects, one whose worship encompassed many forms.

Some aspects of Dionysus appealed primarily (but not exclusively) to women or to men, whereas others attracted significant numbers of both sexes. In Macedonia and elsewhere, Dionysus' patronage of wine primarily attracted men, partly because many Greeks considered female wine-drinking as, at best, problematic, and partly because wine-drinking was embedded in social activities that excluded women: *symposia* and some public festivals.[107] Many cities, however, had Dionysiac festivals celebrating wine or including dramatic performances and processions that may well have involved all citizens, not just men.[108] There must have been much regional variation.[109] Greeks considered women more vulnerable to emotion and ecstatic possession, and many sources associate ecstatic Dionysiac experience with women. Female Dionysiac worship, though it inspired masculine distrust and temporarily gave greater freedom to those women who participated, thereby reinforced the existing order and, to some degree, validated male stereotypes about female nature.[110] Some Dionysiac bands were all female and departed from the city to the mountains;[111] participants (maenads) in these seemed and looked wild,[112] if not as wild as male imagination has made them.[113] Evidence, however, suggests that the wildness of maenads was emotional and involved neither sexual activity nor wine.[114] Whatever their ecstatic experience, such bands also organized conventional festivals held at regular intervals.[115] By the late fifth century, some men belonged to such groups, and later this was more common.[116] City cults of Dionysus, sometimes with female priests, also existed.[117] Both men and women could choose to become initiates in Dionysiac cults, often associated with Orphism,[118] ones that focused on Dionysus as not just a god of life but a god of rebirth. Initiation guaranteed a blessed afterlife.[119] Such beliefs, judging by Macedonian burials, were popular in Macedonia.[120] Evidence is a problem for all of these Dionysiac cults: myth, literature, and art provide abundant Dionysiac material, but distinguishing reality from myth or male fantasy can be difficult.[121]

We can describe the varying aspects of the cults of the god, but it's not clear how differently they were seen by participants. Some individuals participated in several different kinds of Dionysiac experience,[122] but others clearly focused on only one aspect and might even have been hostile to other varieties. Plutarch, for instance, was obviously very uncomfortable with Olympias' highly emotional, personal, and female-dominated cult, yet he himself was an initiate of a cult of Dionysus that seemed focused on the hope of rebirth to a better life (*Mor.* 611d–e). Not everyone, however, would have shared Plutarch's discomfort. If, as Duris claimed, Olympias did go to battle dressed as a Bacchant, to the beat of a Dionysiac drum, then this was immensely successful as a strategy. She may have recalled a story (Polyaen. 4.1) about how a band of Macedonian maenads once turned away an enemy army.[123] The Macedonian army's religious sensibilities were not those of Plutarch, a learned gentleman from central Greece, many centuries removed from the world of Olympias and Alexander. Apparently Macedonians found the image of Olympias as a Dionysiac worshiper a compelling one, perhaps one that summarized the two things Diodorus (19.11.2) said made the army go over to Olympias: her reputation or authority and the benefits her son had secured for his people. What for us seems exotic and disconcerting was for them familiar and yet powerful: the daughter, the wife, the mother of kings leading her army into battle, dressed to show the support of a popular deity, part of the dynasty's ancestral religion, a favorite of her son and husband.

Obviously, her Dionysiac experience could and probably did signify something quite different to Olympias herself. In virtually all aspects of her life, she tried to exercise power and influence over others when it was possible to do so. She took pride in her high birth and distinguished ancestry. Doubtless she enjoyed organizing the activities of what may have been a group of women taken from the Macedonian elite, perhaps adding her own ancestral customs to Macedonian ritual, reveling in a ritual role that allowed her to act out her position (at least by the period of Alexander's later childhood) as the dominant woman at court. Although Dionysiac cult may have offered only illusory freedom to most female participants, if Duris' testimony is to be believed, Olympias actually managed to use it to acquire greater power and prestige. Though Olympias, as far as we know, never asserted herself against either her husband or her son in any significant way, she certainly did so against other men, most notably Antipater and Cassander. She may have savored the male reaction engendered by those upsetting snakes. Even if the story about her pet snakes is a fiction, her Dionysiac experience probably provided her with personal and emotional solace as well. Though she exercised a degree of independence and control over her own life, if only after the death of Philip, that was unusual in the Hellenic world, and most of her attempts to assert herself against various male figures ended, as we have seen, in failure. She would therefore have needed a transcendent experience as much as, if not more than, the typical Greek woman.[124] Although, thanks to sexual stereotyping and contemporary political propaganda, our sources exaggerate the degree to which emotion motivated Olympias, her actions suggest that she was a person with strong feelings. Her role in Dionysiac cult, particularly during the reign of Philip, when her life was otherwise quite limited, may have provided a means to express these feelings in a comparatively acceptable way. Apart from those who would take seriously the idea that Olympias was cuckolding Philip with a divine snake, few would now believe that Olympias' Dionysiac experience, like that of other elite women, was in any way sexual.[125] Plutarch's assertion (*Alex.* 2.5) that Olympias was interested in both Orphic and Dionysiac rites may well mean that she was, like others in the Macedonian elite, also an initiate in the Dionysiac cult associated with rebirth.[126]

While Olympias' intense and personal religiosity may well have influenced the development of a similar religious sensibility in her son,[127] and certainly her focus on Aeacid ancestry had a profound effect on Alexander's emulation of Achilles, her Dionysiac beliefs and activities are less likely to have shaped his. Both certainly had interests in Dionysiac experience but, whereas Olympias' revolved around ecstatic female cult, perhaps some sort of civic cult, and hopes for the afterlife, Alexander's Dionysiac interests related to *symposia* and to emulation of Dionysus as the conqueror of the East. Moreover, Alexander's attraction to Dionysus largely related to the later period of his life, not to his early years, when maternal influence would seem more likely.[128] In short, though mother and son shared an enthusiasm for Dionysus, that enthusiasm manifested itself in conventionally gendered ways.[129]

Since her husband Philip II came close to asserting his divinity and that of his dynasty (and some would say did more[130]) and her son first advanced claims to divine sonship and ultimately to divinity itself,[131] we must address Olympias' possible role, both active and passive, in these developments. No royal woman received cult until at least ten years after the death of Olympias, and when female royal cult began, it occurred in the context of the need of Alexander's Successors to legitimize their rule.[132] Nonetheless, some evidence implies that Philip may have included Olympias (and his mother[133]) in his flirtation with divinity, that Alexander may have contemplated her deification, and that Olympias may herself have inspired her son's belief in his divine or semi-divine nature. We must therefore consider Olympias' part in the early stages of the development of ruler cult.

While Philip II most famously approximated divine status for himself when he arranged for the inclusion of a statue of himself to be marched along with those of the twelve Olympian gods at the wedding festival for his daughter (Diod. 16.92.5), he also authorized the construction of a building that hinted at the divinity of his immediate family. Pausanias (5.17.4, 20.9–10) describes a round building at Olympia, within the sacred area of the Altis, constructed by Philip some time after his great victory at Chaeroneia in 338, which housed five large statues of the king himself, his father Amyntas, his son Alexander, his mother Eurydice,[134] and Olympias.[135] The Philippeum looked like a temple, was placed where one would expect a temple to be, and the statues it protected were made of gold and ivory, a fabrication previously associated only with images of the gods.[136] Thus the building, unlike the procession at Cleopatra's wedding, intimated that not only Philip but each member of his immediate family was *isotheos* (equal to a god) and perhaps more. The presence of Olympias' image in the Philippeum group demonstrates the definition of his dynasty that Philip wanted to present to the Greek world. He included her statue (and the implied allusion to divinity) because she was the mother of his heir, not because he did or did not like her. Its inclusion cannot be used to date the Philippeum.[137] Here was Philip's official, semi-divine family.[138]

According to Curtius (and he alone), Alexander, after his nearly fatal wounding while fighting the Malli in India, told his close associates that, after long reflection, he intended to have his mother "consecrated to immortality" after his death. Alexander justifies or explains this action as the greatest reward for his labors and tasks, and commands them to accomplish it if he dies too soon to do it himself (9.6.26). At the end of his work, when Curtius is summing up Alexander's character (10.5.30), he alludes to the king's decision to consecrate Olympias "among the immortals" as part of his general piety toward his parents. No other source refers to Alexander's determination to deify his mother after death, but in the light of Philip's posthumous cults, Alexander's hope for the deification of Hephaestion, and his own lifetime cult, the notion is unsurprising, though not necessarily historical. The failure of other sources to mention Alexander's intention is not reassuring: it could be a Roman fiction based on posthumous cults for several imperial women or material taken from the *Alexander Romance*. Alexander, of course, claimed divinity on the basis of his actions, which he deemed great enough to merit elevation to divine status. If the story about Olympias is true, Curtius implies that Alexander believed his mother deserved divine status not because of any actions of her own but because of his. Parental piety apart, a deified mother matched to a deified father certainly strengthened Alexander's own claims; traditionally divine status required both parents to be divine, not just one. We know nothing of how Olympias reacted to Alexander's plan, though it is difficult to imagine her objecting to it.[139] In any event, much like her inclusion in the quasi-divine dynastic group in the Philippeum, Olympias' supposed posthumous cult did not derive from any action of her own.

In contrast, many scholars believe that Olympias herself first suggested to Alexander that he was the son of god, whether Zeus Ammon or some other.[140] Little convincing evidence survives that would either support this belief or deny it. In antiquity, views apparently differed as to whether Olympias inspired Alexander's conviction that he was the son of a god. Plutarch (*Alex.* 3.2) preserves opinions on both sides. He cites Eratosthenes for the story that, as Alexander departed for Asia, Olympias told him alone something secret concerning his birth and urged him to do nothing unworthy of his origins, obviously implying that she had confided that his birth was divine. Others, he observes, insisted that she denied any part in the idea and wittily urged her son to cease slandering her to Hera.[141] Plutarch, of course, in his account of the snake sleeping by Olympias' side and more explicitly in the immediately preceding passage (3.1), connects Philip, but not Olympias, to acceptance of the idea that a god, rather than Philip, had fathered Alexander. Arrian (4.10.2) claimed that Callisthenes, Alexander's official historian, referred contemptuously to Olympias' lies about Alexander's birth, insisting that Alexander's participation in divinity depended instead on his history of the king's exploits. For a variety of reasons, it is quite unlikely that Callisthenes said or wrote any such thing.[142]

From a purely chronological point of view, it is possible that Olympias' could have been Alexander's first inspiration for the views that became public at Siwah. Although one cannot establish exactly when Alexander first became convinced privately that he was the son of Zeus, it must have preceded his extraordinary trip to consult the oracle of Zeus Ammon at Siwah in 331: the visit apparently confirmed rather than suggested divine sonship.[143] Moreover, his understanding of his birth clearly derived from Greek not Egyptian concepts[144] and thus likely originated in his early years in Macedonia. Public references to his conviction (often in the nature of objections to it) are comparatively frequent after this.[145]

In the absence of strong evidence, one can only assess what is plausible. Those who believe that Olympias was the likely instigator of her son's conviction that his father was a divinity adduce a variety of reasons or (frequently) none at all: Olympias' intense religiosity, her dislike of Philip, her belief that the snake in question was Dionysus (Zeus Ammon presumably later being substituted), her ambition for herself and for her son.[146] Majority opinion these days sees Alexander as fervently religious and genuinely convinced, first, of his divine paternity and, later, of his own divinity, all based on his unprecedented victories and wealth.[147] Obviously, if we conclude that Alexander believed that he was the son of a god, it becomes more likely that Olympias did as well, or, minimally, that she did not deny it. While one can comparatively easily imagine that her sensibilities were such that she became convinced that a god in the form of a snake had impregnated her with Alexander, it is far less likely that Olympias originated the idea, especially early in Alexander's reign or late in Philip's. Greek women, especially elite or royal Greek women, could not risk the charge of adulterous behavior, whether with a man or a divine snake. In the light of Attalus' charges in 338 or 337, Olympias would have been particularly cautious about anything that seemed to justify his remarks.[148] Over time Alexander came to believe not so much that Philip was not his father, but rather that he was the son of both Zeus and Philip.[149] This view, political benefits aside (this was a more acceptable story for those many loyal Macedonian partisans of Philip), may have developed in part to avoid scandalous remarks about Olympias. Tales of Olympias' pseudo-serpent lover in the *Alexander Romance* (see Chapter 6) point to the risks inherent in asserting that anyone other than Philip sired Alexander. Olympias doubtless supported Alexander's claims of divine sonship and divinity, but she was not their inventor.[150]

Olympias' personal religiosity has proved virtually impossible to define, but those aspects of her religious life that involved public action are not. On the one hand, much of her religious activity was typical, on a grand scale, of Hellenic female religious activity. On the other, her involvement, though probably entirely passive or reactive, in the early development of individual and dynastic ruler cult was anything but conventional, although it set a precedent for royal women in the subsequent Hellenistic period.

6 Olympias' afterlife

Olympias' afterlife, that is to say popular tradition and memory of Olympias, her reception, proved surprisingly happy but also surprisingly conventional for a woman so controversial during her actual life time. She even had a better sex life in her afterlife. As we consider the impact of her career and the fortunes of her reputation throughout the rest of the ancient period, it will become clear that the main reason the posthumous image of Olympias quickly became so much blander than the complex and sometimes frightening historical woman is that, serious historical writing apart, little memory of her individual acts and ambitions survived. The disappearance of the Argead dynasty happened shortly after her own death and the demise of the Aeacid dynasty (at least as a ruling family) followed within less than a century. After that, apart from a few obscure surviving Aeacids (see below), she had no descendants and so could be no one's distinguished ancestor whose deeds could be celebrated.[1] She was recalled largely because she was the mother of Alexander. Her reputation rose, fell, and altered with Alexander's.

Despite Cassander's prohibition against it, Olympias was buried somewhere near Pydna, the probable site of her murder. A now lost fragmentary inscription referred to her tomb.[2] One reconstruction of this inscription makes it the memorial for her tomb itself. The inscription attributed her burial to a brave Aeacid.[3] Two other funerary inscriptions indicate that her tomb once stood among or near those of other, less famous Aeacids.[4] In all likelihood, then, her kin buried her secretly, shortly after her death.[5] The tomb and its testimonial verses doubtless had to wait for the death of the last of Cassander's sons. If the Aeacids had not already built the tomb, the period when Olympias' great-nephew Pyrrhus came to control the portion of Macedonia in which Pydna lies would have given them the opportunity.[6] Whether those who buried her were part of the largely female group of *philoi* who underwent the siege with her, including Aeacides' daughter Deidameia (Diod. 19.36.5, 49.4; Just. 14.6.3) or other Aeacids already resident in Macedonia is unknown.[7] In any event, some Aeacids continued to live in the Pydna area. All three of the funerary inscriptions, in addition to employing patronymics, also refer more generally to the Aeacid descent of those commemorated, thus demonstrating the pride in lineage that characterized the clan. Of course, ordinarily Aeacids would have been buried in their homeland. These Macedonian Aeacids, apparently lacking access to their ancestral plot, must have used the tomb of Olympias as a focus for their burials.[8] Certainly the text of the most well preserved of these inscriptions suggests this. It reads, "I am of Aeacid descent, Neoptolemus was my father, my name was Alcimachus, one of those [descended] from Olympias . . ." In this patriarchal society, reference to descent from a woman (so famous a woman no patronymic was needed[9]) is striking, particularly since the speaker has already mentioned his Aeacid descent. Aeacid loyalty apparently continued to be a potent force: the family seemed to embrace the memory of its most famous member, other than Pyrrhus.

The fact that Pyrrhus named his daughter Olympias confirms the conclusion that Aeacids revered the memory of Olympias. Since Olympias was not her original Aeacid name, his choice could only commemorate the mother of Alexander the Great.[10] The career of Olympias II mirrored that of her famous namesake in some respects. Having married her half-brother Alexander II, she became regent for their sons after her husband's death, supposedly antagonized the Epirote Alliance, thus inviting an Aetolian invasion, and arranged the marriage of her daughter to Demetrius II, king of Macedonia. Like Olympias I, a hostile tradition accuses her of poisoning someone.[11] Both her sons predeceased her and the monarchy foundered after her death *c.* 229 (Just. 28.1.1–4, 3.1–8).

Although her kin revered Olympias' reputation, Molossians in general may not have. One could make a good case for the idea that the downward spiral of Molossian monarchy began in the period of Olympias' return to Molossia and was in fact triggered by Aeacides' attempt to relieve Olympias at the siege of Pydna, during her war with Cassander. Nonetheless, granted our poor sources for Molossian history, their tendency to personalize conflicts that were almost certainly broader, their failure to distinguish Molossians from Epirotes in general, and our uncertainty about how Aeacids of the period were related to each other, the reasons for the decline of Molossian monarchy are difficult to determine.

By the time of Aeacides' second attempt to aid Olympias (presumably winter or early spring 316), one Molossian king had died in battle, Molossians had experienced a long female regency, had accepted Aeacides as their new king, and had already followed him into Macedonia once in support of Olympias. The emergence of the Epirote Alliance was a major development in the period that affected the Aeacids. Whatever its origins (see Chapter 4), it placed Molossian kings, already limited monarchs compared to those of Macedonia, under even greater strictures, although it did give them greater military power, as the new commanders of the army of the alliance. During much of this same period, Macedonia had dominated Molossian affairs.

When Aeacides found the mountain passes blocked against his passage into Macedonia by Cassander's troops, his own forces, already unenthused, revolted and Aeacides had to allow those who wanted to leave to do so. He tried to carry on with his small remaining force but could do nothing to help Olympias. Back in Molossia, the troops whom Aeacides had released generated a revolution against him, had a decree of exile passed, and made an alliance with Cassander, who then sent in a general to act as regent. Diodorus commented that this was unprecedented: previously, in Molossia, father had succeeded son on the throne, from the times of the first Neoptolemus (19.36.2–5).

While Diodorus offers no reason for these events, Justin, despite his generally more confused and mistaken narrative, does. He explains (Just. 17.3.16) that Aeacides' constant wars with the Macedonians tired the people and made him unpopular with the citizens. He blames hatred of Aeacides for a near-successful attempt to kill his two-year-old son Pyrrhus (17.3.18). Pausanias, who presents a different order of events, blames Aeacides' troubles on hatred of Olympias (see below), but he also reports that the Molossians finally relented, only to have Cassander send his brother Philip to oppose Aeacides' return to Epirus. Aeacides died of wounds from a battle against Philip (Paus. 1.11.3–4).

Aeacides' downfall was certainly not the result of nationalistic feelings: the fact that the Antipatrids were able to capitalize on the situation suggests that Epirotes were not anti-Macedonian, nor did they resent Macedonian involvement in Epirus. It is possible, though our sources do not recognize it, that divisions existed between the Epirotes generally and the Molossians.[12] Perhaps Epirotes simply thought that Aeacides had not backed the side likely to win and did not want to risk their lives for a losing cause. Certainly there is no sign of popular support for Olympias and comparatively little evidence of dynastic loyalty.

When sources describe either Olympias or Aeacides as "hated," they suggest personal hostility to them as individuals, but narratives of subsequent events in Epirus,[13] which refer to hatred of various other later Aeacids and indicate that the political instability first noted by Diodorus continued, imply that something more than reactions to the personal character of specific rulers lies behind this instability. According to Pausanias (1.11.5), Aeacides' brother Alcetas reigned immediately after the death of Aeacides, but his bad temper had made his father prefer his brother as heir, and when Alcetas returned, he raged against the Epirotes until they killed him and his children and then brought back Pyrrhus. Diodorus describes a more competent Alcetas, but the end result is not much different: Alcetas and his two sons were hostile to Cassander and won at least one battle against one of his generals, despite limited Epirote support. Cassander concluded an alliance with Alcetas but, ultimately, because he treated the common people harshly, they murdered him and two of his sons (Diod. 19.88.1–89.3).[14]

Plutarch tells a somewhat different tale. Aeacides' son, Pyrrhus, despite Cassander's continuing efforts against him (the Aeacid/Antipatrid feud continued) and the reign of another Aeacid branch, regained the throne through outside assistance from an Illyrian king, only to have, in his absence, opposing

Molossians put another Aeacid, Neoptolemus (probably the son of Cleopatra) on the throne (Plut. *Pyrrh*. 3.1–4.1). Pyrrhus, again with outside help (this time from his father-in-law Ptolemy), came back to Epirus. Plutarch says that most Epirotes were happy to see him because of their hatred of Neoptolemus, who had ruled in a harsh and violent manner. Though Pyrrhus at first co-ruled with Neoptolemus, in the end he murdered him, supposedly because Neoptolemus was plotting to do the same to him. According to Plutarch (*Pyrrh*. 4.2–5.7), the most important Epirotes urged Pyrrhus to take sole control. Doubtless with some satisfaction, he parlayed his alleged support for one of Cassander's two warring sons into control of half of Macedonia, contributing to the end of the Antipatrid dynasty (Plut. *Alex*. 6.1–5).

Since Pyrrhus proved the most able and militarily successful of the Molossian kings, the rest of his reign was relatively stable, but troubles similar to the previous ones reappeared after his death. Pyrrhus' son, Alexander II, was exiled and returned only with outside help.[15] The Aetolians threatened during Olympias II's regency.[16] After both her sons died, a crisis developed and was compounded with the death of Olympias II herself. Her only child still in Epirus,[17] Deidameia, died as well. The tomb of Pyrrhus was violated and his ashes were scattered. Pausanias (4.35.3) claims that the dying Deidameia entrusted public affairs to the people.

Individual Aeacids may have been difficult and the absence of a male heir critical, but the implication of this confusing story of dynastic ins and outs is surely that the Molossians, probably from the beginning of the Epirote Alliance *c*. 330, grew increasingly hostile to monarchy in general and less and less loyal to the Aeacid dynasty. Indeed, the dynasty lasted as long as it did in good part only because of support for various Aeacids from outside powers. Olympias and her daughter may have brought with them expectations of more absolute power generated from their experience of Macedonian monarchy. They and subsequent Aeacids, all extremely proud of their lineage, seem to have reacted to developing anti-monarchic views by being or trying to be more absolute, not less. This may be the explanation for the references to popular "hatred" of various members of the dynasty and also for loyalty within the Aeacid dynasty (despite the frequent turnover in rule, there was, remarkably, only one dynastic murder).

Finally, it is not coincidence that the conclusion of the two known eras of extended female regencies marked periods of precipitate decline in royal power, nor that, when the only heir in the direct line was a woman, the Epirotes abolished the monarchy. Although Molossians allowed women more powers and independence than many Greek peoples, including the Macedonians (see Chapter 1), female rule for any lengthy period made the Molossians turn away from monarchy. Female rulers were not accepted as military leaders and lacked the experience to do a reasonable job, even if accepted. This was an important problem because the third century was a time of prolonged military threat for Molossia.[18] Moreover, Greeks may have come to object to monarchy exactly because women had a role in it. People often saw royal women as if they were translucent vessels of a kind of dynastic entity; in a sense, they could epitomize and symbolize the entire royal family in a way that royal males, permitted much more individual careers, could not. Olympias, high-handed mother of the invincible conqueror, may have embodied what the Epirotes came to detest: Aeacid monarchy.

Outside of Molossia, in the rest of Greece, memory of Olympias was faint. In Macedonia itself, unlike most of the other Successors, Cassander made comparatively little use of links to Alexander.[19] After all, he had not shared in the great expedition or fought by Alexander's side as had the others. Cassander did, as we have seen, attempt to build a bridge to the Argeads by means of his marriage to Thessalonice, Philip II's daughter. However, Cassander stressed a link to Philip, not Alexander: he named his oldest son Philip (rather than naming him, as tradition required, after his own father), although he did name one son Antipater, after his father, and another (perhaps his youngest) Alexander. In the circumstances, Cassander could hardly do otherwise than de-emphasize Alexander: Cassander had murdered not only Olympias, but both of Alexander's sons and, probably, both of their mothers. Many continued to blame him and his family for the death of Alexander. He destroyed the entire house of Alexander (Paus. 9.7.2).[20] Naturally, there was no place for commemoration of Olympias during the reign of Cassander and, as we have already noted, as yet, not even a tomb.

Once Cassander's dynasty imploded, because of a nasty combination of incompetence and matricide, things could have been different. The Antigonids, firmly established on the Macedonian throne by the 270s, claimed to be Heraclids and apparently stressed their descent from the Argeads in particular.[21] Antigonus Gonatas may well have been the person responsible for the creation of the Great Tumulus at Vergina, a structure that protected the last Argead rulers buried in Macedonia.[22] He or Antigonus Doson dedicated a monument at Delos to Apollo that housed twenty-one statues of his ancestors. While this group very likely included his Argead predecessors, all the statues may have been male.[23] If, however, they were not, Olympias could have been commemorated there. Obviously, if any statues of Olympias had been erected in Macedonia previously (see Chapter 4), they might have remained in place.

Since memory of Olympias was so often linked to memory of Alexander, one wants to know what the popular view of Alexander in Hellenistic Macedonia was. On the one hand, popular support for the Argead clan survived Alexander's death, and Cassander moved gingerly in arranging the murders of Alexander's close kin. Diodorus (19.52.4) says that Cassander delayed the murder of Alexander IV and his mother because he feared the reaction of "the many" to the death of Olympias, and Antigonus got a good response from Macedonian troops in Asia when he attacked Cassander for his murder of Olympias and treatment of Alexander IV and Roxane (Diod. 19.6.1–3). On the other, there was certainly no popular revolt against Cassander:[24] his Argead marriage and half-Argead sons, his political and military competence, and his reassuring connection to Antipater, as well as fear of opposing him, all help to explain this. The only enduring political order in Macedonian society until 323 had been the Argead clan. The disappearance of that clan could have caused more trouble than it immediately did, primarily because Cassander offered a smooth transition to a dynasty already familiar to the Macedonians.

After the collapse of his dynasty, however, the popularity of the Argeads in general and Alexander and his family in particular may have surged. Cassander's son Antipater, who murdered his mother, literally severed their living link to the Argeads and managed, at the same time, to remind people of all those other Alexander kin Antipatrids had killed or been suspected of killing. Macedonia plunged into nearly twenty years of chaos, during which no dynasty established itself and Macedonia experienced a decline in manpower. Despite the likelihood that Alexander as well as the Successors were responsible for this situation,[25] the Argead past began to look secure and heroic. The Argeads in general, and Olympias with them, grew more likeable the longer they were gone.

Outside of Macedonia, it is difficult to know what, if any, attention Olympias' memory received.[26] One intriguing piece of information suggests that later generations of Greeks rewrote the Argead past, removing one visible sign of the dynastic importance of Olympias and her mother-in-law Eurydice, their statues in the Philippeum. By the time Pausanias visited Olympia in the mid-second century CE, the images of Olympias and Eurydice had been placed in the nearby Heraeum (Paus. 5.17.4). The date of their removal from the Philippeum is unknown. Their displacement could have been an honor, intended to associate them with Hera and other gods and heroes placed in the temple, or the statues could have been removed in order to destroy the dynastic image Philip had constructed and to dissociate the women of the Macedonian royal family from political power.[27] While I find the latter possibility far more likely than the former, another eventuality seems even more plausible. Considering that both statues, not just that of Olympias, were moved, the change in location is probably not connected to the period of the late fourth and early third century when Olympias still had many surviving enemies but Eurydice, however controversial she may have been in her own day, was just a distant memory.[28] The removal more likely occurred close to Pausanias' day, during the period of the Second Sophistic, and constitutes an example of the kind of sanitized classicizing then going on about the Hellenic past. The agenda must have been gender, rather than partisan political, propaganda and resembles the view of Plutarch (a Second Sophistic writer) on Olympias and other politically powerful women (see the Appendix).

The wars of the Successors inspired a considerable body of propaganda of which, at most, only much altered fragments survive. One of these concerns Olympias. The so-called *Liber de Morte Testamentoque Alexandri* (Book about the Death and Testament of Alexander) is probably one of these scraps of partisan literature. It preserves a fairly lengthy treatment of Alexander's last days and his supposed will. The document appears at the end of one version of the *Alexander Romance* and was appended to the *Metz Epitome*. The *Liber de Morte* combines obviously unhistorical elements, often but not always similar to elements of the *Romance*, with many details suggesting knowledge of the period immediately after Alexander's death. The testament provides a detailed version of the story that Antipater and his family poisoned Alexander, but one that makes Olympias' role critical. According to *Liber de Morte*, Alexander ordered Craterus to replace Antipater because he was treating Olympias so badly. Antipater, fearful of Alexander, then decided to murder him. Alexander's will consistently refers to himself as the son of Ammon and Olympias, allows Olympias to retire to Rhodes or anywhere else she likes, and says she should receive the same income she did during his life and have gilded statues of herself (as well as those of Alexander, Ammon, Heracles, and Philip) set up at Olympia and Delphi. More generally, *Liber de Morte* paints a very negative picture of Antipater and his sons, and contains a number of references to Rhodes and the Rhodians, not simply plans for Olympias' Rhodian retirement.[29]

Today, majority scholarly opinion considers the testament a product of the political period between autumn 317 and about 305.[30] The image of Olympias that *Liber de Morte* presents bears no resemblance to the complex historical Olympias, apart from brief reference to her quarrel with Antipater and withdrawal to Epirus. In this work, she is Alexander's "Dear Old Mum," a person to whom things happen, not an actor in events. Even the somewhat racy sex life the *Romance* allots Olympias is absent from the testament. Ammon is Alexander's father, but not some sorcerer dressed up like him; Olympias is as respectable as Heracles' mother, deceived by a god who either took the form of her husband or somehow combined with him.[31] While it is possible that the origins of this work date back to the last year of Olympias' life and to Polyperchon or Ptolemy, the sentimental picture of Olympias and Roxane more likely dates to a period after their deaths and those of Alexander's sons, but soon after. The testament's airbrushed Olympias is unlikely to have been produced while the real person was still alive, making trouble, getting besieged, and then being murdered or (depending on your point of view) executed. The concern for Olympias' income in retirement seems oddly bourgeois. The dumbed-down, prettified Olympias of *Liber de Morte* is probably the product of the decade or so after her death and that of the rest of Alexander's immediate family (Thessalonice excepted), when sentiment in Olympias' favor and that of the Argeads in general was still powerful but no longer practical, something that could be manipulated by one of the Successors. In the testament, Olympias matters mostly because she slept with a god and so bore Alexander.

On the whole, the same statement applies to Olympias' part in the *Alexander Romance*. Her character in the *Romance* proper[32] differs from the staid figure of the testament, though she is still very far from the historical woman. Many versions (recensions) of the *Alexander Romance* exist, in many different languages, from many historical periods. My focus will be the *Greek Alexander Romance*, the apparent ultimate source for all the other variations of the story, east and west.[33] The *Greek Alexander Romance* developed gradually. The earliest-known manuscript dates to the third century CE, but elements in the *Romance* go back to the third century BCE. Some scholars believe that no unified text existed before the third century CE, but today more believe that someone wrote down a version of the *Romance* quite early, possibly in the third century BCE, and probably in Alexandria. Certainly some of the constituent elements in the *Romance* existed by that date.[34] Its author is anonymous, although some manuscripts attributed authorship to Callisthenes, Alexander's official historian. Granted that Callisthenes died well before Alexander and that the *Romance* narrates the death of the king, Callisthenes cannot have written it. The author is therefore sometimes referred to as "Pseudo-Callisthenes."

In any event, a variety of elements went into the creation of the *Romance*: a conventional if showy historical writer, some sort of epistolary narrative, traditional Egyptian tales and popular stories about the last native pharaoh, Nectanebo, a rhetorical/philosophical debate set in Athens, wonder tales, and adventure stories. In general, the fabulous element in the *Romance* grew with the passing of time, but, especially in its earlier versions, it retains material that, though not found in respectable histories, may in fact be historical. For instance, the *Romance* provides us with the story that Antipater sponsored Alexander's recognition as king. Many scholars accept this story as truthful. The *Romance* offers a popular story of the life of Alexander, one in which Olympias plays an important role.[35]

Olympias in the *Romance* differs from the historical Olympias most dramatically in terms of her sexuality. Historical writers barely refer to Olympias' sexual self. Plutarch's claim that Philip fell in love with her (*Alex.* 2.1) might suggest that she was attractive, but he mentions nothing directly about her appearance. The snake that Plutarch describes as sleeping with her (*Alex.* 2.4) hints at her sexuality, but for Olympias' husband, it is sexually off-putting. Apart from Justin's incorrect belief (9.5.9) that Philip had divorced Olympias for infidelity (a belief possibly derived from the *Romance*), historical sources focus on Olympias as mother, to some degree as a political figure,[36] but not as a sexual being. In the *Romance*, two different men (Nectanebo and Pausanias), upon seeing her, thanks to her beauty, desire her and plot to gain sexual possession of her (1.4, 24). When Alexander meets Candace, queen of Meroe, a woman who was unusually tall and godlike in appearance, the *Romance* comments that Alexander could have mistaken her for his mother (3.22).

It is not simply men who take risks in order to obtain control of Olympias' sexuality; she herself takes sexual risks. Worried that Philip is about to divorce her because she has not produced a child, Olympias consults the supposed prophet Nectanebo (she is not aware that he had been a king) and he instructs her to have intercourse with a god, thus producing a son, one who will avenge her for Philip's bad treatment (1.4). In reality, it is Nectanebo, disguised as the god Ammon, who has a sexual relationship with Olympias and becomes the father of Alexander, but Olympias believes it is the god (1.7).[37] Nonetheless, she knowingly commits adultery, albeit with a divinity, and the narrative makes it clear that she wants to continue the relationship and enjoys having sex with her supposed divine lover (1.7). Despite a handy vision sent by Nectanebo, Philip never quite accepts the divine identity of Olympias' lover, so her sexual fidelity remains an issue. When Pausanias too lusts after Olympias, she resists his blandishments and bribes, so he assassinates Philip in order to seize her, only to have his evil plan thwarted by Alexander.

The *Greek Alexander Romance* consistently portrays Olympias' adultery in a surprisingly sympathetic way,[38] whereas Philip receives less kindly treatment. Alexander's own actions typify the ambivalent but non-judgmental attitude toward Olympias' sexual activities that characterizes the *Greek Romance*. When Alexander was working out the details of his parents' reconciliation, he told Philip that Olympias "had given him no cause for complaint," but when he addressed his mother, he reminded her that Philip "knows nothing of your sin" (i.e., that his father was not Ammon but Nectanebo) and urges her to beg for reconciliation since "a woman should be ruled by her husband" (1.22).

While both historical authors and the *Romance* portray the relationship between Olympias and her son as close and both make frequent references to their letters to each other, the historical sources, as we have seen, generally treat the relationship (or at least Olympias' role in it) in a negative way, suggesting that it was often conflicted because of Olympias' demands, whereas the *Romance* pictures a serene (with the possible exception of the letters of Philip and Olympias to Zeuxis about Alexander's schoolboy allowance[39]), intimate, and sometimes touching bond between mother and son.[40] Alexander defends his mother against his father's bad treatment and rejection (1.20), insults from Cleopatra's guardians (1.21), and Pausanias' attempted rape (1.24), and he manages the reconciliation between Philip and Olympias. After his departure, Alexander and his mother write frequently (she is always his "sweet mother"; 2.22, 3.27, 33), he sends her spoils (1.28), arranges for her to send back Persian royal regalia for his bride Roxane, but also tells Roxane to respect his mother (2.22). He even arranges for a priestess for Olympias (so presumably a cult; 2.21). He says that he misses his mother very much (2.23) and, when he hears an oracle predict his imminent death, asks if it will not at least be possible to embrace his mother one more time before he dies (3.17). Alexander even gives Olympias advice intended to help her accept his death (3.33). In historical sources, their relationship is largely fodder for jokes and axioms about the bad qualities of women, but in the *Romance* their dealings, if sentimentally portrayed, seem nonetheless genuinely affectionate.

Compared to the historical Olympias, Pseudo-Callisthenes' Olympias plays a largely (though not entirely) passive role in events. She does take the initiative to consult a prophet (1.4), but only after a servant has suggested it. She sets up further meetings with "Ammon" (1.6) but Nectanebo has manipulated her into this circumstance. As we have seen, she is the object of sexual desire but not clearly in charge of her own sexuality. When Alexander's murder of Nectanebo reveals the truth about his deception of her, Olympias "berated herself for having been made a fool of by Nectanebo's magic arts and tricked into adultery" (1.14), suggesting that she expected better of herself. Alexander has to save her from various threats to either her person or her reputation and she obeys his behests. Because Olympias in the *Romance* is so unthreatening, it does not depict her as a person who violates gender roles, as the historical authors often do. Only in Alexander's reminder to his mother that wives should obey husbands is there any sign of interest in reasserting conventionality or any sense that it has been challenged.

Perhaps the element that contributes most to the ambivalent attitude of the *Romance* toward the character of Olympias is the problematic identity of Alexander's father. While the narrative certainly begins with the idea that Alexander had one biological father, the mortal Nectanebo (1.14), matters do not remain so straightforward. The narrator sometimes refers to Alexander as the son of Philip and Olympias (1.38, 2.5, 21). One might simply interpret this as a reference to the people who actually brought him up. When, however, Alexander visits Siwah, he says that Olympias has told him his father was Ammon and the god confirms this with a vision (1.29). Soon after Alexander affirms that Nectanebo was indeed his father (1.34), yet a subsequent passage refers to Alexander as the son of Ammon and Philip (1.35). At some point, Alexander's male parent becomes the god, not some sleazy down-at-the-heel and unemployed magical pharaoh. The *Romance* honors the multiple traditions about Alexander's parentage in a way that not only contradicts its own main narrative but problematizes Olympias' choices.

In the Hellenistic period, during which the traditions behind the *Romance* were developing and perhaps the *Romance* itself was being written, many physical images of Olympias may have been created, but none survive that can with certainty be identified with her. The statue of her at Olympia may well have remained visible until late antiquity and could have served as a model for other images of her, but we have no notion of what it looked like.[41] Moreover, comparatively few images of any Hellenistic royal women have been identified because Greek artistic tradition idealized and generalized female images far more than male, making it difficult to distinguish royal women from ordinary women, on the one hand, and from goddesses, on the other. Ptolemaic royal women's comparatively realistic portraits appeared on coins, making it possible to identify some sculptural images as theirs, but this was not the usual situation. In practice, unless a portrait has an inscription naming the subject, the attributes (for instance, a scepter or a

cornucopia) that accompany the image may be the only basis for identification of a woman. Since royal women were often equated with goddesses
and so shown with their attributes, deciding whether an image is, for instance,
Arsinoe as Aphrodite or simply Aphrodite can be difficult.[42] As we have seen,
the statue found at Vergina in the sanctuary of Eucleia, dedicated by
Eurydice, Philip II's mother, has been interpreted as an image of Eucleia or
as one of Eurydice. The head of the statue, though beautiful, is so generalized
that, whether it was intended to represent Eurydice or not, it suggests little
of any specific human being. Moreover, images of one person might allude
to the qualities of another, divine or mortal, by resembling them.[43]

Since we know of no specific physical attributes associated with Olympias
at this period and no labeled images of her survive from the Hellenistic
period, the only way to recognize a possible image of her is in association
with her son. Certainly, at all periods, her image in literature and art is
far more present than that of her husband Philip.[44] If an image seems to be
that of Alexander and appears with that of a woman, one must consider
Olympias a more likely companion to the king than any of his wives,
as Olympias' prominence in the *Romance* suggests. Greeks tended to ignore
Alexander's wives because they were Asian. Moreover, Roxane, the only wife
who produced a child, was not of royal birth. Olympias had a distinguished
royal Hellenic lineage, fame that surpassed her daughter-in-law's, and
she was believed to have had a close relationship with her son.

In this context, some scholars have identified the paired images on two
large cameos, one in Vienna (Figure 6.1) and the other in St Petersburg
(Figure 6.2), as those of Alexander and Olympias.[45] Others have recognized
in these figures various Ptolemaic or Julio-Claudian royal pairs. As this variety
in opinion implies, the dating of the cameos has also continued to be an issue.
Dates assigned to the cameos range (whether based on stylistic, technical, or
iconographic grounds, or some combination of these) from the third century
BCE to the first century CE.[46] Certainly, the current state of the argument
cannot rule out the possibility that the images on either cameo were intended
to be those of Alexander and Olympias.

On both cameos the heads of a male and female appear in superimposed
profiles, facing to their right, with the male profile in the foreground. Both
cameos idealize and generalize the female figure more than the male.[47] The
cameos, however, differ in a number of details. On the Vienna cameo the
male figure wears a helmet with a snake decoration on its dome, a bearded
head (Zeus Ammon?) on the side, and a thunderbolt on the cheekpiece. The
St Petersburg cameo's mane has a partially visible decorated breastplate (an
aegis with a gorgon's head and a bearded head) as well as a differently shaped
helmet (like the helmet on the Vienna piece, this one is also decorated with
a snake, but one with wings, above a laurel wreath). The image of the woman
on the Vienna cameo wears a diadem and veil whereas only a laurel crown
rests on the head of the woman in the St Petersburg cameo.[48] Furthermore,
the somewhat more individualized male head on the Vienna cameo contrasts

Figure 6.1 Vienna Cameo
Source: Kunsthistorisches Museum, Vienna

more dramatically with the accompanying female head than is the case with the more generalized features of both the man and the woman on the St Petersburg cameo.[49] The contrast in treatment of the man and the woman is present on both, but greater on the Vienna cameo. Some features on each cameo suit the "Macedonian" identification fairly well, but others, most notably the absence of some standard features of Alexander portraiture, do not.[50] On the other hand, both the male and (especially) the female profiles lack the comparative realism of Ptolemaic royal portraits.[51] Besides, many rulers imitated Alexander and so might have been depicted with attributes associated with him, without intending to depict him.[52]

The iconography of a couple in superimposed profiles first appeared on Ptolemaic coins, initially those relating to deification of a royal pair,[53] although later examples might also be taken to refer to co-rule, since later Ptolemaic women did co-rule. Most of the paired Ptolemaic coin images

Figure 6.2 Gonzaga Cameo
Source: State Hermitage Museum, St Petersburg

preserved detailed, individualized heads and most of the pairs commemorated were royal spouses. Cameos from the early Roman Empire period copy the idea of these superimposed profiles, but the faces on the cameos, especially those of the women, are more idealized, divinized to some degree, and, if identifications are correct, often represent non-marital pairs, like a mother and son. If we recognize Alexander and Olympias in the Vienna and/or St Petersburg cameos, then we have representation of them that implies the divinity of both and divorces them from Philip. Granted the stories that claimed the first Ptolemy was, in fact, Philip's bastard,[54] such a Philipless construct better fits the early Imperial period than the Ptolemaic. If this later dating is correct, then the image on the cameos has been filtered through the culture and classicizing modes of the early Roman Imperial period.

By the later first century BCE, all of the dynasties of Alexander's Successors had fallen to Roman might and the Roman state itself had been transformed from an oligarchic republic to a monarchy, ruled by the men we call emperors. However, because the first emperor, Augustus, created this monarchy by, in essence, denying that he was a monarch, the emperors of the first two centuries of the Imperial period (the so-called Principate) usually followed his model, playing the role of first citizen in public art. The reality was that they had become the heirs of Alexander's Successors and, like them, received indirect and direct cult worship. By the end of the second century CE, the denial of the existence of monarchy had lost its usefulness and for the rest of Imperial period in the West (the so-called Dominate), emperors ruled and portrayed themselves in more absolute ways.

These succeeding transformations of the Roman state directly impacted on the image of Alexander and, therefore, that of his mother. All the major extant written accounts of Alexander's reign date from the period of Roman domination and virtually all from the Imperial period. People living in the Roman period shaped much of what we know about Alexander. For instance, in all likelihood, the Romans gave Alexander his epithet "the Great," in acknowledgment of his skill as a military commander.[55]

Recognition of the Roman origin of much of our knowledge of Alexander has generated a large body of scholarship about views of Alexander in the Roman period and the degree to which various Roman leaders imitated him, tried to surpass his accomplishments, claimed that they had done so, and employed his image for their own ends. Naturally, with so much work in this area, considerable variety of opinion exists.[56] During the period of the Republic, most likely Alexander was a figure too troubling to risk imitating.[57] Those who did might have it used against them. Alexander was a monarch and Romans of the Republican period loathed the idea of monarchy. Moreover, he lacked the virtues of sobriety and self-control the elite supposedly valued, and he prized Eastern culture too much. Worse yet, his heirs were currently confronting Roman armies. More often than not, Roman Republican generals saw themselves as competing successfully against him and his record. In the early Empire period, even though emperors had become world rulers like Alexander, the pretense that they were not monarchs limited the ways in which they could safely use him as a model. Augustus, for instance, while in Egypt, visited Alexander's tomb and employed his image for a time on his signet ring, but he replaced it soon enough with his own (Suet. *Aug.* 50).

Things began to change in the second century CE and not simply because emperors stopped pretending not to be world rulers. This was the period of the Second Sophistic, when emperors could employ images of themselves as Greek philosophers, Greek dominated high literary culture, and the general culture of the Empire became Graeco-Roman. Many cities reconnected to their Greek past, a past that often (whether this was fiction or fact) connected to Alexander. Hadrian and his successors sponsored the political integration of local Greek elites into the Empire.[58] Second Sophistic writers paid much attention not only to Alexander,[59] but to Homer, the model for so much in Alexander's self-constructed image.[60]

As the second century ended and the third began, two other factors contributed to an atmosphere in which Alexander became an ever more attractive figure, not simply to emperors who tried to connect to his fame but to the general population. Septimius Severus (r. 193–211 CE), the founder of the dynasty of the Severi (193–235), came from North Africa. Most of the other rulers of the dynasty were actually descendants or kin of his wife, Julia Domna, rather than of Severus himself. Julia Domna was from the Greek East, Syria, from the family of the priests of the sun god, and her clan may well have had (or at least claimed to have had) connections to the Seleucids.[61] Two members of the dynasty, Aurelius Antoninus (hereafter referred to by his nickname, "Caracalla"; b. 188, r. 211–17) and Alexander Severus (b. 205, r. 222–35), were perhaps the most famous and enthusiastic of all Alexander emulators (see below), but subsequent emperors also came from the Greek East. In addition, in this same period, Roman armies confronted a reborn Persian Empire. Naturally, the memory of the man who had conquered the last one was heartening to recall for both ordinary soldiers and emperors. This is the backdrop for the dramatic growth in popularity of the *Alexander Romance*. Even in the fourth century, as we shall see, Alexander's image could be useful to emperors of the period and meaningful to their people.

Until the third century CE, little trace of Olympias in the Roman world survives. This is hardly surprising since her image, whether visual or literary, conjured up the idea of dynasty in general and deified kings more particularly. As we have seen, one or more of the "Great Cameos" may depict her and her son and date from the early Imperial period, but this is far from certain. Similarly, a painting from a Roman villa that some have identified as Olympias is more likely some other royal Macedonian woman, or perhaps not even that.[62] Of course, many images, now lost, of Olympias may have existed and we may have failed to recognize her (granted the difficulties involved in identification already discussed) in images we do have.

Literary references to Olympias tend to focus on the snake, but the picture of Olympias in these sources varies considerably. Legends about the fathering of various Roman leaders by divine serpents may have developed during the Republican period, implicitly and sometimes explicitly mimicking the story of Olympias and the serpent.[63] Cicero (*De Div.* 2.66.135) preserves a story in which Olympias' pet serpent appears to Alexander in a dream, telling him where to find a cure for the wound his friend Ptolemy had suffered. While this story does connect Olympias to a snake, it is much closer to the probably historical story in Plutarch about her pet snakes, with overtones of her as a person connected to magic/poison. Aulus Gellius (*N.A.* 13.4.1–3), citing the late Republican writer Marcus Varro, tells a version of the anecdote also told by Plutarch (*Alex.* 3.2) in which Olympias, supposedly hearing that Alexander was claiming that his father was Zeus Ammon, joked that he was getting her into trouble with Hera. In Gellius' version, Alexander called himself the son of Zeus Ammon in a letter to Olympias, but the more striking aspect of the Gellius passage is its insistence not only on Olympias' wittiness, but on her good qualities in contrast to her son's bad ones. She is prudent and wise while he is savage; she advises cautiously and courteously that he should give up his foolish claim, one inspired by the flattery of his court and his own success. Lucian (*Dial. Mort.* 13.390, 25.382), writing in Greek in roughly the same period, has Alexander claim that the idea of his divine birth came from his mother and the prophets of Ammon, not himself. In Macedonia, at Veroea, where games in honor of Olympias' son began to be celebrated, inscriptions from the second century CE preserve the memory of three women who bore her name, almost certainly in commemoration of Alexander's mother.[64] Revival of interest in Alexander in Macedonia may well have predated the Severi but (see below) they were probably the main stimulant.[65]

Obviously, the construction of Roman gender roles, however it changed over the generations, had an effect on the image of Olympias in Roman culture. Despite the political influence and considerable independence of elite women in both late Republican and Imperial Rome, the Roman female ideal was of quietness, privacy, simplicity, and self-denial.[66] Clever imperial women managed to have their power described and justified in terms that fitted these conventions, but even they had to conform to this image or face criticism or even death. Nonetheless, though more so with some dynasties than others, women of the imperial family formed a significant aspect of the public presentation of imperial power, receiving titles, appearing on coins, and sometimes achieving deification after their deaths. As a generalization, mothers of emperors received a more positive reception than wives or daughters in written sources, and public presentation tended to stress an imperial woman's role as mother of heirs more than, for instance, the same woman's role as wife.[67] Roman gender expectations, combined with continuing anti-monarchical tradition, help to explain the largely negative picture of Olympias in the historical sources. She transgressed most of these expectations and her pride in her birth and royal status still did not play well in the early Imperial period, when the name of monarchy, if not the fact, still inspired fear. Her personal qualities, seemingly an exaggeration of those very qualities of her son's that so worried the Romans, were even more upsetting in a woman.

As we have seen with the Severi, "Alexander mania"[68] developed and endured through much of the third century. We should probably take the sometimes bizarre details that the historical accounts provide about these two cousins' fondness for Alexander with a large pinch of salt, but no good reason exists to doubt the idea that Alexander was vital to each one's public presentation and he probably had a personal meaning for each as well.[69] According to the *Scriptores Historiae Augustae*, Caracalla tried to equal Alexander (2.1), and Herodian (4.8.1) mysteriously asserts that the emperor, while campaigning near Macedonia, suddenly "was Alexander."[70] The *Scriptores Historiae Augustae* report that Alexander Severus, the first of the emperors to bear the eonqueror's personal name,[71] read the life of Alexander and tried to imitate him (30.3) and that he wanted to seem to be Alexander (64.3), though he supposedly rejected the senate's offer of the epithet "the great" (5.5). Imitation of the Macedonian was particularly relevant for Alexander Severus since he had to deal with a new Persian Empire that conceived itself as the heir to the Achaemenid Empire that Alexander had destroyed (Herodian 6.2.2).[72]

The women of the Severan dynasty, part of the Syrian elite, played a vital role in it. After the death of Septimius Severus, several of them acted as regents and, even after their sons came of age, continued to exercise considerable power. This power, their good education, and their literary patronage did not go uncriticized, particularly because of their origins in the Hellenistic East and because of the extreme behavior of one of their sons, Elagabalus (r. 218–22). Nonetheless, one cannot help but wonder if Olympias' role in the life of her son played a part in his appeal to both Caracalla and Alexander Severus.[73]

A group of twenty large gold medallions, discovered early in the twentieth century at Aboukir, outside of Alexandria, demonstrate that the Alexander imitation of the Severi was not limited to the conqueror himself, but included his mother. Some date these medallions to the reign of Caracalla or Gordian III, but they probably were produced during the reign of Alexander Severus.[74] No one knows the intended purpose of these medallions, but many believe that they were offered as prizes or commemoratives at games in Alexander's honor given somewhere in the eastern part of the Empire, possibly in Macedonia itself.[75] The collection clearly includes examples of the standard image of Alexander (turned head, upward-turning glance), what most consider a beardless portrait of Caracalla, and images of a woman usually identified as Olympias. Five of the medallions depict a highly conventionalized female image in profile on the obverse, in three different versions: veiled, facing right holding a rod around which a snake twines; veiled and diademed, facing right holding part of veil (Figure 6.3); veiled and diademed, facing left, holding a scepter, and wearing a snake bracelet. Two exemplars of the first type were found; on the reverse of one appeared Athena feeding a snake and on the other Perseus and Andromeda. The reverses of the two exemplars of the second type both show semi-nude women riding on sea creatures, although one creature has the head of a bull whereas the other is a hippocamp. The reverse of the third type also shows a partially clad female on a seagoing bull.[76]

Granted that the male images include and thus (by implication) link a Severan male with Alexander, the female images almost certainly represent

Figure 6.3 Olympias on one of the Aboukir medallions
Source: Walters Art Museum, Baltimore

a woman from one of the two royal families. Portrait traits for Severan women, particularly their hairdos, are well established[77] and the busts do not resemble theirs, thus suggesting that the image is intended to be that of Olympias.[78] Though none of the exemplars of the three types bears a legend identifying Olympias by name, not only their context in the group of medallions but the marked resemblance between the types on the medallions and on later Roman contorniates (fourth century CE bronze medallions made in Rome with Latin labels; see below), some of which do bear the legend "Olympias," make the identification all but certain.[79] Quite apart from similarities to the contorniates, the snake rod (type 1) and snake bracelet (type 3) seem to allude to Olympias.[80] Though different interpretations have been offered, three of the reverses associated with the "Olympias" medallions tend to confirm the identification. The female rider of a sea creature is most easily understood as a Nereid (a daughter of the sea god Nereus), most likely the most famous of them, Thetis, mother of Achilles and founding mother of Olympias' Aeacid dynasty.[81]

In any event, the medallions seem to place Caracalla, and probably his clan, in the family of Alexander and Olympias.[82] No image in this collection can be tied to Philip, and the snake, so often associated with Alexander's story in this period, makes an appearance only as a cult object.[83] Despite the blandness of the Olympias images on medallions, coin portraits of Ptolemaic royal women probably constitute their prototype.[84] The medallions present three different interpretations of Olympias, each using the same generic profile: Olympias the modest Greek woman;[85] Olympias the religious devotee; and Olympias the ruler or woman of power. Despite the interest of Caracalla, at least, in Heracles, the Aboukir medallions appear to celebrate Alexander as victor and, oddly, as Aeacid, and Caracalla as his doppelgänger and kin. These medallions constitute almost the last evidence we have for a comparatively snakeless and somewhat historical Olympias. As the third century progressed and the fourth century began, the *Alexander Romance*, rather than more sober historical accounts, clearly became the main, if not yet the exclusive, source of images and stories about Alexander and his mother.[86]

Late Roman coins and the contorniates demonstrate the continued popularity of Alexander and Olympias, however romanticized. A series of eight Alexander coin types minted by the Macedonian community after 231, when Alexander Severus restored its ancient privileges, includes an image of a woman, reclining on a couch or chair, feeding a snake from a dish.[87] A close relationship exists between the Macedonian coin images and later contorniates.[88] (Contorniates were probably connected to the chariot races in Rome, where Macedonian charioteers were popular.)[89] That the woman on the Macedonian coin is Olympias is largely confirmed by a similar labeled image produced in the next century on the reverse of a contorniate (Figure 6.4).[90] Like other contorniates, the obverse shows the familiar and traditional image of Alexander as Heracles with the lion headdress, but the reverse shows a semi-nude woman reclining on a couch with a dolphin backrest while apparently feeding a snake and supporting his head at the same time. This time the identity of the female figure is not in doubt: the inscription above her reads "Olympias" and below her "*regina*" (queen).[91] While the contorniate could allude to Olympias' keeping of pet snakes, her semi-clothed state and the presence of the scene on an object whose obverse shows Alexander himself suggest that Zeus Ammon, not a domestic pet, is intended.[92] Another contorniate type shows a veiled woman in profile, holding a scepter. On the reverse (with one exception) appears a seated Alexander (identified by a legend) with a shield.[93] This image, so similar to those on the Aboukir medallions, has been identified as that of Olympias.

Yet another type of contorniate provides a remarkable representation of Olympias. Olympias (some exemplars bear a legend with her name while others do not) wears the lion headdress of Heracles and carries his club.[94] The standard interpretation of this contorniate image has been that it depicts Olympias as Omphale,[95] the Lydian queen who owned Heracles while he

Figure 6.4 Olympias feeds the snake, contorniate

Source: British Museum, London

was a slave, for whom he performed various tasks (often said to be those usually given to women), and by whom he may have had children. Omphale, once a threatening symbol of Eastern decadence and the feminization of male power (e.g., Cleopatra and Mark Antony), had become a respectable figure by the Severan period. Imitation of Heracles by Roman rulers had become popular and the Syrian origin of Julia Domna, wife of Septimius Severus, made associations with the East good. Paired statues of husbands and wives as Heracles and Omphale may have become common. Omphale also had Dionysiac associations possibly relevant to Alexander and Olympias.[96] Nonetheless, Heracles' attributes had long been connected to the images of Macedonian kings and a Heracles with a lion headdress appeared on many Macedonian coins, most famously those of Alexander himself. Alexander coins with a lion headdress were endlessly imitated. In a sense, it is as though Olympias is shown on the contorniate as Alexander. This oddly Heraclid Olympias invokes a gender-bending image of her that one suspects the historical Olympias might have enjoyed.[97]

A villa from Baalbeck (ancient Heliopolis) in Syria contained a cycle of mosaics (now much damaged) about the life of Alexander that probably dates to the later fourth century CE and, more clearly than either the Macedonian coins or the contorniates, demonstrates that the source for the story of Alexander and Olympias has now become the *Romance*. One panel is generally well preserved, but heavily damaged in the upper-left area. On the panel, one scene, to the left, shows Olympias on a couch with a snake that sits on her lap; Philip (labeled) sits near her, albeit partially turned away. Behind the couch on which the two sit is a heavily damaged male figure carrying some sort of rod. Ross has argued that the scene (as well as the others pictured) illustrates an episode from the *Romance* (10.1), when the serpent's spectacular sudden appearance with Olympias convinces Philip that a divine snake really did father Alexander.[98] To the right of the first scene is another, showing the birth of Alexander. In the foreground, with partially surviving name labels, a newborn Alexander is bathed by a nymph. In the background, a woman (Olympias' name label is partially preserved) reclines on a couch and is attended by a female servant (also labeled) who stands behind her. (Scenes of the birth of Alexander, looking much like medieval births of Jesus,[99] often appear in medieval illuminations of the *Romance*.)[100]

As the Roman Empire in the West faded, the tradition of the story of Alexander and Olympias survived through the *Romance* into medieval and early modern times, but that is another story. Augustine (*De civ. D.* 8.5, 12.11) knows about Alexander and Olympias, but he knows them entirely from the letter tradition ultimately incorporated into the *Romance*. Elite women in Christian Constantinople and the rest of the Greek East continued to be given the name of Alexander's mother,[101] but the world that produced the historical Alexander and Olympias, as well as the one that had preferred the tale of serpent-divinity fathers, was gone. The *Romance* would prosper and endure, but the Alexander and Olympias it depicted had less and less resemblance to the various versions of mother and son popular in antiquity. If Olympias really did first invent the story of her divine snake lover, then the irony is that her snake tale swallowed the memory of the real woman.

Appendix
Olympias and the sources

My purpose in this section is to provide a short discussion of the nature of the evidence about Olympias offered by each of the major extant sources.[1] This is not intended to be an exercise in source criticism, although reference will occasionally be made to conventional views about the sources of authors under discussion. Instead, I want to characterize and describe the representation of Olympias each major ancient source offers.[2] I will not solely be concerned with whether a given writer presents a hostile or comparatively positive picture of Olympias (often, of course, the same writer does both), but will also note what the source tells us about Olympias and what it omits. My focus will be on literary sources, but I will also look at what the orators contemporary to Olympias tell us, as well as what inscriptions and images offer.

Diodorus Siculus wrote a universal history of the ancient Mediterranean world some time in the second half of the first century BCE.[3] Scholars believe that Diodorus generally employed one major source for his narratives of a given period of time, but that he supplemented this major source with material taken from others and sometimes added his own comments, often of a moralizing sort.[4] As his major source for Alexander's reign, common opinion generally favors Cleitarchus, an Alexandrian writer who may have written soon after Alexander's death and who probably stressed the colorful aspects of the conqueror's career. Hieronymus of Cardia, once an associate of Olympias' ally Eumenes and later an adherent of Antigonus and his family, is Diodorus' probable main source for events after Alexander's death (books 18–20 in Diodorus). Scholarly opinion of Hieronymus is high, though there is recognition of his bias in favor of Eumenes and Antigonus. He may well have had access to Eumenes' correspondence.[5] The most striking aspect of Diodorus' treatment of Olympias[6] is his uneven coverage: he barely mentions her during the reign of Alexander but provides considerable detail about her activities in the period after her son's death. There is one obvious explanation for this discrepancy in coverage. Diodorus, with his broad scope and necessarily brief accounts of specific events, tends to focus on public events. Even allowing for omissions of his and other sources (whose existence we know about from inscriptions and the orators), Olympias probably was much less active in public events during Alexander's reign than she was later. But her greater public role in the later period is probably not the only reason why Diodorus has more to say about her after her son's death. The many details Diodorus furnishes about Olympias' actions and policies (often relating to correspondence) in the era of the Successors strongly suggest that Hieronymus' association with Eumenes gave him access to insider information (and correspondence) dealing with Olympias.

Other than innocuous references Diodorus makes to Olympias in order to identify her more obscure kinfolk (16.72.1, 91.4), only four passages mention Olympias prior to Alexander's death. Diodorus alone reports that the king's mother (presumably Olympias, as I have argued; see Chapter 3) warned Alexander by letter against Lyncestian Alexander (17.32.1) and only he says that Olympias and Antipater both demanded that the Athenians give up Harpalus to them (17.108.7). In his account of the death of Hephaestion, Diodorus mentions in passing the story that Olympias and Hephaestion quarreled by letter (17.114.3). He also refers to the quarrel between Olympias and Antipater and insists that, as relations between Alexander and Antipater cooled, Alexander's piety toward his mother led to his desire to please her in all matters, and so Antipater, for this and other reasons, plotted success-fully to kill Alexander. Diodorus claims many other historians concealed the plot because of the subsequent power of Antipater and Cassander. The latter remained hostile to Alexander even after his death, murdered Olympias, and refused her body burial (17.118.1–3).[7] Diodorus' account of Olympias' actions during her son's reign implies that she was aggressive, but his narrative is much more overtly hostile to Antipater and his clan.

Although Diodorus' narrative of the military and political events after Alexander's death pays much more attention to Olympias, in most of this narrative, his treatment of Olympias consists of matter-of-fact reference to her actions as part of her alliance with Polyperchon. Diodorus' report of the letter she sent to Eumenes, apparently in reference to Polyperchon's offer to return her to Macedonia and put her in charge of her grandson, makes Olympias look both cautious and politically acute: she sees through the subterfuges of the various "guardians" (18.58.3). As we have seen (Chapter 4), the implication of his narrative is that Olympias' cause was lost because of Polyperchon's series of military failures, beginning with the siege of Megalopolis (18.74.1), as well as because of Aeacides' inability to return to Olympias' aid. There are two exceptions to Diodorus' generally neutral account of the decline of Olympias' fortunes: his version of her violent actions after her return to Macedonia and his account of her final days.

Diodorus (19.11.1–11) not only provides a detailed account of her murders of Philip Arrhidaeus and Adea Eurydice that is highly sympathetic to them,[8] but he also repeatedly and explicitly condemns Olympias' actions. According to the narrator, she did not take advantage of her good luck in a humane way and condemned Adea Eurydice to a punishment he considered more severe than her husband's (wrongly, I believe; see Chapter 4). He judges that

Olympias' lack of compassion meant that her own death was merited and comments that by actions contrary to law (or custom) she satisfied her anger but made many Macedonians hate her savagery and recall Antipater's deathbed warning not to let a woman be first in the kingdom. He concludes with the statement that this situation made it clear that a change would come in Macedonia. This section differs from most of Diodorus' previous account of Olympias' actions in a number of respects: it is far more detailed, sometimes unbelievably so; it is replete with moralizing; and it seems to imply that Olympias lost to Cassander because of her treatment of Adea Eurydice and Philip Arrhidaeus, Nicanor, Cassander's supporters, and the tomb of Iolaus, an implication at odds with the rest of his narrative. Diodorus very likely supplemented his narrative here because he saw an opportunity for moralizing,[9] creating something of a conflict with the rest of his account by doing so. Hieronymus may not have been the source for this section of narrative. May I suggest this not only because it differs stylistically from the main body of the account, which presumably was drawn from Hieronymus, but because, as a close associate of Eumenes and later Antigonus, Hieronymus would likely have been sympathetic to Olympias and hostile to Cassander?[10]

Diodorus' description of the siege of Pydna and the events leading to Olympias' death (19.49.1–51.4) is as detailed as his version of Olympias' atrocities (in contrast to the rest of his narrative), yet generally paints a somewhat sympathetic picture of Olympias. The details Diodorus provides about the siege are more believable than those that appear in his account of the earlier incident, suggesting that his source for the siege had spoken to eyewitnesses. Diodorus notes that Olympias had no one to speak for her at her "trial," recounts the story that Cassander attempted to trick her into an escape bid that he could use to murder her, indicates that only the kin of those she had slain were willing to kill her, and comments positively on her bravery in the face of death. Certainly there is no reassertion of the idea that her death was deserved. Diodorus' narrative seems to characterize her death and that of Aristonous as consequences of vendettas rather than justice. His treatment of Cassander is not sympathetic (19.51.1, 2, 4, 52.4–5).

Diodorus is the most important source for Olympias' actions after Alexander's death and, apart from his lengthy condemnation of her actions after her victory, he is not a particularly hostile one. His focus on action and public events and his brevity tend to prevent him from displaying marked bias during much of his narrative. While his text contains hints that, like most Greek males, he found some of Olympias' actions inappropriate for a woman, it is only in his inclusion of Antipater's supposed deathbed warning that he directly indicates that he understands her to have acted in a way that was not only bad, but womanish. On the other hand, he admires the brave death of Olympias herself (and of Adea Eurydice). His dramatic and overtly hostile coverage of Olympias' brutal actions after her victory obscures the fact that his account is otherwise comparatively objective in its treatment of her, provides considerable helpful information, and displays only modest sex and gender prejudice, at least in comparison to other Greek sources.[11]

About 200 CE Justin (Marcus Junianus Justinus) wrote an *epitome* (a shortened version) of a world history composed by Pompeius Trogus in Latin during the reign of Augustus (31 BCE–14 CE). Justin's narrative contains many errors and is sometimes so compressed that it makes little sense, but it is the only extant narrative for some periods of Hellenistic history and contains material not found elsewhere that one cannot immediately discard. Little consensus exists about the sources of Pompeius Trogus, though Cleitarchus was probably the ultimate source of much of his material dealing with the reign of Alexander. Yardley has argued convincingly, based on his study of the language in the text, that Justin, not Pompeius Trogus, dominates the diction and expressions of the book.[12] The *Romance*, or perhaps the tradition building toward the creation of the *Romance*, may also have shaped his portrait of Olympias.[13]

Like Diodorus, Justin recounts events from Olympias' life from the time of her marriage to Philip until her death. He pays even less attention than Diodorus to her actions during her son's reign (though, like Diodorus he claims that Olympias' charges about Antipater were the partial reason for Antipater's decision to assassinate Alexander). Justin's representation of Olympias is significantly more hostile than that of Diodorus (though not exclusively so). Interestingly, though, he displays almost no interest in the incident which generated Diodorus' strongest condemnation—Olympias' violent acts after her victory—and instead focuses his hostility on Olympias' supposed involvement in Philip's death. Although Justin mentions Olympias' murder of Cleopatra and her baby (9.7.12) and terms it revenge, this crime does not interest him either.

Justin insists that Philip repudiated Olympias for adultery with the divine serpent (9.5.9, 11.3–6, 12.16.2). This supposed repudiation is already Olympias' motivation for involvement in Philip's assassination (9.5.9, 7.2), though Justin says that both Olympias and her son encouraged and supported the assassin (9.7.1, 8). Only Justin reports that Olympias tried to get her brother to attack Philip, a plan Philip short-circuited by arranging the marriage between her daughter and her brother (9.7.7). It is in the details of Olympias' involvement in the assassination plot that Justin demonstrates antagonism so considerable as to make his account implausible: she has horses ready for the assassin's getaway; she puts a wreath on the crucified head of the assassin (Justin says only she could have dared to do so); she has Pausanias cremated over Philip's tomb and provides a tomb for him; and she dedicates the murder weapon under her childhood name. Justin comments that she acted as though she were afraid that her involvement in the crime would not be known (9.7.1–14). He seems to take the divine snake seriously as Alexander's parent and even includes a scenario similar to that in the *Romance*: Olympias confesses her adultery to Philip and he announces that Alexander is not his son.

Justin's version of Olympias' life after her son's death fluctuates between considerable criticism and high praise, but, on the whole, he admires her for living up to her high birth and male kin by managing a heroic death. He baldly states that she had Adea Eurydice and Philip Arrhidaeus killed, but offers no details (14.5.10). He follows this information with the observation that she did not live long herself, but his condemnation apparently focuses not on her elimination of the royal pair but on her murder of other members of the Macedonian elite: "Acting more like a woman than a ruler, she caused indiscriminate slaughter of the nobility and transformed favor into hatred" (14.6.1). In Diodorus' account, Olympias' slaughter is clearly political, an action, however brutal, against an opposing faction she blamed for her son's death. In Justin's, she is simply randomly savage, for no reason, and this savagery, not even understood as revenge, Justin sees as somehow feminine.

Justin's account of Olympias' death is as over-the-top in a positive way as is his description of her involvement in Philip's murder in a negative way. According to Justin, Cassander has to bribe the kin of those she killed to accuse her. Justin criticizes those who condemned her as ungrateful. Rather than avoiding death, Olympias goes out to meet her would-be assassins, dressed in royal attire and accompanied by maids, and so overawes them that they do not murder her. The soldiers Cassander then dispatches do the task, but Olympias faces them, does not act like a woman but like a brave man, upholding the glory of her ancient line. Justin says that you could see Alexander in his mother's death (14.6.6–13). His narrative of Olympias' dramatic death scene recalls his earlier (12.16.3) discussion of her lineage: her fame came from her clan, a family going back to the distant past, and from the fact that her father, brother, husband, and all her ancestors had ruled, although no one's name was more famous than that of her son. Justin's Olympias is most dangerous when she acts like a woman, most admirable when she acts like a man, and most remarkable for the way in which she encapsulates the distinction of the males of her family. His portrayal of her is inconsistent and makes no sense of her life or aims. He uses her career as an excuse for narrating dramatic scenes and extreme behavior. This is in keeping with what Justin states as his general guide for inclusion of material in his narrative: pleasure or material for moral examples (*Praef.* 4).

Quintus Curtius Rufus wrote a lengthy Latin narrative of Alexander's reign at a date much debated,[14] but more likely than not in the mid-first century CE. Substantial portions of his work are missing, including the first two books. Like Diodorus and Justin, he may well have used Cleitarchus as a source, but he also employed others, including Alexander's contemporaries Ptolemy and Aristobulus. Scholars once had little respect for Curtius' narrative, but many now value his political analysis, despite the Roman coloring it often displays, although they remain suspicious of his highly rhetorical approach and recognize that he sometimes invents material.[15]

Whereas the first two authors we have discussed produced historical narratives that covered long periods of time, Curtius' work dealt only with Alexander's reign. We have already noted that both Diodorus and Justin say little about Olympias' actions during that reign, so perhaps it does not surprise that Curtius (and Arrian, who covers the same period) devoted comparatively little attention to her. Other than three passing references that picture an affectionate relationship between mother and son,[16] Curtius tells us only two things about Olympias; for both he is our sole source among ancient historians. He reports that Alexander wanted to have his mother deified after her death. Alexander mentions the idea after his grave wound in Malli city, describing it as the greatest reward for his efforts and hoping that, if he is not able to do it, others will (9.6.26–7). Curtius brings it up again when, at the end of his work, he sums up Alexander's admirable qualities, among which he includes his piety to his parents, notably his vengeance for Philip's murder and his decision to "consecrate" Olympias (10.5.30).

The other "nugget" of information about Olympias that Curtius furnishes is much more political, though that is not how Curtius sees it. According to him, Amyntas, son of Andromenes, claimed that when Alexander sent him back to Macedonia on a recruiting trip, he warned him that Olympias was hiding eligible young men and that he should ignore anyone's concern other than the king's. His actions led Olympias to make charges against him (7.1.37–9; see discussion in Chapter 3). Olympias' motivation, according to Amyntas, was not so much political as emotional. He mentions her concern for her son, her anxiety of mind, her false imaginings, wishes that she were more prudent (7.1.36) and insists that she has accused them because they put Alexander's interests before the gratitude of a woman (7.1.40). He concludes that since Alexander is the source of his mother's anger, he is the one to soothe it (7.1.40). The entire episode is recounted in Amyntas' speech and, as transcribed, stresses gender roles to a degree that obscures what was going on. Why Olympias' motherly anxiety would have anything to do with her attempt to protect her favorites is never explained. In Curtius, Olympias is not so much sinister as a typical woman: irrational, emotional, and easily irritated, but still, somehow, a concerned mother beloved by her doting son.

Scholars typically refer to the three authors we have so far discussed in a collective way, as the "Vulgate" tradition, often ascribing their similarities to a common general dependence on Cleitarchus. Nonetheless, we have discovered marked differences in their treatment of the figure of Olympias. Until comparatively recently, scholars automatically preferred the testimony of either of the two non-Vulgate Alexander authors to that of the Vulgate. This tendency has dissipated in the latest scholarly generation to a considerable degree, as has the inclination to exaggerate the similarities in the Vulgate sources and ignore similarities between Vulgate and non-Vulgate sources. As our examination of the treatment of Olympias in the three

Vulgate writers suggests, even if all three made considerable use of the same sources, each writer made choices that led to significant differences in point of view and the amount of information conveyed.

Arrian (Lucius Flavius Arrianus) was born in the first century CE and lived until about 160. A Greek from Bithynia, a student of the Stoic philosopher Epictetus, he rose to the rank of consul, held the governorship of Cappadocia, and commanded Roman troops against the Alan invasion. Arrian wrote a number of works, some military in nature, but his most famous is the *Anabasis of Alexander*. His work is eulogistic, scanting or omitting much that might make Alexander seem unpleasant, but remains valuable because, as he tells us, he depends primarily on two authors who accompanied Alexander on the expedition, Aristobulus (some sort of engineer) and Ptolemy (Alexander's bodyguard, close personal associate, and later king of Egypt). Though not without error and sometimes limited by Ptolemy's bias, Arrian generally produces dependable military information.[17] The quality of his political analysis, however, is best demonstrated by his conviction that it would be more shameful for Ptolemy to lie than for any other person to do so since he was a king (1.1.2).

Granted Arrian's focus on military matters and his desire to make Alexander admirable in a comparatively uncomplicated way, Arrian naturally has little interest in Olympias. As we have already noted, most of the other sources pay little attention to her actions during the reign of her son. Arrian mentions Olympias only five times, and four of these passages offer little information. On the occasion of Harpalus' return from his first flight from Alexander's service, Arrian mentions the exiles of Harpalus and other close friends of Alexander. Unlike Plutarch, he makes no mention of the Pixodarus affair in terms of their exile but he does give a similar chronological context by explaining that it happened when Philip was suspicious of Alexander after Philip's marriage to "Eurydice" (either a mistake or another name for Cleopatra) and dishonored Olympias (3.6.5). Arrian also refers to Callisthenes' supposed assertion that he would make Alexander divine rather than to Olympias' lies about Alexander's birth (4.10.2), to a letter Alexander wrote to Olympias about India (6.1.4), and to Alexander's possible desire to see his mother again (mentioned in a speech attributed to Coenus as an incentive for Alexander to turn back; 5.27.7). These last three references recall material in the *Romance*.[18]

Arrian, however, also provides an account of Olympias' quarrel with Antipater and its connection to Alexander's decision to replace him (7.12.5–7), which, despite its obvious gender stereotyping and implausible political analysis, offers more details than any other source about what Olympias and Antipater actually said about each other (see discussion in Chapter 3). Arrian insists that Alexander did or said nothing to indicate that he did not hold Antipater in as high regard as before—then, unfortunately, there is a lacuna in the manuscript (7.12.5–7). Despite Arrian's apologetic analysis, his comparatively detailed discussion of the famous quarrel (based, one suspects, on Ptolemy's somewhat sanitized version) portrays a difficult but powerful Olympias whose influence has come to surpass Antipater's.

Plutarch, unlike the other authors so far discussed, did not conceive of his works as historical writing. As he himself said, he wrote "lives not history" (*Alex*. 1.2), the famous collection of "parallel" lives of famous Greeks and Romans. He also wrote a series of essays on a great variety of topics, collectively known as the *Moralia* (each essay has an individual title as well). Plutarch, a native of Chaeroneia in central Greece, was roughly contemporary with Arrian. Like Arrian, he was well educated and had friends in high Roman places. He may also have resembled Arrian in holding consular rank and in functioning as a governor, but this is debatable.[19] However, Plutarch and Arrian were certainly two of the stars of the Second Sophistic.

Plutarch, more than any other ancient author, shaped the standard negative image of Olympias found in so many secondary works, but that has happened largely because generations of scholars have privileged his biography of Alexander over the testimony of his essays.[20] Plutarch filled that biography with references to Olympias, most of them substantial in nature, and the great majority of them extremely negative.[21] Olympias fascinates as well as repels Plutarch and so he simply discusses her more than do other authors. Moreover, with his focus on character and therefore on the youth of the subjects of his lives, the scope and structure of his biographies inevitably required more discussion of parents and family. Plutarch also frequently includes stories and information about Olympias in his many essays. Surprisingly, however, in the *Moralia*, he paints a much more flattering picture of her, one so different as to be nearly unrecognizable as the same character described by the same author in his biography of Alexander.[22]

Plutarch's *Alexander* tells us more about Olympias' early life and the period of her marriage than the work of any other author: how she and Philip met, her dreams of her son's future greatness, the story of the sexy snake so off-putting to Philip, her religious activities and their extreme nature, her possible but doubted role in the story of Alexander's divine birth, and the fact that Alexander's early tutor was her kinsman (*Alex*. 2.1–2, 4–6, 3.2, 5.4). Despite his dislike of Olympias' religiosity, Plutarch does not make her the villain of the story until he turns to the period at the end of Philip's reign. Though he does concede that Philip's marriages and affairs caused upsets in his *oikos*, creating a situation that generated problems between the king and Alexander, he claims that Olympias made it worse because of her bad personal character (*Alex*. 9.3). The rest of Plutarch's account of Olympias' actions during Philip's life largely confirms this picture of her as a troublemaker: she is involved in convincing Alexander to intervene in the marriage planned for his half-brother and she incites Philip's assassin to act (*Alex*. 10.1, 4). Plutarch does, however, blame Attalus and Cleopatra (*Alex*. 10.4) for Pausanias' rape, and Attalus alone (*Alex*. 9.4) for the quarrel that leads to Alexander and Olympias' self-imposed exile.

Plutarch continues to portray Olympias as a source of trouble during her son's reign, usually insisting that Alexander dutifully honored her (*Alex.* 25.4, 39.7) but did not allow her to lead him into bad acts or let her meddle in public or military affairs (*Alex.* 10.4, 39.7). The final sections of the biography highlight Olympias' continued troublemaking: she invents (he implies) the story of the involvement of Antipater's clan in Alexander's death years after the fact, using it to excuse her own brutal acts, and Plutarch reveals that Philip Arrhidaeus' mental problems were the consequence of Olympias' drugs or potions (*Alex.* 77.1, 5). He does include one story about Olympias that seems more admirable: she worries that her son's generosity will impoverish him (*Alex.* 39.5). And he clearly involves Olympias in Alexander's claim of divine sonship, though he does not offer any view on whether it was her idea or not (*Alex.* 3.2). Some of the information Plutarch provides clearly contradicts his insistence that Alexander allowed his mother no influence: Alexander kept her letters secret, was affected by her complaints against Antipater, and did nothing to stop the faction his mother and sister had formed against Antipater, merely commenting on which had made the better choice (*Alex.* 39.5, 7, 68.3).[23]

Although the image of Olympias Plutarch creates in the *Moralia* shares some traits with that in the *Alexander*, the overlap is comparatively narrow. In both the *Alexander* (39.5) and the *Moralia* (180d, 333a, 340a), Alexander allows Hephaestion to read secret correspondence from Olympias, sealing his friend's lips, but in one of the *Moralia* passages (180d) the contents of the latter are specifically said to contain charges against Antipater. In both works, Plutarch recounts (*Alex.* 3.4–5; *Mor.* 105b) the story that Philip hears three good things at the same time, the last being that Olympias has borne him a son. Plutarch provides the information about Olympias' name-changes in the *Moralia* (401b) alone, but this contradicts nothing in the *Alexander*.

Perhaps the most striking example of the difference in treatment of Olympias in the two works is an incident mentioned in both, but differently treated. In the *Alexander* (9.4), Plutarch does not involve Olympias directly in the quarrel or the subsequent reconciliation: he specifies that Attalus caused the quarrel between himself, Alexander, and Philip at the wedding and he has Demaratus blame Philip for the discord in his *oikos*, thus leading Philip to persuade his son to return (*Alex.* 9.6). Nonetheless, since this account was immediately preceded by Plutarch's description of Olympias' difficult character and its tendency to worsen tensions between father and son (9.3) Plutarch strongly implies that Olympias' manipulation of her son's fears was the ultimate, if indirect, cause of the quarrel. In the *Moralia*, Olympias' involvement in the quarrel and reconciliation is described as direct. Plutarch says that Philip's wife and son had quarreled with him, and reports that Demaratus convinced Philip to reconcile with *both* of them. (Many scholars ignore the second passage in favor of the first, for reasons not usually discussed.) Whereas one story implied that the entire incident was really

Olympias' fault[24] (though she was not present) and mentioned only the reconciliation of father and son, the other made no such implication and specified
that the reconciliation included both.

The essays include three incidents not mentioned in the *Alexander* that
portray Olympias and her relationships in a more favorable way and characterize her in a manner that is at odds with the representation in the biography.
One story (*Mor.* 141b–c) begins with Olympias acting in what appears to
be a heavy-handed way but concludes by projecting a very different picture.
Philip's erotic interest in a Thessalian woman had led to charges that she had
gained his interest by means of *pharmakon* (drug or spell; see Chapters
2 and 5) and Olympias therefore quickly acts to gain control of the woman.
However, once she meets and speaks to the woman, notes her good appearance, and realizes that she lacked neither good birth nor wit, Olympias
remarks that the false accusations should be forgotten and comments that
the woman is herself the *pharmakon*. Plutarch proceeds to comment on what
a good model for a wife this behavior is.[25]

Elsewhere in the essays Plutarch portrays Olympias as a model mother too.
Making the point that individuals exemplify various virtues in different ways,
he mentions (*Mor.* 243d) the variety of exempla offered by several pairs
of people with similar admirable traits. He specifies that Cornelia (the
proverbially virtuous and self-sacrificing mother of the Gracchi) was not high
minded in exactly the same way as was Olympias.

Perhaps most remarkable of all is a passage (*Mor.* 799e) that praises the
Athenians because, having intercepted Philip's mail, they did not break the
seal of a letter addressed from Philip to Olympias, thus choosing not to
publicize a private message from an absent husband to his affectionate wife.
These stories depict a very different woman from the difficult troublemaker
of the *Alexander* and a very different royal marriage from the one presented
there.[26]

While I would agree with the view that Plutarch generally was uncomfortable with aggressive and politically active women unless he could understand
them as acting in this fashion in support of (rather than manipulating)
male kin or some larger community,[27] such generalizations do not explain
the differences noted between the representations of Olympias in both of
Plutarch's works. Indeed, the depiction of women in general and Olympias
in particular, which is the basis for these generalizations, derives largely or
entirely from Plutarch's Lives. Obviously, Plutarch's beliefs did not change
from one genre of work to another, but something else must have. Moreover,
as the differences in the depiction of Olympias in the two kinds of work
indicate, the issue is not so much what Olympias' personal and character
traits were in any absolute way, but rather how Plutarch chose to understand
and describe them. He chose to represent the jealous virago of one work as
the charmingly complacent (to Plutarch anyway) wife of the other.

The reasons for the dramatically different portrayals of Olympias in
Plutarch's works are probably multiple. Certainly one reason Olympias is so

unpleasant in the biography is that Plutarch employs her character, and to some degree that of Philip, as a foil for that of Alexander; they make him look good by being bad. Plutarch tries to palm off on Olympias bad or unattractive features of Alexander.[28] Many (though hardly all) of the unpleasant stories about Olympias in the *Alexander* are prefaced by words or phrases translatable as "it is said," "the story is," or something similar,[29] or Plutarch may attribute them to another source without offering his own views on the veracity of the source.[30] Whether or not Plutarch intended to distance himself from testimony he considered dubious but entertaining by employing such terms,[31] most readers fail to notice the specifics of his diction and simply understand that he has stated such and such. Of course, each essay in the *Moralia* has its own agenda, often quite a different one from that in the *Alexander*.

Pausanias, another Greek author of the Second Sophistic era, composed a multi-volume description of Greece and its monuments that contains material about Olympias, small in quantity but of considerable importance,[32] much of it information found nowhere else. Though the foundations of the Philippeum have endured, it is only because of Pausanias (5.17.4, 20.9–10) that we know that the statues in the building included images of Olympias and her mother-in-law as well as those of Philip, his father Amyntas, and his son Alexander. Although Justin also reports that Olympias killed both Cleopatra and Cleopatra's baby (9.7.12), Pausanias, the only other author to accuse Olympias of the murder of mother and daughter in a clear manner, allots to them a uniquely awful death: Olympias dragged them on to a bronze vessel over a fire and so burned them to death (8.7.7). Pausanias also provides much of what we know about the dynasty of Olympias' birth and her role in it: he mentions but disputes information about the violation of Molossian royal tombs by Lysimachus (1.9.8), the revolution caused by Aeacides' attempt to help Olympias (1.11.3–7), her return to Macedonia from Epirus (1.25.4), the later history and sad end of the Aeacid dynasty in Epirus (4.35.3–5), Olympias' death at the hands of Cassander, and the subsequent tragic end of the house of Antipater and Cassander, punishment, he says, for Cassander's treatment of Alexander's kin (9.7.2–3). Pausanias' reputation for accuracy is not high, but his generally hostile portrait of Olympias and her family may arise from blaming the decline of Greece (and therefore Roman conquest) on Philip and the Macedonians.[33] Pausanias, nonetheless, seems unusually well informed about Aeacid politics, if hostile to the dynasty until it neared its end. He must have had a Molossian or Epirote source, apparently one unsympathetic to the Aeacids in general and Olympias in particular.[34]

Many of our sources, even those otherwise critical of Olympias, admire and even focus on her physical bravery in the face of death. One should be aware that this was the expectation of royal women: Plutarch, for instance, otherwise portrays Cleopatra the Great as a barbaric, luxury-loving woman who corrupted Antony, but he saw (*Ant.* 85.4–8) her suicide (accomplished to prevent her enemy Octavian from marching her in his triumph) as proof that she was a true offspring of a royal clan.[35] Justin, as we have seen, makes a similar reversal about Olympias. Whereas in general it was bad for a woman to be man-like, it was not if bravery and a brave death were the issues. Then a woman was living up to the standards of her male kin.[36] This expectation often leads to lengthy descriptions of death scenes, the details of which (for instance, Adea Eurydice's pious treatment of her husband's corpse or Olympias' wearing of royal garb and accompaniment by maids) may be suspect.

Recognition, however, that aspects of these female heroic deaths suggest artifice does not lead inevitably to the conclusion that the accounts are not historical, perhaps even in their seemingly improbable details. Just as we recognize that epic and tragedy affected ancient writers' values but were also employed by them,[37] it is important to recognize that women like Olympias and Adea Eurydice used and were used in a similar way by Homer and the tragic writers. As each faced death, the models for behavior in this circumstance were present in Homer and, especially, in tragedy. While we have more information about how Alexander shaped his own public presentation, we should not forget that Olympias and other publicly active women may have done the same. Surely, as her murderers approached, Olympias knew that the Argead house was dying. She may have gone to her death playing the tragic queen she really had become.

I have already commented on the comparative paucity of material, other than highly personalized anecdote, that deals with Olympias' life during her son's reign. It is important to realize that we would not know that she did, in fact, play a meaningful public role during her son's reign if a contemporary inscription and speech had not survived. Olympias' double appearance on a list as the recipient of grain from Cyrene, in a form suggesting she was functioning as the head of a large state (*SEG* IX 2), and Hyperides' repeated allusions to her power, alone and in association with the Macedonians (Hyp. *Eux.* 19–20, 25), provide otherwise unknown material demonstrating that she did more than harass her son by letter. Another inscription tells us that she asked the authorities at Delphi to turn Persian loot she controlled into gold crowns for Apollo (*SIG* I 252N. 5ff). While literary sources did inform us that Alexander had sent his mother plunder, only the inscription reveals what she chose to do with it (see Chapter 3).

Currently, no securely identified contemporary image of Olympias is known. As we have seen, the only physical images we can be certain were intended to represent her were produced many centuries after her death. As such, they may tell us something about her reception in Roman times but not about her public image in her own day. Should this situation change— for instance, should a coin or some other object appear that reproduced the statues in the Philippeum—we might learn a great deal.

This brief survey of Olympias' varying fate in the extant sources should convince the reader of two things. Characterizations of Olympias' personality cannot be treated as objective fact, no matter how appealing the anecdote in which they are imbedded. More specifically, Plutarch's characterization of Olympias in his *Alexander* is no more or less reliable than the quite different image of her he offers in his essays. Neither can function as a dependable basis for evaluating her career or policies. That said, the few surviving contemporary inscriptions and speeches relevant to Olympias' life become vital sources in themselves as well as important correctives to material from narrative sources.

List of terms

Aeacid Royal house of Molossia, the descendants of Aeacus.

Alexander Romance A historical novel about Alexander that developed in antiquity and endured in a plethora of forms until the Renaissance.

Argead Royal house of Macedonia, the descendants of Argeas (also known as the Temenids).

basileia Kingdom or monarchy.

contorniate Roman cast medallions, fourth to fifth century CE, possibly connected to the games.

epitome Shortened, summary version of a literary work.

Hetairos (Pl. *Hetairoi*) Companion (later called *Philoi*), a member of the group of elite men who traditionally accompanied and served (personally, administratively, militarily) the Macedonian king. Ordinarily there would have been a small inner circle within the larger group. The term is also applied collectively to an even larger body, the Macedonian cavalry.

Hypaspist A member of the king's personal foot guard, an elite infantry unit within the Macedonian army.

maenad A female worshiper of Dionysus, usually assumed to be inspired to ritual frenzy.

oikos The household, the house, a royal house.

philia Friendship and affection, including formal and informal good relations between states and/or individuals.

Philos (Pl. *Philoi*) Friends, family members, those with whom one has good relations, possibly of a formal sort. In Hellenistic times, this term was used instead of *Hetairos*.

polis (Pl. *poleis*) City-state, often refers to the public community of citizens.

Royal Youths (Sometimes called Pages) Elite youths under (roughly) eighteen who served and guarded the king. They accompanied him on the hunt and in battle.

Somatophulax Bodyguard, ordinarily Macedonian kings' seven bodyguards, typically their closest associates. Occasionally ancient authors apply the term to other groups that guarded the king.

Successors (*Diadochoi*) The generals of Alexander who contended for control of his empire after his death. Many became kings.

timé Honor, often external in nature, signifying the esteem of others.

xenia Ritualized friendship or guest friendship, a bond between people belonging to separate *poleis* or communities.

Notes

1 Olympias the Molossian

1 Cross 1932: 9, followed by Heckel 1981b: 80. The degree of Hellenization of Molossia outside the royal family is debatable; see Whitley 2001: 400.

2 Some (Cross 1932: 6–8, 100–2; Hammond 1967: 490; Ameling 1988: 663) believe (on the basis of Pind. *Nem*. 7.64–6) that Pindar was a Molossian *proxenos* (formal friend in Thebes of the Molossian state) and that he referred to the descent of Molossian kings from Neoptolemus; others (Perret 1946: 8–11; Woodbury 1979: 121–3) reject it. Heckel 1981b: 80–1, ns. 9 and 10, though recognizing evidentiary problems, argues convincingly that it is likely the genealogy goes back to Pindar.

3 Plut. *Pyrrh*. 1.3 asserts that Achilles received cult in Epirus under the cult name "Aspetus."

4 Hammond 1967: 505, citing Athenian desire for Molossian alliance and interest in flattering the king Tharyps, then present or recently present in Athens. See Robertson 1923; Perret 1946.

5 Hammond 1967: 505 thinks that Euripides may have invented Andromache's marriage to Helenus.

6 Heckel 1981b: 82.

7 Homer more often calls the most notorious son of Priam "Alexandros" than he does "Paris." "Troas" replicates the name of Priam's city, Troy. See below for the likelihood that Olympias' earliest name was Polyxena, the name of a daughter of Priam.

8 Klotzsch 1911: 54–5; Cross 1932: 32 is non-committal; Macurdy 1932a: 23 considered the suggestion possible whereas Heckel 1981b: 81, Ameling 1988: 663, and Mortensen 1997: 5 take it as a certainty. However, an inscription from Epidaurus (*IG* IV² 1.122 *iama* 31) complicates the matter. It refers to a woman named Andromacha, married to a man named Arybbas. (See further discussion of this inscription below.) Tod 1948: 2.217, following Dittenberger, the original editor of the inscription, thinks that her husband was an Aeacid but does not consider the possibility that he was the king himself. Klotzsch 1911: 229 considers it likely that the inscription refers to the king. Assuming that this Andromacha was a royal wife, her "Trojan" name could mean one of several things: Arybbas and Neoptolemus both married members of the Chaonian royal house, possibly sisters; a Chaonian marriage had occurred earlier and this generation chose to emphasize genealogy by name choice, just as the Aeacids claimed descent from Achilles long before they chose names suggesting that descent; Andromacha was, like Troas, an Aeacid by birth as well as by marriage.

9 Perret 1946: 5.

10 Ameling 1988: 658, 664. Many authors refer to Alexander's Aeacid origins, suggesting that he, like his mother, stressed them: Arr. 4.11.6; Paus. 1.9.10; Vell. 1.6.5; Curt. 8.4.26; Plut. *Alex.* 2.1; Diod. 17.1.5. Arrian (1.11.8) even reports a story which has Alexander sacrificing at the tomb of Priam, asking for him not to be angry at the *genos* (clan or house) of Neoptolemus, of which he was the descendant. Greek focus on the male line of descent is normal; Alexander's apparent stress on his maternal descent is unusual.

11 Ameling 1988: 664.

12 See Carney 2000a: 275–6 and Ameling 1988 for references and discussion.

13 See discussion of the actions of Olympias and other royal women as possibly influenced by Greek literature, particularly Greek tragedy in Carney 1993a: 315–16 and Carney 1993b: 51–4.

14 Mortensen 1997: 25 suggests the character of Polyxena in *Hecuba* as a model.

15 Demand's discussion of recent women's and gender studies in the Greek world (Demand 2002: 31–41) prefers the earlier scholarship to more recent work which she is inclined to see to some degree as apologetic for Athenian democracy and anti-feminist. In my view, Pomeroy's association of the subordination of women and the development of democracy (Pomeroy 1975: 78) remains persuasive. Like Demand, I find much recent work too rosy on the situation of women. The reaction of Greek writers to Olympias (see Carney 1993b: 33–4) makes only too clear how powerful the polarity paradigm remained for centuries. However, I also value the recognition that public and private, *polis* and *oikos*, were not always antagonistic opposites (e.g., Foxhall 1989: 22–43), that what people said was not always what they did, and that women need to be understood as actors and negotiators within the system (e.g., Goldberg 1999: 146).

16 For instance, recent work has demonstrated that the *gunaikonitis* (women's place) so frequently mentioned by Greek writers was not, as was previously assumed, a physical place but rather an idea (Morgan 1985; Jameson 1990; Nevett 1995; Goldberg 1999: 149–58). Similarly, statements that women were unseen even by male kin (Lys. 3.6–7) were taken too literally (Cohen 1989).

17 Carney 1993a: 315–18.

18 Variants of the tale appear in Diod. 11.56.1–3; Plut. *Them.* 24.1–3; Nep. *Them.* 7; Stesimbrotus *FGrH* 107 F 3. As Hammond (1967: 493) notes, "Phthia" is the name of at least two Aeacid women. Hammond seems to consider the story historical, but Woodbury 1979: 122 is less certain.

19 Dillon 1997: 185.

20 See discussion in Carney 2000c: 35–7. Both Molossia and Macedonia were more Hellenized by the time documents indicating the legal and social circumstance of ordinary women are available, but this probably means that it is significant that Macedonian documents indicate that women's legal situation was much like that of their southern Greek sisters (Pomeroy 1984: 3; Tataki 1988: 433). On the other hand, Hammond (1989: 5) is probably right to conclude that women's lives were somewhat less narrowly circumscribed in Macedonia than in the south.

21 See Cabanes 1976: 407–13; 1980: 329, 333, who connects the comparative independence of Molossian women to the nature of Molossian society, particularly to pastoral transhumance. The absence of a *kurios* (guardian) is particularly striking (see Cabanes 1976: 412, especially n. 45). While the Buthrotum documents Cabanes discusses date to the third and second centuries, the inscriptions discussed below are much earlier, yet suggest a similar situation.

22 As is demonstrated by an inscription (*SEG* XV 384) dated to the reign of Olympias' father Neoptolemus. Harvey 1969: 228 suggests that one grant is given to a widow, the other to a woman with a living husband. While these

grants are doubtless honorific for some circumstance unknown to us, Harvey rightly notes (1969: 228–9) that they clearly honor the women, not their sons or husbands. See also Larsen 1964 and 1967.

23 Carney 2000c: 28. Recently, based on archaeological evidence from Macedonia, some scholars have entertained the idea of a larger role in drinking for elite Macedonian women, despite contradictory literary evidence. Female burials do not typically include the sets of banqueting vessels so commonly found in male burials, but Hoepfner (Hoepfner 1996: 13–15) has suggested that the double *andron* (dining-room) pattern found in the palace at Vergina/Aegae, private houses at Pella, and elsewhere may have been intended for separate but parallel male and female *symposia*. The "Palmette Tomb" at Lefkadia may signify that elite Macedonian women sometimes banqueted with men (Rhomiopoulou 1973: 90). Kottaridi 2004a: 140 and 2004b: 69 and Lilibaki-Akamati 2004: 91 believe, based on an elaborate late Archaic female burial at Aegae and other such burials of the period (the presumption is that these are the graves of royal women), that such royal women were priestesses who, among other things, participated in public banquets and *symposia*. In terms of Molossia, Plutarch (*Pyrrh.* 5.5–6) refers to a komos (revel or band of revelers) at the house of Cadmeia attended by her brother Neoptolemus, apparently herself and at least one other respectable woman. Cadmeia and Neoptolemus were Aeacids, probably Olympias' grandchildren (see Chapter 4). The evidence, such as it is, supports the notion that such Macedonian women engaged in *symposia* more than it does the idea that they attended mixed *symposia*.

24 See Carney 2000c: 29, n. 113 for references.
25 Cole 1981: 230, followed by Carney 2000c: 29.
26 Pomeroy 1977: 61; Cole 1981: 230; Carney 2000c: 29.
27 Carney 2000a: 29.
28 On the variability of southern Greek perceptions of Epirote ethnicity, see Malkin 2001.
29 Hammond 1967: 1–45; Cabanes 1980: 328–9.
30 Lévêque 1957: 92–3.
31 Lévêque 1957: 91.
32 Hammond 1967: 510 notes growing signs of wealth in late fifth and fourth-century graves and in the archaeological remains from Dodona.
33 For instance, an Athenian decree re-granted citizenship to Arybbas and his descendants. Moreover, Arybbas may have won two Olympic victories and one Pythian victory, apparently in the chariot race (Tod *GHI* 2. 173, l. 48). Panhellenic competition in chariot racing was literally the sport of kings.
34 Strabo 7.7.11 says that Dodona was originally controlled by the Thesprotians, not the Molossians (see Hammond 1967: 453, 491); if so, Dodona cannot have been the original seat of the Molossian kings. Decrees of the Molossian state set up at Dodona in the fourth century (Hammond 1967: 525–30) suggest that it did become some sort of central seat of government. Later Pyrrhus made Passaron (modern Arta) his capital (Cabanes 1980: 345), but it was a Corinthian foundation and did not even pass into Aeacid control until 294 BCE.
35 Three authors, all of Roman date, are the major narrative sources: Pausanias 1.11.2–5, 4.35.3–5; Plutarch *Pyrrh.* 1.1–3.3; Justin 17.3.1–21. This is not an impressive list. Pausanias' reputation in terms of accuracy is poor, his sources uncertain, and his material often overtly hostile to Olympias and other members of her dynasty. See Habicht 1998: 95–109 and Carney 1993b: 37, n. 21. Justin, the epitomator of an earlier Roman history, has an equally poor reputation for dependability and his florid account is also often hostile to

Olympias. Plutarch, the great biographer, is generally a much more creditable source, but the passage in question is simply a quick summary of the Aeacid past and present, written to put the career of Pyrrhus, Olympias' great-nephew and the best known of Molossian kings, in context. See further discussion of these authors in the Appendix.

36 For instance, Just. 17.3.16 calls Aeacides the brother of Alexander (I), thus making him the son of Neoptolemus and brother of Olympias whereas Plut. *Pyrrh*.1.3 calls him (correctly) the son of Arybbas and Troas. This identity problem becomes extreme in the period after the death of Alexander the Great; see below, Chapter 3.

37 The incident, if historical (see above), would date to *c*. 470 BCE

38 Cross 1932: dated his reign to *c*. 440–*c*. 400, but Franke 1954 to *c*. 430–385. Heckel 1981b: 81, n. 11 suggests that he is the same man said to have been the lover of Menon of Pharsalus (Xen. *Anab*. 2.6.28); see Chapter 2.

39 Hammond 1967: 508 points out that the earliest-known inscribed Molossian decrees date to *c*. 370, though the institutions they describe may have developed earlier.

40 See Hammond 1967: 525–6 for discussion of a Dodonian decree dated between 370 and 368 that lists only Neoptolemus, son of Alcetas, as king.

41 Pausanias 1.11.3 says that Molossian monarchy was unified through the reign of Alcetas, but that his sons, having first formed factions against each other, then changed their minds and ruled equally, each abiding by the agreement. Granted that only Neoptolemus' name follows his father's on the list of Athenian allies, the co-reign would appear to have been a subsequent development.

42 Heskel 1988: 194 suggests *c*. 361.

43 Cross 1932: 15 may go too far in describing it as a kind of hereditary "magistracy" but he is right to point out that the neighboring Chaonians actually did turn their monarchy into a kind of magistracy (two members of the royal house chosen annually). Hammond 1967: 549 notes that the Molossian kings had no power to coin in their own names (Alexander I did, but only during his Italian campaign).

44 Cross 1932:16; Cabanes 1980: 342–4, who assumes the chief magistrate (called a *prostates*) was elected and meant to defend the interests of the common people against the king. Just. 17.3.12 mentions a *"senatus,"* presumably some sort of council, perhaps made up of tribal representatives, in connection with the reforms of Tharyps. Hammond 1967: 528 cites inscriptions showing changes.

45 Cabanes 1980: 341 asserts that the exchange of oaths signified that a king who broke his oath could be overthrown, citing Diod. 19.36.4 and Plut. *Pyrrh* 4. The Diodorus passage, however, describes the overthrow of Aeacides by one faction while another was absent on campaign with him. Though Diodorus does refer to a public decree of expulsion, he goes on to say that such a thing had never happened before. The Plutarch passage describes the expulsion of Pyrrhus by a faction, but again lacks a clear legal or constitutional context. See further Chapter 6.

46 Cross 1932: 32 dates Molossian acquisition of coastline to *c*. 373, when the Molossian king Alcetas was able to help the Athenians move foot soldiers from the coast to Corcyra (Xen. *Hell*. 6.2.10); Hammond 1967: 523 dates the acquisition of coastal territory to *c*. 380–60.

47 Mortensen 1997: 15.

48 Paus. 1.11.3 reports that Arybbas and Neoptolemus, the sons of Alcetas, contended for power at one point. He tells us (1.11.5) that Arybbas expelled his older son, Alcetas, in favor of his younger one, Aeacides; after the death of

Aeacides, Alcetas briefly took power only to be murdered (along with his children) and replaced by Aeacides' son Pyrrhus. The identity of the Aeacids who then contended against Pyrrhus is under dispute (see Chapter 3) but they were probably descendants of different royal brothers.

49 So Ogden 1999: ix–xxxiv.

50 Cross 1932, followed by Lévêque 1957: 102, thinks Arybbas' sons were by different mothers. They could well have been. Plut. *Pyrrh.* 1.3 says that Aeacides was the son of Arybbas and Troas. This is confirmed by the fact that Justin 7.6.11 says Arybbas was married to Troas, daughter of Neoptolemus and sister of Olympias and strongly suggested by the fact that one of Aeacides' daughters was named Troas (Plut. *Pyrrh.* 1.4), as Herzog 1931: 73 observed. Alcetas was probably not Troas' son. Pausanias 1.11.5 says merely that Alcetas was the older of Arybbas' two sons and not his father's favorite. It is likely, however, that Arybbas had married before his marriage to Troas, granted that he and Troas were a generation apart in age. If the Andromacha of Epirus, wife of Arybbas, who made a trip to Epidaurus, was indeed the wife of Arybbas the king (see above, n. 8), then she was probably the earlier wife (*contra* Klotzsch 1911: 229 who forgets the testimony of Plutarch (*Pyrrh.* 1.3)). Herzog 1931: 73–4 argued that Andromacha and Troas were one and the same person. Olympias and other Macedonian royal women were known by different royal names, but my view is that one should assume that women referred to by different names are in fact the same woman only when an ancient source indicates that they were known by more than one name, as in the case of Olympias (see Carney 2000c: 33, n. 133). Dillon (1997: 185, 189; 2002: 30) assumes that the husband of Andromacha is King Arybbas. The most reasonable conclusion is that Andromacha was an earlier wife of Arybbas and that she had a son who could have been Alcetas, but could also have been a child who died young.

51 For instance, Reuss 1881: 161, referring to the fact that Neoptolemus' name follows his father's on the document that lists them as members of the Second Athenian confederacy, assumes that Neoptolemus must have been the older brother whereas he may, in fact, simply have been the more favored.

52 Arybbas and Neoptolemus, as we have noted, ultimately shared rule (Paus. 1.11.3) and Pyrrhus briefly shared power with another Aeacid named Neoptolemus (Plut. *Pyrrh* 5.1). Alcetas, son of Tharyps, was expelled (Diod. 15.13.1–3). Arybbas was expelled, as was his son Aeacides (Just. 17.3.17), as was *his* son Pyrrhus (Plut. *Pyrrh.* 4.1).

53 Parallels are often made between the two kingdoms and peoples: see Cross 1932: 24; Hatzopoulos 2003: 51–64.

54 Archaeology offers examples over centuries of similarities in material culture and trade between the two regions. For instance, Hammond 1967: 401 notes considerable similarity in the tumulus burials of northern Epirus and of Vergina in Macedonia in the Iron Age.

55 Dell 1970: 116.

56 Cabanes 1980: 347–9, citing the reign of Philip as a turning point.

57 Greenwalt 1988a.

58 Though some historians reject the erotic part of the tale, they accept the idea of a Samothracian betrothal. Cole 1984: 17, n. 127, however, implausibly rejects it as a literary cliché based on the need to explain how the supposedly secluded Greek woman could meet a male. As already discussed, women were frequently publicly active in cult areas. Moreover, Plutarch's account (*Alex* 2.1) specifically mentions Arybbas' consent and so presumed presence.

59 See Carney 1992a: 170, n. 3 for references to Greek marital practice and to that of Philip.

60 Mortensen 1997: 23, ns. 138 and 139, rightly notes that, even in later periods, most of the cult's visitors came from the northern Aegean, not central Greece, and that though sailors might constitute something of an exception, the Molossian royal family had no connection to any seagoing tradition. See further Chapter 5.

61 Griffith 1979: 215; Errington 1975b: 49; Mortensen 1997: 6.

62 Mortensen 1997: 8 notes that Macedonia was clearly better placed to give aid against the Illyrians than the Athenians, later certainly allies of Arybbas.

63 Hammond 1967: 533; Mortensen 1997: 6. Mortensen puts this effort in the broader context of Philip's attempts to stabilize the borders of Macedonia, as did earlier his marriage alliances. Whether the Illyrian incursion into Molossia came before or after Philip's defeat of Illyrian forces is uncertain; see Mortensen 1997: 7.

64 Satyrus (*ap.* Athen. 557c) asserted that Philip's marriage to Olympias brought him the Molossian kingdom. Literally this cannot have been true since Arybbas remained king for some years yet (see Chapter 2). Reuss 1881: 162 doubts, despite the remark of Satyrus, that her marriage brought with it any Molossian territory. Griffith 1979: 215 suggests that Olympias brought Orestis as part of her dowry. No ancient source confirms this. See Mortensen 1997: 12 for arguments against this suggestion. Ellis 1976: 61–2 suggests that Philip's primary motivation for the Molossian alliance was to prevent the possibility of the Molossians returning to their traditional Athenian alliance. Bosworth 1971b: 104 argues that the marriage was meant to conciliate Upper Macedonia.

65 Cabanes 1976: 101; Carney 1987a: 41 terms the marriage the initial move in Philip's "plan" to control Molossia. While Mortensen 1997: 8, n. 37 rightly doubts that there literally was a formal plan, the pattern is similar to the series of actions that led to Philip's domination of Greece and equally difficult to pinpoint when potential became plan.

66 Lane Fox 1973: 44; Cole 1984: 16–17. Mortensen 1997: 19–22 argues that Argead patronage began a few years earlier, in the reign of Philip's brother Perdiccas III, surmising that Philip may have completed his brother's projects. See further discussion in Chapter 5. For our purposes, the relevant point is that this was a shrine recently developed under Argead patronage.

67 Mortensen 1997: 23. Apart from the difficulty for Molossians to reach the island sanctuary, one must also note that it focused on providing safety for those who traveled by sea (not much of a Molossian problem) and that it was, even much later, largely patronized by peoples of the northern Aegean.

68 *Contra* Mortensen 1997: 89.

69 Mortensen 1997: 24.

70 Cole 1984: 21, 39–40. Mortensen 1997: 24, n. 147 argues that *FGrH* 70 F 120 does not demonstrate that the festival was held before Hellenistic times, but, of course, this does not mean that it was not. See Clinton 2003: 50–78, especially 67–8.

71 Cleopatra, sister of Alexander the Great and widow of Alexander of Molossia, acted as her own marriage broker and also worked in concert with her mother; Cynnane, half-sister of Alexander the Great and widow of his cousin Amyntas, expressed the desire not to remarry (which Alexander apparently rejected) and gave her life in an attempt to bring about the marriage of her daughter Adea Eurydice to Philip Arrhidaeus. Hellenistic examples of royal widows brokering or attempting to broker marriage alliances can also be found. See Carney 2000c: 21, 123–7, 129–31).

72 Mortensen 1997: 15.

73 As we shall see in Chapter 2, Philip already had several wives and may already

have had two children, one of them male. Mortensen 1997: 15 believes that Arybbas would have negotiated from a position of greater strength than the guardians of Philip's other wives. This could be true, but the order and circumstances of all Philip's marriages are so controversial (see Chapter 2 and Carney 2000c: 52–7) that certainty or even probability is difficult.

74 *IG* IV² 1.122 *iama* 31; see discussion above, especially in n. 8 and in Dillon 1997: 185, 189 and 2002: 30.

75 See Chapter 2 for a discussion of the factors that affected the status of a royal wife when her husband had many wives.

76 See general discussion and references in Carney 2000c: 18–23.

77 See Blundell 1995: 119–28.

78 As Mortensen 1997: 30, n. 189 observed, Plutarch seems to regard these as nicknames or epithets, not genuine name-changes. Pomeroy 1984: 10 seems to agree, whereas Heckel 1981b: 82 understands them as actual changes in name. Plutarch's terminology, *paronomia*, seems to support the views of Pomeroy and Mortensen rather than that of Heckel.

79 Heckel 1981b: 79, followed by Mortensen 1997: 25–35.

80 Carney 1991a; 2000c: 32–4

81 Heckel 1981b: 80–2 connects it to Aeacid claims of descent from Achilles via Neoptolemus, pointing out that Polyxena was connected to Neoptolemus in myth (Eur. *Tro.* 260 ff., *Hec.* 218ff., 521ff.). Mortensen 1997: 25, noting that the mythic connection was a grim one (Neoptolemus murdered Polyxena) suggests that the name choice may reflect the heroic character of Polyxena in Euripides' *Hecuba* and that it may have been a common name in the Chaonian dynasty.

82 Mortensen 1997: 26–9 prefers to connect the name to a possible puberty rite in honor of Aphrodite. See further discussion on this issue in Chapter 5.

83 Milns 1968: 17. Heckel 1981b: 82–4 connects the name choice to her betrothal/initiation at Samothrace, making the rites a kind of *proteleia* (sacrifices offered before marriage) for her wedding. Pomeroy 1984: 10 believes that the name could have been taken on either occasion. See further discussion in Chapter 5.

84 Heckel 1981b: 85 (followed by Pomeroy 1984: 10; Mortensen 1997: 29) argues that it was not a "maiden name" since it was the last one listed by Plutarch, that it is unlikely that one young woman would have had three separate names in so brief a period, that it had no precedent within the Aeacid house (though it was known in the Argead house), and that it can be connected to a known event. Heckel suggested that she was remembered as "Olympias" because she died so soon after assuming this final name, before it became common usage.

85 Pomeroy 1984: 10.

86 No physical description of Olympias survives and all ancient images of her date from many centuries after her life and are highly idealized (see Chapter 6). One could take it as suggestive that her son was fair skinned, with a somewhat ruddy tone (Plut. *Alex.* 4.2) and supposedly not particularly tall (Arr. 2. 12. 6).

87 Mortensen 1997: 36 argues that Olympias would not have expected so distant a marriage because there is little reason to think earlier Aeacid brides had traveled so far.

88 Mortensen 1997: 36 speculates that the children of Neoptolemus would not have liked their uncle Arybbas because he had "semi-usurped their father's throne." Moreover, we do not know if Olympias was close to her sister and brother (though subsequent events might imply that she was: see Chapter 2 for her dealings with her brother and Chapter 4 for the extraordinary loyalty her

sister's son Aeacides demonstrated to her) or whether her mother was still alive. On mother–daughter ties, see discussion in Chapter 2.

2 Olympias, wife of Philip II

1   On Philip's reign, see Ellis 1976 and Cawkwell 1978. On general Macedonian history in this period, see Hammond and Griffith 1979 and Errington 1990.
2   On the developing nature of Macedonian monarchy and institutions, see Borza 1992.
3   See recent discussion and references in Heckel 2003: 205–6. Carney 1981: 227–8 rejects the term "Page."
4   My description of Macedonian monarchy is in accord with the currently dominant view, but until comparatively recently scholars understood Macedonian monarchy in more constitutional terms and some continue to do so. See Borza 1990: 231–48 for discussion and references on this controversy and for his conclusions.
5   Borza 1990: 166–71.
6   See Greenwalt 1989: 22–28; Carney 2000c: 23.
7   On this passage, see the discussion of Tronson 1984: 116–26. He argues that the list is chronological, that the "*kata polemon*" (in connection with a war) observation is Athenaeus' not Satyrus', that this is a list of wives not concubines. See Carney 2000c: 52–6 for a lengthier exposition of arguments given here; see also Ogden 1999: 17–20, who reaches similar conclusions. My translation of the Satyrus passage is nearly identical to that in Carney 2000c: 53.
8   Athenaeus wrote in the late second century CE and used the setting of a *symposium* to collect excerpts from a long list of earlier ancient authors on a variety of subjects. In many cases, these excerpts are all that remains of the authors' works. See further Baldwin 1976: 21–42; Hawley 1993: 73–91; Braund and Wilkins 2000. Satyrus the Peripatetic was active in the third century BCE and wrote a series of lives of famous men, now preserved only by citations from late Ancient authors like Athenaeus. Extant fragments imply that he was prone to gossip, sensationalism, and moralizing: see Tronson 1984: 117–18; Hawley 1993: 73–91.
9   Carney 2000c: 54, n. 9.
10 Tronson 1984: 121, followed by Carney 2000c: 55.
11 Carney 2000c: 55–6.
12 Some scholars assume that, since Nicesipolis was Pheraean, Philip could not have married her before 353 or 352 (so Ehrhardt 1967: 296–7; Griffith 1979: 677; Ellis 1981: 112, n. 16; Green 1982: 143). Tronson 1984: 122; Sawada 1993: 38, n. 98; Carney 2000c: 60–1 find an earlier date more likely. Martin 1982: 68–9 considers it possible.
13 Whether Olympias or Nicesipolis was his fifth wife, virtually all agree that Meda came next. Since the only known reference to Meda is the Satyrus passage, estimated dates for the marriage vary from 342 to 339. See references in Carney 2000c: 68, n. 69.
14 Apart from his own marriage to Cleopatra, Philip arranged the marriage of his daughter Cleopatra, tried to arrange the marriage of Arrhidaeus (see below), and probably arranged the marriage of his daughter Cynnane to his nephew Amyntas (the date of this marriage can only be estimated; see Carney 2000c: 69–70, 132).
15 See discussions and references to the marriage of each wife in Carney 2000c: 57–68.
16 For instance, Heckel 2003: 199, citing the statements of Satyrus in Athenaeus

(13.557e) and Plutarch (*Alex.* 9.4). However, Plutarch makes a similar claim about Philip's marriage to Olympias; in her case, we know enough about her family to realize that it is unlikely to have been true but the mystery of Attalus and Cleopatra's origins (see below) obscures the issue for the last marriage. See below for the argument that Philip married Cleopatra because Attalus was already important.

17   Carney 1991b.

18   See discussion in Ogden 1999: xiv–xix, xxvi–xxx, 3–5, 17–29.

19   See general discussion and references in Greenwalt 1989: 36–38; Carney 1991b: 154–72; Carney 2000c: 26–7; Mortensen 1999: 802.

20   On the absence of a clear pattern of succession, see Greenwalt 1989 *contra* Hatzopoulos 1986. Both Goody 1966: 25 and Stafford 1983: 173 point out that, world-wide, well-defined methods of choosing heirs to the throne are rare. Stafford links this truth to the importance of women in succession politics since struggles for the throne tend to enhance the importance of a mother to her son.

21   See discussion of factors affecting the status of wives in Ellis 1976: 213, 254, n. 96; Prestianni-Giallombardo 1976–7: 96; Greenwalt 1989: 25–6; Carney 1992a: 171–2; Mortensen 1999: 798–801; Carney 2000c: 25–7. Greenwalt 1989: 39–40 places greater emphasis on ethnicity as a factor than most other scholars.

22   See Demand 1994: 17 for discussion and references. Speaking of Greek marriage in general, she says, "In order to establish her position in her new family the bride had to produce a child, preferably a son. Only the birth of a child gave her full status as a *gyne*, woman-wife." See also Carney 1992a: 170, ns. 2 and 3.

23   Mortensen 1999: 803 observes that the king's sexual favor advantaged a wife in the production of heirs and so wives may have competed for his sexual favor. This, however, would only signify before the birth of children, particularly male children, and, of course, granted the vagaries of human fertility, even an unfavored wife might produce a son as the result of one sexual encounter with her husband whereas a wife the king found more attractive might, even after many such encounters, remain childless. The sexual favor of the king could also have been a factor in the status of childless wives. On fertility in polygamy, see further references in Carney 2000c: 25.

24   Two possible examples: Ptolemy's preference for the children of Berenice over the children of Eurydice or Lysimachus' developing preference for the children of Arsinoe over those of Nicaea. Even here one must consider that a preference for the children of a younger, more recent wife, means that a king bypasses for a longer period the awkwardness that Philip and other rulers experienced when their heirs neared or reached adulthood (see discussion in Lund 1994: 196–8; Fredricksmeyer 1990: 300–15; Carney 2000c: 174–5).

25   See Clignet 1970: 34, 41, 51 for discussion of similar situations in other cultures.

26   See Mortensen 1999: 801–5 and Clignet 1970: 30–1, 45, 52–3, who says that tensions in polygynous marriages decline when each wife is separately housed, the senior wife has distinctive privileges, and the duties and rights of each wife are clearly defined. My own view (see below) is that only the first of these factors was present at Philip's court and thus there were tensions, but that they were not equally present among all wives (see further below). Mortensen's view (1999: 806–7) that tensions were generally modest and that the troubles generated by Philip's last marriage have distorted our understanding of Macedonian polygamy is attractive (although I see a greater degree of competition than she): the main problem was not polygamy in itself but the events surrounding Philip's last wedding.

27 Heckel 1992: 213 suggests that Phila, who was apparently childless, nonetheless might have been able to use her influence on behalf of her birth family.

28 *Contra* Mortensen 1999: 803, who thinks that Olympias' status was very high immediately, that she was perhaps pre-eminent from the start. Her conclusions derive from the degree of importance she places on family as a factor affecting the status of wives as well as from her understanding of the importance of the Molossian alliance. She believes that wives who had very young children did not have much advantage because so many children died. As noted, I consider the production of children the major factor, even children who were still infants.

29 See Carney 2000c: 40–6 for discussion and references on the career of Eurydice. She was almost certainly dead by 346, and may well have died much earlier.

30 Since the date of his mother's marriage, as with all of Philip's marriages, is uncertain, so is the date of his birth. The only certainty is that Philip planned that he marry Pixodarus' daughter in (roughly) spring 336 (see below for discussion) and this probably means that he was at least twenty; see further discussion in Carney 2000c: 62, ns. 47 and 48 and Ogden 1999: 39.

31 Carney 2001.

32 Mortensen 1999: 804 doubts that there would have been much tension between Philinna and Olympias when their sons were quite young, perhaps because she considers that high infant mortality would have meant that the issue was not serious until they were older. My own view is the reverse: these two had an early advantage as the mothers of the king's only sons. Later, when Arrhidaeus' problems were evident, tensions may have decreased, but early on they must have seemed near rivals for the succession.

33 See Carney 2000c: 61–2. As discussed, Philip's marriages generally had a political aspect and the Satyrus passage makes that explicit in terms of his two Thessalian marriages. No political gain accrues when a king marries a prostitute or a woman of obscure social standing.

34 Greenwalt 1985a: 71; Hammond 1994: 29; Carney 2000c: 61 suggest that the negative stories of Philinna's origins derive from propaganda from the period of the Successors, from the fact that her family was not royal, and from Greek misunderstanding of polygamy. Ogden 1999: 25–6 argues persuasively that an additional and perhaps primary factor in the slanders against Philinna and her son was the competition between the two royal wives with sons (Olympias and Philinna) to achieve each son's succession, the kind of competition that Ogden has termed "amphimetric." As he notes, in the Pixodarus incident (see discussion below), mentioned by Plutarch (*Alex.* 10.2), Alexander has his agent term Arrhidaeus a bastard (*nothos*) and charges of bastardy are common features of disputes between royal sons by different mothers.

35 Ogden forthcoming. Daniel Ogden was kind enough to offer me a copy of his paper in manuscript form.

36 Ogden forthcoming. See further discussion of religion and magic in terms of Olympias in Chapter 5.

37 Plutarch (*Alex.* 78.5) says that his mental limitations did not exist while he was still a boy (*pais*). This presumably means that they became obvious late in childhood or early in adolescence. In modern times, mildly retarded people (the category that I have argued most appropriate for Arrhidaeus) are often not recognized as such until they begin schooling and the discrepancy between their skills and the average begins to increase (Carney 2001: 63–89, especially 80, n. 80).

38 This represents a modification of my earlier view. Carney 1992a: 172 argues for a brief period of dominance, failing to note the significance of the choice of

Aristotle and the likely point at which functionality issues would indicate retardation.

39 See further discussion in Chapter 5.

40 See discussion and references in Carney 2000c: 25.

41 See Heckel forthcoming on the importance of this point, based on Aeschin. 3.223.

42 On homoerotic activity at the Macedonian court, see Carney 1981 and 1983 and more recent discussions in Mortensen 1997: 119–27 and Reames-Zimmerman 1998: 153–9.

43 In addition to his relationships with the two men whose rivalry led to his assassination and his possible relationship with Olympias' brother, Philip, while a hostage as a young boy in the house of the Theban general Pammenes (Plut. *Pelop.* 26.4–6), may also have been the general's *eromenos* as the Suda s.v. *Karanos* claims (accepted by Griffith 1979: 205; Ogden 1996: 122; Mortensen 1997: 145, n.67)

44 Heckel 1981a: 53; Carney 1987a: 42, n. 23, 46, 53; O'Brien 1992: 12–14, 16–19: Ogden 1999: 22. Jouanno 1995: 213 argues that the Vulgate tradition (Justin, Curtius, Diodorus, and, in this case, Plutarch) stresses the mother–son relationship and sentimentalizes it. Her arguments tend to oversimplify the representation of Olympias in these sources and to exaggerate the similarity and the sentimentality of their representation of Olympias. See below and the Appendix.

45 For instance, Wirth 1973: 120 speaks of a "mother complex."

46 On Alexander's sexuality, see Carney 2000c: 97–100.

47 Stafford 1978: 79–100; Carney 1987a: 37 and 2000c: 31; Ogden 1999: 22.

48 Fredricksmeyer 1990 provides an excellent description of the competitive yet not entirely hostile relationship between Philip and Alexander. See discussion in Lund 1994: 196–8; Fredricksmeyer 1990: 300–15; Carney 2000c: 174–5 about the difficulties that develop between a ruler and his adult heir.

49 See Mortensen 1997: 168, fig. 5 for a chart illustrating Philip's probable absences between the time of Alexander's birth and 340, when, while his father was gone, he took over the kingdom.

50. Other examples of Alexander as an Aeacid: Arr. 4.1.26; Just. 11.2.1, 12.15.1, 16.3; Paus. 1.9.8; Curt. 8.4.26; Diod. 17.1.5; Strab. 13.1.27. See Ameling 1988. See Chapter 1 for discussion of Aeacid ancestry.

51 Lewis 2002: 42 suggests that the problem is primarily evidentiary. Foley 2003: 113–37, utilizing a variety of evidence, contends that the mother–daughter relationship was close and did endure past a daughter's marriage. Foley points to expectations that mothers play a role in their daughter's wedding preparations and in the birth of the daughter's first child. Pomeroy 1997: 126 notes some continuation of mother–daughter ties. Demand 1994: 4, however, argues that a close relationship between women and their daughters-in-law was more likely than one between mother and daughter, partly because daughters married so young and because sons (and thus their wives), not daughters, were responsible for the care of elderly parents.

52 See further Carney 2000c: 75–6, 89–90, 123–8.

53 Justin 8.6.7 says that Alexander was twenty when Philip put him on the Molossian throne, but the date of Alexander's accession and Arybbas' expulsion is uncertain thanks to conflicting statements in our sources. The majority of scholars believe that it happened in 343 or 342 and that Alexander was therefore substantially younger than Olympias, but Errington 1975a and Heskel 1988 have made a strong case for dating Alexander's accession to much earlier, perhaps to 349 (see discussion and references in Heskel 1988).

54 Cross 1932: 38.

55 Mortensen 1997: 127.
56 Mortensen 1997: 128 observes that "this situation is so alien to our own culture that it is difficult to imagine the etiquette involved."
57 Mortensen 1997: 128 surmises that this was the case. There is a hint of evidence. Plutarch's narrative (*Pyrrh.* 5.3–5) of the early exploits of Pyrrhus (Olympias' great-nephew) includes an incident in which Pyrrhus' cupbearer Myrtilus asked Pyrrhus for a gift and was rejected. A certain Gelon, an adherent of Pyrrhus' rival co-king Neoptolemus, noted his irritation and dined with him, possibly seducing him, and persuaded him to join a conspiracy against Pyrrhus (in fact, Myrtilus was a double-agent and informed Pyrrhus). Myrtilus' expectation of favor, based on Macedonian court intrigues, could imply that Myrtilus was Pyrrhus' lover (see Carney 1983: 262–3). Xenophon (*Anab.* 2.6.28) refers to a Thessalian named Menon who had sexual relationships with several men, including a certain Tharyps, probably an Epirote and possibly an Aeacid, granted his name (so Heckel 1981b: 81, n. 11).
58 Mortensen 1997: 128 assumes that a sexual relationship between one's husband and a younger brother was, "perhaps, offensive," but also notes that it was probably an honor for a brother to have such a relationship with the king. She cites the case of Thebe (Plut. *Pelop.* 28.4–5), wife of the Pheraean tyrant Alexander, whose younger brother he had made his lover. Plutarch refers to the tyrant's *hubris* (outrage, sometimes a euphemism for rape) and clearly indicates that Thebe hates her husband because of his actions, but Plutarch's diction, particularly his use of *hubris* (see Carney 1992a: 181, n. 36), could well mean that this was not seduction but rape. See below for possibility that Olympias' reaction and young Alexander's honor might be situationally determined, not shaped by a general view of such relationships.
59 Diodorus states that Arybbas was dead and that Philip backed Alexander against Aeacides, Arybbas' son.
60 Heckel 2003: 204, 214 suggests that two men from Acarnania (a region neighboring Epirus and dependent upon it at some periods), Philip the doctor and Lysimachus, Alexander's tutor (see Chapter 1), had some connection to Olympias and may have been selected by her. So also Fredricksmeyer 2003: 255.
61 His nurse was Lanice, daughter of Dropidas and sister of the famous Cleitus "the Black," whom Alexander would later kill while in a drunken rage. On Lanice, see Berve 1926: 2.231 and on Cleitus see Heckel 1992: 34–7.
62 Plutarch terms him a *suggenes* (of the same kin or descent) of Olympias and stresses his dignity and blood relationship. He was known for his austerity and strictness (Plut. *Alex.* 25.4). Alexander supposedly (Plut. *Alex.* 25.4–5) sent him five hundred talents' worth of frankincense and a hundred of myrrh for having inspired him as a boy with the hope of conquering spice-producing regions. Plutarch says that the gift was sent after the successful conclusion of the siege of Gaza, at the same time as he sent rich plunder to Olympias and Cleopatra. Whatever the literal truth of the tale, it associates these three Aeacids. See Berve 1926: 2.235–6; Hamilton 1969: 14, 58, 66.
63 Berve 1926: 2.85 notes his Epirote name and high status (he was one of the seven royal bodyguards or *Somatophulakes*: see Heckel 1992: 257–9) and suggests that he was related to the Aeacid house. See further Heckel 2003: 204, n. 29. Arrian (3.5.5) mentions him as a bodyguard of Alexander who died in Egypt in 332/1. Heckel 1992: 261 suggests that he became a bodyguard under Philip and argues (1992: 257) that during the reign of Philip, the *Somatophulakes* had only one duty, guarding the person of the king. If he was an Aeacid, his rank suggests the importance of the Molossian alliance.
64 We know he was active during Alexander's reign and a companion of the king.

The possibilities that he was connected to Alexander of Molossia and that he was a Royal Youth are my own ideas. On Neoptolemus' career during Alexander's reign and in the Successor era, see Berve 1926: 2.273 and Heckel 1992: 300–2. Heckel suggests that he may have been related to Arybbas the *Somatophulax* and raises the possibility that Perdiccas, with whom he was associated after the death of Alexander, was also related. Perdiccas came from the Upper Macedonian royal dynasty of Orestis (Curt. 10.7.8) and Heckel points out that Aeacids intermarried with some of the Upper Macedonian dynasties and that Perdiccas' brother's name, Alcetas, was also common in the Aeacid house. Bosworth 1988: 104, noting the surprising fact that Neoptolemus was given command of the whole *Hypaspist* group when Alexander was moving to divide larger commands, suggests that his relationship to Alexander was a factor. Of course, Aeacid (as opposed to Argead) kin were no threat to Alexander.

65 Heckel 1992: 300, n. 2.
66 O'Neil 1999a: 5 assumes that this was Olympias' choice, but the greater likelihood is that it was Philip's.
67 The Vergina palace used to be dated to the era of Cassander, but recently the reign of Philip II has been suggested. See discussion and reference in Saatsoglou-Paliadeli 2001: 210, n. 33.
68 Carney 2000c: 27–9, especially n. 107; Ogden 1999: 273–7; Mortensen 1999: 799–802. Here I differ markedly from Mortensen, who imagines royal women to be much removed from the rest of the court. She cites a conversation with Akamatis (1999: 800, n. 20) for the idea that the distribution of loom weights in private houses at Pella indicates that women were housed in the upper stories. Apart from recent research that suggests a more complex picture (see below), this would only demonstrate that private apartments were upstairs. Virtually the entire ground floor of the Vergina palace was devoted to public rooms, so private apartments, male and female, would necessarily have been upstairs.
69 Jameson 1990; Nevett 1995; Goldberg 1999.
70 Mortensen 1999: 201–2. She points out that the differing educations of the children of Philip by different wives suggest some degree of separation, though she prefers to picture them in separate quarters within the same structure. Ogden 1999: 273–7 seems to imply a similar view.
71 Carney 2000c: 27–9 *contra* Mortensen 1999: 799–801. On their possible presence at drinking parties, see Chapter 1, n. 23.
72 On the occupations and activities of royal women, see Carney 2000c: 29–31. Despite Curtius (5.2.18–20), one should not believe that Olympias and Alexander's sisters did basic weaving for the household; see discussions in Briant 1994: 286, n. 9; Carney 2000c: 29, n. 117; Mirón-Pérez 1999; *contra* Lilibaki-Akamati 2004: 91, who seems unfamiliar with relevant recent scholarship.
73 Heckel 1979: 389–92; 1981a: 54.
74 On Cleopatra, see Carney 2000c: 72–5. Although all other sources name her Cleopatra, Arrian 3.6.5 once refers to her as "Eurydice." There are two known cases in which sources report that a royal woman's name was changed, at some significant point in her life (Olympias is one; see Chapter 1) and two other cases (including this one) where this may have happened, but it is not certain because, as in the case of Cleopatra, a person who seems to be the same individual has different names in different texts. The name she is given in Arrian could be a mistake or it could be an example of a significant name-change. "Eurydice," if that was her name at some point, was not a "throne" name (*contra* Heckel 1978: 155–8; see instead Badian 1982b; Carney 1991a:

159–60, especially n. 30) but it could be allusive of Philip's mother, Eurydice (Carney 2000c: 33). In any event, as Ogden 1999: 24 concludes, the name-change, if it happened, tells us nothing about her relative status.

75 On Attalus, see Berve 1926: 2.94; Heckel 1992: 4–5.

76 Carney 1992a: 174. In the case of Olympias and Alexander, however, the uncertainty should, by this point, have been low, whereas earlier, when the potential for more sons of an age close to Alexander's was a real one, there would have been greater cause for anxiety.

77 Borza 1983.

78 Most scholars conclude that Philip had no intention of removing his son from his position as presumed heir at the time of his departure for Asia, whatever his long-term intent might have been. See Borza 1990: 208; Ellis 1981: 118 for references.

79 Whitehorne 1994: 35–6 rightly points out that sons born to Cleopatra might have been able to reach adulthood before Philip died. He argues that their more purely Macedonian bloodlines (a problematic issue, as I have suggested) would then have given them/him the advantage, that "Alexander might hardly be in the race." Had Philip lived another twenty years, such might have been the case, but it does not in any way explain his actions in 337. He had no other viable heir then and would not for years yet. While Satyrus' list of Philip's wives and children gives Cleopatra only a daughter, Europa, Pausanias (8.7.7) says that Cleopatra was murdered with a male infant and Justin (9.7.12), though referring to the murdered infant as female, also mentions a son of Philip, Caranus (11.2.3). Heckel's argument (1979: 285–303) that Satyrus should be prized over Justin and Pausanias for a variety of reasons has won general acceptance, but see *contra* Green 1991: 103, 112, 115, 141–2. In any event, even if Cleopatra did bear a male child, it could only have been an infant at the time of Philip's murder and thus not yet a meaningful replacement for Alexander.

80 See Berve 1926: 2.30–1.

81 Carney 2000c: 68–71 *contra* Heckel 2003: 199, n. 9, who argues that "there was no pressure on Philip to take another bride at this time." Since Attalus' identity remains obscure, it is difficult to assess what kind of pressure Philip might have been under from him, but Philip's need for more sons is self-evident. I have suggested (Carney 2000c: 70–1) that Philip may have chosen Olympias to avoid choosing a bride from the families of Antipater and Parmenio and thus inevitably offending one or the other. Heckel 2003: 199, n. 9 points out that Philip could have arranged for Alexander to marry Cleopatra, but, granted his failure to arrange any marriage for Alexander (see below), this probably speaks to his general reluctance to find his son a bride rather than any particular preference for Cleopatra.

82 Carney 1992a: 176, 180.

83 *Contra* Heckel 2003: 199, n. 9, who believes that his importance derived from Cleopatra's marriage, not the reverse.

84 Carney 2000c: 73, n. 105.

85 See discussions and references in Ogden 1999: 21–4. Hatzopoulos 1986 suggested, as part of his theory about ordered Macedonian succession, that the term referred to the idea that Alexander had not been born "in the purple." This theory has not gained support: see a convincing refutation in Greenwalt 1989. Similarly, Prestianni-Giallombardo 1976–7: 102–4 has not gained support for her suggestion that Attalus' language referred not to Alexander's personal legitimacy or lack of same, but to his legitimacy as a successor; see Ogden 1999: 21 for refutation.

86 Milns 1968: 28; Hamilton 1969: 24; Lane Fox 1973: 503; Bosworth 1988: 21

all suggest that Attalus may have referred to adultery (some mention ethnicity too and express no preference), but the context seems always to be the snake story, thus implying that none think that Olympias was literally guilty. Since the story of his divine fatherhood almost certainly post-dates the reign of Philip, it is unlikely that Attalus referred to that.

87 Plutarch's tale of the snake sleeping by Olympias' side, which raises the possibility that Philip thought the snake was a god in disguise (*Alex*. 2.4), does not offer support for its truth but rather implies the opposite. Neither do other references to Alexander's divine fatherhood (see Chapters 5 and 6 for further discussion).

88 Ogden 1999: 21.

89 Carney 1992a: 175.

90 On the lives and treatment of Roxane and Stateira, see Carney 2000c: 106–7, 108–9, 146–8.

91 Eurydice's ethnicity is controversial (see discussion and references in Carney 2000c: 41), but much of the controversy has centered on the ethnicity of her father, who may have been Lyncestian or Illyrian. Since at least two sources (*Suda* s.v. "Karanos"; Lib. *Vit. Dem.* 9) refer to her as Illyrian and a passage in Plutarch's corpus (*Mor.* 14c) seems to as well, it is difficult to doubt that some of her ancestry was Illyrian.

92 Ogden 1999: 21 argues that this must have been the case. Macedonians, as we have seen, were not at this period much inclined to written law and systematic behavior, least of all Philip and Alexander themselves.

93 Whether or not Alexander believed that Philip really contemplated some change in the succession, toleration of the insult threatened his *timé*; see Carney 1992a: 176–7 for the Homeric context and values involved in the quarrel.

94 Badian 1963: 244, n. 8 suggests that he may have gone to Langarus of the Agrianes, a good friend to Alexander during Philip's reign and in the troubles other Illyrians caused immediately after Philip's death (Arr. 1.5.2). Whitehorne 1994: 37 sees his Illyrian exile as far more sinister, suggesting a Molossian–Illyrian alliance against Macedonia that would generate a war behind him if he departed on his eastern campaign. While one cannot rule out this possibility —or at least the idea that Alexander wanted Philip to worry that it might be true—it seems a comparatively unlikely one. Both Alexander and Philip had Illyrian friends (kin) and enemies and the Molossians had, at best, problematic dealings with them.

95 Whitehorne 1994: 35.

96 Justin (9.7.2) is the only source that claims she was, apparently because he did not understand that Philip was polygamous. Scholars other than Fears 1975: 126 do not accept the idea of repudiation; see references in Ogden 1999: 20, n. 114.

97 Satyrus' language (*ap*. Athen 557e) is less clear since he simply describes where each went into exile, not how they got there. Whitehorne 1994: 37 seems to imagine her making a separate decision, a possibility in Satyrus' version of events, but more puzzlingly adds that she "felt her own honour to have been as much impugned as Alexander's." My view would be that this was not a distinction that she or the rest of the court could make; if Alexander's legitimacy or ability to inherit was at stake, whether for reasons sexual, ethnic, or political, then so was hers. She seems to have taken a more active role in events after the departure for exile.

98 Carney 1992a: 178–9; Whitehorne 1994: 37.

99 On royal lovers, political violence and regicide, see Carney 1983. See recent discussion of royal same-sex relationships at the Macedonian court in

Mortensen 1997: 119–26 and forthcoming; Reames-Zimmerman 1998: 160–4 and 1999: 81–9.

100 Granted that Justin's next sentence asserts that Olympias was trying to persuade her brother to go to war with Philip, if Justin's testimony has any worth, Olympias was unlikely to be one of the relatives urging reconciliation.

101 Plutarch twice reports that Philip quarreled with *both* his wife and son (*Mor.* 70b and 179c). (His *Alexander*, as we have seen, gives Olympias only an indirect role in the quarrel, citing her temperament as the reason why her son was inclined to respond to slights.) Justin's account of Olympias' actions after the death of Philip (Just. 9.7.10–14) deserves little credence (see below) but it does indicate that Olympias was in Aegae immediately after Philip's death, although it is not clear whether she had recently arrived or not. Yardley's translation (Yardley and Develin 1994: 90–1) seems to assume that she had just come, but the Latin is not so clear. Moreover, she could have been in Macedonia, but not Aegae. Some scholars have doubted the reconciliation, but the majority have accepted it: see references in Carney 1992a: 178, n. 25.

102 Some scholars (Badian 1960: 246; Fears 1975: 128; Griffith 1979: 682; Whitehorne 1994: 39–40) have suggested that the marriage was meant to cut Olympias out of the picture and substitute her daughter. Heckel 1981a: 53 makes the most cogent case for understanding the marriage of Cleopatra and Alexander in this way, but see also Macurdy 1932a: 30–1; Ellis 1976: 219, 304, n. 32; Carney 1987a: 44 and 1992a: 178. The interpretation of the marriage as an insult and displacement to Olympias misunderstands what the quarrel had been about, what it took to resolve it, and implicitly imposes assumptions about modern marriages on ancient royal marriages. Diodorus tellingly refers to the bride as Philip's daughter by Olympias and to the king of Molossia as Olympias' brother. Mortensen 1997: 205–6 suggests that Olympias may have proposed the marriage alliance herself. Whitehorne 1994: 40 sees the marriage as damaging to both Olympias and Alexander, supposing that she would have opposed the marriage, perhaps because he understands her as the primary actor in the quarrel with Philip.

103 Ellis 1981: 135–6 and Hatzopoulos 1982a: 59–66 argue that it should be rejected; Fredricksmeyer 1990: 303 doubts it but does not reject it; see *contra* Develin 1981: 95; Bosworth 1988: 22; Carney 1992a: 179.

104 On Pixodarus in general, see Ruzicka 1992: 120–34. Whitehorne 1994: 38–9 makes the interesting suggestion that Pixodarus' initial offer to Arrhidaeus was made in ignorance of his mental limitations, possibly on the assumption that Arrhidaeus as "first-born" would inherit. While this is possible, the Hecatomnids had played a prominent role in eastern Mediterranean power politics for some time and it is hard to believe that Pixodarus would have been ignorant of the facts. Indeed, he may have assumed that his daughter would "co-rule" as his two sisters had and that Arrhidaeus' mental problems were convenient rather than the reverse. Once offered, however, the chance of a marriage to Philip's presumptive heir, he could not resist; see further Carney 2005.

105 Badian 1960: 246 speaks of his "isolation" in this period, though noting Antipater's continuing presence and presumed support. Heckel 1986: 302 cautions that many of Alexander's friends (and presumably his mother) remained at court.

106 Carney 1992a: 180 contends that Alexander, Olympias, and his friends, used as they were to judging their situation by Philip's actions, may, rightly or wrongly, have seen Philip's plan for Arrhidaeus as an indication that he was not ruling the latter out of the succession and viewed the omission of Alexander from the list of royal marriages as a kind of reminder that he had not behaved

correctly. In turn, Alexander's reactions may suggest not under-confidence (that he feared his succession was in immediate jeopardy) but over-confidence in his father's tolerance of continued divergence from his policy.

107   The chronology of the Pixodarus episode is notoriously difficult so caution must be used in interpreting its significance in relationship to other events. Fredricksmeyer (1990: 303), for instance, argues that the exile of Alexander's friends happened before the incident. See further Carney 1992a: 179–80, n. 30.

108   Arist. *Pol.* 1311b; Diod. 16.93–4; Just. 9.6.4–7.14; *P.Oxy.* 1798. On the murder of Philip, see references in Carney 1992a: 169, n. 1.

109   Plutarch (*Alex.* 10.4) implicates both. See further discussion in Chapter 3.

110   Carney 1983: 260–3.

111   We do not know whether Philip even planned to take Alexander with him on the expedition; his death meant that Alexander would not only go but command.

112   Justin's narrative (9.7.9–14) makes Olympias publicly embrace Philip's murder by her treatment of the assassin's remains and by her erection of a tomb for him. It is therefore particularly implausible; public admission of patricide or complicity in patricide was too great a risk, though unprovable suspicion of it could prove beneficial.

113   Here I follow Carney 1992a: 183–9.

114   Griffith 1979: 484.

115   Bosworth 1971b: 93–105, followed by Heckel 2003: 199, advocated the idea of an Upper Macedonian conspiracy lying behind Pausanias; see *contra* Ellis 1981: 120–1. As Heckel notes, Amyntas, son of Perdiccas, may not have been involved, at least not willingly. Any Macedonian candidate, however, had some of the same risks that Alexander did in terms of the public image of Macedonia and good reason to think that waiting until Philip departed would be wise.

3 Olympias, mother of the king, Alexander the Great

1   O'Neil 1999a: 5 implausibly assumes that Olympias voluntarily played a modest role in Philip's reign. He extends his assumption to the reign of her son, though the stories about her conflicts with Antipater and others, the public role attested by the inscriptions, and the testimony of Athenian orators all demonstrate that she played a considerably greater role in Alexander's reign.

2   See discussion, references, but not necessarily conclusions in Worthington 2003. Worthington, while accepting the view that Alexander's primary motive for the destruction of Thebes was to warn other Greek powers against revolt, adds an additional possible motive, support for a pretender, possibly Alexander's cousin Amyntas. His hypothesis is interesting, though dependent on an unusual reconstruction of the much debated order of events after Philip's murder.

3   See Berve 1926: 2.30–1; Badian 1963: 244; Ellis 1970: 68–75, 1971: 15–24; Griffith 1979: 702–4; Bosworth 1971b. Curtius (6.9.17, 10.24) has Alexander claim that Amyntas plotted against Alexander's life (with the collusion of Philotas), while Justin (12.6.14) and Arrian (*FGrH* 156 F 9.22) give no motive for Alexander's action.

4   The brothers may have been scions of one of the formerly independent dynasties of Upper Macedonia (see Carney 1980: 23–4, 1992a: 184, n. 44; Heckel 1992: 357). Arrian (1.25.1–2) and Justin (11.1.2–3) say that two of the brothers had a role in the murder of Philip and imply that the third brother (another Alexander) did as well, but escaped blame because of his early support for Alexander. Curtius (7.1.6–7) explicitly blames Alexander, son of Aeropus,

for colluding at the death of Philip (he does not mention the other brothers) and adds that Alexander's marriage to a daughter of Antipater led to his evading punishment. On later charges of conspiracy against Lyncestian Alexander, see below. Thus the king almost certainly executed the two brothers as murderers of Philip. He may have done this simply to create plausible scapegoats and lessen doubts about his own involvement (Badian 1963) and/or because they had their eyes on the throne or separate rule and supported Pausanias. As Plutarch's observation indicates, their presence was somehow destabilizing and Alexander moved to eliminate the risk.

5   *Contra* Ellis 1982: 70, who believed that Attalus had a chance, primarily because he rejects the stories of Attalus' insult at Cleopatra's wedding. See Chapter 2.

6   On Attalus, see Heckel 1992: 4–5. Diodorus (17.2.3–6, 5.1–2) claims that Attalus was a potential rival for the throne, popular with the troops, and that having initially colluded with the Athenians, he changed his mind and attempted to ingratiate himself with Alexander by sending on to him an incriminating letter of Demosthenes. Obviously, Alexander may simply have used charges of treason to justify his murder of Attalus (so Badian 1963: 249–50), but it is equally possible that Attalus was guilty, very reasonably doubting that he could survive long if Alexander remained in charge (see Baynham 1998c: 147). Diodorus' account stresses the caution of Alexander's agent Hecataeus: he brings with him considerable troops, waits for an opportunity, and then kills Attalus by treachery. Curtius claimed (7.1.3) that Parmenio was Alexander's agent in the death (as Heckel 1992: 5 observes, Attalus' death could hardly have been brought about without the approval of his co-commander). Minimally, these accounts suggest that Attalus was a serious problem, one all concerned treated with caution.

7   It is possible that Cleopatra's bones were among those found in the burials under the Great Tumulus at Vergina, burials widely viewed as royal (see Carney 1991a: 1–26 for an overview, with particular reference to the female burial). Controversy continues to surround the occupants of Tombs I and II at Vergina. A woman, presumably royal, was buried in each tomb. While I am now inclined to believe that Tomb I, where fragments of the bones of an adult male, a woman, and a newborn were found, was the burial of Philip, Cleopatra, and Europa and that Tomb II housed the remains of Philip Arrhidaeus and his wife Adea Eurydice (see Bartsiokas 2000: 511–14; Themelis and Touratsoglou 1997; Palagia 2000; Carney 2004), rejecting this view would not substantially affect my analysis of the death of Cleopatra and its motivation. Granted Alexander's supposed disapproval of Olympias' actions, it is not difficult to fit the circumstances of the burial of the woman in the antechamber of Tomb II to the death of Cleopatra (see Borza 1981: 85, n. 24, Carney 1991a: 18, ns. 8 and 9).

8   Granted the general problems with the chronology of events immediately after the death of Philip, dating the deaths of Cleopatra and her baby either absolutely or relative to other deaths is difficult, but our sources imply that she was killed soon after Philip's death. I believe that her death preceded that of Attalus, who survived long enough after that to manage some long-distance conspiring against Alexander (see above). Ellis 1982: 70–2; Burstein 1982: 159–61; Baynham 1998c: 147 argue that both events happened somewhat later and that, whether or not Cleopatra's death preceded or followed that of Attalus, he did not know about it when he corresponded with Alexander.

9   Satyrus (*ap.* Athen. 557d), generally considered an accurate list of Philip's wives and their children (at least those who survived long enough to be known), gives Cleopatra only one child, a daughter named Europa. Justin

(9.7.12) says the murdered baby was female, in contradiction to Pausanias' statement. Elsewhere, Justin may refer to a son of Cleopatra's. He claims (11.2.3) that, in the period after the murder of Philip, Alexander had Caranus, a son by a stepmother (name unspecified), killed, because he was a rival for the throne. Justin, as we have seen, attributes to Alexander the deaths of not only his stepmother but brothers (12.6.14). Though some accept the idea that Cleopatra had a son as well as a daughter (see Green 1991: 103, 112, 115, 141–2; Unz 1985: 171–4), most scholars accept Heckel's argument (1979: 285–303) that Cleopatra had only one child, a daughter.

10 See Carney 1993b: 37, n. 21 for references to discussions of Pausanias' credibility as a source.
11 See further Carney 1993b: 38.
12 If, as I have suggested (Carney 2000c: 73), Cleopatra was an Argead, the threat to Alexander and Olympias would have been even greater.
13 Modern scholarship often assumes that these murders were personal and unnecessary in a way that dynastic murders by males were not and that this presumed (rarely argued) lack of pragmatic policy motivation made Olympias' actions worse. As noted, the crime had practical advantages and does not justify a more negative treatment of Olympias than that of various male Macedonians who committed similarly brutal acts (see Carney 1993b: 38–41 for discussion and references).
14 Whitehorne 1994: 44.
15 Ogden 1999: x, 20–9.
16 Whitehorne 1994: 44 calls Plutarch's inclusion of Cleopatra in the plot "ridiculous," because he thinks that her pregnancy (tricky to date in itself, let alone relative to Pausanias' rape) meant that she "would have been out of circulation."
17 Olympias herself killed Adea Eurydice, Cassander murdered Olympias, and all three of Alexander's sisters were murdered.
18 Views about the moral capacities of women and how they differed from those of men varied with time, place, and the individual in the Greek world, but generalizations are certainly possible. See Dover 1974: 98–102; Harris 2003: 130–43 comments on the generality of the view that women, like children and barbarians, were particularly susceptible to anger, yet were excluded from the legitimate anger of men. Justin (14.6.1), referring to Olympias' slaughter of pro-Cassander members of the Macedonian elite, terms her actions more like those of a woman than a monarch; see Chapter 4.
19 See Carney 1993b: 38 for a list of some dynastic murders in the period immediately after the death of Alexander. See Carney 1983: 260–72 for a discussion of Macedonian regicides, successful and attempted. Justin (8.3.10–11) reports that Philip II killed at least one of his half-brothers and probably all three. Plato (*Gorg.* 471a–b) claims that Archelaus murdered his uncle and cousin and his very young half-brother.
20 See Mortensen 1992: 156–71, followed by Carney 2000c: 40–6, on Eurydice's career and the probable falsity of charges against her.
21 Justin (11.5.1) asserts that Alexander killed all of his stepmother's kin to whom Philip had given high military and civilian office, but Heckel 1992: 5–12 argues convincingly that Alexander spared a nephew of Cleopatra and that Justin exaggerated. More generally, Heckel observes that, at the time of Philip's assassination, Alexander did not immediately eliminate all possible enemies, but merely the most obvious.
22 See Carney 1993b: 50–4 for lengthier discussion and references on this point. Plutarch's story (*Mor.* 253C–D) about the deaths of the wife and daughters of the tyrant Aristodemus is illustrative. When the tyrant was killed, his wife

hanged herself in her own chamber rather than face the crowd attacking the house, and the virtuous Megisto (who had helped to bring down the tyrant) did not save the girls but persuaded the crowd to allow them to hang themselves, sparing them rape and slaughter at the hands of the mob.

23 Carney 1993b: 53, n. 63. Such a death obviated the fear of rape in association with female death and maintained the expectation that women remained primarily private. The murders of Stateira (Plut. *Alex*. 77.6) and Alexander's sister Cleopatra (Diod. 20.37.3) were the work of women, though men were also indirectly involved.

24 See Carney 1993b: 40–1 for references. Golden 2003: 24: "Generalizations are of limited use: parents probably did not care for their daughters just as they did for sons, fathers' and mothers' feelings probably differed, children of different ages were not treated the same, one's own children counted for more than others (as is true even in supposedly child-centered societies today). Nevertheless, there is ample evidence that parents loved the children they decided to raise." Oakley 2003: 178 argues that the practice of exposure indicates that parents did not generally have the level of attachment to newborns that they did to those who had spent more time with the family.

25 See Pomeroy 1997: 84, ns. 61 and 62 for a typical example of this mentality: an Attic curse that condemned to destruction and bad reputes not only Diocles' enemies, but their wives or husbands and children.

26 Diodorus (14.37.6) reports that Orestes, a boy, succeeded Archelaus but was killed by his guardian Aeropus, doubtless an Argead and possibly his uncle (see Hammond 1979: 134–6, 170; Mattingly 1968: 474; Borza 1990: 178). Cassander arranged the deaths of both of Alexander's sons (Just. 15.2.5; Paus. 9.7.2; Diod. 20.28.2–4). The half-brother Archelaus murdered (see above) was supposedly a small child.

27 Dover 1974: 180–1 lists some of the many passages in Greek literature where this sentiment is voiced. See also Blundell 1989: 26–31; Mitchell 1997: 14. Thucydides (7.68.1 is a good example of the acceptability of the revenge ethic: "Let us consider both that it is entirely acceptable, in dealing with adversaries, to claim satisfaction of the anger in one's heart in vengeance upon the aggressor, and also that retaliation upon enemies, which will be possible for us, is proverbially the greatest of pleasures."

28 Dover 1974: 180–4, 190–201. He does, however, warn (1974: 191–2) against over-generalization: "Greek frankness in admitting that revenge is enjoyable, the obvious *contra*st between careful justice and Christian love . . . have all combined to exaggerate the cold or fierce aspects of Greek morality and to play down the credit which the Greeks gave to diffidence, trustfulness, peaceableness and magnanimity."

29 One reason for caution is that modern writers seem inclined to ascribe Olympias' motivation to vengeance when they do not make similar assumptions about her male contemporaries (see Carney 1993b: 30–1 for discussion and examples).

30 Bosworth 1971b: 104 argues that Alexander's fear of dividing Macedonia along regional lines deterred him from marrying a Macedonian; Baynham 1998c: 141–52 focuses on the potential problems in choosing a daughter of Antipater or Parmenio (or both); Carney 2000c: 96–100 makes some arguments similar to Baynham's (neither had the other's argument available to her), but has a broader focus, putting Alexander's marriage policy in the context of Philip's and his treatment of his sisters' marriage plans, as well as considering the impact of his delayed marriage on Olympias and his sister.

31 Baynham 1998c: 151 points out that had Alexander married at this time and left behind a baby or pregnant wife, the potential for feuding and intrigue

would have been increased. Antipater and Olympias certainly managed a feud anyway, but the existence of children and a wife with a child would only have added to the complexity of her situation and would probably have weakened it. Doubtless Olympias hoped for an heir at some point, but she may not have been in a rush for a grandson.

32 See Lane Fox 1973; Bosworth 1988; Green 1991 for major accounts of the reign of Alexander.

33 See Heckel 2003: 197–225 for a recent discussion of the factions and factionalism at Alexander's court. While I do not agree with all of his conclusions, Heckel's overview of the dynamics of the Macedonian court is compelling.

34 Her name is restored to the inscription in line 5: Ὀλ[υμπιά]δι. See further Chapter 5.

35 For instance, Athenaeus (14.659f) quotes from a letter of Olympias to Alexander in which she urges him to buy a slave cook who knows various rituals from her. See further Chapter 5.

36 On Antipater's career, see Berve 1926: 2.46–51; Kanatsulis 1958/9, 1968; Adams 1984; Heckel 1992: 38–49; Baynham 1994; Blackwell 1999: 33–80, 102–6, 110–16.

37 See Carney 1995: 367–91 for the view that, in the Argead period, office-holding was not "the way in which power was understood and allotted in Macedonian society," that kingship was primarily understood not as an office held by an individual but as the possession of the royal clan, that any kind of substitute kingship was not, therefore, seen as a well-defined office, and that Antipater's position in Macedonia during Alexander's campaign was not so clearly defined as to justify the assumption that he had sole power.

38 So Macurdy 1932a: 31. Apart from the complete absence of evidence, the idea is implausible for the reasons stated. Olympias may well have hoped or even understood that she and Antipater were to work together and she may not have understood herself as under his control. If we knew more about the nature of their quarrel (see below), we would know more about what each one's expectations might have been.

39 Blundell 1995: 160–8; Dillon 2002: 1, *passim*. As Kron 1996: 139 notes, female priesthoods tended to be hereditary in elite families. On Olympias and religion, see Chapter 5.

40 See discussion in Jones 1999: 2–3. Certainly, as Jones 1999: 51 notes, ties between Greek cities and states were defined and reinforced by their common religion and shared worship of the same gods.

41 See Jones 1999: 1–56; Erskine 2002; see also below. Mosley 1973: 78 says that the diplomatic relations of monarchs and tyrants tended to be even more personal and direct than those of cities.

42 Mosley 1973: 1, 78. A passage in Aeschines (3.223) not only exemplifies this situation but demonstrates how easily, even in a minor way, royal women got involved in the process. Aeschines refers to Ctesiphon's engineering of the arrest of a certain Anaxinus of Oreus, ostensibly on grounds that he was shopping for Olympias. The charge was obviously a cloak for suspicions that Anaxinus was spying for Philip while appearing to honor his obligations to his *xenos* (guest friend) or *philos* (friend). What we cannot know is whether his task obliged Olympias as well as her husband; in all probability it did since the proffering of gifts or favors automatically led to the expectation of return.

43 Jones 1999: 14. Herman 1987: 29 comments that, in various ways, *xenia* (ritualized guest friendship) "mimicked" aspects of blood kinship and, in effect, created supplemental kin. *Xenia* was an important aspect of international dealings. Mitchell 1997: 122 observes that there was comparatively

little development of diplomatic terminology other than that associated with personal relationships.

44 As Mitchell 1997: 4 observes, Greeks were "not coy about the emphasis placed on reciprocity" even in *philia* relationships involving kin, generally considered one's closed *philoi*. See Blundell 1989: 31–42; Mitchell 1997: 1–26 on the nature of *philia* and the importance of reciprocity.

45 Even Aristotle (*Nic. Eth.* 1157b–1158a) includes women (specifically husbands and wives) in some such relationships. Despite the understanding of blood relationships as solely the creation of males as made famous in the *Oresteia*, much evidence, particularly that relating to royal dynasties, assumes that both mothers and fathers were kin of their children; consider, for instance, Alexander's pride in his descent from Achilles, the supposed ancestor of his mother Olympias' family. Similarly, Alexander's interest in marrying Darius' daughter and the hostility of the Macedonian elite after his death to his sons by Asian women both indicate that they understood children as the kin of both parents. Herman 1987: 34–5 argues that *xenia* relationships involving women are rare, but his discussion deals largely with mythic figures, not Macedonian royal women. In any event, *xenia* and *philia*, though part of a collection of overlapping terms expressing friendship and kinship (Herman 1987: 19), are not identical. As discussed below, *philia* (and its cognates) is used repeatedly in terms of various royal Macedonian women.

46 So Blackwell 1999: 91.

47 Herman 1987: 47, 69 observes that special gestures of *euergesia* (benefaction) could initiate the end of hostility between parties and the first step toward *philia* or *xenia* relationships, relationships that could endure for generations. Erskine 2002: 105 observes that individual acts of benefaction can always be understood as part of a continuing relationship rather than as isolated instances.

48 The inscription does not specify for what group either one acted, but Blackwell (1999: 89–91) plausibly suggests that Olympias was acting for Macedonia and Cleopatra for Molossia. He argues that the size of the shipments sent to Olympias (second only to Athens on the list) suggests that she received grain for Macedonia and that the difference in the quantity each one received suggests that they did not receive the shipments for the same country.

49 Blackwell 1999: 89.

50 See discussion and references in Kron 1996: 141, 166–7 and Dillon 2002: 10–11, 25, who suggest a mix.

51 Mendels 1984: 139; Blackwell 1999: 89 believes the shipments were "Alexander's doing" and argues that they date between 334/3 and 331, probably earlier rather than later. Kingsley 1986: 169–71 and Blackwell 1999: 97 connect the shipments to the Persian counter-offensive against Alexander of 334/3. Garnsey 1988: 159–62 wants to tie the inscription to known grain crises and prefers 328/7.

52 Mendels 1984: 138–9 points to the absence from the Cyrene edict of some of Antipater's newer friends and suggests that the shipments indicated Alexander's support for his mother against Antipater. Garnsey 1988: 161 rejects political consideration as the primary explanation for the presence or absence of names from the list, preferring to emphasize climate. On Olympias and Antipater, see further below.

53 Blackwell 1999: 101. Mendels 1984: 138–9 suggests that the Cyrene edict indicates the emergence of two power blocs or "zones of influence," one the Antipatrian, the other Alexandrian.

54 Worthington 1984: 48 rejects the idea that either Antipater or Olympias demanded Harpalus, though he terms Olympias' participation "more

questionable," and concludes that only Philoxenus, Alexander's governor of Cilicia, demanded Harpalus (Hyp. 5.8). See *contra* Blackwell 1999: 18–27, 88. Worthington, perhaps influenced by the values of the *polis* world, seems simply to assume that Olympias' actions could not possibly have legitimacy.

55 Mendels 1984: 144.

56 While nothing directly associates either individual with Harpalus' career, suggestive circumstances exist for both, particularly for Olympias. Harpalus' family (his aunt was one of Philip's wives), formerly the royal house of the Upper Macedonian area of Elimeia, was prominent in Philip's and Alexander's courts (see Heckel 1992: 213–21) and Harpalus was one of the friends of Alexander Philip sent into exile after the Pixodarus affair (Plut. *Alex.* 10.3; Arr. 3.5). Since Plutarch tells us that Olympias and friends of Alexander had helped to precipitate the attempted marriage with Pixodarus' daughter (Plut. *Alex.* 10.1) and Philip sent them into exile apparently in response to their "bad" advice, it seems likely that Olympias and Harpalus had worked together. When Harpalus fled from his responsibilities the first time (see discussion and references in Heckel 1992: 215–17), he did so in association with a certain Tauriscus, who then went on to Olympias' brother, campaigning in Italy (Arr. 3.6.7). As we have noted, the Aeacids probably had ties to several of the Upper Macedonian royal houses. The Tauriscus association might suggest a connection to that of Olympias (Jaschinski 1981: 12–18 goes too far in thinking this somehow connects to Alexander of Molossia becoming king of Macedonia). Antipater had worked closely with Alexander before his father's death and gave him critical support at the time of Philip's murder, so he too may have been part of the group that included Harpalus, supporting Alexander.

57 Diodorus says that the Athenians "πεπολυωρηκότες" her. Geer 1962: 191 translates this as "had great respect for Olympias," but *LSJ* translates it as "having observed her carefully." While the verb can signify either "care" or "respect," Geer's translation makes more sense in the context of a passage about her previous honors and Athenian hopes for her help.

58 This phenomenon is more obvious after the death of Alexander, when Hellenistic dynasties began to develop, but observable in the continuing relations of his mother and sister with the dynasties of their births. Indeed, before that, Macedonian wives born to foreign dynasties could have been active in dealings between two states, though no evidence currently supports such a possibility.

59 Livy (8.24.17) said that Olympias was present when her brother's ashes were returned for burial and Pausanias (1.11.3) seems to imply that her arrival in Molossia was associated with her brother's death, as might Hyperides (*Eux.* 25). As Blackwell 1999: 98 notes, if his dating and attribution of the grain shipments (see above) are correct, Olympias cannot have left Macedonia before 333. The combined testimony of Curtius (4.6.20, 7.1.38) and Diodorus (17.49.1) would appear to demonstrate that Olympias was still in Macedonia in late 332 or early 331. Curtius (7.1.38) has Amyntas, son of Andromenes, squabble with Olympias at that time over his seizure as recruits of a group of young men of military age whom Olympias had been sheltering. (On the historicity of this incident, see below and the Appendix.) Hammond 1980: 474 tried to discredit the Livy passage, but his contentions (part of his general argument (473–6) that Olympias held an office, the *prostasia*, and then exchanged it with her daughter) are not persuasive: see Carney 1987a: 50–3, 1995: 367–76.

60 Pausanias (1.1.3) surely overstates when he claims that Olympias returned to Epirus out of "fear" of Antipater. So long as Alexander lived, Olympias cannot

have had cause to fear for her life at Antipater's hands. It is possible that Antipater had reason to fear Olympias. Plutarch (*Alex*. 39.6) has Alexander warning Antipater to watch out for plots against him, but he makes no connection to Olympias, even though his next section deals with her. Many people, of course, had reason to plot against Antipater.

61 Macurdy 1932a: 33 imagines an incident in which Alexander tells her to stop "meddling," but no such incident is attested in our sources. (See Carney 1987a: 53, n. 52 for references to those who have accepted this myth.) Macurdy's fiction seems to be based on Plutarch (*Alex*. 39.7), but, quite apart from the dubious truth of the passage itself (see above), it simply says that Alexander did not allow Olympias to meddle in his affairs or military matters, that he bore her complaints, and that Antipater failed to realize that he was more affected by his mother's upsets than by Antipater's letters.

62 Macurdy 1932a: 33 considers the acquittal of Amyntas, son of Andromenes, despite Olympias' attempts to blacken his name with her son (Curt. 7.2.36–40), a humiliation that would have forced her departure. Assuming Curtius' testimony is accurate (see Appendix), his acquittal would have been embarrassing to Olympias but hardly a major issue, particularly since it happened in Asia. Green 1991: 458 suggests that she left because she was losing her struggle with Antipater whereas Cross 1932: 48 (followed by Blackwell 1999: 101) argues that she hoped to escape Antipater's control and influence. Both could easily be true.

63 No ancient source directly names this royal brother and sister as the children of Alexander and Cleopatra. Some accept this identification, but others do not. See further discussion in Chapters 4 and 6.

64 See Cabanes 1980: 324–51 for a discussion of the role of Epirote women in terms of property ownership. Cabanes notes that they could function as heads of family, if widowed, or at least as deputies until their sons were of age.

65 In the later third century, Olympias II (widow and half-sister of Alexander II) acted as regent for her two young sons (Justin 28.1.1). It may be significant that both Olympias II and Cleopatra were members of the Aeacid dynasty by blood as well as marriage.

66 *SEG* IX 2. Cleopatra also sold grain to Leocrates, which ultimately went to Corinth (Lycurg. *Leoc*. 26). The grain, probably surplus from that shipped to her from Cyrene, was likely sold in 333/2 or a little earlier: see Kingsley 1986: 169–70 *contra* Oliverio 1933: 34–5. See also Blackwell 1999: 96–8.

67 Aeschines (3.242) mentions an embassy sent to Cleopatra to bring condolences *c*. 331/30 and around 330 she appeared (*SEG* XXIII 189) as *thearodoch* (an official who receives envoys sent to consult oracles or present offerings), perhaps for the new Epirote Alliance. See below for the possible date and circumstance of the initiation of the alliance.

68 The date of this development is unknown and discussion about it tends to connect to a scholar's view about whether the alliance was a sign of Aeacid weakness or strength; see below. Those who think it a sign of Aeacid strength (Cabanes 1976: 177–81) tend to date it to the reign of Alexander of Molossia while those who see it as weakness (Hammond 1967: 537, 1980: 472) date it after his death, so to 331–325. Franke 1954: 42 thought that Olympias may have been behind the alliance. Cross 1932: 42–3 connects its formation to Olympias' move to Molossia while Blackwell 1999: 101, though not embracing that idea, comments that, once the alliance existed, Olympias probably could enjoy a "greater degree of autonomy from Pella and Antipater."

69 Hammond 1967: 562; Errington 1975b: 41.

70 See Blackwell 1999: 101, n. 73, for a discussion of the evidence. Hammond 1967: 559, 1980: 472, who ties the date of the formation of the alliance to *SEG*

XXIII 189 and so dates it after 331, argues that the formation of the alliance was a sign of Molossian weakness, probably a plan of Antipater, approved by Alexander the Great in order to enfeeble the Molossians and Chaonians. Cabanes 1976: 177–81 views the alliance as an indication of Molossian strength and so believes that it may have formed while Alexander of Epirus was still alive.

71 Hammond's idea (1980: 472) that Alexander of Macedonia would have been involved as well is believable only if the alliance was created during Alexander of Molossia's lifetime; everything indicates considerable cooperation between the Macedonian Alexander and his mother and sister.

72 The reign of Pyrrhus was something of a temporary reversal of this trend, primarily because his military success, greater than that of any other Aeacid, attracted support. Even in Pyrrhus' reign, however (see Chapter 4), signs of weakening allegiance to the monarchy were visible.

73 Despite this passage and cooperative actions after the death of Alexander (see Chapter 4) and the absence of a single example of conflict between mother and daughter, a scholarly myth arose that mother and daughter had quarreled and the quarrel occasioned Cleopatra's departure (see Carney 1987a: 53, n. 53 for references). Macurdy 1932a: 34, while accepting the possibility of friction between the two, considers it possible that Cleopatra may have been sent by Olympias to watch and/or trouble Antipater. This suggestion certainly better suits available evidence and the known behavior of the pair.

74 Alexander's apparent acceptance of or at least indifference to his mother's actions appears to contradict Plutarch's earlier (*Alex.* 39.7) assertion that he did not allow his mother to interfere. Hammond 1967: 559 implausibly suggests that the dispute was about Molossia, though the passage certainly does not support that view. Whether Alexander ever said anything like this is uncertain since the situation it describes is at odds with the literal truth, as evidenced by other sources.

75 Had Craterus actually arrived and replaced him, then he would have had the role that had been Antipater's. Thus mother and daughter could hardly have had exclusive control of the two realms, as the passage seems to imply.

76 See also Mendels 1984: 141. As already noted, Hammond's view (1980: 473–6) that the situation referred to in this passage was part of some exchange of formal office and related to Alexander's attempt to replace Antipater with Craterus is implausible. He thought that Olympias needed to be consoled for her supposed loss of the *prostasia* by offers of divine honors (mentioned only by Curtius 9.6.26, 10.5.30) and that Olympias' grandson Neoptolemus was, at this point, replaced by her nephew Arybbas (see Chapter 4 for discussion).

77 Blackwell 1999: 95–6 argues that a more general reading of the passage would allow one to date the situation Plutarch mentions to somewhat earlier, to a period before his return from India.

78 See Seibert 1972: 4–5 for a summary, as well as discussion in the Introduction and Appendix.

79 Droysen 1877: 399–405 and Kaerst 1887: 107–17 first articulated this case-by-case principle. On the whole, this principle continues to dominate, but has not necessarily led to general agreement on the authenticity of a given letter. See Introduction and Appendix.

80 *Contra* Tarn 1949: 2.301 who imagines Olympias and Cassander doctoring original letters of Antipater, Alexander, and Olympias, as they had access to them, in order to serve their political goals in the age of the Successors. Political rewriting may well have occurred, but much of the correspondence seems irrelevant to such concerns.

81 Asirvatham 2001: 95, 100 discusses Plutarch's use of Olympias as a foil to demonstrate Alexander's good, Hellenic qualities.

82 On the advice theme in terms of Parmenio, see Carney 2000a.

83 Arr. 3.6.5; Plut. *Alex.* 10.3. See above for Harpalus, who was probably from the Upper Macedonian royal house of Elimeia. Ptolemy was somehow related to the royal family (see Heckel 1992: 222–7, especially n. 40). Many years later Olympias' daughter died trying to reach Ptolemy, in order to marry him (Diod. 20.37.3–6). Nearchus was the son of a Cretan immigrant to Philip's court (see Heckel 1992: 228–33). Erigyius and his brother Laomedon (on Arrian's list of those exiled but not Plutarch's) were also sons of a Greek immigrant, from Mytilene.

84 See Chapter 2 for their careers. Arybbas died fairly early in the campaign, but Neoptolemus lived on into the Successor era. Having been allied with Eumenes (certainly a friend of Olympias; see below), he later became his enemy, and Eumenes ultimately killed him in battle (see Heckel 1992: 300–2). Doubtless his change of side meant that he became Olympias' enemy as well, but he may nonetheless have been a supporter during Alexander's lifetime.

85 For Eumenes, a Greek immigrant, see Heckel 1992: 346–7; for Polyperchon, a Tymphaean, who, *c.* 317, sponsored Olympias' return to Macedonia, see Heckel 1992: 188–204; for Leonnatus, a relative of Alexander's grandmother Eurydice and so possibly Lyncestian, and the first member of the elite Olympias' daughter sought to marry (probably at Olympias' instigation) after her brother's death, see Heckel 1992: 91–106; for Aristonous, of Eordaean origin, who fought loyally for Olympias during her war with Cassander, see Heckel 1992: 275–6; for Perdiccas, a member of the Orestian royal house, to whom the dying Alexander gave his ring and whom Olympias wanted her daughter to marry, see Heckel 1992: 134–63.

86 Heckel 2003: 197–8, 219 stresses the changeable and complex nature of groupings.

87 Heckel 2002: 85–6.

88 On the historicity of this incident, see further discussion in the Appendix. Blackwell 1999: 103–4 suggests that these young men were part of an overly large bodyguard and that Olympias, in the year of the war with Agis, hoped to use to advantage a small military force. That may be true. However, the Curtius passage focuses on the avoidance of military service (Bosworth 2002: 71 argues that the incident suggests general reluctance for military service in Asia) and does not indicate that these young men were already soldiers. Heckel 1992: 177 thinks that three of the young men named by Curtius were brought to Asia to serve as "Pages" or Royal Youths since Amyntas brought fifty grown sons of elite Macedonians for this purpose (Curt. 5.1.42).

89 Plutarch's account of the Pixodarus affair gives Philotas a role which implies that he might have been the one who informed Philip about the marriage negotiations that Olympias and Alexander's friends had encouraged (Badian 1960: 327 thinks he tried to reconcile father and son and Heckel 1992: 25 thinks it more likely that Philip simply wanted him there as a model of good behavior); certainly he was present for Alexander's humiliation (Plut. *Alex.* 10.3) and the failure of a policy Olympias had championed. Late in Philip's reign, Parmenio, Philotas' father, had apparently supported the faction of Attalus against that of Alexander—one of his daughters married Attalus (Curt. 6.9.18) and he and Attalus commanded the preliminary Asian expedition together. In order to survive, Parmenio collaborated in the elimination of Attalus (see Heckel 1992: 14–15 for references). So, though there is no direct evidence, Olympias could certainly have disliked Philotas and his family.

90 Heckel 1992: 178, while noting their subsequent obscurity, argues that Amyntas remained popular enough so that a conviction would have been difficult. Alexander also managed to look moderate while actually indicating what would happen to those who continued to support the views of Philotas.

91 On the life of Lyncestian Alexander and his probable connection to the royal house, see Berve 1926: 2.17–19; Carney 1980: 23–33; Heckel 1992: 357–8. The guilt of any of the sons of Aeropus is uncertain.

92 He was first governor of Thrace and later commander of the important Thessalian cavalry (Arr. 1.25.2).

93 So Badian 1963: 248.

94 Carney 1980: 28. In-laws generally proved a disposable commodity among the Macedonian elite. It was the Lyncestian's importance that had led to his marriage to a daughter of Antipater and his own importance that saved him, not his father-in-law's influence. Heckel 1992: 357 seems to consider both factors equally causative. Badian 1963: 248 suggests that Lyncestian Alexander's prompt action at the time of Philip's assassination was the result of Antipater's forewarning but Green 1991: 112 attributes it to his shrewdness and Fears 1975: 130, n. 62 thinks mere friendship inspired him. Carney 1980: 29, n. 21 suggests that Alexander's treatment of the Lyncestian parallels his subsequent sparing of the sons of Andromenes (see above).

95 Bosworth 2000: 59, n. 18 argues that this interpretation is based on a misreading of Diodorus and that, in fact, one cannot determine from his narrative when the letter was received.

96 See Heckel 1992: 358, n. 29 and 2003: 210–13 for further variations in what remains of Curtius' account and on the many problems in the sources' treatment of the incident and the difficulties of resolving chronological issues.

97 Diodorus does not refer to Olympias by name in this passage, though nearly all scholars have assumed that she is the one referenced. Tarn 1949: 2.68 irrationally assumed that the reference was to Darius' mother Sisygambis, whom Alexander treated like a mother, and uses this assumption to criticize Diodorus' accuracy, since Alexander had not yet met Sisygambis. Welles 1963: 207, n. 1 rejected Tarn's view and judged that a warning by Olympias was "very credible." More recently, Abramenko 1992: 1–8 has argued that Diodorus' phrase alluded to Ada of Caria. While Alexander did function as a kind of adoptive son to Ada (see Carney 2003: 248–9 for references), this would hardly lead Diodorus to refer to Ada in this manner. Like Heckel 2003: 211, n. 59, I find the argument implausible.

98 Alexander of Lyncestis was not, however, executed until 330 (see references in Carney 1980: 32).

99 Arrian's account is often preferred over that of Diodorus, but Bosworth 1980: 164 and 2000: 59–60 connects it to Olympias' hostility to Antipater and argues that Olympias' letter, a general warning against the Lyncestian rather than charges about a specific conspiracy, was written earlier and simply used by Alexander at this point.

100 My translation puts more weight on the loss of friends than the loss of wealth but I believe that the entire passage is about both. See Hamilton 1969: 104 and see further Plut. *Alex.* 41.1–2, where wealth and arrogance are associated with an unwillingness to perform tasks for the king.

101 See Hamilton 1969: 104 for references.

102 Two other Plutarch passages relate to gifts to the elite. Plut. *Alex.* 15.2–3, referring to the period just before Alexander's Asian campaign, has Alexander impoverishing himself by gifts of property and wealth to companions, though Perdiccas declines any gift. Plut. *Mor.* 342D–E tells much the same story. In both passages, Plutarch claims that Alexander gave away most of his

possessions. Hamilton 1969: 37 rightly judges that this is a "romantic exaggeration," but the idea that the king had to reward his companions with considerable wealth is real enough; Philip had done the same.

103 Bosworth 1996a: 130–1 connects Alexander's gifts to his claims of divinity rather than Macedonian monarchy. See *contra* Roisman 2003a: 307. Like Roisman 2003a: 308, I find Mitchell's argument (1997: 171–2) that Alexander's extravagant giving imitated Persian royal gift-giving implausible. Not only did Alexander, as noted, give gifts before the departure for Asia, but Philip did so as well (*FGrH* 156 F 224, 225b). On the importance of wealth and gift-giving for kings, see Austin 1986: 459–60, though Bosworth 2002: 268 cautions against making royal wealth too significant. As already noted (see above), gift-giving often established and then confirmed *philia*.

104 See Roisman 2003a: 306–9 for discussion and references on gift-giving in general and Alexander's in particular. He does not, however, discuss Olympias' cautions and tends to focus on the limitations gifts imposed on the king's Companions, rather than the limitations they imposed on the king.

105 On Hephaestion, see Berve 1926: 2.169–75; Heckel 1992: 65–90; Reames-Zimmerman 1998, 1999.

106 Welles 1963: 456, n. 1 observes that his usage can "hardly mean anyone but himself." Since Hephaestion supposedly tells Olympias to stop being difficult and threatening "us," he cannot be speaking of himself and the king together.

107 In *Alex.* 39.5, Plutarch says that Olympias often warned Alexander against the ambitions of members of his court and that Alexander kept this correspondence secret with the exception of one occasion when Hephaestion read a letter of hers along with the king (supposedly this was his custom, but not, presumably, for letters from Olympias). Alexander did not keep him from reading the letter but put his seal ring to Hephaestion's lips. *Mor.* 180D tells much the same story except that Plutarch specifies that the letter contained secret accusations against Antipater (in this version it is less clear that this incident was an exception). *Mor.* 333A simply calls the letter secret and comments that Alexander acted with a friend's faith. *Mor.* 340A has Alexander reading his mother's secret letter silently to himself, when Hephaestion joins him and Alexander cannot force himself to restrain his friend.

108 One wonders why Olympias would have written to Hephaestion rather than to her son if she were dissatisfied with his friend. It was certainly not her procedure when dissatisfied with Antipater. The "quotation", with its odd use of the first-person plural, seems especially spurious. Plutarch's frequently repeated story, even with all its variations, presents a contradictory picture.

109 Carney 2003: 239–42.

110 See Heckel 2002: 81–95, especially 82–4.

111 It is difficult to say whether this comment is Arrian's own or that of Antipater.

112 According to the story (as Arrian terms it), Alexander quipped that Olympias was charging him high rent for his nine-month lodging.

113 A lacuna follows.

114 As do modern writers: see Badian 1961: 36–40; Bosworth 1988: 161–2; Heckel 1992: 42; Baynham 1994: 337–46.

115 The cause of his death has been the source of endless speculation. While the long history of Macedonian regicide and the conspiracies of Alexander's reign make it impossible to rule out assassination, in recent scholarship, only Bosworth 1971a has taken the possibility very seriously. Moreover, the nature of evidence in the ancient sources makes diagnosis of any sort difficult. See Borza and Reames-Zimmerman 2000, and Reames-Zimmerman 2001 for discussion and references.

4 Olympias on her own, 323–316

1 For general narratives of this period see: Préaux 1978; Will 1979–82; Green 1990; Shipley 2000; Erskine 2003: 17–89.
2 Austin 1986: 455–7 warns against understanding the Hellenistic world as balance-of-power politics based on a false analogy to nineteenth-century Europe and stresses the continuing importance of conquest.
3 See discussions in Shipley 2000: 1–32; Bosworth 2002: 19–28 (for the period of the Successors); Erskine 2003: 1–15. The scarcity of narrative sources is critical. For this last period of Olympias' life, Diodorus, preserved fragments of now lost works by Arrian and others, and several of Plutarch's lives are major sources. No inscriptional evidence relevant to Olympias' career in this period has as yet been found, other than that associated with her tomb (see Chapter 6).
4 See brief discussion and references in Bosworth 2002: 279. My preference is for the "high" chronology he champions. In some cases, the chronological dispute makes comparatively little difference in one's understanding of events and motivation but in others the difference is meaningful. Readers should refer to this volume's "Significant events" but understand that another historian might offer a different chronology.
5 On his functionality, see Carney 2001: 63–89.
6 On Barsine, see Carney 2000c: 101–5, 149–50.
7 See Carney 2000c: 118–19, ns. 12, 13, and 14. Soon after Alexander's death, his generals began to perform acts previously limited to kings. Diodorus frequently describes generals as aiming at *basileia* (rule), indicating that the Successors began to think and act like kings well before their delayed assumption of a royal title. This in turn implies that none of them realistically expected the Argead dynasty to survive, at least through the male line.
8 Carney 2000c: 115–17.
9 See Bosworth 2002: 29–63 for a discussion and references, not necessarily conclusions.
10 Bosworth 1993: 420–7 contends, contrary to the general view, that the infant Alexander IV was not proclaimed king until about a year after his birth.
11 On the role of lament and women in perpetuating vendettas, see Alexiou 1974: 21–2; Holst-Warhaft 1992: 118, 144.
12 Alexiou 1974: 17–22; Holst-Warhaft 1992: 115–19.
13 Carney 2000c: 14.
14 Holst-Warhaft 1992: 103.
15 See Wolohojian 1969: 268 for this variant of 3.33 and its translation.
16 See references in Carney 2000c: 34.
17 Austin 1986. Bosworth 2002: 247, however, rightly warns against too narrow a reading of the importance of wealth and plunder.
18 Carney 2000c: 131–2.
19 Despite Errington 1975a: 148, the fact that Cleopatra rather than Leonnatus took the initiative indicates her importance, not the lack of it. See further Carney 2000c: 124.
20 See Heckel 1992: 91–106; Carney 2000c: 124.
21 Macurdy 1932a: 36; Errington 1970: 60; Heckel 1992: 104.
22 Diodorus (18.12.1) mentions that Antipater, hoping for military assistance, offered a daughter to the satrap of Phrygia. He calls this satrap Philotas. Since Leonnatus was, in fact, the satrap of Phrygia (so even Diod. 18.3.1), this is presumably an error (Errington 1970: 60). Moreover, Olympias and Cleopatra later attempted to counter another marriage alliance involving another daughter of Antipater, lending credence to the idea that they had done it before.

23 Diod. 18.33–36.5; Plut. *Eum.* 5–7; Arr. *FGrH* 156 F 26. Diodorus and Justin, based on Antigonus' claims, report these secret negotiations, but not all historians believe that Antigonus was telling the truth. Some even believe that Cleopatra did actually marry Perdiccas, though there is no proof; see Carney 2000c: 292, n. 31.

24 See Carney 2000c: 126–7.

25 Plutarch (*Pyrrh.* 2.1), narrating later Molossian events, refers to the "the children of Neoptolemus" and later mentions (*Pyrrh.* 4.1) the rule of a Neoptolemus with whom Pyrrhus once shared power and whom he later murdered (5.1, 7). Granted that the father of Alexander of Molossia was Neoptolemus, that eldest sons were typically named after their paternal grandfather, that this Neoptolemus' sister's name was Cadmeia (5.5), a name associated with victory against Thebes—the victory of her uncle the Macedonian Alexander—the "children of Neoptolemus" were probably the descendants of Neoptolemus, father of Olympias and Alexander, and the Neoptolemus who shared rule with Pyrrhus was Cleopatra's son (so Berve 1926: 2.186, 273; Hammond 1967: 558; Garoufalias 1979: 188–90 *contra* Reuss 1881: 168–71; Cross 1932: 42; Lévêque 1957: 99–100). Reuss 1881: 169 doubts that Cleopatra would have left Molossia if she had such a son since he supposes that her departure somehow signified his renunciation of the throne. This is not convincing. Cleopatra could leave her mother in charge of her son and pursue marriage, something she and Olympias needed, as we have noted.

26 A similar circumstance in the next century, with another Olympias (II) as regent, contributed to the end of Aeacid monarchy: see Hammond 1967: 591–3 and Chapter 6. Olympias II also sought outside military aid when her sons were too young to rule.

27 Whether or not Aeacides shared rule with Neoptolemus at this stage, Olympias' favoring of Aeacides hardly required abandoning her grandson (so Reuss 1881: 169–70) since he was so young that he would not be able to rule for many years.

28 Diodorus' diction in this passage suggests that this was a faction only, not all the Molossians. This certainly is the implication of the rest of the list of allies opposing Antipater. For instance, Diodorus also refers to "the Thessalians except for the Pelinnians."

29 Hammond 1967: 561. See *contra* Treves 1942: 148; Errington 1975b; Heskel 1988. Hammond believed that Arybbas, rather than replacing young Neoptolemus as king, became co-king with him and that when Arybbas died, Aeacides succeeded him as co-king with Neoptolemus. There is no evidence of their shared kingship, but Aeacids before and after this did share kingship.

30 Cross 1932: 43. Plutarch (*Pyrrh.* 1.4) says that Aeacides married Phthia, a daughter of Menon the Thessalian, an important leader of the forces arrayed against Macedonia in the Lamian War. This too would imply that when the war began, Aeacides' family opposed the Macedonians.

31 Cross 1932: 44 continued to believe that Aeacides got the throne because Antipater hoped he would work against Olympias, though he recognized that Aeacides, in fact, pursued the opposite policy.

32 Hammond 1967: 561.

33 Cross 1932: 47, n. 1 suggests that Aeacides, rather than his older brother, became king because Aeacides was the son of Olympias' sister Troas whereas Alcetas, Cross supposed, was the son of another wife. However, Pausanias (1.11.5) specifically says that Arybbas had banished his elder son because of his ungoverned temper.

34 By the time of the siege of Pydna, Olympias' grandson Alexander IV had been

betrothed (or actually married) to Aeacides' daughter Deidameia (Plut. *Pyrrh.* 4.2). This "marriage" not only confirmed the personal alliance between Olympias and her nephew but typifies the general dynastic loyalty of the Aeacids. Marriage within the dynasty had grown frequent: Arybbas married his niece Troas, Alexander his niece Cleopatra, and Deidameia was supposed to marry her cousin.

35   Since they could hardly count on the survival of the male line of the family, mother and daughter pursued marriage alliances for Cleopatra.

36   All three passages in Diodorus about her *epimeleia* (personal guardianship; see below) make it contingent upon her return to Macedonia, something that did not happen until the fall of 317. Hammond 1988a: 131 wrongly assumes that she accepted Polyperchon's offer immediately but that she did not need to return to Macedonia to accept it.

37   See Heckel 1992: 188–204 for an overview of his career and Wheatley 1998.

38   On the meaning of Polyperchon's offer and the significance of *prostasia*, see discussion and references in Carney 2000c: 138–9; Mirón-Pérez 2000: 36; and Bosworth 2002: 48–57.

39   O'Neil 1999a: 5 sees Olympias as "only reluctantly" taking up an important role in Macedonia at this point, because of the absence of a male defender for her grandson. She was certainly cautious, but nothing suggests that she did not want to exercise power. Her caution related to legitimate fears about safety (and, one suspects, success).

40   On the career of Cassander, see Berve 1926: 2:201–2; Fortina 1965; Adams 1977, 1979, 1984. Adams 1979 argues that Cassander did briefly participate in the early part of Alexander's campaign, in Asia Minor.

41   Bosworth 2002: 246–78.

42   Since Antipater had not made his eldest son his successor, Cassander must have had mixed feelings about his father and his father's policies. Initially, therefore, he may not have planned to continue his father's hostility to Olympias, but events led him in that direction. His marriage to Thessalonice and his possible earlier marriage to a daughter of Amyntas and Cynnane (see Palagia 1999, based on a funerary inscription, and Tataki 1988: 85, n. 26 for references to the inscription) suggest that he was trying to exclude Alexander's part of the Argead family from rule but ally himself with what was left of the other branches of the dynasty.

43   Gregory 1995: 27–8 concludes that Cassander had good relations with his siblings, in contrast to the murderous ways of many of the Successors. If so, Olympias' elimination of one brother and disrespect for the remains of another would have been particularly offensive.

44   Most recently, see Carney 2000c: 132–7.

45   For Cynnane, see Carney 2000c: 69–70, 129–31.

46   Polyaenus 8.60. O'Neil 1999a: 6 suggests that his narrative may have been "embellished" in order to make her seem less Greek. Polyaenus' account of Cynnane, however, does not focus on her "otherness" (for instance, he never characterizes her actions as barbaric or unwomanly) but rather on her skill as a warrior. The substance of Polyaenus' picture, as O'Neil concedes, is supported by Arr. *FGrH* 156 F 9.22–3. Cool 2005: 64–6 reports on burials of warrior women in Roman Britain who may have been Illyrian. See also Carney 2004: 184–7. Hatzopoulos 1994: 81, n. 3 is not convincing when he suggests stories about troops of Macedonian maenads possibly armed with daggers (Polyaen. 4.1) explain these accounts about the military training of royal Macedonian women. I am aware of no story about Olympias' military training. Cynnane and Adea Eurydice had multiple associations with the army and were not understood as Macedonian but Illyrian.

47 Arr. *FGrH* 156 F 9.23. Bosworth 2002: 12, n. 26, seems to believe that Adea Eurydice's marriage was not her mother's plan, contrary to the views of others (Macurdy 1932a: 49; Heckel 1983–4: 195; Carney 2000c: 129–30), apparently because he does not read the Arrian passage as others have. Granted the efforts of Antipater, Olympias, and Cleopatra, and the general surge in marriage alliances in the period immediately after Alexander's death, it is hard to imagine why else Cynnane would have risked the dangers of her trip. Had she simply wished to avoid Antipater's control, closer and safer havens were available, most obviously among Illyrian kin.

48 Hornblower 1981: 161 pictures Cassander as the catalyst, exploiting the existing hostility between the two branches of the Argeads by supporting Philip Arrhidaeus.

49 *Heidelberg Epitome FGrH* 15 F1 and App. *Syr.* 52 assert that Philip Arrhidaeus had been allotted kingship only until Alexander IV reached his majority. While this assertion is probably not literally true (see Carney 2001: 83, n. 108), it is likely enough that Philip Arrhidaeus would have ceased to be king if Alexander IV managed to stay alive long enough to rule without a guardian.

50 Hammond 1988a: 141 blames it on Cassander's decision to stay in Tegea, suggesting that he may have wanted Adea Eurydice to fail, or at least expected her to.

51 Since Adea Eurydice accompanied her mother on the escape from Antipater's forces, it is possible that she was involved in that small-scale military activity, but, if so, we do not know it. Diodorus (19.11.2) refers to it as "her" army but this need not indicate who commanded it. The sources mention various men throughout her career who assisted her, but none is given a military title and the only person mentioned in terms of this encounter is Polycles, whom Diodorus (19.11.3) refers to as an advisor. While it is possible that she did not even plan to participate in the battle, the desertion of her army is hardly proof that she did not (so, oddly, O'Neil 1999a: 7, n. 17) but rather the event that prevents us from knowing if she did. If Duris is right, both women presented themselves in the guise they thought would most impress their armies (and foes).

52 Macurdy 1932a: 41 suggests that Olympias may have recalled a story (Polyaen. 4.1) about how Macedonian maenads once turned away an opposing army. See further Chapter 5.

53 Macurdy 1932b: 256–61 argues that Alexander IV and his mother remained in Polyperchon's control until his forces and those of Aeacides met, on the Macedonian border. If so, Olympias would have met her grandson for the first time at this critical moment.

54 Adams 1984: 86 believes that they deserted because they did not want a battle "without a competent commander." Perhaps, but then one wants to know why they had followed them to begin with.

55 Carney 1993b and 1994b.

56 See Carney 1993b: 50–4 for discussion of forced suicide and suicide and royal women. Aelian (*V.H.* 13.36) also briefly mentions the story of the choices offered her and her preference for the noose. See also Chapter 3.

57 See Appendix for a discussion of the contrast this passage presents to the rest of Diodorus' material about Olympias. Hornblower 1981: 121 surmises that Hieronymus, Diodorus' presumed source, derived this account from "court gossip" and Hieronymus therefore included a reference to a servant (the presumed witness) to make a somewhat unbelievable tale less so. However, see below for the possibility that both Adea Eurydice and Olympias may have modeled their behavior at death on tragedy.

58 See ἀνόσιος in *LSJ*. Bartsiokas 2000: 513–14, in his recent reexamination of the male bones from Tomb II at Vergina, concluded that they showed physical signs of having been first inhumed for some time before being cremated (*contra* Musgrave 1985), a conclusion that supports an identification of the male as Philip Arrhidaeus, not his father Philip II.

59 See Berve 1926: 2.274.

60 Arr. 7.27.1–3; Just. 12.13.6–9 (which includes a second cupbearer son of Antipater, Philip, in the plot); Curt. 10.10.14–19; Plut. *Alex* 77.2, *Mor.* 849F.

61 Kurtz and Boardman 1971: 197.

62 He attributes it to Hieronymus' prejudice against kings, particularly Lysimachus. He argues that Lysimachus would not have treated the graves of Alexander's ancestors so badly, nor would Pyrrhus later have allied himself with Lysimachus, had this really happened. Elsewhere, Pausanias (1.13.7) claims that Hieronymus gave a biased treatment of Pyrrhus because of his need to please Antigonus (Gonatas). Hornblower 1981: 17 considers that it is "less certain" that Hieronymus was dependable in his treatment of historical figures, though later (74) she says that, in this passage, Pausanias gave only a confused version of what Hieronymus said. My view is that it would be a mistake to prize Pausanias' view over that of Hieronymus.

63 Edson 1970: 23.

64 Though manuscripts read "CCC," editors have often emended this to "XXX." (See references in Carney 1993b: 49, n. 52.) However, Yardley and Heckel 1984: 255 reject the emendation.

65 See Billows 1990: 11, n. 26, and n. 27 for a useful list of atrocities by various Successors.

66 On Macedonian political trials, see O'Neil 1999b. Bauman 1990: 128–70 also discusses Macedonian political trials but his discussion is limited by lack of familiarity with Macedonian constitutional issues and a tendency to assume that the Macedonians acted like the Athenians.

67 O'Neil 1999b: 31, 46.

68 Unless, of course, our sources fail to mention it. Hammond 1988a: 140, n. 3 apparently assumes they did since he believes that Olympias got the assembly to condemn the supporters of Cassander. More likely, just as Alexander did not risk trying Parmenio in person (if he tried him at all) and Cassander did not take the risk for Olympias, Olympias feared a trial that would put the royal couple in front of a group of Macedonians. See further below.

69 Macurdy 1932a: 45 thinks so, but the sources do not compare her actions to those of the men.

70 Holst-Warhaft 1992: 118.

71 Mirón-Pérez 2000: 35 believes that the remark is authentic because Macedonians really did not like or accept female rule. The issue is not, however, the truth of the generalization attributed to Antipater, but whether he said it, especially on his deathbed. Long literary tradition attributes witty or memorably appropriate remarks to the dying famous. This particular deathbed remark probably originated in Cassander's propaganda against Olympias, either while she was still alive, or after her death, when he needed to justify that death.

72 One could, perhaps, imagine that he was also thinking of Adea Eurydice since she too had opposed him, as had Olympias' daughter Cleopatra (see above).

73 When Diodorus (19.35.1) speaks of Cassander's reactions to events in Macedonia, he mentions the murders of Philip Arrhidaeus and Adea Eurydice and Olympias' maltreatment of his brother's tomb, but omits the deaths of Cassander's supporters.

74 For instance, Bosworth 2002: 249, commenting on Lysimachus' slaughter of five thousand Illyrian troops under his own command, says, "He was well advised to do so." Lysimachus had reason to fear that his Illyrian troops might revolt and turn against him, so Bosworth considers the massacre appropriate because it makes pragmatic sense.

75 Carney 1993b.

76 Errington 1977: 478–504 and Billows 1990: 60, 86–105 (see further references in Bosworth 2002: 279, n. 1) support the more drawn-out chronology and date the siege of Pydna to winter 316/15. See Bosworth 1992: 55–81 for arguments for the chronology that puts the siege of Pydna in winter 316/15. Bosworth 2002: 280–4 provides a helpful chronology of events, reflecting his views.

77 See Heckel 1992: 193–9 for a detailed discussion.

78 Hornblower 1981: 225 understands Diodorus' statement about the make-up of her entourage to be critical of Olympias. Since she was forced to withdraw to the city and hardly chose to have non-combatants with her rather than more soldiers, this seems to misread the passage.

79 To my mind, their disarray confirms the view that Cassander moved quickly north. His forces consistently arrived at critical points before their opponents. Justin (14.6.4) says he reached Pydna by rapid or forced marches. As Adams 1984: 87 notes, his enemies were "caught utterly flatfooted."

80 On Polyperchon's subsequent inglorious career, see Heckel 1992: 200–4; Wheatley 1998.

81 Justin (14.6.2) attributes Olympias' withdrawal to her "distrust of the Macedonians." If his comment refers to civilian Macedonian opinion, it is incorrect (see below), but he may be speaking about Cassander's Macedonians.

82 Diodorus (19.35.5) lists Roxane, Alexander IV, Thessalonice (a daughter of Philip II by another wife), Deidameia, daughter of Aeacides, the daughters of Attalus, and other kin of Olympias' most important friends. Justin (14.6.2–3) has much the same list, though he confuses Alexander IV with his half-brother Heracles.

83 His behavior seems inexplicable, particularly granted that his subsequent actions suggest that he remained loyal. Even if he were waiting for aid from Eumenes (see below), that would not have signified if Olympias and her grandson fell into Cassander's control. Perhaps he simply lacked sufficient troops to mount a defense of Pydna.

84 Olympias and officers loyal to her may have hoped for help, direct or indirect, from Eumenes. Aristonous' position at Amphipolis, not helpful for confronting Cassander, might suggest an interest in connecting to reinforcements from the east. Similarly, Diodorus' statement (19.50.8) that Aristonous was reluctant to surrender in part because he did not know of Eumenes' death only makes sense if he thought that Eumenes' survival would aid him. Although Olympias' ability to get valuable intelligence, even over great distances, was generally good, Cassander's blockade and siege may have prevented her from knowing about his situation, just as, apparently, it did Aristonous.

85 On Eumenes' final campaign, see Bosworth 2002: 98–168. Although the absolute date of the deaths of Olympias and Eumenes is disputed because of the general chronological controversy (see above), there is general agreement that they happened at about the same time. See Errington 1977: 487.

86 Hammond 1967: 562 assumes that the Epirotes did not know that the enemy they were advancing against was the Macedonian army. Diodorus (19.36.3) contradicts this assumption since he says that the majority of Epirotes had set out for a campaign against the Macedonians unwillingly. Cassander's control of the passes, however, rather than their more general discontent, seems to have been the trigger for their rebellion.

87   Pausanias may intend to attribute Epirote hatred of Olympias to her savagery in the fall of 317, but it is difficult to determine if that is his meaning, or whether he refers to more general dislike. Diodorus' account focuses on policy—opposition to war against Macedonia—rather than hatred of either figure. Clearly all these factors could interrelate. For more on Olympias' possible impact on subsequent Molossian history and the continuation of the Aeacid/Antipatrid feud, see Chapter 6.

88   Pausanias (11.3–5) also provides a narrative of these events but, apparently conflating Aeacides' two campaigns in support of Olympias, asserts that Aeacides' troops refused to accompany him on both occasions. This assertion is contradicted by the narratives of both Diodorus and Justin, as we have seen.

89   Adams 1977: 23 makes the excellent point that, while Cassander demonstrated skill as a general, his success also depended on a collection of very competent officers who, for instance, repeatedly reached critical mountain passes in time to command them.

90   Polyaenus and Diodorus offer differing accounts of an attempted escape by Olympias in a quinquireme, just prior to her surrender. According to Polyaenus (4.11.3), before the fall of Pydna, Polyperchon tried to arrange for Olympias' escape, but Cassander thwarted the plot and this in turn convinced Olympias that Polyperchon could not be trusted, so she surrendered. In Diodorus (19.50.4–5), Olympias herself tried to launch the ship, was betrayed by a traitor, Cassander seized the quinquireme, and Olympias then recognized that she had no choice but to negotiate for surrender.

91   Diodorus offers this explanation of Cassander's failure to honor his promise: Aristonous' reputation as a royal bodyguard of Alexander and Cassander's eagerness to eliminate any able to revolt. See below on identity of the agents of his death.

92   Pausanias (9.7.2) does not clearly describe a trial.

93   Briant 1973: 298–9; Bauman 1990: 162; O'Neil 1999b: 45.

94   Curtius (6.11.38) describes stoning as an ancestral Macedonian custom, but, though Curtius twice reports that the Macedonians stoned Philotas to death (6.11.38, 72.1), Arrian (3.26.3) says they killed him with javelins. Stoning may have been a common but not exclusive punishment (see O'Neil 1999b: 31–2). Elsewhere in Greece it was not a legal punishment but a common mob action.

95   Women, even at the point of death, still needed to maintain sexual modesty. Justin's account therefore gives Olympias a death that is partly masculine (killed by men with weapons in public) and partly feminine. See Carney 1993b: 52–4 for discussion and references.

96   These stories of varying and multiple escape attempts do not inspire much confidence in their veracity, but they could be true. A surprising number of other stories of royal female escapes, often in disguise, survive, but their popularity does not necessitate their falseness; see further Carney 2000c: 175, n. 91.

97   O'Neil 1999b: 46 points to the parallel with Parmenio: neither Alexander nor Cassander risked allowing them a public defense because of their powerful support and the dubious case against them. See above on Olympias' treatment of Philip Arrhidaeus and Adea Eurydice.

98   Bauman 1990: 163 considers and rejects this possibility on the dubious grounds that the punishment—no burial—does not fit the crime of murder but rather treason. Picturing the Macedonians as concerned about such legal niceties is implausible.

99   Hatzopoulos 1996: 273–6. While his view rationalizes Diodorus to a degree that is somewhat implausible, his idea that Olympias had a right to speak and

would have, if proceedings not been halted, better fits Macedonian culture than Adams' suggestion (1977: 22, n. 23) that, like Athenian women, she had no right to speak in assembly.

100 See discussion and references in Bauman 1990: 162–3.

101 Bosworth 1994: 65; O'Neil 1999b: 32, 41.

102 O'Neil 1999b: 40.

103 So Hatzopoulos 1996: 273–6, who believes that the murder of Olympias, like the equally controversial murders of Cleopatra, Alexander IV, and his mother, was disguised, in this case by an attempt to make it look like a vendetta on the part of the families of those Olympias had killed.

104 Mirón-Pérez 2000: 46–52, following Vernant's view that in Homeric society the wife represented the royal hearth and marriage, connects this to the role of the king's wife as "perpetuator and transmitter of sovereignty" and argues that power could be understood as a woman's dowry when a man who wanted to rule (e.g., Cassander) married a king's wife. My view is that these are quite different circumstances.

105 Hammond 1988b: 145, 167 doubted Diodorus' statement about the "pages" (Royal Youths) because he thought Alexander IV was too young to have any, but see Burstein 1977 and Heckel 1980 for epigraphic confirmation of the existence of Alexander IV's Royal Youths.

106 As Bosworth 2002: 41 notes, Cassander was able to use Philip Arrhidaeus, even after his death, to legitimize his own position.

107 On these events and their dates, see Carney 2000c: 145–52.

108 *Contra* Gruen 1985: 254, who doubts that this was the intention of Cassander and others, even at the time of the murder of Alexander IV.

109 See Carney 1993b: 53 for references and the Appendix.

110 Bosworth 2002: 253–5 stresses the importance for Hellenistic kings of Homeric battle action, single combat, and general prowess, all in imitation of Alexander. See Cohen 1995 on the influence of Homer on Macedonian elite culture and Carney 2000a: 273–85 on Alexander's manipulation of his imitation of Achilles.

111 Justin's account, with Olympias going out to meet her murderers, makes this explicit. In Diodorus, with the mention of the royal house, there is the possibility that she was killed indoors, but this was hardly a private death and the means, the sharp blade, was more masculine than feminine.

112 Justin's version has her death approximate a forced suicide and he mentions her concern for bodily modesty, both features of the appropriate female death, but other aspects of his account of her end are, as discussed, more masculine. Diodorus' version makes her death overtly masculine.

113 So also Porphyry *FGrH* 260 F 3.3.

114 So Garland 2001: 101–3. But see *contra* Griffin 1980: 47.

115 Whitehorne 1983: 137. See Garland 2001: 101 for discussion of the Boeotian refusal in 424 to allow the burial of the dead because they had committed sacrilege. In Sophocles, it is treason or betrayal of *philia* that inspires Creon's refusal to bury Polyneices (*Antigone* 21–36, 198–210) and Agamemnon to refuse burial to Ajax (*Ajax* 1052–63). Pausanias' version (9.7.2) of Olympias' death as execution by stoning, though probably mistaken, may come from its common popular use against traitors (Bowra 1944: 49) or from the fact that Macedonians did sometimes employ it as a method of execution. See above.

116 So Whitehorne 1983: 133–4.

117 *Contra* Whitehorne 1983: 134, who seems to consider Achilles' treatment of the body of Hector and Hector's fear of mutilation as unique. Apart from the behavior of the other Greek heroes in terms of Hector's corpse already discussed, the Aiantes not only strip the dead Imbrius of his armor, but cut off

his head and toss it back among the Trojans, so that it lands at Hector's feet (*Il.* 16.200–5). See Tritle 1997 for discussion and references.

118   Griffin 1980: 46–7.

119   See also Hegesias of Magnesia *FGrH* 142 F 5.

120   So (explicitly) Tritle 1997: 123 and (implicitly) Bosworth 1988: 68 *contra* Atkinson 1980: 341 and many others (see references in Bosworth 1980: 258).

121   Cohen 1995: 491.

122   Lacey 1968: 148–9; Kurtz and Boardman 1971: 143; Whitehorne 1983: 130, 137. Thus the idea of what Whitehorne 1983: 137 terms "posthumous exile."

123   Griffin 1980: 160. Thus, though Themistocles had been convicted of treason and the Athenians had therefore denied him burial, his relatives secretly brought him to Athens and buried him there (Thuc. 1.138.6).

124   He appropriated the role of kinsman to bury Adea Eurydice and Philip Arrhidaeus, suggesting that they were defined as the legitimate royal family. His treatment of Alexander IV, even before his murder, in keeping with his treatment of Olympias' body, implies the illegitimacy of that part of the Argead family.

5   Olympias and religion

1   For general discussions, see Kraemer 1992: 22–49; Blundell 1995: 160–8; Dillon 2002.

2   See discussion in Jones 1999: 2–3. Certainly, as Jones 1999: 51 notes, ties between Greek cities and states were defined and reinforced by their common religion and shared worship of the same gods.

3   On female pilgrimage, see Dillon 1997: 183–203.

4   Kraemer 1992: 22.

5   Blundell 1995: 166.

6   By the fourth century, priestesses began to dedicate statues of themselves (Kron 1996: 146).

7   Zeitlin 1982: 129–57; Bremmer 1984: 285. Cohen 1991: 238 discusses the phenomenon of "simultaneous norm-validation and norm-non-adherence." See below on this phenomenon in terms of women in the cult of Dionysus.

8   Blundell 1995:160

9   On religion in Macedonia, see Ginouvès 1994: 106–16; Hatzopoulos 1994. See also Baege 1913; Düll 1977.

10   Le Bohec-Bouhet 2002.

11   In the remains of the funeral pyre placed on top of slabs covering Derveni Alpha were the carbonized remains of an Orphic text (see Themelis and Touratsoglou 1997: 30, 194, 205–6 and Laks and Most 1997).

12   Tomb I at Vergina contains a fresco that depicts the rape of Persephone and, perhaps, Demeter herself (Andronicos 1984: 86–97, Drogou *et al.* 1996: 73–5). Also at Vergina, inside the "Tomb of Eurydice" or "Tomb of the Throne" was an oversize throne, its back painted to depict Hades and Persephone in a chariot (see Ginouvès 1994: 154–61).

13   Kottaridi 2004a: 140 and 2004b: 69; and Lilibaki-Akamati 2004: 91. Kottaridi 2004b: 69 sees the presence of objects connected to sacrifice and feasting as indications of priestly duties. As with other burials at Vergina/Aegae, the difficulty is that, in the absence of an inscription with a name, we have no way to determine which were royal and which non-royal burials. The burials in question are quite rich and may well have been royal, but there is no certainty.

14   See Carney 2000c: 41 for references and discussion.

15   See discussion and references in Mortensen 1992, and Borza 1992: 308–9, Carney 2000c: 40–6.

16 The inscription does not specify the nature of the dedication. See discussion of its possible nature in Saatsoglou-Paliadeli 2000: 402.

17 Some scholars have failed to note that the passage is probably not a genuine work of Plutarch (see discussion in Mortensen 1992: 159, n. 16) and are unaware (e.g., Hammond 1994: 184; Saatsoglou-Paliadeli 2000: 401–3) of emendations to the text (see Robert and Robert 1984: 450–1; Wilhelm 1949: 625–33). Consequently, with a different understanding of the content of the inscription, they reach conclusions about its significance different from my own. Though the passage does not identify this particular Eurydice as the mother of Philip II, the discovery of the inscriptions at Vergina which give the same patronymic (see below) have led to the virtual certainty that the *Moralia* passage refers to the mother of Philip II.

18 Since the dedication itself did not survive, we do not know the location of the inscription.

19 The first inscribed statue base was found in 1982, the second in 1990. See, most recently, Saatsoglou-Paliadeli 2000: 392–7.

20 *AR* 2002–3: 61 reports the discovery of the head of a statue from the adjoining sanctuary of the Mother of the gods which is identified (reason not reported) as that of Eurydice.

21 A headless statue was found near the second inscribed statue base; the plinth of this statue fits the second statue base; subsequently a head was excavated (Saatsoglou-Paliadeli 2000: 396). Hammond 1994: 184 identified the statue as Eurydice herself and, without further explanation (other than a reference to the so-called tomb of Eurydice, a structure the original excavator attributed to her but for which attribution there is no specific evidence) concludes that this means she was probably "worshiped after her death as a goddess." While Eurydice certainly had at least one portrait statue (in the Philippeum) and may well have had another (see below), nothing has survived so it is hardly possible to identify her image, particularly since Greek artists tended to produce only the most generalized images of women (see further Chapter 6). The statue could represent Eucleia (so *AR* 1990–1: 56), or perhaps Eurydice as Eucleia.

22 As Dillon 2002: 3 notes, Plato (*Laws* 909e–910a) complained that women were peculiarly inclined to dedicate shrines and altars. One can rarely tell whether female dedicators funded the dedications themselves or through their male relatives (Dillon 2002: 25), particularly since (as Kron 1996: 155 notes), law or custom often obliged men to pay for female activity. Similarly, we have no information as to whether Eurydice herself or one of her royal sons paid for the construction of the complex. In any event, since the statue base inscriptions do not mention her husband or sons but only Eurydice and (through the patronymic) her father, they put emphasis on her rather than her Argead family.

23 The current excavator of the Eucleia shrine (Saatsoglou-Paliadeli 2000: 394) thinks that the inscriptions date to the mid-fourth century (or possibly a little later). The last literary reference to Eurydice dates to roughly 368. It is extremely likely that she was dead by 346 at the latest (Carney 2000c: 45).

24 So Saatsoglou-Paliadeli 2000: 397. Kron 1996: 139–40 points out that priesthoods, in the Hellenic world typically held by elite women, dramatically increased the social status of the women who held them. In a monarchy like Macedonia, one would expect that royal women, therefore, would be priestesses of appropriate cults, especially in the two capitals.

25 Saatsoglou-Paliadeli first (1987: 742) associated it with Philip's victory at Chaeroneia (following Andronicos 1984: 50–1) but has now (2000: 395) suggested (responding to the criticism of Borza 1992: 193 and Mortensen 1992: 164) that the shrine commemorated Eurydice's successful intervention

in 368 with the Athenian general Iphicrates, when she safeguarded the throne for her remaining sons. This is a more attractive suggestion, though troubles in Macedonia in that period could mean that the actual dedication happened later.

26 Borza 1992: 192–3.

27 My views have changed somewhat since Carney 2000c: 44–6. Saatsoglou-Paliadeli 2000: 395 assumes that the Vergina cult was associated with victory.

28 See discussions in Cabanes 1988; Pötscher 1988; Dakaris 1998: 6–10; Vokotopoulou 2001. They differ on the significance of the epithet "Naos" and on the aspect of Zeus on which the cult focused. Over the passage of time, other deities also found a place at the site, among them Dionysus (Hammond 1967: 510–11; Parke 1967: 150–2; see below).

29 Some differences appear to relate to change in practice over time, but not all. See Parke 1967: 80–6; Dakaris 1998: 13–14; Vokotopoulou 2001: 654, 663.

30 Parke 1967: 113, based on a survey of the surviving lead-inscribed tablets from Dodona then available, followed by Vokotopoulou 2001: 77, based on a much larger collection of tablets (now about 1300). However, if responses to cities were taken back to them (so Dakaris *et al.* 2001: 511), there may have been more involvement of that sort than the tablets imply. Like Samothrace (see below), the great majority of patrons, however, were local.

31 Dakaris 1998: 13 points out that the first temple dates to about the time the Molossians came to control Dodona (*c.* 410–385 *contra* Cross 1932: 6). Additions and changes to the shrine in the course of the fourth century made it look more like a conventional Greek sanctuary.

32 As Dakaris 1998: 18 points out, the structure obviously existed by the time of Hyperides' speech (*c.* 330; see below). He suggests that the Dione temple was built between 350 and 330, when the sacred precinct was surrounded by a stone wall. Parke 1967: 142 believes that the shrine was under construction at the time and that the Athenians had been asked by the oracle to provide the cult statue. Hyperides' language (see below) implies, however, that the seated image already existed and that the Athenians were adding to and improving something that already existed.

33 Parke 1967: 142, who also assumes that Olympias was regent of Molossia at the time; as we have seen, this is not certain (see Chapter 3).

34 Vokotopoulou 2001: 65, citing the fact that there was very little construction until the second half of the fourth century, connects it to Olympias' marriage. She seems to assume that Argeads would have funded the building. Another possibility is that the Aeacids, competitive as they were with the Argeads (see Chapters 1 and 2) funded more building for that reason. If the building occurred after 334, as seems to be the case for Dione's sanctuary, it may have been the work (and funding) of Olympias and/or Cleopatra, granted their apparent role in Molossia (see Chapter 3).

35 Parke 1967: 142–3 notes that before and after Chaeroneia, the Athenians had looked to northwestern Greece for support against Macedonia, and suggests that their extravagant gifts to Dione were meant to gain them goodwill in that region. For earlier Athenian consultation of Dodona, see Parke 1967: 139–42

36 Diodorus (18.4.5) includes in the list of projects in Alexander's last plans the construction of six very expensive temples at Delos, Delphi, Dodona, Dion, Amphipolis, and Cyrnus. The list is clearly panhellenic, but Olympia is not on it, even though Dodona, Dion, and the mysterious Cyrnus are. The authenticity of Alexander's "last plans" has sometimes been doubted: see Bosworth 1988: 164–5 and 2002: 59, n. 112. Vokotopoulou 2001: 651 believes that Alexander had plans for Dodona.

37 See Asirvatham *et al.* 2001: i–xv for discussion and references on the problematic nature of the categories of "religion" and "magic," on the tendency to describe as magic the actions of those one considered "Other." Olympias, as a woman and a Molossian, obviously is liable to be treated as "Other," as Plutarch clearly does.

38 Asirvatham 2001: 95 argues that another factor that contributes to Plutarch's treatment of Olympias is his use of her as a foil to Alexander, the immoderate barbarian as opposed to her Hellenic son. See also Appendix.

39 Ogden forthcoming points out that *pharmaka* can signify not only herbs or poisons but also spells.

40 As Ogden forthcoming notes, in the *Alexander Romance* (4–7, 12), Olympias has a relationship with the magician king Nectanebo. See Chapter 6 for further discussion.

41 Cross 1932: 4 seems to accept Aelian's testimony at face value.

42 Asirvatham 2001: 99. They are stories he reports as something others say or they are beliefs he attributes to Philip.

43 Justin (11.11.3–6) makes this explicit. According to him, Olympias confessed to Philip that Alexander's father was not Philip but a big snake. This leads Philip to repudiate Olympias on grounds of adultery with the snake and Alexander to pursue the claim of divine birth for his own reasons as well as to clear his mother's name. Asirvatham 2001: 102 points to the oddity that in the *Alexander Romance*, Nectanebo appears to Olympias as Ammon in the guise of a snake (i.e., dressed in a snake suit). The version in the *Romance* clearly derives from the references in more conventional historical sources to Alexander's belief that he was the son of Zeus Ammon.

44 This is the central thesis of Ogden forthcoming. See also Ogden 1999: 21–7 and Chapter 2 on succession struggles in Macedonia between rival wives for the succession of their sons.

45 Aelian (see above) makes the association for Molossian women but Thessalian women (see Ogden forthcoming for references) were much more commonly associated with witchcraft, and Ogden discusses some passages which may indicate that Philinna too was said to employ witchcraft.

46 Mortensen 1997: 76–83 has an excellent discussion of Olympias and snakes. Asirvatham 2001: 102 seems to believe that tame snakes are somehow not credible and therefore concludes that Lucian *Alex.* 6–7 (which not only mentions snakes in Pella but alludes to the story about Olympias sleeping with them) derives from his skepticism and is not to be taken seriously. See *contra* Mortensen 1997: 82 who takes the Lucian passage more literally, as I do. So also Dillon 2002: 144.

47 See Asirvatham 2001: 97–8 for some of the possibilities. Saatsoglou-Paliadeli 1991: 15–17 and 2000: 391, discussing the discovery of a colossal marble snake in a deposit in the antechamber of Temple II in the Eucleia sanctuary complex at Vergina, connects it to Zeus Melichius. At the moment nothing connects Olympias to this sanctuary. Even if Saatsoglou-Paliadeli is correct, the nature and benefits of the cult would be uncertain. Burkert 1985: 201 considers him a god of the underworld and implies that his rites related mainly to reconciliation of the dead, whereas Cook 1965: 2.1091–60 associates the cult with purification of blood guilt and perhaps fertility.

48 On this, see Mortensen 1997: 79.

49 Plutarch says that the use of snakes in this manner "astonished (or terrified)" the men. As Mortensen 1997: 73 points out, this probably means that it was a practice unfamiliar to them.

50 Carney 1987a: 41, n. 16; O'Brien 1992: 13; argued at length by Mortensen 1997: 76–7, especially n. 177; Dillon 2002: 144.

51 Carney 1987a: 41, n. 16; Mortensen 1997: 82–3. She cites Lucian *Alex.* 7 on the sale of tame snakes in the Pella market place. See also Cic. *De Div.* 2.135 and above.

52 Other than Plutarch, there is only the highly dubious statement of Justin (9.7.13) that Olympias dedicated to Apollo the sword of Philip's assassin, for secrecy's sake, under the name Myrtale, which she had borne as a little girl. Granted that, as the daughter of a king, her name was well known, this would hardly have constituted concealment.

53 Maxwell-Stuart 1972: 151.

54 Pliny (*NH* 36.4.25) mentions statues of Aphrodite and Pothos and cult for them at Samothrace in his own day. Mortensen 1997: 27 rejects the idea that the cult existed earlier, considers it likely that the statue in question was not that of Aphrodite but the Great Mother, and so concludes that Olympias' name-change cannot have been associated with Aphrodite at Samothrace. In fact, the evidence for Aphrodite at Samothrace, like that for her role at Dodona, is of a later date. Moreover, Cole 1984: 86 notes that elsewhere the Samothracian gods were worshiped in concert with Aphrodite.

55 Heckel 1981b: 83–4.

56 *Contra* Heckel 1981b: 84, who believes that myrtle was associated with fertility rites in general. As to whether one may consider the Samothrace cult a fertility rite, see below.

57 Maxwell-Stuart 1972: 155–6.

58 Mortensen 1997: 26–7 denies any association of the cult with myrtle, marriage or fertility, in this period.

59 Mortensen 1997: 27–9.

60 Maxwell-Stuart 1972: 145–7, 159–61.

61 Maxwell-Stuart 1972 discusses the growing association of the plant with the Eleusinian mysteries, but implies that it may also have symbolized the general power of life (sexuality) and eternal life, not necessarily in association with the Eleusinian mysteries in particular. Certainly wreaths of myrtle appear in male and female burials in Macedonia, including those in the Great Tumulus at Vergina (Carney 1991a: 21).

62 See discussion in Chapter 1.

63 Cole 1984: 17, n. 127 implausibly rejects it as a literary cliché based on the need to explain how the supposedly secluded Athenian woman could meet a man. Quite apart from the assumption that Macedonian/Molossian behavior modeled Athenian, the dedications of elite women at panhellenic sites demonstrates that there is nothing implausible in the idea of Olympias' attendance at the shrine. The cliché and embroidery relate to the erotic part of the story.

64 Cole 1984: 40.

65 See Lane Fox 1973: 44; Cole 1984: 16–17; and discussion in Chapter 1. Mortensen 1997: 19–22 argues that Argead patronage began a few years earlier, in the reign of Philip's brother Perdiccas III, although surmising that Philip may have completed his brother's projects. For our purposes, the relevant point is that this was a shrine recently developed under Argead patronage.

66 Mortensen 1997: 24.

67 Cole 1984: 21, 39–40. Mortensen 1997: 24, n. 147 argues that *FGrH* 70 F 120 does not prove that the festival was held before Hellenistic times, but, of course, nor does it mean that it was not. See, however, Clinton 2003: 50–78, especially 67–8.

68 As Mortensen 1997: 23 observes, the sanctuary was difficult to reach, and even in later periods was largely patronized by those from the northern Aegean area and sailors.

69 See Chapter 1. Molossia had been landlocked until comparatively recent times.
70 Mortensen 1997: 23 points to the discrepancy between the benefits of the cult and Molossian experience. On the nature of the cult's benefits, see Cole 1984: 6; Burkert 1985: 284. While Cole believes that the cult promised eternal salvation, Burkert points out that there was no mention of such a possibility.
71 See discussions in Cole 1984: 1–6, 26–37; Burkert 1985: 281–5; Clinton 2003; Schachter 2003. The gods of the sanctuary are called simply *theoi* (gods) or *theoi megaloi* (Great Gods). Their number, sex, and identity are not known. Though some writers connect the Cabiri to Samothrace, others do not, and their name appears on no inscription at Samothrace.
72 On ordinary female initiates, see Cole 1984: 42. No Greek female *epoptai* (those who had achieved the highest grade of initiation) are known (Cole 1984: 46). In the Hellenistic period, a woman from Miletus dedicated a large building with three rooms (Cole 1984: 21) and Arsinoe, probably during the period of her marriage to Lysimachus, then ruler of Macedonia, dedicated a huge eponymous structure at Samothrace (see Carney 1994a: 125, n. 7 for references and discussion).
73 Cole 1984: 19 implausibly prefers the possibility of Philip Arrhidaeus to Olympias. His probable absence in Asia and his mental limitations make him an unlikely choice for building supervisor (see further Carney 2001). Olympias, an initiate, known to have been given great wealth by Alexander and to have made expensive dedications, seems a more likely choice, even for the period after her return to Molossia. Some non-royal Macedonian may have supervised on Alexander's behalf.
74 See references in Cole 1984: 11, n. 148; Carney 2001: 70, n. 35. Since the names of both kings appear on the inscription, it presumably predates Olympias' control of her grandson.
75 Macurdy 1932a: 24 (followed by Heckel 1981b: 84–5), basing her supposition on Plutarch's statement (*Alex.* 3.8) that Philip heard about the birth of their son the same day he heard of his Olympic victory.
76 Some scholars date the wedding to October 357: Beloch 1922–: 68; Prestianni-Giallombardo 1976–7: 96, n. 46; Green 1991: 30. Hatzopoulos 1982b: 37–42 suggests that the wedding took place in concert with the Macedonian festival of Zeus Olympius, a new year festival held every October. Hatzopoulos' argument depends on the belief that the wedding of Olympias' daughter to Alexander of Molossia was tied to the same festival. There are some difficulties with his argument (see discussion in Mortensen 1997: 32–4; Le Bohec-Bouhet 2002: 44–5). Wedding festivals for major marriage alliances became the norm in the Hellenistic period, based on the model of the wedding of Olympias' daughter (Carney 2000c: 203–7); Hatzopoulos' argument assumes that the model predated the wedding of Cleopatra. Mortensen 1997: 34 hypothesizes that Aegae was the traditional place not only for royal funerals but for royal weddings.
77 Mortensen 1997: 31 argues that the occasion for a name-change should be something important in her life. She also wonders (1997: 47, n. 192) whether being given one's name from a horse race, even a famous one, might be less than complimentary. More to the point, the victory in the horse race does not directly relate to Olympias, whereas her wedding and piety to Zeus did. Certainly, as she notes (1997: 35) associating this name-change with Olympias' wedding better explains the fact that our sources call her by no other name than does attaching it to an event that happened several years after her marriage.
78 *Anth. Gr.* 14.114. Fredricksmeyer 2003: 265, n. 56 accepts this obscure oracle as genuine but see also Kaiser-Raiss 1984: 40.

79   I follow Fredricksmeyer 1966: 179–81 in the reading and translation of this text. He, however, does not suggest, as I do, that Olympias' possession of a slave who performs such duties must mean that she had some sort of role, most likely supervisory, in all the sacrifices, not just those she personally performs. This particular letter is especially likely to be genuine since it fills no propaganda need, is so matter-of-fact in tone, and presents Olympias in a conventional role. Its authenticity should therefore be accepted: see Berve 1926: 312. See *contra* Hamilton 1969: 5; Gagé 1975: 7. As we have seen, any letter in sources should be treated with suspicion, but this one deserves less than most.

80   Pausanias (1.23.4) locates the Athenian cult on the Acropolis.

81   Berve 1926: 286 suggests that she made the offering as a response to Alexander's illness in Cilicia.

82   Dillon 2002: 27, for instance, notes that at the Asclepieion in Athens female dedicators outnumber male, contrary to the situation in the majority of cults. He argues (2002: 31) that women, since they were more often at medical risk than men, tended to focus more than men on healing deities.

83   Dillon 2002: 14 believes that women were the main dedicators to *kourotrophic* (child-nourishing) deities.

84   Dillon 2002: 18 notes that female dedications at Athenian sanctuaries ceased to be outside but rather were placed within temples and took on "a standard form, largely of *phialai* . . . jewellery and the like." Olympias' *phiale* was likely of either silver or gold. Dillon notes that of the ten silver *phialai* dedicated at the Erechtheion, eight were dedicated by women. It was a pattern that continued: Phthia, wife of Demetrius II, dedicated a *phiale* to Apollo at Delos (*ID* 407.20).

85   Dillon 2002: 18. Of course, women sometimes poured their own libations and men sometimes dedicated *phialai*.

86   Her name is restored to the inscription in line 5: Ὀλ[υμπιά]δι. Her son also sent her plunder after Granicus (*FGrH* 151 F 1) and quite possibly on other occasions unknown to us.

87   *Eux.* 19 says that he allowed her to dedicate it. Later, discussing her objections to the Athenian dedication at Dodona, he refers to "those who had come from her" (envoys) but there is no suggestion of envoys in terms of the *phiale*.

88   Kosmetatou 2004: 80 seems to suggest that Olympias' Delphic donation was done by proxy.

89   Instead of returning to Molossia by land, over mountain passes, she could have traveled largely by sea, making stops along the way at Athens and Delphi.

90   See discussion of use of slaves in the household of Alexander in Scholl 1987.

91   Since few military items were initially found in the antechamber, almost all on the threshold of the door to the male burial, Andronicos (1984: 179) the original excavator, suggested that these items belonged to the male. Subsequent work has discovered much more military equipment (including, for instance, a cuirass and apparently an entire panoply), distributed throughout the antechamber (Drogou *et al.* 1996: 57, 107–13; Adam-Veleni 2004: 53). One can no longer plausibly ascribe the martial paraphernalia in the antechamber to the male. See further Carney 2004.

92   Although the debate on the identity of the occupants of Tomb II continues (see Carney 1991a: 1–26 for an overview, with particular reference to the female burial), recent work (Bartsiokas 2000: 511–14; Themelis and Touratsoglou 1997; Palagia 2000) adds decisive support to the already compelling arguments of Borza (1987: 105–21), that the occupants were Philip Arrhidaeus and Adea Eurydice.

93   The Greek *orgiasmos* means the celebration of *orgia*. *Orgia*, according to *LSJ*, can refer to secret rites or worship (perhaps to the mystery religions, that is to

say those requiring initiation) or to general rites or worship. English translations of this passage which employ terms like "orgiastic" (Scott-Kilvert 1973: 253) or "orgies" (Perrin 1919, 1958: 227; Asirvatham 2001: 96) deceive and confuse their readers. Whereas the Greek term (and as we shall see Dionysiac practice itself) could refer to festivals at which indiscriminate sexual activity occurred and to those in which it did not, the English terms explicitly indicate sexual activity. In this passage, Plutarch clearly reacts against emotional excess in religion but it is unlikely (see below) that he imagines sexual excess in this context.

94 Macedonian female worshipers of Dionysus: see Dillon 202: 147 and below.

95 Both Perrin 1919, 1958: 229 and Asirvatham 2001: 97 translate ζηλόω as "affect." *LSJ* offer this as one of the meanings of the verb, but it is probably not the best translation of the term in the context of this passage. The Greek term involves the idea of competition and is particularly appropriate in the light of Plutarch's stress on excess, zealousness. The derivative English term, "zealot," conveys some of this sense. Asirvatham 2001: 97–8, especially n. 12, favors "affect" because the author sees Plutarch as picturing Olympias "inauthentic" in these actions as a result of their "intentionality" and later speaks of them as "a calculated effort to play on the superstition of others." (Asirvatham's discussion of this point makes it difficult to determine whether the actual Olympias or merely Plutarch's construct is the one who is manipulative.) Asirvatham insists (2001: 97) that "intentionality seems incompatible with true inspiration." This view seems unreasonable: Plutarch describes a ritual that involves preparation (snakes, sacred baskets, groups of women, ivy) yet this preparation or organization need not have prevented inspiration.

96 Mortensen 1997: 75 observes that Plutarch describes a public procession but not one involving a retreat to the mountains.

97 O'Brien 1992: 13; Mortensen 1997: 76.

98 Bremmer 1984: 284–5; Dillon 2002: 147 *contra* Kraemer 1979: 31.

99 On the role of Dionysus in Macedonia, see Baege 1913: 79–83; Fredricksmeyer 1966 and 2003: 264–5; Goukowsky 1981: 2.8–9; O'Brien 1992: 14–16; Ginouvès 1994: 113–14; Baynham 2000: 258–9.

100 For an overview of Dionysiac cult, see Burkert 1985: 161–7. See also Cole 1980, 1993a, and 1993b; Henrichs 1982.

101 See Henrichs 1978: 121–60; Kraemer 1979: 55–80; Blundell 1995: 165–9; Dillon 2002: 139–52.

102 At Pella, in the House of Dionysus, a floor mosaic of Dionysus on a panther; the famous Derveni krater (see Themelis and Touratsoglou 1997). At Dion, a sanctuary to Dionysus stood (unsurprisingly) near the Hellenistic theater and Pella also had a Dionysus cult (Ginouvès 1994: 114).

103 In Tomb II, in the main chamber: one of the ivory and gold couches, typical of couch decoration in that period, had themes related to both Dionysus and banqueting (Drogou *et al.* 1996: 99), twin kalyxes with a Silenus head on the interior base, two silver pitchers with a Silenus head at the base of the handle, a lantern with a Pan head at the handle base (Andronicos 1984: 150–3, 162–5). Tomb III also contained an ivory and gold couch decorated with figures related to Dionysiac cult (Drogou *et al.* 1996:105), as well as silver cups with heads of Pan.

104 Dillon 2002: 147 discusses a play of Aeschylus about Macedonian female Dionysiacs.

105 On Alexander and Dionysus, see Edmunds 1971: 376–8; Goukowsky 1981: 2; Bosworth 1996a: 119–23 and 1996b: 140–66; Fredricksmeyer 2003: 264–5. Philip's relationship to Dionysus (O'Brien 1992: 14) seems tied to drinking (implied even in his coinage), true of many Macedonians. Most of the

Dionysiac objects from tombs are connected to the *symposia*, possibly not only because Dionysus was a god of wine but because of his connections to the afterlife (see below).

106   Blundell 1995: 165–6.

107   Some scholars believe that the worship of Dionysus as a wine god was an entirely male pursuit (Bremmer 1984: 270), but see Henrichs 1978: 159 and 1982: 139–40; Blundell 1995: 166; Dillon 2002: 148. See Chapter 1, n. 23 for the possibility that royal Macedonian women attended drinking parties and that royal Molossian women may have.

108   Henrichs 1982: 148; Blundell 1995: 166, 168 notes that sources do not specifically mention the presence of women in terms of drinking aspects of spring festivals to Dionysus in Athens, but this is the same conundrum as female attendance at Attic drama during Dionysiac festivals. She does think it likely that women as well as men attended rural wine festivals.

109   Henrichs 1982: 151 remarks on the regional quality of Dionysiac cults.

100   Zeitlin 1982, followed by Blundell 1995: 169; Dillon 2002: 147. As Blundell comments, this phenomenon helps to explain the strange combination of tolerance of the cult by men but also male suspicion or hostility to it.

111   Blundell 1995: 166–7 notes that this form of Dionysiac cult is attested in only some regions of Greece.

112   Dillon 2002: 144.

113   As Blundell 1995: 166 notes, this term, derived from *mania* (madness), had "derogatory connotations," implying male disapproval.

114   Blundell 1995: 168.

115   Blundell 1995: 168; Cole 1993a. The evidence for these civic festivals is Hellenistic; one could assume that the cult became less personal and ecstatic over time or one could conclude (my preference) that classical evidence like the *Bacchae* is shaped by the needs of art and interest in myth, and that Hellenistic documentary evidence tells us more about real cults, evidence probably meaningful for real practice even at an earlier period.

116   Cole 1980: 230; Kraemer 1992: 38–9.

117   Kraemer 1979: 66 and 1992: 41.

118   Dillon 2002: 153–4 concludes women may have been less involved in these rites, partly because he seems to regard them as entirely separate from Dionysus. See Laks and Most 1997 for discussion of the Orphic papyrus found in the remnants of the funerary pyre placed over Derveni A.

119   Cole 1980, 1993b, and 2003. Kraemer 1992: 39–40 pictures these cults as separate to a degree that Cole 1980 does not, although she does consider the possibility of overlap.

120   Cole 2003: 201 notes that tags, badges, and greetings related to the cult found in burials are concentrated in Macedonia though they appear elsewhere as well.

121   Kraemer 1979: 59; Bremmer 1984: 267–9; Blundell 1995: 167–8.

122   Henrichs 1978: 133–48: one woman was both leader of maenads and public priestess of Dionysus. Some types of Dionysiac cult were more periodic than others

123   So Macurdy 1932a: 41. (See discussion in Chapter 4.) Of course, Duris may have recalled the story and based his description upon it. Polyaenus (4.1) recounts the tale of Argaeus, king of the Macedonians, who, short of men, used young women who came down from the mountains waving *thyrsoi* (ritual wands) to scare the enemy: the enemy troops thought they were men, panicked, and retreated. After winning without fighting, Argaeus dedicated a temple to Dionysus Pseudaner (the false man) and gave order to call the young women, whom the Macedonians had previously called Klodones, Mimallones, because they mimicked men.

124 Mortensen 1997: 74–5.
125 See O'Brien 1992: 16, who points out that the women (royal and otherwise) in the *Bacchae* do not engage in sexual activity (they are violent but sexually chaste) and rightly concludes that Olympias was particularly unlikely to have done anything to compromise her status or that of Alexander. Moreover, according to Plutarch (*Alex.* 2.6), only women participated in the ritual Olympias organized.
126 Kraemer 1992: 42. Orphism is so notoriously broad a term that a number of interpretations are possible. See general discussion in Burkert 1985: 296–304 and Robertson 2003 on the relationship between Orphism and Dionysus. Robertson 2003: 220 argues that the development of personal cults happened as a reaction to the decline of communal cults.
127 One cannot prove her influence, but many scholars believe in it (see discussion and references in Fredricksmeyer 2003: 255), primarily because the genuine and emotional nature of Alexander's religious beliefs and practices is now widely recognized (Edmunds 1971; Badian 1981; Bosworth 1996b: 140). This, in turn, has made belief in Olympias' influence more likely than it was when many scholars, like Plutarch himself, tried to rationalize Alexander's religion. No evidence directly connects Philip to such an individualized religiosity; although, like Alexander, he may well have believed that his extraordinary accomplishments raised him to the level of the gods. (See further below.)
128 See Bosworth 1996a: 98–132 and 1996b; Fredricksmeyer 2003: 264–5, who notes that the idea that Alexander believed Dionysus to be his ancestor is probably false.
129 Implied by O'Brien 1992: 14.
130 Fredricksmeyer 1979, 1981, 1982 argued that Philip planned to acquire divine honors and establish dynastic ruler cult as part of his desire to create a more absolute monarchy and that he actually received cult in one sanctuary, but Badian 1981, especially 67–71, though accepting that Philip had "pretensions" to divinity, denied that he actually received lifetime cult anywhere. Badian's views have dominated (Borza 1992: 249–50; O'Brien 1992: 202; Schumacher 1990: 438–9).
131 See recent discussions and references in Fredricksmeyer 2003: 270–8.
132 Carney 2000b: 31–40.
133 Saatsoglou-Paliadeli 2000: 397–400 discusses a statuary base found near Vergina inscribed on the side, rather than the front, with the name of Eurydice and her patronymic. She suggests not only that this once supported an image of Eurydice but that, granted the position of the inscription and the shape of the base, that Eurydice's statue was part of a group of at least three statues and perhaps included all five figures once in the Philippeum. Thus, an image of Olympias could have been part of this second, possibly dynastic monument.
134 The end of the text of Paus. 5.17.4 is corrupt, but the Eurydice referred to can only be Philip's mother: see Lapatin 2001: 116–17, especially n. 198.
135 See Carney 2000b: 24–30; Lapatin 2001: 115–19. See also Huwendiek 1996. See discussion in Chapter 2. Lapatin's discussion is important, but marred by his limited understanding of the political situation in the Macedonian court. I intend to discuss the political significance of the Philippeum at greater length elsewhere. In what follows, I supplement my 2000b conclusions with material from Lapatin.
136 Lapatin 2001: 118, though agreeing that the gold and ivory materials imply connections to divinity, warns against overemphasis on this point because "There is no evidence that chryselephantine materials alone signified divinity." In fact, the fabrication is typical of the ambiguity of the entire construct. Lapatin also observes that the images of Philip and the twelve Olympians

marched in the wedding procession for Cleopatra, daughter of Philip, could have been chryselephantine; Diodorus (16.92.5) says they were expensive and elaborate and that Philip's was suitable for a god but does not precisely describe the materials of which they were made.

137 Fredricksmeyer 1979: 53 rightly rejects the view of Badian 1981: 71 (followed by Huwendiek 1996: 156; Lapatin 2001: 116–17) that her image would not have been included if the building had been completed in the last years of Philip's reign. As I have argued here and elsewhere (Carney 1992a; 2000b: 25, n. 20), this dating depends on mistaken assumptions about Macedonian royal marriage in general and particularly that of Philip and Olympias. This building was a political construct. It was about power, not personal affection.

138 Though Alexander may well have had to supervise the completion of this monument after his father's death, it is wrong to claim, as Lapatin 2001: 118 does, that the dynastic image it generated "served Alexander's interests more than his father's." Philip had seven wives and at least one other son. The troubles associated with Attalus' public questioning of Alexander's legitimacy as heir (see Chapter 2), troubles which Philip did everything he could to end, are why Philip would have been sure to include Olympias and Alexander. He could hardly hope for a successful reconciliation if he did otherwise. Moreover, Philip had more reason than Alexander to include his own parents. In both cases, the selection of those to be commemorated from a much larger possible pool (for instance, apart from Philip's other wives and children, there was Amyntas' other wives and Philip's two royal brothers) indicates a definition of the central part of the dynasty.

139 Scholarly acceptance of the idea has varied and even those who take it seriously do not necessarily agree about the reasons behind it. Macurdy 1932a: 34 accepts the planned cult as historical, supposing that Alexander intended it as compensation for her "defeat in the contest with Antipater." One doubts that Olympias, however much she might have liked the idea of the cult, would have acknowledged her "defeat;" certainly her subsequent actions do not suggest this. Hammond 1980: 475 also accepts it, but on the dubious grounds that it was compensation for a change in Olympias' constitutional position. See also Berve 1926: 2.286; Momigliano 1934: 174; Edmunds 1971: 380. Strasburger 1939: col. 179 does not accept it.

140 For instance, Anson 2003: 123.

141 Entertaining though this remark is, it is unlikely to be true. Once Alexander had begun to assert that he was the son of a god, Olympias was hardly likely to contradict him.

142 Bosworth 1995: 76 rejects the notion that the historical Callisthenes would have referred to Olympias' views at all, let alone in such a way. Moreover, one must doubt that he would have dared to put into writing the notion that Alexander approached divinity not because of his heroic acts but because of Callisthenes' recording of them. Justin (11.11.3–4) reports that Olympias confessed to Philip that a big snake, not Philip, was Alexander's father, so Philip publicly repudiated both and Alexander therefore invented the claim to divine birth. This story, obviously influenced by the *Romance*, deserves no credence.

143 See Anson 2003: 123 for discussion. Asirvatham 2001: 96 is uncertain whether to accept Olympias as the originator. She also argues that Plutarch's belief (or assertion) that she was is part of his depiction of her as a barbarian foil to Alexander.

144 Fredricksmeyer 2003: 271–2.

145 Plutarch (*Alex*.27.5) cites a letter (rather than other sources) from Alexander to his mother about his visit to Ammon in which Alexander reveals that the oracle had offered certain secret prophecies that he would tell only to her on

her return. Quite apart from the usual doubts about the authenticity of letters, this particular reference mirrors Olympias' secret conversation with her son in a suspicious manner and seems oddly unnecessary unless one concludes that the secret information that Alexander would tell only to his mother was that he was not simply the son of a god but a god himself. See Hamilton 1969: 72 for references to those who consider the letter genuine and other possible explanations of his statements, the least implausible of which is Tarn 1949: 2.354, who imagines that the priest offered some spiritual explanation of Alexander's relationship to Ammon.

146 Berve 1926: 2.287; Hamilton 1969: 4–5; Wirth 1973: 120; Brunt 1976: 1.477; Badian 1996: 19; Fredricksmeyer 2003: 272.
147 See discussion and references in Bosworth 1996b: 140–2.
148 I have changed my views since Carney 1987a: 61, n. 68. Hamilton 1969: 5 makes the bizarre assumption that Olympias might have made these claims prior to the death of Philip and that Attalus was, in fact, capitalizing on them.
149 Bosworth 1988: 283–4; Fredricksmeyer 2003: 274; Anson 2003: 124.
150 Bosworth 1995: 76. Anson 2003: 124 seems to believe that the idea was, to some degree, inspired by both Olympias and Philip.

6 Olympias' afterlife

1 The Attalids also claimed to be Aeacids, but their interest seems to have been in Achilles, Pyrrhus, and perhaps Alexander. I am not aware of direct Attalid reference to Olympias. See Kosmetatou 1995: 138–44 and 2003: 168; Scheer 2003: 222–3.
2 Plutarch (*Mor.* 747f–748a) quotes two lines of elegiac poetry about Olympias: "Her father and husband and son were kings, and her brothers and her ancestors. Greece calls her Olympias." Plutarch says nothing about the origin of these verses; they could, like the lines from a dedication by Olympias' mother-in-law Eurydice (see Chapter 5), be copied from an inscription or they could simply be elegiac poetry. The failure to mention the Aeacids directly seems to suggest the latter since (see below) this is very different from the known funerary inscriptions.
3 See discussion and references in Edson 1949; Robinson 1953; Oikonomedes 1982. Edson believes that the inscription, first discovered by Oikonomos, was part of another tomb but referred to the tomb of Olympias, whereas Oikonomedes (whose arguments I find more generally persuasive, although oddly personal at times) deduced that this inscription appeared on the actual tomb of Olympias. The inscription itself, once found near Makriyialos (the general area of ancient Pydna), is now lost.
4 One of these inscriptions, once seen by Heuzey in Kitros (near Makriyialos), is also lost. The text of this inscription is the least well preserved of the three, but clearly refers (Edson 1949: 92; Oikonomedes 1982: 16) to the *genna* (offspring or race/clan) of Neoptolemus. The third inscription (*SEG* XII 340), also found at Makriyialos, has the best-preserved text. It is an elegiac epigram that commemorates a three-year-old child, Alcimachus, son of Neoptolemus (see Robinson 1953).
5 Edson 1949: 93 assumes that the need for secrecy, granted the contents of Cassander's edict, necessitated her burial close to the place of her death. The text of the Oikonomos inscription, as reconstructed by Oikonomedes (1982: 13), may imply secret burial: "Olympias; whose corpse the noble—enos, one of the brave clan of Aiakos, concealed in the embrace of measureless earth."
6 Edson 1949: 93, followed by Oikonomedes 1982: 13.
7 Edson 1949: 94–5 considers various possibilities, including the survival of

some Aeacids who refugeed to Macedonia after the collapse of the Molossian monarchy. Obviously some Aeacids must have been present around the time of Olympias' death to arrange her secret burial. Neoptolemus (see Chapters 3 and 4), Olympias' probable relative, had died bravely in battle against Eumenes (Diod. 18.31.5; Just. 13.8.8), but other members of his immediate family could have been present. Edson 1949: 86 dates the Alcimachus inscription quite late in the first century BCE (Robinson 1953: 151 prefers mid-second century) and has suggestions about how Aeacids might have remained in Macedonia despite the demise of Macedonian monarchy. Robinson 1953: 153–6 also speculates on their identity.

8 Edson 1949: 94 makes this suggestion. Robinson 1953: 155, n. 5 attacks it, though it seems quite plausible.

9 Robinson 1953: 156 considers and rejects the possibility that the "Olympias" the inscription refers to was not the mother of Alexander but her namesake, Olympias II, the daughter of Pyrrhus (see below). Olympias II died in Epirus, but her daughter had married the king of Macedonia, so Olympias II's remains could have been brought to Macedonia. The failure of the inscription to provide a patronymic, however, strongly suggests that the Olympias in question is the more famous one.

10 One could attribute the name choice to the kind of Alexander imitation that characterized Pyrrhus (see Goukowsky 1978: 1.116–18) as well as the Successors, but the names of his other children do not necessarily suggest that: "Helenus" refers to the supposed Trojan branch of the Aeacid descent; "Ptolemy" to Pyrrhus' father-in-law and patron; "Alexander" not only to Pyrrhus' Aeacid descent, but to the earlier king and not necessarily to the Macedonian Alexander.

11 Her son Pyrrhus, in Ovid, *Ibis* 307f.

12 Plutarch, however, refers to factions among the Molossians (Plut. *Pyrrh.* 2.1).

13 See Hammond 1967: 567–71, 588–92.

14 Cross 1932: 48 terms the assassins of Alcetas "nationalist," but they appear to have been supporters of democracy.

15 Hammond 1967: 590 sees Alexander II's reign as stable and prosperous, but external pressures and a succession crisis quickly removed that stability, as Cross 1932: 92–3 recognizes.

16 Cross 1932: 95 suggests that in these years the Molossians remained loyal to the dynasty but the Epirotes generally did not.

17 Aeacids, as we have seen, did survive in Macedonia, even if Phthia, Demetrius II's wife, had no children of her own (see Carney 2000b: 190–3). Nereïs, the Aeacid wife of the tyrant Gelo of Syracuse, kept the dynasty's memory alive by dedicating statues of the last members of the dynasty at Delphi and Olympia (*SIG* 453) and her sons used quasi-Molossian images on their coinage (see Hammond 1967: 592 for references).

18 Hammond 1967: 591. Cabanes 1980: 345–6 considers the inability of the last Aeacids to defend against these military threats critical. My own view is that, although important, this was not the only factor.

19 See Goukowsky 1978: 1.108–11 for the memory of Alexander during the reign of Cassander. See also Cohen 1997: 114–16 for discussion and references. The theme of the "hatred" of Cassander for Alexander is, as both scholars argue, a silly one, but a number of factors necessarily limited Cassander's use of the image of Alexander, though he certainly did employ it, most obviously in his coinage.

20 Carney 1997a: 213–14 attributes some of this blame to Antigonid propaganda via Hieronymus, but also considers popular sympathy.

21 Edson 1934: 216–17; Bohm 1989: 27–51; Huttner 1997: 159–74.

22 Andronicos 1984: 62 made this plausible suggestion; obviously it would be a particularly appropriate action for a ruler trying to establish his legitimacy. See also Errington 1990: 65–6; Carney 1992b: 5. Most scholars have accepted this suggestion.

23 On the monument and its remains, see Courby 1912; Edson 1934. Courby 1912: 81 denied that any of the statues were female and Edson 1934: 218 accepted this view. Le Bohec 1993: 239 suggested that there could have been royal women in the group. My view is that their inclusion is unlikely in the light of the narrow public presentation of Antigonid monarchy.

24 Bosworth 1986: 11.

25 Recent scholarship has disputed the degree to which Macedonian manpower was reduced, and, if it was, whether Alexander was responsible. Bosworth, who initially argued that Alexander alone was responsible (1986), has now moderated his views and attributes the decline in manpower to the wars of the Successors as well as those of Alexander. See Bosworth 2002: 64–97 for discussion and references.

26 See Bohm 1989 on Alexander imitation in the later Hellenistic period.

27 Mirón-Pérez 1998: 223.

28 Here I reject my earlier view (Carney 2000c: 24, n. 17) for reasons stated below.

29 For an English translation of *Liber de Morte*, see Stoneman 1991: 148–55. See Seibert 1984 and 1990; Heckel 1988; Baynham 1995 and 1998b; Bosworth 2000: 16–17, 207–41; Baynham 2000: 242–62 for discussion and references on the date, political circumstances, and general nature of *Liber de Morte*.

30 Heckel 1988 argued for autumn 317 or spring 316; Seibert 1984 and 1990 suggests a date between 315 and 305; Bosworth 2000 and Baynham 1995, 1998b, and 2000 suggest *c.* 308. Much depends on whether one considers the Rhodian references interpolations or integral to *Liber de Morte*.

31 Baynham 1998b.

32 Jouanno 1995: 211–30 discusses Olympias in the context of her relationship to Alexander. Apart from differences in our views and conclusions, my discussion concentrates on the Greek version of the *Alexander Romance* whereas hers deals with various forms of the *Alexander Romance*.

33 All references to the *Romance* will be to the Greek version unless otherwise stated, and the translation will be that of Stoneman 1991.

34 On the dating problem, see recent discussions in Stoneman 1996 and Jouanno 2002: 13–55.

35 On the history and early development of the *Alexander Romance*, see discussion and references in Gunderson 1970; Stoneman 1991: 1–32, 1994, 1996: 602; Jouanno 2002. Jouanno 1995: 229 notes that Olympias is a less prominent figure in later recensions than in earlier ones.

36 Jouanno 2002: 181, n. 322, for instance, points out that in the *Romance*, Attalus' insult loses all political context; by implication, Olympias can be only a sexual being.

37 Many of Olympias' remarks to Nectanebo are double entendres (Jouanno 1995: 222 implausibly insists that her honesty is never in doubt), so the narrator raises the possibility that Olympias knows perfectly well that her lover is Nectanebo, not a god, but, as Stöcker 1976 points out, in this version of the *Romance* the narrator finally states that Olympias does not know his true identity and she later (1.14) blames herself when she discovers the truth.

38 In other versions, the narrator is more critical. For instance, in the Armenian version, the narrator blames Olympias (1.15) for her actions: "Now depraved Olympias carried on in this fashion, revealing her true nature through force of magic" (translation of Wolohojian 1969: 29).

39   An exchange of letters between Zeuxis, Aristotle, Alexander, and Philip and Olympias (they write and receive these letters jointly) was probably part of the Greek *Romance*, although it is preserved in Armenian and Latin versions and is not translated in Stoneman 1991. These letters portray Alexander as giving so many gifts to his friends that he wants more allowance and his parents as reluctant to provide it. Thus the exchange pictures Olympias and Philip acting together, in accord, and implies some conflict and disagreement between them and their son.

40   Jouanno 1995: 230 sees this as the sole similarity between the figure of Olympias in the historical sources and in the *Romance*. She also notes (1995: 224) that the theme of secret knowledge/conversation between mother and son that appears in some historical authors in terms of Alexander's birth continues in the *Romance*. Her reading of the historical sources, however, makes them closer in tone to the *Romance*, more sentimental, than is my view; see Appendix.

41   Bieber 1964: 23 suggests that this image depicted Olympias with a snake. One doubts that Philip would have agreed to this. Granted that the Philippeum must have been completed very early in his reign, Alexander would have been only slightly more likely to do so. Andronicos (1984: 129–31) originally thought that the small ivory heads from the couch in the main chamber of Tomb II at Vergina were portraits and suggested that one might be Olympias, but later stepped back from this claim. Smith 1988: 62–3 doubts that any of the heads are female, let alone portraits.

42   Smith 1988: 2, 43, 48, 89. See further Carney 2000b: 26–30.

43   Smith 1988: 48.

44   Papisca 1999: 864–5; she connects his decline to the rise of the *Romance*, but the process could easily have happened in reverse order.

45   See Figs. 11 and 12 in Pollitt 1986: 24.

46   See discussion and references in Plantzos 1997, especially 123–6. See also Bieber 1964: 23, 57–8; Pollitt 1986: 23–9; Oberleitner 1985: 32–5 and 1992; Hertel 1989; Seidmann 1993: 85–7; Bernhard-Walcher *et al.* 1994: 90.

47   The apparent youth of both female images is likely more idealizing, an allusion to divinity, and so *contra* Bieber 1964: 46 not a reasonable guide to acceptance or rejection of any identification.

48   Bieber 1964: 57 implausibly sees the same facial features in the Vienna female image and the female head on the Aboukir medallions and fourth century CE contorniates (see below), but the headdress of the Vienna woman is similar to that on the Aboukir examples. Certainly the veil and diadem of the Vienna cameo resembles that worn by Ptolemaic royal women. Hertel 1989: 419 sees a dolphin on the front of the Vienna woman's diadem, notes the dolphin backrest on the contorniate, but unconvincingly argues that dolphins refer to sexuality and thus Zeus Ammon.

49   Plantzos 1997: 125.

50   The snake decoration on both helmets, the possible heads of Zeus Ammon, and the thunderbolt on the helmet of the Vienna cameo would be suitable for Alexander, but as Pollitt 1986: 24 notes, the profiles, even that on the Vienna cameo, do not much resemble coin profile images of Alexander.

51   Plantzos 1997: 126.

52   Pollitt 1986: 24. Stewart 2003: 64 refers to images "infected with Alexander's iconography."

53   Pollitt 1986: 271, 74. Under Ptolemy II, coins depicting his parents as the Savior Gods appeared.

54   See Heckel 1992: 222 for discussion and references.

55   See Green 1978: 9.

56 See Spencer 2002 for its bibliography. Her focus, however, is literary, so the bibliography is scant for art historical topics. For those, see Hannestad 1993, Stewart 2003, and below. Moreover, she does not deal with late Roman evidence of either sort.

57 So Green 1978; Gruen 1998; Stewart 2003: 56–9. Spencer 2002: 167 sees the context for Roman views of Alexander, no matter how varied, as a persistent Roman "ambivalence" relating to Greek power and Greek figures of power.

58 Hannestad 1993: 66; Woolf 1994; Elsner 1998: 3–7; Spencer 2002: 177–8; Stewart 2003: 63–5.

59 See Vermeule 1986; Stoneman 2003: 325–45 and 2004: 167–86.

60 See Zeitlin 2001.

61 Vermeule 1982: 67–8.

62 On the Boscoreale frescoes, Simon 1958 identified Alexander (mirrored in a shield), and seated male and female figures as Philip and Olympias, and interpreted the scene as one predicting the birth of Alexander, perhaps deriving from some Antigonid monarch. Stewart 1993: 279, n. 46 rejects her argument. Schoder 1982 interprets the seated female figure as Roxane.

63 Livy 26.19.5–8; Sil. 13.637–44; *Vir Ilus* 49.1; Dio. 16.39. Dating the origin of these tales is difficult (Gruen 1998: 182). Aulus Gellius (*N.A.* 6.1.1), a Latin writer from the first half of the second century CE, prefaces his story about a snake visiting the mother of the future Scipio Africanus with the statement that what is said in Greek literature about Olympias, wife of Philip and mother of Alexander, is also recorded about Scipio's mother. Suetonius (*Aug.* 94) tells the tale about Augustus but does not mention Olympias directly. See also Dio. 45.1.23.

64 Tataki 1988: 90, 106, 238, 326.

65 Gagé 1975: 1.

66 Kleiner and Matheson 2000: 1–16 for a general sketch.

67 For general discussions of imperial women and their public presentation, see Kleiner and Matheson 1996: 27–100 and 2000: 17–42, 77–100; and Wood 1999.

68 Stewart 2003: 61.

69 See discussion in Blázquez 1990; Espinosa 1990; Millar 1993: 142–4; Baharal 1994 (who argues unconvincingly that Caracalla's personal identification with Alexander had no political context or inspiration); Zeitlin 2001: 239–41; Stewart 2003: 61–2.

70 Diodorus (78.7–8.3) claims that Caracalla collected the supposed belongings of Alexander for his own use, had Alexander's images set up throughout the Empire, raised a 16,000-strong phalanx of Macedonians outfitted in what he believed to be period-appropriate gear, once wrote to the senate that Alexander had entered his body, favored Macedonians, reenacted Alexander's visit to Troy and the tomb of Achilles (78.16.7; so also Herodian 4.8.4), and tried to marry the daughter of the Parthian king he was campaigning against, in obvious imitation of Alexander (79.1.1; also Herodian 4.10.2). Herodian (4.8.1–3) offers more specifics: he dressed as a Macedonian, ordered statues whose heads combined those of Alexander with his own, urged his officers to take the names of Alexander's generals, and made an offering at Alexander's tomb (4.8.9).

71 Herodian (5.7.3) asserts that he changed his name from that of his grandfather, Alexianus, because of his admiration for the conqueror, the man so admired by his cousin Caracalla. Herodian was apparently unaware that "Alexander" is simply a Hellenized version of his grandfather's name.

72 Herodian also mentions specifics about his Alexander obsession: he had a nurse named Olympias whose husband was named Philip (13.3) and he placed Alexander among his ancestors in a shrine (31.4).

73 Vermeule 1982: 68 refers to Alexander Severus' mother Julia Mamaea as a "veritable Olympias" and suggests that she and her advisors may have been the source of his Alexander emulation. Gagé 1975: 11 suggests that Mamaea consciously revived the memory of Olympias. Nau 1968 argues that Julia Domna identified herself with Olympias, but her arguments do not convince.

74 Gold bars and gold Roman coins were parts of the same find. See discussion and references in Dressel 1906; Yalouris *et al.* 1980: 103–4, 115, Pl. 5, Figs. 10, 11, 33; Vermeule 1982: 67; Savio 1994/5; Stewart 2003: 62–3. The uncertain provenance of the medallions once led to questions about their authenticity, but most scholars now accept them as genuine (see Vermeule 1982: 62–3 for references). The Tarsus medallions, contemporary with these, also linked to Caracalla, do not depict any figure identifiable as Olympias. One of the images is commonly identified as that of Philip, though it could represent a mature Caracalla, the fictive father of Alexander Severus (see Vermeule 1982: 61, 69).

75 Some associate the medallions with Macedonian games at Veroea *c.* 225–50 (Ninou 1980: 45), perhaps to Gordian III's visit to the games in 242. Yalouris *et al.* 1980: 103 connect them to Severus Alexander's reconfirmation of Macedonia's privileges in 231. Vermeule 1982: 63–7 is less sure.

76 Dressel 1906: 10–11, 17–19. See chart in Dressel 1906: 69 of obverse/reverse types. Two remain at the Walters Art Gallery, but the third is now in Thessaloniki.

77 See Wood 1986: 52–3, 59–60, 62, 64, 74–5, 125–6; Kleiner and Matheson 1996: 81–4, 86–9.

78 Vermeule 1982: 69–70 suggests that the "Olympias" figure on the Aboukir medallions could refer to one of the Severan royal women. The hairdo of the portrait makes his hypothesis, plausible in the abstract, somewhat difficult to accept: see Kleiner and Matheson 1996: 81–4. While one can imagine that the artist intended to allude to one of the Severan women as well as Olympias, the generic nature of the image (see below) seems poorly adapted to such an intention; a more portrait-like representation would seem necessary if one wanted to allude to one of these women.

79 Dressel 1906: 31–3; Alföldi and Alföldi 1990: 2.85.

80 Dressel 1906: 33.

81 Hertel 1989: 419 considers Europa a possible identification of the figure on the bull-headed creature (Ninou 1980: 45 sees either Europa or a Nereid) but sees Thetis for the hippocamp. Yalouris *et al.* 1980: 103 connects Thetis to Alexander's and (by implication) Caracalla's imitation of Achilles, but it can hardly be an accident that the reverse seems to show the female divine ancestress of the Aeacids. The other two reverses are more problematic, although one could simply associate Athena's snake with that of Olympias on the obverse. Toynbee 1944: 69, n. 52 suggests that Perseus and Andromeda could allude to Olympias' affection for her husband. Such a suggestion would be implausible if one considered only the historical Olympias, but is conceivable (though not easily) if applied to the developing character of Olympias in the *Romance*.

82 Yalouris *et al.* 1980: 103.

83 The snake on the rod seems much closer to Plutarch's account of Olympias' ritual and domestic use of snakes than to the later tale of her union with a divine snake, let alone the *Romance*'s sexual relationship with Nectanebo in the guise of a snake.

84 Dressel 1906: 38; Alföldi and Alföldi 1990: 2.86 against Nau's views.

85 Dressel 1906: 19 points to holding of the veil as a universal female gesture in Greek art.

86 Gagé 1975: 16 argues that the Severi were the last Alexander revivers for whom the historical Alexander, not the character in the *Romance*, was the main inspiration.
87 Gaebler 1906, Tafel V, nos. 3 and 5, Tafel XI, no. 25; Bieber 1964: 22; Stewart 2003: 62. The revival included games and Alexander's cult.
88 Dressel 1906: 31.
89 Many uses have been suggested. See Yalouris *et al.* 1980: 117; Stewart 2003: 65.
90 Bieber 1964: 22, n. 20; Yalouris *et al.* 1980: 116–17, Figs. 34–7.
91 Alföldi and Alföldi 1976: 10.1, Tafel 1, nos. 1–11.
92 Ross 1963: 17–21 is inclined to connect the image to Plutarch; so also Gagé 1975: 10. Dressel 1906: 31 connects the coin and contorniate images of Olympias and the snake with the *Romance*. Vermeule in Yalouris *et al.* 1980: 116 suggests that the Olympias figure (Fig. 34) was copied from a Hellenistic relief or painting of Olympias as a "divine banqueter" and was brought to Rome as booty. The 700th anniversary of Alexander's birth fell in 344; some associate the contorniates with that: see Stewart 2003: 65–6.
93 Alföldi and Alföldi 1976: 1.18, Tafel 22, nos. 7–12, Tafel 23, nos. 1–2. The exceptional reverse shows a bestiarius (gladiator).
94 Alföldi and Alföldi 1976: 1.19–20, Tafel 23, nos. 3–6. The reverses for this Olympias type refer to gladiatorial games, the story of Heracles, or to the goddess Roma.
95 Dressel 1906: 33; Alföldi and Alföldi 1990: 2.86.
96 Kampen 1996. On ruler imitation of Heracles, see Palagia 1986; Huttner 1997.
97 Dressel 1906: 333; Alföldi and Alföldi 1990: 2.86 point out, however, that though the attributes of this Olympias type are unconventional, the figure's pose (particularly the way she holds the club) resembles that of the more conventional Olympias figure on the other contorniates (and the Aboukir medallion) rather than images of Omphale.
98 On the Alexander mosaic at Soueidié/Baalbeck, see Chehab 1958: 43–50 and 1959: Pls. XI–XXVI; and Ross 1963. Ross 1963: 3–9 bases his argument on the text of the *Romance* and the tradition of medieval picture cycles that accompanied it. He believes that the damaged figure behind the couch on which Olympias and Philip sit is Nectanebo. See *contra* Chehab 1958: 49–50, who thinks that the mysterious figure is a divine messenger and that the scene represents the annunciation to Olympias of Alexander's divine origin.
99 Chehab 1958: 48.
100 A fragment of a second panel above the first survives. What remains is the head of a bald philosopher, labeled "Aristotle." This third scene presumably dealt with Alexander's education. See Ross 1963: 13–15, who suggests that rest of the damaged Aristotle panel may also have shown the taming of Bucephalus.
101 See, for instance, McLynn 1998: 228–9.

Appendix: Olympias and the sources

1 See Carney 1993b: 29, especially n. 1. Jouanno 1995 examines the representation of Olympias' relationship to Alexander in the sources, but I am not aware of a general discussion of Olympias' role in the ancient sources. I do not find Jouanno's thesis, that the "Vulgate" authors (she includes Plutarch in this category) idealize the relationship between mother and son to such a degree that they conceal difficulties between the two, persuasive or supported by the texts. Most of the texts, as we shall see, focus on Alexander's piety toward his mother but often show him resisting her desires, or being said to do so by

ancient authors. Many stress gender difference and Olympias' failure to follow the correct gender pattern.

2   See Baynham 2003 for an insightful overview of the sources for the life of Alexander and scholarship about them. This Appendix, of course, deals with material from the period of the Successors as well.

3   On Diodorus and his work, see Sacks 1990.

4   Sacks 1990: 107.

5   On Hieronymus and his dependability, see Brown 1946–7 and Hornblower 1981: 18–75.

6   See Casevitz 1985 on Diodorus' general treatment of women.

7   Diodorus does not refer to Cassander's refusal to bury Olympias again when he narrates the events leading up to her death and its aftermath.

8   Brown 1946–7: 689 and Hornblower 1981: 281 are skeptical about the historicity of these details. My view (see Chapter 4) is that Olympias probably did allow Adea Eurydice to kill herself and that Adea Eurydice may have acted much like a tragic queen, though some details of the incident are probably not dependable.

9   Sacks 1990: 107 emphasizes Diodorus' tendency to add to and embroider material when a possibility for moralizing arose whereas Westlake 1969: 314 believes that Hieronymus was not given to such an approach. Duris (see arguments in Carney 1993b: 44, n. 40) is a more likely source for this passage. Hornblower 1981: 121–2 accepts Hieronymus as the source, believing he had access to eyewitness and possibly to partisan accounts.

10   See Carney 1993b: 42–4. Edward Anson, in private conversation, suggested that Hieronymus could have blamed Olympias for Eumenes' death because of her poor strategy. While Olympias ultimately disregarded Eumenes' advice to stay put in Molossia and Hieronymus could have blamed her for that, several things make Anson's hypothesis unlikely. Diodorus' narrative, as we have noted, focuses on a series of military failures (primarily those of Polyperchon), failures that often forced Olympias to take military matters in hand, although this was clearly not her original intention. The chronology of events Anson assumes (i.e., for Olympias' failure to have happened in time to have contributed to Eumenes' death) is very tight. Anson's suggestion also depends to some degree on the controversial date of composition of Hieronymus' work, since, if Hieronymus had taken this view, he would have appeared to justify Cassander's actions against Olympias' family, something Antigonus, Hieronymus' patron, would not have approved.

11   Casevitz 1985: 122 exaggerates the hostility of Diodorus' portrayal of Olympias, primarily because his discussion is so brief.

12   Yardley 2003.

13   See Riley 2001 for a discussion of his general treatment of women.

14   See Baynham 1998a: 201–19.

15   See Baynham 1998a for an overview of his work; see Atkinson 1980, 1994 for commentaries. McKechnie 1999 launched an overall attack on Curtius' work on the grounds that it was entirely shaped by perceived parallels between Curtius' day and Alexander's. I do not find McKechnie's arguments convincing; see discussion in Carney 2001: 68–70.

16   Alexander refers to Olympias as his "sweetest mother" (5.2.22); Philip the doctor refers to Olympias and Alexander's sisters as an incentive for his recovery from an illness (3.6.15); and in a speech Alexander says that he would rush home to his *parens* (parent; mother) and sisters if duty did not call (6.2.5).

17   See Stadter 1980 for an overview of Arrian's work; see Bosworth 1980, 1995 for commentaries.

18   *Contra* Jouanno 1995: 212–13, who stresses Arrian's differences from the

Vulgate and the Vulgate's similarity to the *Romance* in its depiction of the relationship between Alexander and Olympias. See *Greek Alexander Romance* 1.30, 3.17, 27.

19 See Hamilton 1969 for a commentary on Plutarch's life of Alexander; Stadter 1965, Badian 2003, and Pelling 2002 for his skills as an historian. See also Stadter 1992.

20 So Carney 1997b: 29. On broader categories of women in Plutarch, see Le Corsu 1981; Blomquist 1997. All these discussions, however, tend to focus largely or exclusively on the lives.

21 I am not as inclined as some (see Jouanno 1995: 214, n. 8) to attribute Plutarch's negative picture of Olympias in the *Alexander* to his sources. He read widely and chose from his readings. Propaganda from Olympias' day doubtless existed and survived, but that does not explain why Plutarch preferred it for the *Alexander* but not necessarily for the *Moralia*.

22 Plutarch's *Eumenes* includes references to Olympias (12.2, 13.1) dealing with her public activities in connection to Eumenes. These passages accept Olympias' political activity in a matter-of-fact way and do not comment on it. The first passage testifies to Eumenes' loyalty as shown by his insistence on swearing oaths to Olympias and the kings and in the second a letter from Olympias, hoping to safeguard her grandson against plots on his life, invites him to come to Macedonia, take charge, and rear Alexander IV.

23 While I would agree that many of Olympias' actions reported by Plutarch in the *Alexander* can be interpreted as attempts (if extreme ones) by Olympias to safeguard her son's interests (indeed, I have often done that), Jouanno 1995: 215 does not persuade when she suggests that Plutarch means to suggest this view without explicitly stating it. As we have seen, he describes her several times over as an unpleasant troublemaker, not an obsessive mother.

24 So also Blomquist 1997: 80.

25 The essay is devoted to advice for bride and groom.

26 Plutarch's essays also contain a quotation (*Mor.* 747 F) of a two-line elegy for Olympias. Its origin is unknown. Since Plutarch does not comment on these lines and quotes them for technical purposes, they do not aid the current discussion. See brief discussion in Chapter 6.

27 Blomquist 1997; Asirvatham 2001: 100.

28 Asirvatham 2000: 104–12 and 2001: 95, 100. She focuses on the topic of religion and the need to make Alexander seem Hellenic, but one could extend her point to other areas.

29 For instance, 2.1, 4, 5, 3.1, 77.5. See Badian 2003: 27–9.

30 For instance, he cites (3.2) Eratosthenes for the story that Olympias told the departing Alexander the secret of his birth but then he mentions a contradictory story by unnamed others.

31 Badian 2003: 27–9 considers this practice an indication that he is "hedging" about the veracity of entertaining or morally useful stories. Asirvatham 2001: 97 sees it as a distancing device, for somewhat different reasons, a practice known in Arrian and other writers as well. However, Cook 2001 argues, against the conventional view, that Plutarch's usage is not at all intended to cast doubt on included material, thus rejecting the notion that Plutarch was either "hedging" or distancing himself.

32 See Heer 1979: 55–7 on Pausanias' treatment of women.

33 Habicht 1998: 95–109 discusses Pausanias' dependability and his condemnation of Philip's policies (109). Palm 1959: 63–74 thinks that Pausanias did blame Philip for the beginning of the process that led to Roman conquest.

34 Habicht 1998: 98 believes that Pausanias worked from memory and employed many sources.

35 Blomquist 1997: 79.
36 Carney 1993b: 29, n. 1.
37 For instance, see Mossman 1988.

Bibliography

Abramenko, A. 1992. "Die Verschwörung des Alexander Lyncestes und die „μήτηϱ τοῦ βασιλέως" Zu Diodor XVII 32,1." *Tyche* 7: 1–8.

Adams, W. L. 1977. "The Dynamics of Internal Macedonian Politics in the Time of Cassander." *AM* 3: 2–30.

—— 1979. "Cassander and the Crossing of the Hellespont: Diodorus 17,17,4." *AncW* 2: 111–15.

—— 1984. "Antipater and Cassander: Generalship on Restricted Resources in the Fourth Century." *AncW* 10: 79–88.

Adams, W. L. and E. N. Borza. 1982. *Philip II, Alexander the Great and the Macedonian Heritage*. Lanham, MD.

Adam-Veleni, P. 2004. "Arms and Warfare Techniques of the Macedonians." In Pandermalis 2004: 47–64.

Adcock, F. and D. J. Mosley. 1973. *Diplomacy in Ancient Greece*. New York.

Alexiou, M. 1974. *The Ritual Lament in Greek Tradition*. Cambridge.

Alföldi, A. and E. Alföldi. 1976 and 1990. *Die Kontorniat—Medaillons*. Vols. 1 and 2. Berlin.

Allan, W. 2000. *The Andromache and Euripidean Tragedy*. Oxford.

Ameling, W. 1988. "Alexander und Achilleus." In W. Will and J. Heinrichs (eds.), *Zu Alexander der Grosse. Festschrift G. Wirth zum 60 Geburtstag am 9.12.86.* Vol. 2, 657–92. Amsterdam.

Andronicos [Andronikos], M. 1984. *Vergina: The Royal Tombs*. Athens.

Anson, E. M. 2003. "Alexander and Siwah." *AncW* 34: 117–30.

Asirvatham, S. R. 2000. *Macedonia and Memory: The Legacy of Alexander in Second Sophistic Rhetoric and Historiography*. Unpublished dissertation, Columbia University. New York.

—— 2001. "Olympias' Snake and Callisthenes' Stand: Religion and Politics in Plutarch's *Life of Alexander*." In Asirvatham *et al.* 2001: 93–125.

Asirvatham, S. R., S. O. Pache and J. Watrous (eds.). 2001. *Between Magic and Religion: Interdisciplinary Studies in Ancient Mediterranean Religion and Society*. Lanham, MD.

Atkinson, J. E. 1980, 1994. *A Commentary on Q. Curtius Rufus' Historiae Alexandri Magni*. Vols. 1 and 2. Amsterdam.

Austin, M. M. 1986. "Hellenistic Kings, War, and the Economy." *CQ* 36: 450–66.

Badian, E. 1958a. "Alexander the Great and the Unity of Mankind." *Historia* 7: 425–44.

—— 1958a. "The Eunuch Bagoas." *CQ* 8: 144–57.

—— 1960. "The Death of Parmenio." *TAPA* 91: 324–38.

—— 1961. "Harpalus." *JHS* 81: 16–43.

—— 1963. "The Death of Philip II." *Phoenix* 17: 244–50.

—— 1964. "The Struggle for the Succession to Alexander the Great." In *Studies in Greek and Roman History*, 262–70. Oxford.

—— 1981. "The Deification of Alexander the Great." In *Ancient Macedonian Studies in Honor of Charles F. Edson*, 27–71.Thessaloniki.

—— 1982a. "Eurydice." In Adams and Borza 1982: 99–110.

—— 1982b. "Greeks and Macedonians." In Barr-Sharrar and Borza 1982: 33–51.

—— 1988. "Two Postscripts on the Marriage of Phila and Balacrus." *ZPE* 73: 116–18.

—— 1996. "Alexander the Great between Two Thrones and Heaven: Variations on an Old Theme." In D. Fishwick and A. Small (eds.), *Subject and Ruler: The Cult of the Ruling Power in Classical Antiquity*. Journal of Roman Archaeology supplement 17, 11–26.

—— 2003. "Plutarch's Unconfessed Skill: The Biographer as a Critical Historian." In T. Hantos (ed.), *Laurea internationalis: Festschrift für Jochen Bleicken zum 75. Geburtstag*, 26–44. Stuttgart.

Baege, W. 1913. *De Macedonum sacris*. Dissertationes Philologicae Halenses 22. Halle.

Baharal, D. 1992. "The Portraits of Julia Domna from the Years 193–211 and the Dynastic Propaganda of L. Septimius Severus." *Collection Latomus* 51: 110–20.

—— 1994. "Caracalla and Alexander the Great: A Reappraisal." *Collection Latomus* 227: 524–67.

Baldwin, B. 1976. "Athenaeus and His Work." *Acta Classica* 19: 21–42.

Barr-Sharrar, B. and E. N. Borza (eds.). 1982. *Macedonia and Greece in Late Classical and Early Hellenistic Times*. Studies in the History of Art 10. Washington, DC.

Bartsiokas, A. 2000. "The Eye Injury of King Philip II and the Skeletal Evidence from the Royal Tomb II at Vergina." *Science* 288: 511–14.

Bauman, R. A. 1990. *Political Trials in Ancient Greece*. London and New York.

Baynham, E. J. 1994. "Antipater: Manager of Kings." In Worthington 1994: 331–56.

—— 1995. "An Introduction to the Metz Epitome: Its Traditions and Value."*Antichthon* 29: 60–77.

—— 1998a. *Alexander the Great: The Unique History of Quintus Curtius*. Ann Arbor.

—— 1998b. "The Treatment of Olympias in the *Liber de Morte Alexandri Magni*: A Rhodian Retirement." In W. Will (ed.), *Alexander der Grosse—eine Weltroberung und ihr Hintergrund*, 103–16. Bonn.

—— 1998c. "Why Didn't Alexander Marry before Leaving Macedonia? Observations on Factional Politics at Alexander's Court in 336–334 *BC*" *RhM* 141: 141–52.

—— 2000. "A Baleful Birth in Babylon: The Significance of the Prodigy in the *Liber de Morte*—An Investigation of Genre." In Bosworth and Baynham 2000: 242–62.

—— 2003. "The Ancient Evidence for Alexander the Great." In Roisman 2003b: 3–30.

Beloch, K. J. 1922–3. *Griechische Geschichte*. Vol.3, 1 and 2. Berlin and Leipzig.

Bernhard-Walcher, B. *et al.* 1994. *Trésors des Empereurs d'Autriche*. Vienna and Quebec.

Berve, H. 1926. *Das Alexanderreich*. Vol. 2. Munich.

Bieber, M. 1964. *Alexander the Great in Greek and Roman Art*. Chicago.

Billows, R. A. 1990. *Antigonos the One-Eyed and the Creation of the Hellenistic State*. Berkeley.

Blackwell, C. W. 1999. *In the Absence of Alexander: Harpalus and the Failure of Macedonian Authority*. New York.

Blázquez, J. M. 1990. "Alejandro Magno, modelo de Alejandro Severo." In J. M. Croisille (ed.), *Neronia IV: Alejandro Magno, modelo de los emperadores romanos*, Collection Latomus 209, 25–36. Brussels.

Blomquist, K. 1997. "From Olympias to Aretaphila: Women in Politics in Plutarch." In J. Mossman (ed.), *Plutarch and His Intellectual World*, 73–98. London.

Blundell, M. W. 1989. *Helping Friends and Harming Enemies: A Study in Sophocles and Ethics*. Cambridge.

Blundell, S. 1995. *Women in Ancient Greece*. Cambridge, MA.

Le Bohec, S. 1993. "Les Reines de Macédoine de la mort d'Alexandre à celle de Persée." *Cahiers du Centre Glotz* 4: 229–45.

—— [as Bohec-Bouhet]. 2002. "The Kings of Macedon and the Cult of Zeus in the Hellenistic Period." In Ogden 2002: 41–58.

Bohm, C. 1989. *Imitatio Alexandri im Hellenismus: Untersuchungen zum politischen Nachwirken Alexanders des Grossen in hoch-und späthellenistischen Monarchien*. Munich.

Borza, E. N. 1981. "The Macedonian Royal Tombs at Vergina: Some Cautionary Notes." *ArchN* 10: 73–87.

—— 1983. "The Symposium at Alexander's Court." *AM* 3: 45–55.

—— 1987. "The Royal Macedonian Tombs and the Paraphernalia of Alexander the Great." *Phoenix* 41: 105–21.

—— 1992. *In the Shadow of Olympus: The Emergence of Macedon*. Princeton.

Borza, E. N. and J. Reames-Zimmerman. 2000. "Some New Thoughts on the Death of Alexander the Great." *AHB* 31: 22–30.

Bosworth, A. B. 1971a. "The Death of Alexander the Great: Rumour and Propaganda." *CQ* 21: 112–36.

—— 1971b. "Philip II and Upper Macedonia." *CQ* 21: 93–105.

—— 1980. *A Historical Commentary on Arrian's History of Alexander*. Vol. 1. Oxford.

—— 1986. "Alexander the Great and the Decline of Macedonia." *JHS* 106: 1–12.

—— 1988. *Conquest and Empire*. Cambridge.

—— 1992. "Philip Arrhidaeus and the Chronology of the Successors." *Chiron* 22: 56–81.

—— 1993. "Perdiccas and the Kings." *CQ* 43: 420–7.

—— 1994. "A New Macedonian Prince." *CQ* 44: 57–65.

—— 1995. *A Historical Commentary on Arrian's History of Alexander*. Vol. 2, Oxford.

—— 1996a. *Alexander and the East: The Tragedy of Triumph*. Oxford.

—— 1996b. "Alexander, Euripides, and Dionysos: The Motivation for Apotheosis." In R. W. Wallace and E. M. Harris (eds.), *Transitions to Empire: Essays in Greco-Roman History 360–146 BC, in Honor of E. Badian*, 140–66. Norman, OK.

—— 2000. "Ptolemy and the Will of Alexander." In Bosworth and Baynham 2000: 207–41.

—— 2002. *The Legacy of Alexander: Politics, Warfare and Propaganda under the Successors*. Oxford.

Bosworth, A. B. and E. J. Baynham (eds.). 2000. *Alexander the Great in Fact and Fiction*. Oxford.

Bottin, C. 1925. "Les Tribus et les dynastes d'Épire avant l'influence macédonienne." *Musé Belge* 29: 62–6.

Bowra, C. M. 1944. *Sophoclean Tragedy*. Oxford.

Braund, D. and J. Wilkins (eds.). 2000. *Athenaeus and His World: Reading Greek Culture in the Roman Empire*. Exeter.

Bremmer, J. N. 1984. "Greek Maenadism Reconsidered." *ZPE* 55: 267–86.

Briant, P. 1973. *Antigone le Borgne*. Paris.

—— 1994. "Sources gréco-hellénistiques, institutions perses et institutions macédoniens: continuités, changements et bricolages." *Achaemenid History* 8: 283–310.

Brown, T. S. 1946–7. "Hieronymus of Cardia." *AHR* 52: 684–96.

Brunt, P. A. 1976. *Arrian: History of Alexander and Indica*. Vol. 1. Cambridge, MA.

Burkert, W. 1985. *Greek Religion*. Trans. J. Raffan. Cambridge, MA.

Burstein, S. M. 1977. "IG II 56 1 and the Court of Alexander IV." *ZPE* 24: 223–5.

—— 1982. "The Tomb of Philip II and the Succession of Alexander the Great." *EchCl* 26: 141–64.

Cabanes, P. 1976. *L'Épire de la mort de Pyrrhos a la Conquête Romaine (272–167 av. J.C.)*. Paris.

—— 1980. "Société et institutions dans les monarchies de Grèce septentrionale au IV siècle." *REG* 113: 324–51.

—— 1988. "Les Concours des *Naia* de Dodone." *Nikephoros* 1: 49–84.

—— 1993. *L'Illyrie méridionale et l'Épire dans l'Antiquité-II*. Paris.

Carlsen, J., B. Due, O. S. Due, B. Poulsen (eds.). 1997. *Alexander the Great: Reality and Myth*. 2nd edn. Rome.

Carney, E. D. 1980. "Alexander the Lyncestian: The Disloyal Opposition." *GRBS* 21, 1: 23–33.

—— 1981. "The Conspiracy of Hermolaus." *CJ* 76: 223–31.

—— 1983. "Regicide in Macedonia." *PP* 211: 260–72.

—— 1987a. "Olympias." *AncSoc* 18: 35–62.

—— 1987b. "The Career of Adea Eurydice." *Historia* 36: 496–502.

—— 1987c. "The Reappearance of Royal Sibling Marriage in Ptolemaic Egypt." *PP* 237: 420–39.

—— 1988 "The Sisters of Alexander the Great: Royal Relics." *Historia* 37: 385–404.

—— 1991a. "The Female Burial in the Antechamber of Tomb II at Vergina." *AncW* 22: 17–26.

—— 1991b. "'What's in a Name?': The Emergence of a Title for Royal Women in the Hellenistic Period." In S. B. Pomeroy (ed.), *Women's History and Ancient History*, 154–72. Chapel Hill.

—— 1992a. "The Politics of Polygamy: Olympias, Alexander, and the Death of Philip II." *Historia* 41: 169–89.

—— 1992b. "Tomb I at Vergina." *ArchN* 17: 1–10.

—— 1993a. "Foreign Influence and the Changing Role of Royal Macedonian Women." *AM* 5, 1: 313–23.

—— 1993b. "Olympias and the Image of the Royal Virago." *Phoenix* 47: 29–56.

—— 1994a. "Arsinoe before She Was Philadelphus." *AHB* 8: 123–31.

—— 1994b. "Olympias, Adea Eurydice, and the End of the Argead Dynasty." In Worthington 1994: 357–80.

—— 1995. "Women and Basileia: Legitimacy and Female Political Action in Macedonia." *CJ* 90: 367–91.

—— 1997a. "The Curious Death of the Antipatrid Dynasty." *AM* 6: 209–16.

—— 1997b. "Were the Tombs under the Great Tumulus at Vergina Royal?" *ArchN* 19: 33–44.

—— 2000a. "Artifice and Alexander History." In Bosworth and Baynham 2000: 263–85.

—— 2000b. "The Initiation of Cult for Royal Macedonian Women." *CP* 95: 21–43.

—— 2000c. *Women and Monarchy in Macedonia*. Norman, OK.

—— 2001. "The Trouble with Philip Arrhidaeus." *AHB* 15: 63–89.

—— 2003. "Women in Alexander's Court." In Roisman 2003b: 227–52.

—— 2004. "Women and Military Leadership in Macedonia." *AncW* 35, 2: 184–95.

—— 2005. "Women and *Dunasteia* in Caria." *AJP* 126: 67–91.

Casevitz, M. 1985. "La Femme dans l'oeuvre de Diodore de Sicile." In *La Femme dans le monde méditerranéen*. Travaux de la Maison de l'Orient 10. Vol. 1, 113–35. Lyon.

Cawkwell, G. 1978. *Philip of Macedon*. London.

Chehab, M. 1958 and 1959. "Mosaiques du Liban", *Bulletin du Musée de Beyrouth*, 14–15: 29–52, Pls. XI–XXVI.

Clignet, R. 1970. *Many Wives, Many Powers: Authority and Power in Polygamous Families*. Evanston.

Clinton, K. 2003. "Stages of Initiation in the Eleusinian and Samothracian Mysteries." In Cosmopoulos 2003: 50–78.

Cohen, A. 1995. "Alexander and Achilles—Macedonian and 'Myceneans.'" In J. B. Carter and S. P. Morris (eds.), *The Ages of Homer: A Tribute to Emily Townsend Vermeule*, 483–505. Austin.

—— 1997. *The Alexander Mosaic: Stories of Victory and Defeat*. Cambridge.

Cohen, D. 1989. "Seclusion, Separation and the Status of Women in Classical Athens." *G&R* 36: 3–15.

—— 1991. *Law, Sexuality, and Society: The Enforcement of Morals in Classical Athens*. Cambridge.

Cole, S. G. 1980. "New Evidence for the Mysteries of Dionysos." *GRBS* 3: 223–38.

—— 1981. "Could Greek Women Read and Write?" In Foley 1981: 219–46.

—— 1984. *Theoi Megaloi: The Cult of the Great Gods at Samothrace*. Leiden.

—— 1993a. "Procession and Celebration at the Dionysia." In R. Scodel (ed.), *Theater and Society in the Classical World*, 25–38. Ann Arbor.

—— 1993b. "Voices from beyond the Grave: Dionysus and the Dead." In T. H. Carpenter and C. A. Faraone (eds.), *Masks of Dionysus*, 276–95. Ithaca.

—— 2003. "Landscapes of Dionysos and Elysian Fields." In Cosmopoulos 2003: 193–217.

Cook, A. B. 1965. *Zeus: A Study in Ancient Religion*. Vol. 2, part 2. New York.

Cook, B. L. 2001. "Plutarch's Use of λέγεται: Narrative and Design and Source in *Alexander*." *GRBS* 42: 239–60.

Cool, H. 2005. "Rescuing an Old Dig." *Archaeology* 58, 2: 61–6.

Le Corsu, F. 1981. *Plutarque et les femmes dans les Vies parallèles*. Paris.

Cosmopoulos, M. B. (ed.). 2003. *Greek Mysteries: The Archaeology and Ritual of Ancient Greek Secret Cults.* London and New York.

Courby, F. 1912. *Exploration archéologique de Délos, V. Le Portique d'Antigone.* Paris.

Cross, G. N. 1932. *Epirus: A Study in Greek Constitutional Development.* Cambridge.

Dakaris, S. 1964. *Hoi Genealogikoi Muthoi ton molosson.* Athens.

Dakaris, S. 1998. *Dodona.* 3rd edn. Athens.

Dakaris, S., A. Ph. Christidis, and J. Vokotopoulou. 2001. "Les Lamelles oraculaires de Dodone et les villes de l'Épire du Nord." In J. Vokotopoulou (ed.), *Studies on Epirus and Macedonia.* Vol. 2, 511–16. Athens.

Dell, H. J. 1970. "The Western Frontier of the Macedonian Monarchy." *AM* 1: 115–26.

—— 1980. "Philip and Macedonia's Northern Neighbors." In Hatzopoulos and Loukopoulos 1980: 90–9, 240–1.

Demand, N. 1994. *Birth, Death, and Motherhood in Classical Greece.* Baltimore.

—— 2002. "Gender Studies and Ancient History: Participation and Power." In S.M. Burstein, N. Demand, I. Morris, and L. Tritle (eds.), *Current Issues and the Study of Ancient History.* Publications of the Association of Ancient Historians 7, 31–44. Claremont, CA.

Develin, R. 1981. "The Murder of Philip II." *Antichthon* 15: 86–99.

Dillon, M. P. J. 1997. *Pilgrims and Pilgrimage in Ancient Greece.* London.

—— 2002. *Girls and Women in Classical Greek Religion.* London and New York.

Dover, K. J. 1974. *Greek Popular Morality in the Time of Plato and Aristotle.* Berkeley.

Dressel, H. 1906. *Fünf Goldmedallions aus dem Funde von Abukir.* Abhandlungen der königlische preuss. Akademie der Wissenschaften. Berlin.

Drogou, St. and C. Saatsoglou-Paliadeli, P. Faklaris, A. Kottaridou, E.-B. Tsigarda. 1996. *Vergina: The Great Tumulus: Archaeological Guide.* Thessaloniki.

Droysen, G. 1877. *Geschichte des Hellenismus.* 1, 2.2. Gotha.

Düll, S. 1970. "De Macedonum Sacris: Gedanken zu einer Neuarbeitung der Götterkulte in Makedonien." *AM* 1: 316–23.

—— 1977. *Die Götterkulte Nordmakedoniens in römischer Zeit.* Munich.

Edmunds, L. 1971. "The Religiosity of Alexander." *GRBS* 12: 363–91.

Edson, C. 1934. "The Antigonids, Heracles, and Beroea." *HSCP* 45: 213–35.

—— 1949. "The Tomb of Olympias." *Hesperia* 18: 84–95.

—— 1970. "Early Macedonia." *AM* 1: 17–44.

Ehrhardt, C. 1967. "Two Notes on Philip of Macedon's First Interventions in Thessaly." *CQ* 17: 296–301.

Ellis, J. R. 1970. "The Security of the Macedonian Throne under Philip II." *AM* 1: 68–75.

—— 1971. "Amyntas Perdikka, Philip II and Alexander the Great: A Study in Conspiracy." *JHS* 91: 15–24.

—— 1976. *Philip II and Macedonian Imperialism.* London.

—— 1981. "The Assassination of Philip II." In *Ancient Macedonian Studies in Honor of Charles F. Edson,* 99–137. Thessaloniki.

—— 1982. "The First Months of Alexander's Reign." In Barr-Sharrar and Borza 1982: 69–73.

Elsner, J. 1998. *Imperial Rome and Christian Triumph.* Oxford.

Errington, R. M. 1970. "From Babylon to Triparadeisos: 323–320 BC."*JHS* 89: 49–77.

—— 1975a. "Alexander in the Hellenistic World." In E. Badian (ed.), *Alexandre le Grand: Image et réalité*. Foundation Hardt, Entretiens sur l'Antiquitè Classique 22, 145–52. Geneva.

—— 1975b. "Arybbas the Molossian." *GRBS* 16: 41–50.

—— 1977. "Diodorus and the Chronology of the Early Diadochoi, 320–311 BC." *Hermes* 4: 478–504.

—— 1990. *A History of Macedonia*. Trans. C. Errington. Berkeley.

Erskine, A. 2002. "O Brother, Where Art Thou? Tales of Kinship and Diplomacy." In Ogden 2002: 97–116.

—— (ed.). 2003. *A Companion to the Hellenistic World*. Oxford.

Espinosa, U. 1990. "La alejandrofilia de Caracala en la antigua historiografía." In J. M. Croisille (ed.), *Neronia IV: Alejandro Magno, modelo de los emperadores romanos*. Collection Latomus 209, 37–51. Brussels.

Fears, J. R. 1975. "Pausanias, the Assassin of Philip II." *Athenaeum* 53: 111–35.

Foley, H. P. (ed.). 1981. *Reflections of Women in Antiquity*. Philadelphia.

—— 2003. "Mothers and Daughters." In Neils and Oakley 2003: 113–37.

Fortina, M. 1965. *Cassandro, re di Macedonia*. Palermo.

Foxhall, L. 1989. "Household, Gender and Property in Classical Athens." *CQ* 39: 22–44.

De Francisci, P. 1948. *Arcana Imperii*. Milan.

Franke, P. R. 1954. *Alt-Epirus und das Königtum der Molosser*. Erlangen.

Fredricksmeyer, E. A. 1966. "The Ancestral Rites of Alexander the Great." *CP* 61: 179–81.

—— 1979. "Divine Honors for Philip II." *TAPA* 109: 39–61.

—— 1981. "On the Background of the Ruler Cult." In *Macedonian Studies in Honor of Charles F. Edson*, 145–56. Thessaloniki.

—— 1982. "On the Final Aims of Philip II." In Adams and Borza 1982: 85–98.

—— 1990. "Alexander and Philip: Emulation and Resentment." *CQ* 85: 300–15.

—— 2003. "Alexander's Religion and Divinity." In Roisman 2003b: 253–78.

Gaebler, H. 1906. *Die Antiken Münzen von Makedonia und Paionia*. Berlin.

Gagé, J. 1975. "Alexandre le Grand en Macédoine dans la Ière moitié du IIIe siècle ap. J.-C." *Historia* 24: 1–16.

Garland, R. 2001. *The Greek Way of Death*. 2nd edn. Ithaca.

Garnsey, P. 1988. *Famine and Food Supply in the Graeco-Roman World: Responses to Risk and Crisis*. Cambridge.

Garoufalias, P. 1979. *Pyrrhus King of Epirus*. London.

Gauthier, Ph. and M. B. Hatzopoulos. 1993. *La Loi Gymnasiarchique de Beroia*. Athens.

Geer, R. M. 1962. *Diodorus of Sicily*. Vol. 9. Cambridge, MA.

Ginouvès, R. 1994. *Macedonia, from Philip II to the Roman Conquest*. Princeton.

Goldberg, M. Y. 1999. "Spatial and Behavioural Negotiation in Classical Athenian City Houses." In P. M. Allison (ed.), *The Archaeology of Household Activities*, 142–61. London and New York.

Golden, M. 2003. "Childhood in Ancient Greece." In Neils and Oakley 2003: 13–30.

Goody, J. 1966. *Succession to High Office*. Cambridge.

Goukowsky, P. 1978 and 1981. *Essai sur les origines du mythe d'Alexandre*. Vols. 1 and 2. Paris.

Green, P. 1978. "Caesar and Alexander: Aemulatio, Imitatio, Comparatio." *AJAH* 3: 1–26.
—— 1982. "The Royal Tombs of Vergina: A Historical Analysis." In Adams and Borza 1982: 129–51.
—— 1990. *Alexander to Actium: The Historical Evolution of the Hellenistic Age*. Berkeley.
—— 1991. *Alexander of Macedon*. Berkeley.
Greenwalt, W. S. 1985a. "The Introduction of Caranus into the Argead King List." *GRBS* 26: 43–9.
—— 1985b. "The Search for Arrhidaeus." *AncW* 10: 69–77.
—— 1986. "Herodotus and the Foundation of Argead Macedonia." *AncW* 13: 117–22.
—— 1988a. "The Age of Marriageability at the Argead Court." *CW* 82: 93–7.
—— 1988b. "Amyntas III and the Political Stability of Argead Macedonia." *AncW* 18: 35–44.
—— 1989. "Polygamy and Succession in Argead Macedonia." *Arethusa* 22: 19–45.
Gregory, A. P. 1995. "A Macedonian ΔΥΝΑΣΤΗΣ: Evidence for the Life and Career of Pleistarchos Antipatrou." *Historia* 44: 11–28.
Griffin, J. 1980. *Homer on Life and Death*. Oxford.
Griffith, G. T. 1979. Part Two. In Hammond and Griffith 1979: 203–646, 675–721.
Gruen, E. 1985. "The Coronation of the Diadochoi." In J. W. Eadie and J. Ober (eds.), *The Craft of the Ancient Historian: Essays in Honor of Chester G. Starr*, 553–71. Lanham, MD.
—— 1998. "Rome and the Myth of Alexander." In T. W. Hillard, R. A. Kearsley, C. E. V. Nixon, and A. M. Nobbs (eds.), *Ancient History in a Modern University*. Vol. 1, 178–91. Grand Rapids, MI.
Gunderson, L. L. 1970. "Early Elements in the *Alexander Romance*." *AM* 1: 353–75.
Habicht, C. 1998. *Pausanias' Guide to Ancient Greece*. Berkeley.
Hamilton, J. R. 1969. *Plutarch: Alexander: A Commentary*. Oxford.
Hammond, N. G. L. 1931. "Prehistoric Epirus and the Dorian Invasion." *BSA* 32: 131–79.
—— 1956. "The Philaids and the Chersonese." *CQ* 6: 113–29.
—— 1966. "The King of Illyria *circa* 400–167 BC." *BSA* 61: 239–53.
—— 1967. *Epirus*. Oxford.
—— 1978. "Philip's Tomb in Historical Context." *GRBS* 19: 331–50.
—— 1979. Part One and Chapter 20. In Hammond and Griffith 1979: 3–200, 647–76.
—— 1980. "Some Passages in Arrian Concerning Alexander." *CQ* 30: 47–76.
—— 1985. "Some Macedonian Offices c. 336–309 BC." *JHS* 105: 156–60.
—— 1988a. Part One and Part Three. In Hammond and Walbank 1988: 3–196 and 367–617.
—— 1988b. "The King and the Land in Macedonia." *CQ* 38: 382–91.
—— 1989. *The Macedonian State: Origins, Institutions and History*. Oxford.
—— 1991. "The Royal Tombs at Vergina: Evolution and Identities." *BSA* 86: 69–82.
—— 1994. *Philip of Macedon*. Baltimore.
—— 1997. "The Location of Aegae." *JHS* 117: 177–9.
Hammond, N. G. L. and G. T. Griffith. 1979. *A History of Macedonia*. Vol. 2. Oxford.

Hammond, N. G. L. and F. W. Walbank. 1988. *A History of Macedonia*. Vol. 3. Oxford.

Hannestad, N. 1997. "*Imitatio Alexandri* in Roman Art." In Carlsen *et al.* 1997: 61–9.

Harris, G. 1973. "Furies, Witches, and Mothers." In J. Goody (ed.), *The Character of Kinship*, 145–59. Cambridge.

Harris, W. V. 2003. "The Rage of Women." In S. Braund and G. W. Most (eds.), *Ancient Anger, Perspectives from Homer to Galen*, Yale Classical Studies 32, 121–43. Cambridge.

Harvey, D. 1969. "Those Epirote Women Again (*SEG*, XV, 384)." *CP* 64: 226–9.

Hatzopoulos, M. B. 1982a. "A Reconsideration of the Pixodarus Affair." In Barr Sharrar and Borza 1982: 59–66.

—— 1982b. "The Oleveni Inscription and the Dates of Philip's Reign." In Adams and Borza 1982: 21–42.

—— 1986. "Succession and Regency in Classical Macedonia." *AM* 4: 279–92.

—— 1994. *Cultes et rites de passage en Macédoine*. Paris and Athens.

—— 1996. *Macedonian Institutions under the Kings*. Vols. 1 and 2, Mélétèmata 22. Athens.

—— 2003. "Polis, Ethnos and Kingship in Northern Greece." In K. Buraselis and K. Zoumboulakis (eds.), *The Idea of European Community in History*. Vol. 2, 51–64. Athens.

Hatzopoulos, M. B. and L. D. Loukopoulos. 1980. *Philip of Macedon*. Athens.

Havelock, C. M. 1971. *Hellenistic Art*. Greenwich, CT.

Hawley, R. 1993. "'Pretty, Witty and Wise': Courtesans in Athenaeus' *Deipnosophistai* Book 13." *International Journal of Moral and Social Studies* 8: 73–91.

Heckel, W. 1978. "Cleopatra or Eurydice?" *Phoenix* 31: 9–21.

—— 1979. "Philip II, Kleopatra and Karanos." *RFIC* 107: 385–93.

—— 1980. "IG II 561 and the Status of Alexander IV." *ZPE* 40: 249–50.

—— 1981a. "Philip and Olympias (337/6 BC)." In G. S. Shrimpton and D. J. McCargar (eds.), *Classical Contributions: Studies in Honour of M. F. McGregor*, 51–7. Locust Valley, NY.

—— 1981b. "Polyxena, the Mother of Alexander the Great." *Chiron* 11: 79–96.

—— 1983–4. "Kynnane the Illyrian." *RSA* 13–14: 193–200.

—— 1986. "Factions and Macedonian Politics in the Reign of Alexander the Great." *AM* 4: 293–305.

—— 1988. *The Last Days and Testament of Alexander the Great: A Prosopographic Study*. Historia Einzelschriften 56. Stuttgart.

—— 1992. *The Marshals of Alexander's Empire*. London and New York.

—— 2002. "The Politics of Distrust: Alexander and His Successors." In Ogden 2002: 81–96.

—— 2003. "King and 'Companions': Observations on the Nature of Power in the Reign of Alexander." In Roisman 2003b: 197–226.

—— Forthcoming. *Who's Who in the Age of Alexander*. Oxford.

Heckel, W. and L. A. Tritle (eds.). 2003. *Crossroads of History: The Age of Alexander*. Claremont, CA.

Heer, J. 1979. *La Personnalité de Pausanias*. Paris.

Henrichs, A. 1978. "Greek Maenadism from Olympias to Messalina." *HSCP* 82: 121–60.

—— 1982. "Changing Dionysiac Identities." In B. F. Meyer and E. P. Sanders (eds.), *Self-Definition in the Graeco-Roman World*, 137–60 (notes at 213–36). Philadelphia.

Herman, G. 1987. *Ritualised Friendship and the Greek City*. Cambridge.

Hertel, D. 1989. "Eine Darstellung Alexanders d. Gr. und seiner Mutter Olympias: Zur Deutung des. sog. Ptolemäerkameos in Wien." In H.-U. Cain, H. Gabelmann, and D. Salzmann (eds.), *Festschrift für Nikolaus Himmelmann*, 417–23. Mainz.

Herzog, R. 1931. *Die Wunderheilungen von Epidaros: Ein Beitrag zur geschichte der Medzin und der Religion*. Philologus, Supplementband 22, 3. Leipzig.

Heskel, J. 1988. "The Political Background of the Arybbas Decree." *GRBS* 29: 185–96.

Hoepfner, W. 1996. "Zum typus der Basileia und der königlichen Androna." In W. Hoepfner and G. Brands (eds.), *Basileia: Die Paläste der Hellenistischen Könige*, 1–43. Mainz.

Holst-Warhaft, G. 1992. *Dangerous Voices: Women's Laments and Greek Literature*. London and New York.

Hornblower, J. 1981. *Hieronymus of Cardia*. Oxford.

Huttner, U. 1997. *Die Politische Rolle der Heraklesgestalt im Griechischen Herrschertum*. Stuttgart.

Huwendiek, J. 1996. "Zur Interpretation des Philippeion in Olympia." *Boreas* 19: 155–9.

Isager, J. 1997. "Alexander the Great in Roman Literature from Pompey to Vespasian." In Carlsen *et al.* 1997: 75–84.

Jameson, M. 1990. "Domestic Space in the Greek City-state." In S. Kent (ed.), *Domestic Architecture and the Use of Space*, 171–95. Cambridge.

Jaschinski, S. 1981. *Alexander und Griechenland unter dem Eindruck der Flucht des Harpalos*. Bonn.

Jones, C. P. 1999. *Kinship Diplomacy in the Ancient World*. Cambridge, MA.

Jouanno, C. 1995. "Alexandre et Olympias: De l'histoire au mythe." *Bulletin de l'Association Guillaume Budé* 3: 211–30.

Jouanno, C. P. 2002. *Naissance et métamorphoses du Roman d'Alexandre Domaine grec*. Paris.

Kaerst, J. 1887. "Der Briefwechsel Alexanders bei Plutarchs." In *Forschungen zur Geschichte Alexanders des Grossen*, 107–17. Stuttgart.

Kaiser-Raiss, M. R. 1984. "Philip II. und Kyzikos." *Schweizerische Numismatische Rundschau* 63: 27–43.

Kampen, N. B. 1996. "Omphale and the Instability of Gender." In N. B. Kampen (ed.), *Sexuality in Ancient Art, Near East, Egypt, Greece and Italy*, 233–46. Cambridge.

Kanatsulis, D. 1958/9. "Antipatros als Feldherr und Staatsmann in der Zeit Philipps und Alexanders des Grossen." *Hellenika* 16: 14–64.

—— 1968. "Antipatros als Feldherr und Staatsmann nach dem Tode Alexanders des Grossen." *Makedonika* 8: 121–84.

Kingsley, B. 1986. "Harpalus in the Megarid (333–331 BC) and the Grain Shipments from Cyrene." *ZPE* 66: 165–77.

Kleiner, D. E. E. and S. B. Matheson (eds.). 1996. *I Claudia: Women in Ancient Rome*. Austin.

—— (eds.). 2000. *I Claudia II: Women in Roman Art and Society*. Austin.

Klotzsch, C. 1911. *Epirotische Geschichte bis zum Jahre 280 v.Chr.* Berlin.

Kosmetatou, E. 1995. "The Legend of the Hero Pergamus." *Anc Soc* 26: 133–44.
—— 2003. "The Attalids of Pergamon." In Erskine 2003: 159–74.
—— 2004. "Rhoxane's Dedications to Athena Polias." *ZPE* 146: 75–80.
Kottaridi, A.. 2004a. "The Lady of Aigai." In Pandermalis 2004: 139–48.
—— 2004b. "The Symposium." In Pandermalis 2004: 65–72.
Kraemer, R. S. 1979. "Ecstasy and Possession: The Attraction of Women to the Cult of Dionysus." *HThR* 72: 55–80.
—— 1992. *Her Share of the Blessings: Women's Religions among Pagans, Jews, and Christians in the Greco-Roman World*. New York and Oxford.
Kron, U. 1996. "Priesthoods, Dedications and Euergetism: What Part did Religion Play in the Political and Social Status of Greek Women?" In P. Helström and B. Alroth (eds.), *Religion and Power in the Ancient Greek World*, 139–82. Uppsala.
Kurtz, D. C. and J. Boardman 1971. *Greek Burial Customs*. Ithaca.
Lacey, W. K. 1968. *The Family in Classical Greece*. London.
Laks, A. and C. W. Most (eds.). 1997. *Studies on the Derveni Papyrus*. Oxford.
Lane Fox, R. 1973. *Alexander the Great*. New York.
Lapatin, K. D. S. 2001. *Chryselephantine Statuary in the Ancient Mediterranean World*. Oxford.
Larsen, J. A. O. 1964. "Epirote Grants of Citizenship to Women." *CP* 59: 106–7.
—— 1967. "Epirote Grants of Citizenship Once More." *CP* 62: 255–6.
Lévêque, P. 1957. *Pyrrhos*. Paris.
Lewis, S. 2002. *The Athenian Woman: An Iconographic Handbook*. London and New York.
Lilibaki-Akamati, M. 2004. "Women in Macedonia." In Pandermalis 2004: 89–114.
Lloyd-Jones, H. 1973. "Modern Interpretation of Pindar: The Second Pythian and Seventh Nemean Odes." *JHS* 93: 109–37.
Lund, H. 1994. *Lysimachus: A Study in Early Hellenistic Kingship*. London.
McKechnie, P. 1999. "Manipulation of Themes in Quintus Curtius Rufus Book 10." *Historia* 48: 44–60.
McLynn, N. 1998. "The Other Olympias: Gregory Nazianzen and the Family of Vitalianus." *Journal of Ancient Christianity/Zeitschrift fur antikes Christentum* 2: 227–46.
Macurdy, G. H. 1932a. *Hellenistic Queens*. Baltimore.
—— 1932b. "Roxane and Alexander IV in Epirus." *JHS* 52: 256–61.
Maitland, J. 1992. "Dynasty and Family in the Athenian City State: A View from Attic Tragedy." *CQ* 42: 26–40.
Malkin, I. 2001. "Greek Ambiguities: 'Ancient Hellas' and 'Barbarian Epirus.'" In I. Malkin (ed.), *Ancient Perceptions of Greek Ethnicity*, 187–212. Cambridge, MA.
Mari, M. 1998. "Le Olimpie macedoni di Dion tra Archelao e l'età romana." *RFIC* 126: 137–69.
Martin, T. R. 1982. "A Phantom Fragment of Theopompus and Philip II's First Campaign in Thessaly." *HSCP* 86: 55–78.
Mattingly, H. B. 1968. "Athenian Finance in the Peloponnesian War." *BCH* 92: 450–85.
Maxwell-Stuart, P. G. 1972. "Myrtle and the Eleusinian Mysteries." *WS* 85: 145–61.
Mendels, D. 1984. "Aetolia 331–301: Frustration, Political Power, and Survival." *Historia* 33, 2: 129–80.
Millar, F. 1993. *The Roman Near East: 31 BC–AD 337*. Cambridge, MA.

Milns, R. D. 1968. *Alexander the Great*. London.

Mirón-Pérez, M. D. 1988. "Olimpia, Euridice y el origen del culto en la Grecia helenistica." *FlorIlib* 9: 215–35.

—— 1999. "Realeza y labor doméstica en Macedonia antigua." *Geri 1* 17: 213–22.

—— 2000. "Transmitters and Representatives of Power: Royal Women in Ancient Macedonia." *AncSoc* 30: 35–52.

Mitchell, L. G. 1997. *Greeks Bearing Gifts: The Public Use of Private Relationships in the Greek World*. Cambridge.

Momigliano, A. 1934. *Filippo il Macedone*. Florence.

Morgan, G. 1985. "Euphiletos's Lysias I." *TAPA* 112: 115–23.

Mortensen, C. 1991. "The Career of Bardylis." *AncW* 22: 49–59.

—— 1992. "Eurydice: Demonic or Devoted Mother?" *AHB* 6: 155–69.

—— 1997. *Olympias: Royal Wife and Mother at the Macedonian Court*. Unpublished dissertation, University of Queensland. Brisbane.

—— 1999. "Harmony or Hatred? The Inter-relationship of Philip's Wives." *AM* 6, 2: 797–805.

—— Forthcoming "Homosexuality at the Macedonian Court and the Death of Philip II." *AM*.

Mosley, D. J. 1973. *Envoys and Diplomacy in Ancient Greece*. Wiesbaden.

Mossman, J. 1988. "Tragedy and Epic in Plutarch's *Alexander*." *JHS* 108: 83–93.

Mowat, R. 1903. "Le Médallions grec du Trésor di Tarse et les Monnaies de Bronze de la communauté macédonienne." *RN* 4: 1–30.

Musgrave, J. 1985. "The Skull of Philip II of Macedon." In J. W. Lisney and B. S. Matthews, *Current Topics in Oral Biology*, 1–16. Bristol.

Nau, E. 1968. "Julia Domna als Olympias." *Jahrbuch für Numismatik und Geldgeschichte* 18: 49–66.

Neils, J. and John H. Oakley (eds.). 2003. *Coming of Age in Ancient Greece: Images of Childhood from the Classical Past*. New Haven.

Nevett, L. 1995. "Gender Relations in the Classical Greek Household: The Archaeological Evidence." *BSA* 90: 1–29.

—— 1999. *House and Society in the Ancient Greek World*. Cambridge.

Nielsen, I. 1994. *Hellenistic Palaces, Tradition and Renewal*. Aarhus.

Ninou, K. 1980. *Treasures of Ancient Macedonia*. Athens.

Oakley, J. H. 2003. "Death and the Child." In Neils and Oakley 2003: 163–94.

Oberleitner, W. 1985. *Geschnittene Steine: Die Prunkkameen der Wiener Antikensammlung*, 32–5. Vienna.

—— 1992. "Der 'Ptolemaer'–Kameo—doch ein Kamero der Ptolemaer!" In O. Brehm and S. Klie (eds.), *MOUSIKOS ANER: Festschrift für Max Wegner zum 90. Geburtstag*, 329–38. Bonn.

O'Brien, J. M. 1992. *Alexander the Great: The Invisible Enemy*. London and New York.

Ogden, D. 1996. "Homosexuality and Warfare in Classical Greece.' In A. B. Lloyd, *Battle in Antiquity*, 107–68, London.

—— 1999. *Polygamy, Prostitutes and Death: The Hellenistic Dynasties*. London.

—— Forthcoming "A War of Witches at the Court of Philip II?" *AM*.

—— (ed.). 2002. *The Hellenistic World: New Perspectives*. London.

Oikonomedes, A. 1982. "The Epigram on the Tomb of Olympias at Pydna." *AncW* 5: 9–16.

—— 1983. "A New Inscription from Vergina and Eurydice, Mother of Philip II." *AncW* 7: 62–4.

Oliverio, G. 1933. *Cirenaica 2:1: La Stela dei nuovi commandamenti e dei cereali*. Bergamo.

O'Neil, J. L. 1999a. "Olympias: 'The Macedonians Will Never Let Themselves Be Ruled by a Woman.'" *Prudentia* 31, 1: 1–14.

—— 1999b. "Political Trials under Alexander the Great and His Successors." *Antichthon* 33: 28–47.

Palagia, O. 1986. "Imitation of Herakles in Ruler Portraiture: A Survey from Alexander to Maximinus Daza." *Boreas* 9: 137–51.

—— 1999. "The Grave Relief of Adea—A Macedonian Princess." Unpublished paper delivered at the Australian Archaeological Institute, Athens, Greece, April 21.

—— 2000. "Hephaestion's Pyre and the Royal Hunt of Alexander." In Bosworth 2000: 167–205.

Palm, J. 1959. *Rom, Römertum und Imperium in der griechischen Literatur der Kaiserzeit*. Lund.

Pandermalis, D. (ed.). 2004. *Alexander the Great: Treasures from an Epic Era of Hellenism*. New York.

Papisca, M. 1999. "Immagini della *Imitatio Alexandri* in età severiana.I Medaglioni di Tarso." *AM* 6, 2: 859–71.

Parke, H. W. 1967. *The Oracles of Zeus: Dodona, Olympia, Ammon*, Oxford.

Pelling, C. 2000. "Fun with Fragments: Athenaeus and the Historians." In Braund and Wilkins 2000: 171–90.

—— 2002. *Plutarch and History: Eighteen Studies*. London.

Perret, J. 1946. "Néoptolème et les Molosses." *REA* 48: 5–28.

Perrin, B. 1919, 1958. *Plutarch's Lives*. Vol. 11. Cambridge, MA.

Plantzos, D. 1997. "Hellenistic Cameos: Problems of Classification and Chronology." *BICS* 41: 115–31, Pls. 22A–27A.

Pollitt, J. J. 1986. *Art in the Hellenistic Age*. Cambridge.

Pomeroy, S. B. 1975. *Goddesses, Whores, Wives and Slaves: Women in Classical Antiquity*. New York.

—— 1977. "Technikai kai Mousikai: The Education of Women in the Fourth Century and Hellenistic Period." *AJAH* 2: 51–68.

—— 1984. *Women in Hellenistic Egypt*. New York.

—— 1997. *Families in Classical and Hellenistic Greece: Representations and Realities*. Oxford.

Pötscher, W. 1988. "Zeus Naios und Dione in Dodona." In W. Pötscher (ed.), *Hellas und Rom: Beiträge und kritische Auseinandersetuzung mit der inzwischen erschienen Literatur*, 173–207. Hildesheim.

Poulsen, B. 1997. "Alexander the Great in Italy during the Hellenistic period." In Carlsen *et al.* 1997: 161–70.

Préaux, C. 1978. *Le Monde hellénistique: La Grèce et L'Orient de la mort d'Alexandre à la conquête romaine de la Grèce (323–146 av. J.-C.)*. Vols. 1 and 2. Paris.

Prestianni-Giallombardo, A. M. 1976–7. "'Diritto' matrimoniale, ereditario et dinastico nella Macedonia di Filippo II." *RSA* 6–7: 81–118.

Reames-Zimmerman, J. 1998. *Hephaestion Amyntoros: Éminence Grise at the Court of Alexander the Great*. Unpublished dissertation, Pennsylvania State University. Philadelphia.

—— 1999. "An Atypical Affair? Alexander the Great, Hephaistion Amyntoros and the Nature of Their Relationship." *AHB* 13, 3: 81–96.

—— 2001. "The Mourning of Alexander the Great." *Syllecta Classica* 12: 98–145.

Reuss, F. 1881. "König Arybbas son Epeiros." *RhM* 86: 161–74.

Rhomiopoulou, K. 1973. "A New Monumental Chamber Tomb with Paintings of the Hellenistic Period near Leukadia (West Macedonia)." *AA* 6: 87–92.

Richter, G. M. 1965. *The Portraits of the Greeks*. London.

Riley, J. 2001. *The Treatment of Women in Justin*. Unpublished dissertation, University of Newcastle. New South Wales.

Robert, L. and J. Robert. 1984. "3249 Vergina-Aegai." *REG* 97: 450–1.

Robertson, D. S. 1923. "Euripides and Tharyps."*CR* 37: 58–60.

Robertson, N. 2003. "Orphic Mysteries and Dionysiac Ritual." In Cosmopoulos 2003: 218–40.

Robinson, D. M. 1953. "Macedonica: I. the Epigram of Aeacid Alcimachus." In *Geras A. Keramopoullou*, 149–56. Athens.

Roisman, J. 2003a. "Honor in Alexander's Campaign." In Roisman 2003b: 279–321.

—— (ed.). 2003b. *Brill's Companion to Alexander the Great*. Leiden.

Ross, D. J. A. 1963. "Olympias and the Serpent: The Interpretation of a Baalbek Mosaic and the Date of the Illustrated Pseudo-Callisthenes." *Journal of the Warburg and Courtauld Institutes* 26: 1–23.

—— 1988. *Alexander Historiatus: A Guide to Medieval Illustrated Alexander Literature*. Frankfurt.

Ruzicka, S. 1992. *Politics of a Persian Dynasty: The Hecatomnids in the Fourth Century* BC. Norman.

Saatsoglou-Paliadeli, C. 1987. "Eurydika Sirra Eukleiai." *Ametos* 2: 733–44.

—— 1991. "Vergina 1991. Anaskaphe Sto Hiero Tes Eucleias." *AEMTH* 5: 9–21.

—— 2000. "Queenly Appearances at Vergina-Aegae: Old and New Epigraphic and Literary Evidence." *AA* 3: 387–403.

—— 2001. "The Palace of Vergina-Aegae and Its Surroundings." In I. Nielsen (ed.), *The Royal Palace Institution in the First Millennium* BC: *Regional Development and Cultural Interchange between East and West*, 201–14. Athens.

Sacks, K. 1990. *Diodorus Siculus and the First Century*. Princeton.

Savio, A. 1994/5. "Intorno ai medaglioni talismanici di Tarso e di Aboukir." *Rivista Italiana di Numismatica e Scienze Afficini* 96: 73–103.

Sawada, N. 1993. "A Reconsideration of the Peace of Philocrates." *Kodai* 4: 21–50.

Schachter, A. 2003. "Evolutions of a Mystery Cult: Theban Kabiroi." In Cosmopoulos 2003: 112–42.

Scheer, T. S. 2003. "The Past in a Hellenistic Present." In Erskine 2003: 216–31.

Schoder, R. V. 1982. "Alexander's Son and Roxane in the Boscoreale Murals." *AncW* 5: 27–32.

Scholl, R. 1987. "Alexander der Grosse und die Sklaverei am Hofe." *Klio* 69: 108–21.

Schumacher, L. 1990. "Zum Herrschaftsverständnis Philipps II von Makedonien." *Historia* 39: 426–43.

Schneider, R. 1885. *Olympias, die Mutter Alexanders des Grossen*. Zwickau.

Scott-Kilvert, I. 1973. *The Age of Alexander: Nine Greek Lives by Plutarch*. London.

Seibert, J. 1972. *Alexander der Grosse*. Erträge der Forschung 10. Darmstadt.

—— 1984. "Das Testament Alexanders: Ein Pamphlet aus der Frühzeit der

Diadochenkämpfe." In A. Kraus (ed.), *Lande und Reich, Stamm und Nation: Festgabe für Max Spindler*, 247–60. Munich.

—— 1990. "Review of W. Heckel, *The Last Days and Testament of Alexander the Great: A Propographical Study.*" *Gnomon* 62: 564–6.

Seidmann, G. 1993. "Portrait Cameos: Aspects of their History and Function. In M. Henig and M. Vickers (eds.), *Cameos in Context*, 85–95. Oxford.

Shipley, G. 2000. *The Greek World after Alexander 323–30 BC*. London

Simon, E. 1958. *Die Fürstenbilder von Boscoreale*. Deutsche Beiträge zur Altertumswissenschaft 7. Baden-Baden.

Smith, R. R. 1988. *Hellenistic Royal Portraits*. Oxford.

Spencer, D. 2002. *The Roman Alexander: Reading a Cultural Myth*. Exeter.

Stadter, P. 1965. *Plutarch's Historical Methods*. Cambridge, MA.

—— 1980. *Arrian of Nicomedia*. Chapel Hill.

—— 1992. *Plutarch and the Historical Tradition*. London and New York.

Stafford, P. M. 1978. "Sons and Mothers: Family Politics in the Early Middle Ages." In D. Baker (ed.), *Medieval Women*, 79–100. Oxford.

—— 1983. *Queens, Concubines, and Dowagers: The King's Wife in the Early Middle Ages*. Athens, GA.

Stewart, A. 1993. *Faces of Power. Alexander's Image and Hellenistic Politics*. Berkeley.

—— 2003. "Alexander in Greek and Roman Art." In Roisman 2003b: 31–66.

Stöcker, C. 1976. "Der Trug der Olympias: Ein Beitrag zur Erzählkunst antiker Novellistik." *WJA* 2: 85–98.

Stoneman, R. 1991. *The Greek Alexander Romance*. London.

—— 1994. "The *Alexander Romance*: From History to Fiction." In J. R. Morgan and R. Stoneman (eds.), *Greek Fiction: The Greek Novel in Context*, 117–29. London and New York.

—— 1996. "The Metamorphoses of the *Alexander Romance*." In G. Schmeling (ed.), *The Novel in the Ancient World*, 601–12. Leiden.

—— 2003. "The Legacy of Alexander in Ancient Philosophy." In Roisman 2003b: 325–45.

—— 2004. "The Latin Alexander." In H. Hofmann (ed.), *Latin Fiction: The Latin Novel in Context*, 167–86. London and New York.

Strasburger, H. 1939. "Olympias 5." *RE* 18, 1: 177–82.

Tarn, W. W. 1913. *Antigonos Gonatas*. Oxford.

—— 1949. *Alexander the Great*. Vols. 1 and 2. Cambridge.

Tataki, A. B. 1988. *Ancient Beroea: Prosopography and Society*. Athens.

Themelis, P. and J. Touratsoglou. 1997. *Oi Taphoi Tou Derveniou*. Athens.

Tod, M. N. 1946 and 1948. *Greek Historical Inscriptions*. Vols. 1 and 2. Oxford.

Toynbee, J. M. C. 1944. "Greek Imperial Medallions." *JRS* 34: 69–73.

Treves, P. 1942. "The Meaning of *Consenesco* and King Arybbas of Epirus." *AJP* 63: 129–53.

Tritle, L. 1997. "Hector's Body: Mutilation of the Dead in Ancient Greece and Vietnam." *AHB* 11: 123–36.

Tritsch, W. 1936. *Olympias, die Mutter Alexanders des Grossen*. Frankfurt.

Tronson, A. 1984. "Satyrus the Peripatetic and the Marriages of Philip II." *JHS* 104: 116–56.

Unz, R. K. 1985. "Alexander's Brothers?" *JHS* 105: 171–4.

Vermeule, C. 1982. "Alexander the Great, the Emperor Severus Alexander and the Aboukir Medallions." *Revue suisse de numismatique/Schwizerische numismatische Rundschau* 61: 61–79.

—— 1986. *Alexander the Great Conquers Rome*. Cambridge, MA.

Vermeule, E. 1979. *Aspects of Death in Early Greek Art and Poetry*. Berkeley.

Vokotopoulou, J. 2001. "Dodone et les villes de la Grande Grece et de la Sicile." In J. Vokotopoulou (ed.), *Studies on Epirus and Macedonia*. Vol. 2, 649–77. Athens.

Welles, C. B. 1963. *Diodorus VII*. Cambridge, MA.

Westlake, H. D. 1969. "Eumenes of Cardia." In H. D. Westlake (ed.), *Essays on the Greek Historians and Greek History*, 313–30. New York.

Wheatley, P. V. 1998. "The Date of Polyperchon's Invasion of Macedonia and Murder of Heracles." *Antichthon* 32: 12–23.

Whitehorne, J. 1983. "The Background to Polyneices' Disinterment and Reburial." *G&R* 30: 129–42.

—— 1994. *Cleopatras*. London and New York.

Whitley, J. 2001. *The Archaeology of Ancient Greece*. Cambridge.

Wilhelm, A. 1949. "Ein Weihgedicht der Grossmutter Alexanders des Grossen." *Mélanges Grégoire*. Vol. 2, 625–33. Brussels.

Will, E. 1979–82. *Histoire politique du monde hellénistique*. 2nd edn. 2 vols. Nancy.

Wirth, G. 1973. *Alexander der Grosse*. Reinbek bei Hamburg.

Witt, R. E. 1977. "Kabeiroi in Macedonia." *AM* 2: 67–80.

Wolohojian, A. M. 1969. *The Romance of Alexander the Great by Pseudo-Callisthenes*. New York.

Wood, S. E. 1986. *Roman Portrait Sculpture 217–260: The Transformation of an Artistic Tradition*. Leiden.

—— 1999. *Imperial Women: A Study in Public Images, 40BC–AD 68*. Leiden.

Woodbury, L. 1979. "Neoptolemus at Delphi: Pindar, *Nem.* 7.30ff." *Phoenix* 33: 95–133.

Woolf, G. 1994. "Becoming Roman, Staying Greek: Culture, Identity and the Civilizing Process in the Roman East." *PCPhS* 40: 116–43.

Worthington, I. 1984. "Harpalus and the Macedonian Envoys." *LCM* 9: 47–8.

—— 2003. "Alexander's Destruction of Thebes." In Heckel and Tritle 2003: 65–86.

—— (ed.). 1994. *Ventures into Greek History*. Oxford.

Yalouris, N., M. Andronikos, K. Rhomiopoulou, A. Herrman, C. Vermeule. 1980. *The Search for Alexander*. New York.

Yardley, J. 2003. *Justin and Pompeius Trogus: A Study of the Language of Justin's Epitome of Trogus*. Phoenix Supplementary Volumes 41. Toronto.

Yardley, J. and R. Develin.1994. *Justin, Epitome of the Philippic History of Pompeius Trogus*. Atlanta.

Yardley, J. and W. Heckel. 1984. *Quintus Curtius Rufus: The History of Alexander*. London.

Zeitlin, F. I. 1982. "Cultic Models of the Feminine: Rites of Dionysus and Demeter." *Arethusa* 15: 129–57.

—— 2001. "Visions and Revisions of Homer." In S. Goldhill (ed.), *Being Greek under Rome: Cultural Identity, the Second Sophistic and the Development of Empire*, 195–268. Cambridge.

Index

Related titles from Routledge

Women and religion in the First Christian Centuries
Deborah F. Sawyer

Women and Religion in the First Christian Centuries focuses on religion during the period of Roman imperial rule and its significance in women's lives. It discusses the rich variety of religious expression, from pagan cults and classical mythology to ancient Judaism and early Christianity, and the wide array of religious functions fulfilled by women. The author analyses key examples from each context, creating a vivid image of this crucial period which laid the foundations of western civilization.

ISBN10: 0-415-10748-2 (hbk)
ISBN10: 0-415-10749-0 (pbk)

ISBN13: 978-0-415-10748-8 (hbk)
ISBN13: 978-0-415-10749-5 (pbk)

Available at all good bookshops
For ordering and further information please visit:
www.routledge.com